William Batchelder Bradbury

Devotional Hymn and Tune Book for Social and Public Worship

William Batchelder Bradbury

Devotional Hymn and Tune Book for Social and Public Worship

ISBN/EAN: 9783337290641

Printed in Europe, USA, Canada, Australia, Japan

Cover: Foto ©Lupo / pixelio.de

More available books at **www.hansebooks.com**

THE

DEVOTIONAL

HYMN AND TUNE BOOK

FOR

SOCIAL AND PUBLIC WORSHIP.

THE MUSIC ARRANGED AND ADAPTED

BY

WM. B. BRADBURY.

WITH A SUPPLEMENT.

PHILADELPHIA:
AMERICAN BAPTIST PUBLICATION SOCIETY,
530 ARCH STREET.

Entered according to Act of Congress, in the year 1864, by the
AMERICAN BAPTIST PUBLICATION SOCIETY,
In the C'erk's Office of the District Court of the United States, in and for the Eastern District of Pennsylvania.

PREFACE.

THE compilers of this book have endeavored to group together the choicest Hymns and Tunes in the language; embracing the old and familiar Songs of Zion, and the many precious gems that have been more recently added to the treasury of sacred song. That we have *perfectly* succeeded in the execution of this design, we do not for a moment suppose. That hymns and tunes have been omitted, which should have been inserted; and some inserted, which should have been omitted, is possibly true. Nevertheless we confidently believe that we have given to the denomination, and to the Church in general, a greater number of valuable hymns and tunes than can be found, within an equal compass, in any other collection; making the book not only preeminently adapted to the weekly social meetings, but also answering well the wants of the Sabbath Service.

A duplicate copy has been prepared without music.

It is the prayer of those to whom the preparation of this work was committed, that it may be blessed by God as a humble offering of praise upon the altar of the Church of Christ.

Philadelphia, September 1, 1864.

NOTICE.

☞ *The numbers at the right hand in brackets, indicate the numbers of the Hymns in the Edition without Music.*

INDEX OF TUNES.

A Friend that's ever near	161	Hamburg....(L. M.) 58	Rest for the Weary............ 171
Aletta............(7s, 6 lines)	158	Happy Day............ " 116	Retreat............(L. M.) 7
A Light in the Window........	120	Harwell........(8s & 7s double) 88	Rockingham............ " 18
All will be well...............	105	Heaven is my Home........... 203	Rock of Ages.......,...(7s, 6 lines) 159
Amazing Grace........(C. M.)	185	Heber............(C. M.) 34	Rockport...,......(7s, 6s, & 4s) 160
America...............	189	Hebron............(L. M.) 100	Rolland............(L. M.) 208
Amoy...............	74	He Leadeth me............ 225	Sabbath............(7s, 6 lines) 129
Amsterdam.........(7s & 6s)	163	Hendon............(7s) 148	St. Martins............(C. M.) 201
Arlington............(C. M.)	24	Here is no Rest............ 199	St. Thomas............(S. M.) 85
Autumn............(8s & 7s double)	82	Home............(11s) 173	Salzburgh........(8s & 7s, 6 lines) 177
Avon............(C. M.) 164,	205	Homeward Bound............ 147	Saviour, like a Shepherd lead us
Aylesbury............(S. M.)	222	Horton............(7s) 149	&s, 7s & 4s)............ 15
Azmon............(C. M.)	70	How Beauteous are their Feet.. 49	Say, Brothers............ 121
Balerma............(C. M.)	76	Howell............(8s, 7s, & 4s) 21	Shall we know each other...... 226
Banks of Jordan........(C. M.)	141	I'm a Pilgrim............ 9	Shall we meet............ 152
Bartimeus............(8s & 7s)	94	I do believe............(C. M.) 103	Shall we sing in Heaven........ 227
Blessed Bible............	86	Invitation............(8s & 7s) 20	Shining Shore............ 22
Bloomfield Chant........(L. M.)	31	Iowa............(S. M.) 108	Shirland............(S. M.) 84
Boyle............(S. M.)	27	Ives............(7s double) 113	Siloam............(C. M.) 118
Boylston............ "	182	Jesus paid it all............ 126	Silver Street............(S. M.) 123
Braden............ "	48	Joyfully............ 98	Star of Bethlehem (L. M. double) 135
Bremen............(C. P. M.)	39	Just as I am............ 19	State Street............(S, M.) 109
Bright Canaan,............	170	Laban............(S. M.) 122	Stephens............(C. M.) 96
Bright Crown............(C. M.)	102	La Mira............(C. M.) 56	Sweet Hour of Prayer (L. M double
Brown............ " 40,	218	Lanesboro............ " 115	ble)............ 117
Burford............ "	107	Latter Day............ 63	Sweet Land of Rest......(S. M.) 63
Caddo............(C. M.)	124	Lebanon........(S. M. double) 223	Sweet Rest in Heaven........ 42
Canaan............ "	132	Lenox............(H. M.) 186	Suffering Saviour............(C. M.) 197
Captivity............(L. M.)	111	Lischer............ " 61	Tappan............(C. M.) 154
China............(C. M.)	119	Looking Home........(7s & 6s) 36	That Beautiful Land............ 131
Corinth............ "	212	Lottie............(S. M.) 26	The Angels Sing........(S. M.) 67
Coronation............ "	133	Loving Kindness........(L. M.) 59	The Angels' Welcome........ 146
Cross and Crown............ "	196	Marching Along............ 28	The Christian Hero............ 221
Croydon............ "	217	Martyn............(7s double) 80	The Evergreen Shore............ 104
Dedham............(C. M.)	174	Melody............(C. M.) 5	The Garden Hymn............ 23
De Fleury............(8s double)	51	Mercy's Free............ 191	The Golden Shore............ 99
Dennis............(S. M.)	10	Meribah............(C. P. M.) 38	The Heavenly Land............ 8
Dover............ "	33	Meroe............(L. M.) 93	The Penitent............ 202
Downs............ "	155	Missionary Hymn........(7s & 6s) 195	The Promised Land............ 176
Duane Street......(L. M. double)	79	Naomi............(C. M.) 12, 216	The Sinner's Friend............ 43
Duke Street............(L. M.)	78	Nearer my Home............ 220	The Solid Rock............ 52
Dundee............(C. M.)	184	Nearer to Thee............ 211	The Sweetest Name............ 75
Dunlap's Creek............ "	106	Nettleton........(8s & 7s double) 83	There will be no Parting............ 55
Eden............(8s)	50	Northfield............(C. M.) 200	Unity............ 114
Eltham............(7s double)	68	No Sorrow There........(S. M.) 153	Uxbridge............(L. M.) 30
Evan............(C. M.)	90	Nothing but Leaves............ 64	Ward............(L. M.) 64
Even Me............	74	Nuremburg............(7s) 128	Ware............ " 180
Evening Expostulation..(L. M.)	157	Oberlin............(L. M.) 134	We are coming............ 139
Evening Hymn............	92	Oh how happy are they........ 198	Webb............(7s & 6s) 194
Expostulation............(11s)	138	Oh how he loves............ 37	Weep and mourn............(C. M.) 204
Federal Street............(L. M.)	156	Old Hundred............(L. M.) 6	Welcome Home............ 112
Forest............ "	110	Oliphant........(8s, 7s, & 4s) 14	Wells............(L. M.) 192
Forever with the Lord............	62	Olive's Brow............(L. M.) 145	We'll be there............ 224
Foster............(8s)	190	Olivet............(6s & 4s) 188	Will you go............ 29
Fountain............(C. M.)	168	Olmutz............(S. M.) 206	Windham............(L. M.) 193
Frederick............(11s)	172	Ortonville............(C. M.) 44	Wirth............(C. M.) 57
Fulton............(7s)	151	Our Fathers long ago............ 66	Woodland............ " 178
God Calling Yet........(L. M.)	210	O when shall I see Jesus (7s & 6s) 72	Woodstock............ " 140
Going Home............	65	Passing away............ 166	Woodworth............(L. M.) 167
Golden Hill............(S. M.)	142	Penitence............(S. M.) 32	Young Pilgrims............ 87
Goshen............(11s)	136	Peterboro............(C. M.) 16	Zebulun............(H. M.) 60
Gratitude............ "	144	Pleading Saviour........(8s & 7s) 95	Zephyr............(L. M.) 46
Greenville......(8s & 7s double)	89	Pleyel's Hymn............(7s) 150	Zion............(8s, 7s & 4s) 134
Hail to the Brightness............	162	Rest............(L. M.) 214	Zion's Pilgrim............ 127

THE DEVOTIONAL
HYMN AND TUNE BOOK.

MELODY. C. M.

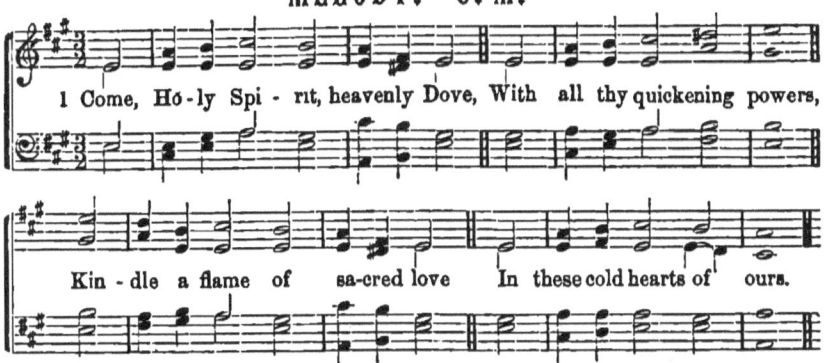

1 Come, Holy Spirit, heavenly Dove, With all thy quickening powers, Kindle a flame of sacred love In these cold hearts of ours.

1. *The Quickening Spirit.* (309)

1 COME, Holy Spirit, heavenly Dove,
With all thy quickening powers,
Kindle a flame of sacred love
In these cold hearts of ours.

2 Look, how we grovel here below,
Fond of these trifling toys;
Our souls can neither fly nor go
To reach eternal joys.

3 In vain we tune our formal songs,
In vain we strive to rise;
Hosannas languish on our tongues,
And our devotion dies.

4 Dear Lord! and shall we ever live
At this poor dying rate?
Our love so faint, so cold to thee,
And thine to us so great?

5 Come, Holy Spirit, heavenly Dove,
With all thy quickening powers;
Come, shed abroad a Saviour's love,
And that shall kindle ours.
WATTS.

2. *Jesus Precious to Them that Believe.* (266)

1 JESUS, I love thy charming name;
'Tis music to my ear;
Fain would I sound it out so loud,
That earth and heaven might hear.

2 Yes, thou art precious to my soul,
My transport and my trust;
Jewels to thee are gaudy toys,
And gold is sordid dust.

3 All my capacious powers can wish
In thee doth richly meet;
Nor to my eyes is light so dear,
Nor friendship half so sweet.

4 Thy grace shall dwell upon my heart,
And shed its fragrance there,—
The noblest balm of all its wounds,
The cordial of its care.

5 I'll speak the honors of thy name
With my last laboring breath,
And, dying, clasp thee in my arms,
The antidote of death.
DODDRIDGE.

OLD HUNDRED. L. M.

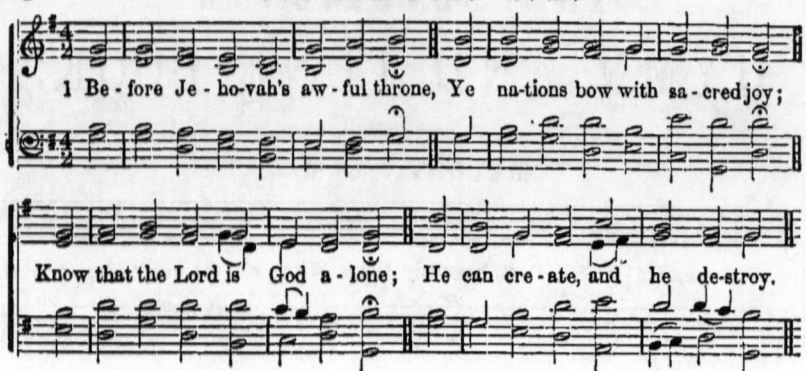

1 Be-fore Je-ho-vah's aw-ful throne, Ye na-tions bow with sa-cred joy; Know that the Lord is God a-lone; He can cre-ate, and he de-stroy.

3.   *The Sovereign Jehovah.*   (179)

1 BEFORE Jehovah's awful throne,
  Ye nations bow with sacred joy;
  Know that the Lord is God alone;
  He can create, and he destroy.

2 His sovereign power without our aid,
  Made us of clay, and formed us men;
  And when, like wandering sheep, we strayed,
  He brought us to his fold again.

3 We are his people; we his care;
  Our souls, and all our mortal frame;
  What lasting honors shall we rear,
  Almighty Maker, to thy name?

4 We'll crowd thy gates with thankful songs,
  High as the heaven our voices raise;
  And earth, with her ten thousand tongues,
  Shall fill thy courts with sounding praise.

5 Wide as the world is thy command;
  Vast as eternity thy love;
  Firm as a rock thy truth shall stand,
  When rolling years shall cease to move.
                                    WATTS.

4.   *Praise to the Great Jehovah.*   (206)

1 BE thou, O God, exalted high;
  And as thy glory fills the sky,
  So let it be on earth displayed,
  Till thou art here, as there, obeyed.

2 O God, my heart is fixed; 'tis bent
  Its thankful tribute to present
  And, with my heart, my voice I'll raise,
  To thee, my God, in songs of praise.

3 Thy praises, Lord, I will resound
  To all the listening nations round;
  Thy mercy highest heaven transcends;
  Thy truth beyond the clouds extends.

4 Be thou, O God, exalted high;
  And as thy glory fills the sky,
  So let it be on earth displayed,
  Till thou art here, as there, obeyed.
                              TATE & BRADY.

5.   *The Indwelling of God Desired.*   (6)

1 COME, gracious Lord, descend and dwell,
  By faith and love in every breast;
  Then shall we know, and taste, and feel
  The joys that cannot be expressed.

2 Come, fill our hearts with inward strength,
  Make our enlarged souls possess,
  And learn the height, and breadth, and length
  Of thine eternal love and grace.

3 Now to the God whose power can do
  More than our thoughts and wishes know,
  Be everlasting honors done,
  By all the church, through Christ, his Son
                                    WATTS.

RETREAT. L. M.
T. HASTINGS.

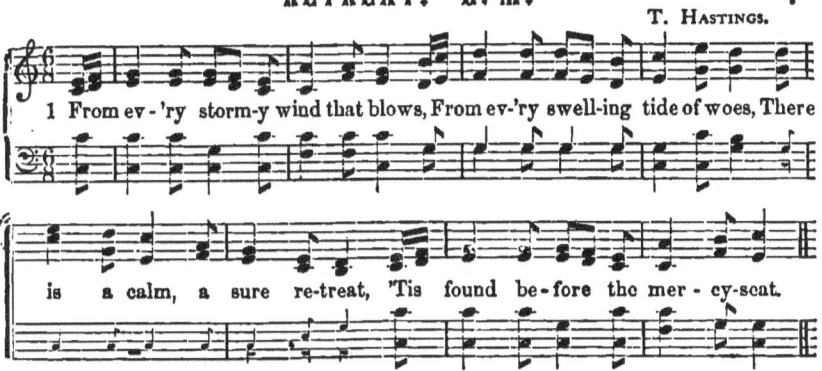

1 From ev-'ry storm-y wind that blows, From ev-'ry swell-ing tide of woes, There is a calm, a sure re-treat, 'Tis found be-fore the mer-cy-seat.

6. *The Mercy Seat.* (412)

1 FROM every stormy wind that blows,
From every swelling tide of woes,
There is a calm, a sure retreat;
'Tis found before the mercy-seat.

2 There is a place where Jesus sheds
The oil of gladness on our heads—
A place of all on earth most sweet;
It is the blood-bought mercy-seat.

3 There is a scene where spirits blend,
Where friend holds fellowship with friend;
Though sundered far, by faith they meet
Around one common mercy-seat.

4 There, there, on eagle wings we soar,
And sin and sense molest no more;
And heaven comes down, our souls to greet,
And glory crowns the mercy-seat.
STOWELL.

7. *Converts Welcomed.* (147)

1 BELIEVING souls, of Christ beloved,
Who have yourselves to him resigned,
Your faith and practice both approved,
A hearty welcome here shall find.

2 Now saved from sin and Satan's wiles,
Though by a scorning world abhorred,
Now share with us the Saviour's smiles;
Come in, ye ransomed of the Lord.

3 In fellowship we join our hands,
And you an invitation give;

Unite with us in sacred bands;
The pledges of our love receive.

4 O Thou, who art the church's Head,
This union with thy blessings crown;
And still revive and save the dead,
Till thousands more thy name shall own.
BEDDOME.

8. *Zion Encouraged.* (539)

1 ZION, awake; thy strength renew;
Put on thy robes of beauteous hue;
Church of our God, arise and shine,
Bright with the beams of truth divine.

2 Soon shall thy radiance stream afar,
Wide as the heathen nations are;
Gentiles and kings thy light shall view;
All shall admire and love thee too.

9. *They that go down to the Sea in Ships.* (516)

1 WHILE o'er the deep thy servants sail,
Send thou, O Lord, the prosperous gale;
And on their hearts, where'er they go,
O, let thy heavenly breezes blow.

2 When tempests rock the groaning bark,
O hide them safe in Jesus' ark!
When in the tempting port they ride,
O keep them safe at Jesus' side.

3 If life's wide ocean smile or roar,
Still guide them to the heavenly shore;
And grant their dust in Christ may sleep,
Abroad, at home, or in the deep.

THE HEAVENLY LAND. P. M.

1. I love to think of the heavenly land, Where white-robed angels are; Where many a friend is gather'd safe From fear, and toil, and care. There'll be no part-ing,

REFRAIN.

There'll be no part-ing, There'll be no parting, There'll be no parting there.

10. *The Heavenly Land.* (426)

1 I love to think of the heavenly land,
  Where white-robed angels are;
  Where many a friend is gathered safe
  From fear, and toil, and care.
    There'll be no parting, &c.

2 I love to think of the heavenly land,
  Where my Redeemer reigns,
  Where rapturous songs of triumph rise
  In endless, joyous strains.
    There'll be no parting, &c.

3 I love to think of the heavenly land,
  The saints' eternal home,
  Where palms, and robes, and crowns
        ne'er fade,
  And all our joys are one.
    There'll be no parting, &c.

4 I love to think of the heavenly land,
  The greetings there we'll meet,
  The harps—the songs forever ours—
  The walks—the golden streets.
    There'll be no parting, &c.

5 I love to think of the heavenly land,
  That promised land so fair,
  O, how my raptured spirit longs
  To be forever there!
    There'll be no parting, &c.

DOXOLOGY.

PRAISE the God of all creation:
  Praise the Father's boundless love
Praise the Lamb, our expiation, —
  Priest and King, enthroned above;
Praise the Fountain of salvation,—
  Him by whom our spirits live;
Undivided adoration
  To the one Jehovah give.

I'M A PILGRIM.

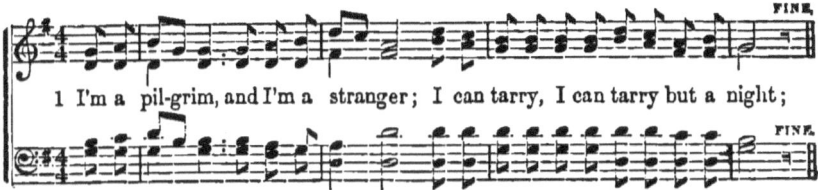

11. *A Pilgrim and Stranger.* (446)

1 I'm a pilgrim, and I'm a stranger;
I can tarry, I can tarry but a night;
Do not detain me, for I am going
To where the fountains are ever flowing.
I'm a pilgrim, and I'm a stranger;
I can tarry, I can tarry but a night.

2 There the glory is ever shining;
I am longing, I am longing for the sight;
Here in this country so dark and dreary,
I have been wand'ring forlorn and weary.
I'm a pilgrim, and I'm a stranger;
I can tarry, I can tarry but a night.

3 There's the city to which I journey;
My Redeemer, my Redeemer is its light;
There is no sorrow, nor any sighing,
There is no sin there, nor any dying.
I'm a pilgrim, and I'm a stranger;
I can tarry, I can tarry but a night.

12. *The Missionary's Farewell.*
TUNE HOWELL, page 21. (519)

1 YES, my native land, I love thee;
All thy scenes, I love them well;
Friends, connections, happy country!
Can I bid you all farewell?
Can I leave you,
Far in heathen lands to dwell?

2 Yes, I hasten from you gladly,
From the scenes I loved so well—
Far away, ye billows, bear me;
Lovely native land, farewell!
Pleased I leave thee,
Far in heathen lands to dwell.

3 In the desert let me labor;
On the mountains let me tell
How he died—the blessed Saviour
To redeem a world from hell!
Let me hasten
Far in heathen lands to dwell.

4. Bear me on, thou restless ocean;
Let the winds my canvas swell—
Heaves my heart with warm emotion,
While I go far hence to dwell.
Glad I bid thee,
Native land—Farewell—Farewell.

S. F. SMITH.

DAN or DENNIS. S. M.

Arranged from H. G. NAGELI.

1 Jesus, who knows full well The heart of ev-'ry saint, In-vites us all our griefs to tell, To pray, and ne-ver faint.

13. *Importunity in Prayer.* (395)

1 JESUS, who knows full well
The heart of every saint,
Invites us all our griefs to tell,
To pray, and never faint.

2 He bows his gracious ear,
We never plead in vain;
Then let us wait till he appear,
And pray, and pray again.

3 Though unbelief suggest,
"Why should we longer wait?"
He bids us never give him rest,
But knock at mercy's gate.

4 Jesus, the Lord, will hear
His chosen when they cry;
Yes, though he may awhile forbear,
He'll help them from on high.

5 Then let us earnest cry,
And never faint in prayer;
He sees, he hears, and from on high
Will make our cause his care.
NEWTON.

14. *Adoption.* (188)

1 BEHOLD, what wondrous grace
The Father has bestowed
On sinners of a mortal race
To call them sons of God!

2 Nor doth it yet appear
How great we must be made;
But when we see our Saviour here
We shall be like our Head.

3 A hope so much divine
May trials well endure;
May purify our souls from sin,
As Christ, the Lord, is pure.

4 If in my Father's love
I share a filial part,
Send down thy Spirit, like a dove,
To rest upon my heart.

5 We would no longer lie
Like slaves beneath the throne;
Our faith shall Abba, Father, cry,
And thou the kindred own.
WATTS.

15. *Joy in the Salvation of Sinners.* (121)

1 WHO can forbear to sing,
Who can refuse to praise,
When Zion's high, celestial King
His saving power displays?

2 When sinners at his feet,
By mercy conquered, fall?
When grace and truth, and justice meet,
And peace unites them all?

3 Who can forbear to praise
Our high, celestial King,
When sovereign, rich, redeeming grace
Invites our tongues to sing?
SWAIN.

16. *Sanctifying Influence.* (302)

1 Come, Holy Spirit, come;
　Let thy bright beams arise;
　Dispel the sorrow from our minds,
　The darkness from our eyes.

2 Convince us all of sin;
　Then lead to Jesus' blood,
　And to our wondering view reveal
　The mercies of our God.

3 Revive our drooping faith,
　Our doubts and fears remove,
　And kindle in our breasts the flame
　Of never-dying love.

4 'Tis thine to cleanse the heart,
　To sanctify the soul,
　To pour fresh life in every part,
　And new-create the whole.

5 Dwell, Spirit, in our hearts;
　Our minds from bondage free,
　Then shall we know, and praise, and love
　The Father, Son and Thee.
　　　　　　　　　Hart.

17. *Prayer for our Children.* (419)

1 Great God, now condescend,
　To bless our rising race;
　Soon may their willing spirits bend
　To thy victorious grace.

2 Oh, what a vast delight
　Their happiness to see!
　Our warmest wishes all unite
　To lead their souls to thee.

3 Dear Lord, thy Spirit pour
　Upon our infant seed;
　O, bring the long'd-for happy hour
　That makes them thine indeed!

4 May they receive thy word,
　Confess the Saviour's name,
　Then follow their despised Lord
　Through the baptismal stream.

Thus let our favored race
　Surround thy sacred board,
There to adore thy sovereign grace
　And sing their dying Lord.
　　　　　　　　　Fellows.

18. *God's Favor Preferred.* (314)

1 Let sinners take their course,
　And choose the road to death;
　But in the worship of my God
　I'll spend my daily breath.

2 My thoughts address his throne,
　When morning brings the light;
　I seek his blessing every noon,
　And pay my vows at night.

3 Thou wilt regard my cries,
　O, my eternal God,
　While sinners perish in surprise,
　Beneath thy holy rod.

4 Because they dwell at ease,
　And no sad changes feel,
　They neither fear nor trust thy name,
　Nor learn to do thy will.

5 But I, with all my cares,
　Will lean upon the Lord;
　I'll cast my burdens on his arm,
　And rest upon his word.

6 His arm shall well sustain
　The children of his love;
　The ground on which their safety stands
　No earthly power can move.
　　　　　　　　　Watts.

19. *Ingratitude Deplored.* (365)

1 Is this the kind return?
　Are these the thanks we owe?—
　Thus to abuse eternal love,
　Whence all our blessings flow?

2 To what a stubborn frame
　Has sin reduced our mind!
　What strange, rebellious wretches we!
　And God as strangely kind!

3 Turn, turn us, mighty God,
　And mould our souls afresh;
　Break, sovereign grace, these hearts of stone,
　And give us hearts of flesh.

4 Let past ingratitude
　Provoke our weeping eyes;
　And hourly, as new mercies fall,
　Let hourly thanks arise.
　　　　　　　　　Watts.

NAOMI. C. M.

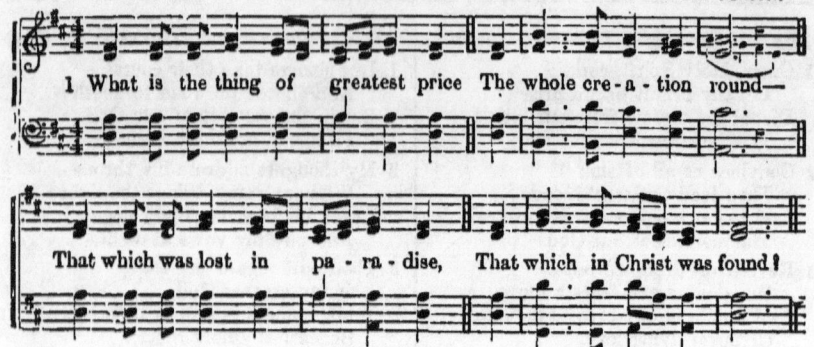

1 What is the thing of greatest price The whole cre-a-tion round— That which was lost in pa-ra-dise, That which in Christ was found!

20. *Value of the Soul.* (45)

2 The soul of man, Jehovah's breath,
That keeps two worlds at strife;
Hell moves beneath to work its death,
Heaven stoops to give it life,

3 God, to redeem it, did not spare
His well-beloved Son;
Jesus, to save it, deigned to bear
The sins of all in one.

4 And is this treasure borne below,
In earthen vessels frail?
Can none its utmost value know,
Till flesh and spirit fail?

5 Then let us gather round the cross,
That knowledge to obtain;
Not by the soul's eternal loss,
But everlasting gain.

21. *Salvation by Faith.* (346)

1 'Tis faith that lays the sinner low,
And covers him with shame;
Renouncing all self-righteousness,
It trusts in Jesus' name.

2 Faith works with power, but will not plead,
The best of works when done;
It knows no other ground of trust,
But in the Lord alone.

3 It gives no title, but receives;
No blessing it procures;
Yet, where it truly lives and reigns,
All blessings it insures.

4 Its sole dependence and its stay
Is Jesus' righteousness;
'Tis thus salvation is by faith,
And all of sovereign grace.

5 The more this principle prevails,
The more is grace adored;
No glory it assumes, but gives
All glory to the Lord.

BEDDOME.

22. *Trust in Immanuel.* (78)

1 DEAREST of all the names above,
My Saviour and my God,
Who can resist thy heavenly love,
Or trifle with thy blood?

2 'Tis by the merits of thy death
The Father smiles again;
'Tis by thine interceding breath,
The Spirit dwells with men.

3 Till God in human flesh, I see,
My thoughts no comfort find;
The holy, just, and sacred Three,
Are terrors to my mind.

4 But if Immanuel's face appear,
My hope, my joy, begin;
His name forbids my slavish fear;
His grace removes my sin.

5 While Jews on their own law rely,
And Greeks of wisdom boast,
I love th' incarnate mystery,
And there I fix my trust.

WATTS.

23. *Parental Solicitude.* (417)

1 How can we see the children, Lord
Thou hast in mercy given,
Remain regardless of thy word,
Without a hope of heaven!

2 How can we see them tread the path
That leads to endless death;
Thus adding to thy fearful wrath,
With every moment's breath?

3 Lord, hear the parents' earnest cry,
And save our children dear;
Now send thy Spirit from on high,
And fill them with thy fear.

4 O, make them love thy holy law,
And joyful walk therein:
Their hearts to new obedience draw;
Save them from every sin.

24. *Converting Grace implored.* (15)

1 Come, Lord, in mercy come again,
With thy converting power;
The fields of Zion thirst for rain,
O, send a gracious shower.

2 Our hearts are filled with sore distress,
While sinners all around
Are pressing on to endless death,
And no relief is found.

3 Dear Saviour, come with quickening power,
Thy mourning people cry;
Salvation bring in mercy's hour,
Nor let the sinner die.

4 Once more let converts throng thy house,
And shouts of victory raise;
Then shall our griefs be turned to joy,
And sighs, to songs of praise.

25. *Resolving to go to Jesus.* (99)

1 Come, trembling sinner, in whose breast
A thousand thoughts revolve—
Come, with your guilt and fear oppressed,
And make this last resolve:

2 I'll go to Jesus, though my sin
Hath like a mountain rose ;
I know his courts, I'll enter in,
Whatever may oppose.

3 Prostrate I'll lie before his throne,
And there my guilt confess;
I'll tell him I'm a wretch undone,
Without his sovereign grace.

4 I'll to the gracious King approach,
Whose sceptre pardon gives;
Perhaps he will command my touch-
And then the suppliant lives.

5 Perhaps he will admit my plea,
Perhaps will hear my prayer;
But if I perish, I will pray,
And perish only there.

6 I can but perish if I go;
I am resolved to try;
For if I stay away, I know
I must for ever die.
JONES.

26. *"Weep with them that Weep."* (506)

1 Lord, may our sympathizing breasts
The generous pleasure know,
Kindly to share in others' joys,
And weep for others' woe!

2 Where'er the helpless sons of grief
In low distress are laid,
Soft be our hearts, their pains to feel,
And swift our hands to aid.

3 Thus may the sacred law of love
Through all our actions shine,
And force a scoffing world to own
The Christian name divine.

27. *Prayer for Submission.* (355)

1 Father, whate'er of earthly bliss
Thy sovereign will denies,
Accepted at thy throne of grace,
Let this petition rise:

2 Give me a calm, a thankful heart,
From every murmur free;
The blessings of thy grace impart,
And make me live to thee.

3 Let the sweet hope that thou art mine
My life and death attend;
Thy presence through my journey shine
And crown my journey's end.
STEELE.

OLIPHANT. 8s, 7s & 4.

Dr. Lowell Mason.

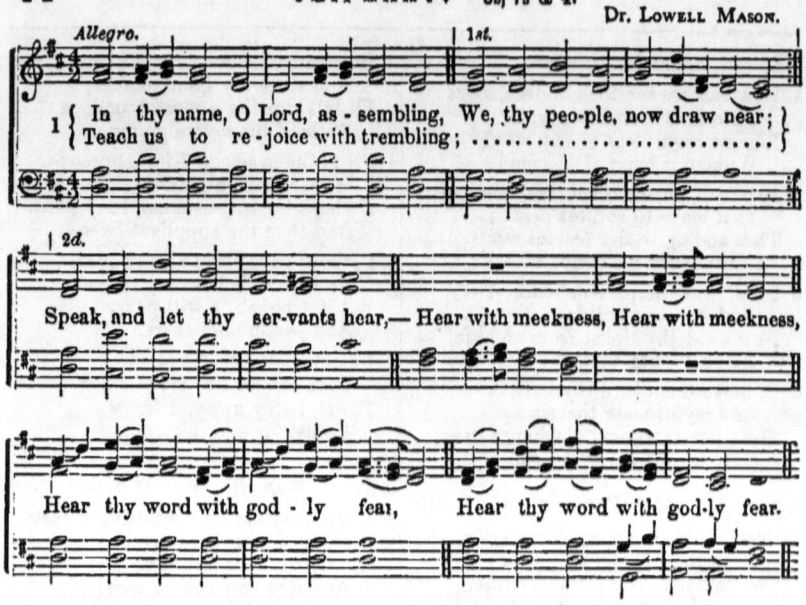

28.   *Spiritual Improvement.*   (1)

1 In thy name, O Lord, assembling,
    We, thy people, now draw near;
  Teach us to rejoice with trembling;
    Speak, and let thy servants hear,—
      Hear with meekness,—
  Hear thy word with godly fear.

2 While our days on earth are lengthened,
    May we give them, Lord, to thee;
  Cheer'd by hope, and daily strengthen'd,
    We would run, nor weary be,
      Till thy glory,
  Without clouds, in heaven we see.

3 There, in worship purer, sweeter,
    All thy people shall adore;
  Tasting of enjoyment greater
    Than they could conceive before,—
      Full enjoyment,—
  Holy bliss, forevermore.

                              Kelly.

29.   *Prayer for a Blessing.*   (7)

1 Come, thou soul-transforming Spirit,
    Bless the sower and the seed;
  Let each heart thy grace inherit;
    Raise the weak, the hungry feed;
      From the gospel
  Now supply thy people's need.

2 O, may all enjoy the blessing
    Which thy word's designed to give?
  Let us all, thy love possessing,
    Joyfully the truth receive,
      And forever
  To thy praise and glory live.

                              Jay.

Doxology.

  Father, Son, and Holy Spirit,
    Thou, the God whom we adore,
  May we all thy love inherit,
    To thine image us restore,
      Vast Eternal!
  Praises to thee evermore.

SAVIOUR, LIKE A SHEPHERD LEAD US. 8s, 7s & 4. 15
Wm. B. Bradbury.

1. Saviour, like a shepherd lead us, Much we need thy tend'rest care;
   In thy pleasant pastures feed us, For our use thy folds pre-pare.
   Bless-ed Je-sus, Bless-ed Je-sus, Thou hast bought us, thine we are,
   Blessed Je-sus, Blessed Je-sus, Thou hast bought us, thine we are.

30. "*Saviour, like a Shepherd lead us.*" (447)

2 We are thine, do thou befriend us,
Be the Guardian of our way;
Keep thy flock, from sin defend us,
Seek us when we go astray.
Blessed Jesus,
Hear, O hear us, when we pray.

3 Thou hast promised to receive us,
Poor and sinful though we be;
Thou hast mercy to relieve us,
Grace to cleanse, and power to free.
Blessed Jesus,
We will early turn to thee.

4 Early let us seek thy favor,
Early let us do thy will;
Blessed Lord and only Saviour,
With thy love our bosoms fill.
Blessed Jesus,
Thou hast loved us, love us still.

31. *God, the Pilgrim's Guide and Strength.* (472)
Tune Oliphant.

1 Guide me, O thou great Jehovah,
Pilgrim through this barren land:
I am weak, but thou art mighty;
Hold me with thy powerful hand:
Bread of heaven,
Feed me, till I want no more.

2 Open now the crystal fountain
Whence the healing streams do flow;
Let the fiery, cloudy pillar
Lead me all my journey through:
Strong Deliverer,
Be thou still my strength and shield.

2 When I tread the verge of Jordan,
Bid my anxious fears subside;
Bear me through the swelling current;
Land me safe on Canaan's side:
Songs of praises
I will ever give to thee.
Wm. Williams.

PETERBORO'. C. M.

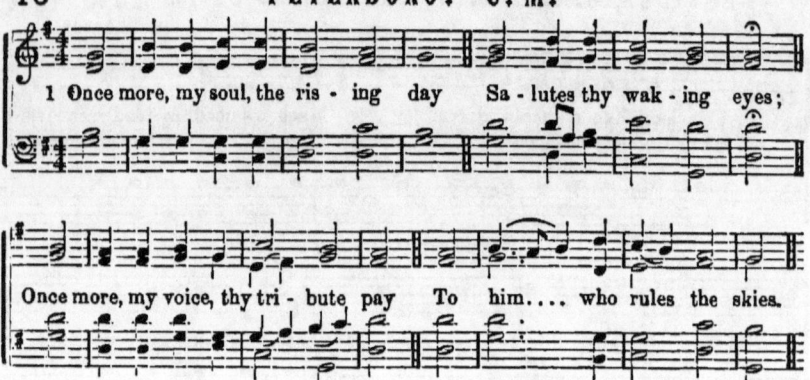

1 Once more, my soul, the ris-ing day Sa-lutes thy wak-ing eyes;
Once more, my voice, thy tri-bute pay To him.... who rules the skies.

32. *Divine Forbearance Acknowledged.* (386)

1 Once more, my soul, the rising day
Salutes thy waking eyes;
Once more, my voice, thy tribute pay
To him who rules the skies.

2 'Tis he supports my mortal frame;
My tongue shall speak his praise;
My sins would rouse his wrath to flame,
And yet his wrath delays.

3 Great God, let all my hours be thine,
While I enjoy the light;
Then shall my sun in smiles decline.
And bring a peaceful night.
WATTS.

33. *Hope of Heaven through Christ.* (584)

1 Blest be the everlasting God,
The Father of our Lord;
Be his abounding mercy praised,
His majesty adored.

2 When from the dead he raised his Son,
And called him to the sky,
He gave our souls a lively hope
That they should never die.

3 What though our inbred sins require
Our flesh to see the dust;
Yet as the Lord our Saviour rose,
So all his followers must.

4 There's an inheritance divine
Reserved against that day;

'Tis uncorrupted, undefiled,
And cannot fade away.

5 Saints by the power of God are kept
Till the salvation come;
We walk by faith as strangers here,
Till Christ shall call us home.
WATTS.

34. *Buried with him by Baptism.* (144)

1 Buried beneath the yielding wave,
The great Redeemer lies;
Faith views him in the watery grave,
And thence beholds him rise.

2 Thus do his willing saints to-day
Their ardent zeal express,
And, in the Lord's appointed way,
Fulfill all righteousness.

3 With joy we in his footsteps tread,
And would his cause maintain—
Like him be numbered with the dead,
And with him rise and reign.

4 His presence oft revives our hearts,
And drives our fears away;
When he commands, and strength imparts,
We cheerfully obey.

5 Now we, blest Saviour, would to thee
Our grateful voices raise;
Washed in the fountain of thy blood,
Our lives shall all be praise.
BEDDOME.

HYMNS.

35. *Spiritual Blessings.* (566)
1 Now, gracious Lord, thine arm reveal,
And make thy glory known;
Now let us all thy presence feel,
And soften hearts of stone.

2 From all the guilt of former sin
May mercy set us free;
And let the year we now begin,
Begin and end with thee.

3 Send down thy Spirit from above,
That saints may love thee more;
And sinners now may learn to love,
Who never loved before.

4 And when before thee we appear,
In our eternal home,
May growing numbers worship here,
And praise thee in our room.
NEWTON.

36. *The Safe Retreat.* (404)
1 DEAR Father, to thy mercy-seat
My soul for shelter flies:
'Tis here I find a safe retreat
When storms and tempests rise.

2 My cheerful hope can never die,
If thou, my God, art near;
Thy grace can raise my comforts high,
And banish every fear.

3 My great Protector and my Lord,
Thy constant aid impart;
O, let thy kind, thy gracious word
Sustain my trembling heart!

4 O, never let my soul remove
From this divine retreat!
Still let me trust thy power and love,
And dwell beneath thy feet.
STEELE.

37. *Goodness of God.* (185)
1 YE humble souls, approach your God
With songs of sacred praise;
For he is good, supremely good,
And kind are all his ways.

2 All nature owns his guardian care;
In him we live and move;
But nobler benefits declare
The wonders of his love.

3 He gave his Son, his only Son,
To save our souls from sin;
'Tis here he makes his goodness known,
And proves it all divine.

4 To this sure refuge, Lord, we come
And here our hope relies;
A safe defense, a peaceful home,
When storms of trouble rise.
STEELE.

38. *Watch and Pray.* (411)
1 THE Saviour bids us watch and pray,
Through life's brief, fleeting hour,
And gives the Spirit's quickening ray
To those who seek his power.

2 The Saviour bids us watch and pray,
Maintain a warrior's strife;
Help, Lord, to hear thy voice to-day;
Obedience is our life.

3 The Saviour bids us watch and pray;
For soon the hour will come
That calls us from the earth away,
To our eternal home.

4 O Saviour, we would watch and pray,
And hear thy sacred voice,
And walk, as thou hast marked the way,
To heaven's eternal joys.

39. *The Spirit's Presence Desired.* (163)
1 SPIRIT divine, attend our prayer,
And make this house thy home;
Descend with all thy gracious power;
O, come, great Spirit, come.

2 Come as the light; to us reveal
Our sinfulness and woe,
And lead us in the paths of life,
Where all the righteous go.

3 Come as the fire, and purge our hearts,
Like sacrificial flame;
Let every soul an offering be
To our Redeemer's name.

4 Come as a dove, and spread thy wings,—
The wings of peaceful love,—
And let the church on earth become
Blest as the church above.

ROCKINGHAM. L. M.
Dr. Lowell Mason

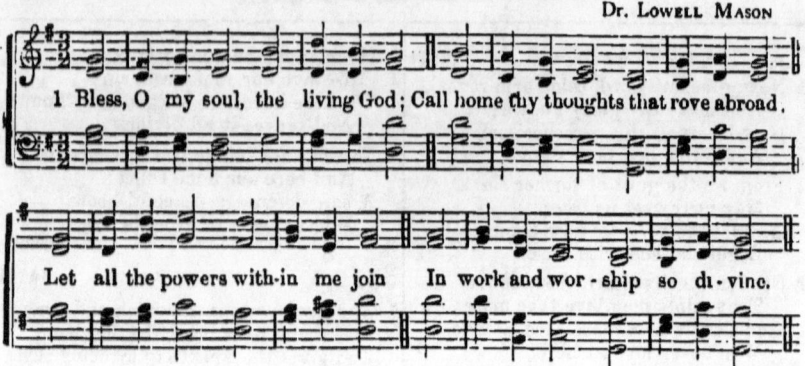

1 Bless, O my soul, the living God; Call home thy thoughts that rove abroad.
Let all the powers within me join In work and wor-ship so di-vine.

40. *The Goodness and Mercy of God Celebrated.* (203)

1 Bless, O, my soul, the living God;
Call home thy thoughts that rove abroad;
Let all the powers within me join
In work and worship so divine.

2 Bless, O, my soul, the God of grace;
His favors claim thy highest praise;
Let not the wonders he hath wrought
Be lost in silence and forgot.

3 'Tis he, my soul, that sent his Son
To die for crimes which thou hast done:
He owns the ransom, and forgives
The hourly follies of our lives.

4 Let every land his power confess;
Let all the earth adore his grace:
My heart and tongue, with rapture, join
In work and worship so divine.
WATTS.

41. *Lord's Day Service Pleasant.* (169)

Sweet is the work, my God, my King,
To praise thy name, give thanks, and sing,
To show thy love by morning light,
And talk of all thy truth at night.

2 Sweet is the day of sacred rest;
No mortal cares shall seize my breast;
O, may my heart in tune be found,
Like David's harp of solemn sound!

3 My heart shall triumph in my Lord,
And bless his works, and bless his word;
Thy works of grace, how bright they shine,
How deep thy counsels! how divine!
WATTS.

42. *Joy of Public Worship.* (172)

1 Great God, attend, while Zion sings
The joy that from thy presence springs:
To spend one day with thee on earth
Exceeds a thousand days of mirth.

2 Might I enjoy the meanest place
Within thy house, O God of grace,
Not tents of ease, nor thrones of power,
Should tempt my feet to leave thy door.

3 God is our sun—he makes our day:
God is our shield—he guards our way
From all th' assaults of hell and sin;
From foes without and foes within.

4 All needful grace will God bestow,
And crown that grace with glory too:
He gives us all things, and withholds
No real good from upright souls.

5 O God, our King, whose sovereign sway
The glorious host of heaven obey,
Display thy grace, exert thy power,
Till all on earth thy name adore.
WATTS.

JUST AS I AM. 8s & 6s.
Wm. B. Bradbury.

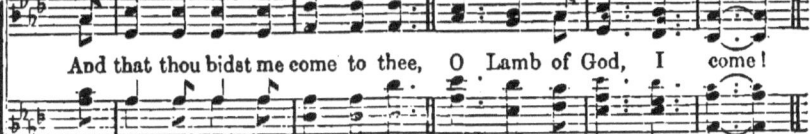

1 Just as I am, with-out one plea, But that thy blood was shed for me, And that thou bidst me come to thee, O Lamb of God, I come!

43. *Going to Jesus.* (106)

1 Just as I am, without one plea,
But that thy blood was shed for me,
And that thou bidst me come to thee,
O, Lamb of God, I come!

2 Just as I am—and waiting not
To rid my soul of one dark blot,
To thee, whose blood can cleanse each spot,
O, Lamb of God, I come.

3 Just as I am—poor, wretched, blind;
Sight, riches, healing of the mind,
Yea, all I need in thee to find,
O, Lamb of God, I come!

4 Just as I am, thou wilt receive,
Wilt welcome, pardon, cleanse, relieve!
Because thy promise I believe,
O, Lamb of God, I come!

5 Just as I am—thy love unknown,
Has broken every barrier down;
Now, to be thine, yea, thine alone,
O, Lamb of God, I come!
Charlotte Elliott.

44. *The Invitation.* (107)

1 Just as thou art,—without one trace
Of love, or joy, or inward grace,
Or fitness for the heavenly place,—
O, guilty sinner, come!

2 Thy sins I bore on Calvary's tree;
The stripes, thy due, were laid on me,
That peace and pardon might be free,—
O, wretched sinner, come!

3 Come, leave thy burden at the cross;
Count all thy gains but empty dross;
My grace repays all earthly loss,—
O, needy sinner, come!

4 Come, hither bring thy boding fears,
Thy aching heart, thy bursting tears;
'Tis mercy's voice salutes thine ears.—
O, trembling sinner, come!

5 The Spirit and the bride say, "Come!"
Rejoicing saints re-echo, "Come!"
Who faints, who thirsts, who will, may come,
Thy Saviour bids thee come.
C. Wesley.

45. *Glory of the Latter Day.* (541)
Tune Rockingham, page 18.

1 Arise, arise: with joy survey
The glory of the latter day;
Already is the dawn begun
Which marks at hand a rising sun.

2 Behold the way, ye heralds, cry;
Spare not, but lift your voices high;
Convey the sound from pole to pole,
Glad tidings to the captive soul.

3 Behold the way to Zion's hill,
Where Israel's God delights to dwell:
He fixes there his lofty throne,
And calls the sacred place his own.

INVITATION. 8s, 7s & 4s.

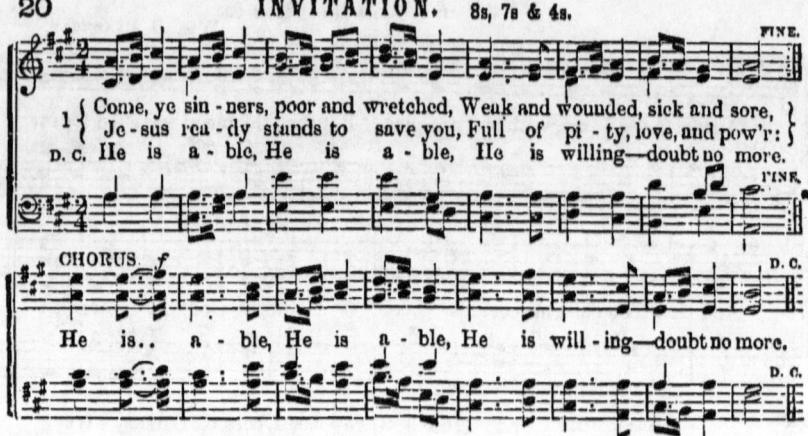

1. Come, ye sinners, poor and wretched, Weak and wounded, sick and sore,
Jesus ready stands to save you, Full of pity, love, and pow'r:
D.C. He is able, He is able, He is willing—doubt no more.

CHORUS.
He is.. able, He is able, He is willing—doubt no more.

46. *Jesus Ready to Save.* (64)

2 Come, ye thirsty, come and welcome;
God's free bounty glorify;
True belief and true repentance,
Every grace that brings us nigh—
Without money,
Come to Jesus Christ and buy.

3 Come, ye weary, heavy laden,
Lost and ruined by the fall;
If you tarry till you're better,
You will never come at all:
Not the righteous—
Sinners, Jesus came to call.

4 Let not conscience make you linger,
Nor of fitness fondly dream;
All the fitness he requireth,
Is to feel your need of him:
This he gives you—
'Tis the Spirit's rising beam.

5. Agonizing in the garden,
Lo! your Maker prostrate lies!
On the bloody tree behold him;
Hear him cry before he dies,
"It is finished!"
Sinners, will not this suffice?

6 Lo! the incarnate God ascended,
Pleads the merit of his blood;
Venture on him, venture wholly,

Let no other trust intrude:
None but Jesus
Can do helpless sinners good.
HART.

47. *Glad Tidings.* (54)

1 SINNERS, will you scorn the message
Sent in mercy from above?
Every sentence, oh, how tender
Every line is full of love:
Listen to it:
Every line is full of love.

2 Hear the heralds of the gospel,
News from Zion's King proclaim:
"Pardon to each rebel sinner;
Free forgiveness in his name:
How important!
"Free forgiveness in his name."

3 Tempted souls, they bring you succor,
Fearful hearts, they quell your fears;
And with news of consolation,
Chase away the falling tears;
Tender heralds!
Chase away the falling tears.

4 Who hath our report believed?
Who received the joyful word?
Who embraced the news of pardon
Offered to you by the Lord?
Can you slight it?
Offered to you by the Lord?
ALLEN.

HOWELL. 8s, 7s & 4s.
WM. B. BRADBURY.

Thou hast said, ex-alt-ed Je-sus, "Take thy cross and fol-low me;"
Shall the word with ter-ror seize us? Shall we from the bur-den flee?
Lord, I'll take it, Lord, I'll take it, And, re-joicing, fol-low thee.

48. *Buried with Christ by Baptism.* (138)

1 Thou hast said, exalted Jesus,
 "Take thy cross and follow me;"
Shall the word with terror seize us?
 Shall we from the burden flee?
  Lord, I'll take it,
 And rejoicing follow thee.

2 While this liquid tomb surveying,
 Emblem of my Saviour's grave,
Shall I shun its brink, betraying
 Feelings worthy of a slave?
  No! I'll enter:
 Jesus entered Jordan's wave.

3 Blest the sign which thus reminds me,
 Saviour, of thy love for me:
But more blest the love that binds me
 In its deathless bonds to thee:
  Oh, what pleasure,
 Buried with my Lord to be!

4 Should it rend some fond connection,
 Should I suffer shame or loss,
Yet the fragrant, blest reflection,
 I have been where Jesus was,
  Will revive me
 When I faint beneath the cross.

5 Fellowship with him possessing,
 Let me die to earth and sin;
Let me rise t' enjoy the blessing
 Which the faithful soul shall win:
  May I ever
 Follow where my Lord has been.
J. E. GILES.

49. *Coronation of the King of Kings.* (233)

1 Look, ye saints;—the sight is glorious;
 See the man of sorrows now;
From the fight returned victorious,
 Every knee to him shall bow:
  Crown him, crown him;
 Crowns become the victor's brow.

2 Crown the Saviour, angels, crown him;
 Rich the trophies Jesus brings;
In the seat of power enthrone him,
 While the heavenly concave rings:
  Crown him, crown him;
 Crown the Saviour King of kings.

3 Sinners in derision crowned him,
 Mocking thus the Saviour's claim;
Saints and angels crowd around him,
 Own his title, praise his name:
  Crown him, crown him;
 Spread abroad the victor's fame.

4 Hark! those bursts of acclamation!
 Hark! those loud, triumphant chords!
Jesus takes the highest station;
 Oh, what joy the sight affords!
  Crown him, crown him,
 King of kings, and Lord of lords.
KELLY.

SHINING SHORE. 8s & 7s.

G. F. Root.

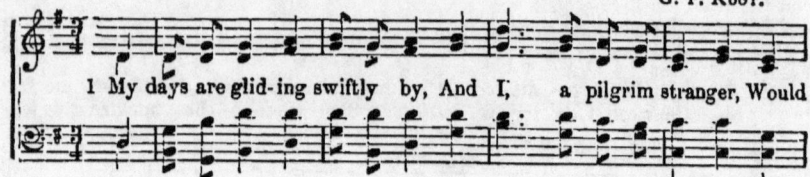

1 My days are glid-ing swiftly by, And I, a pilgrim stranger, Would
not de-tain them as they fly,—Those hours of toil and dan-ger.
D.s just be-fore the shin-ing shore We may al-most dis-cov-er.

CHORUS.

For now we stand on Jordan's strand, Our friends are passing o-ver; And

---

50. *The Shining Shore.* (451)

2 We'll gird our loins, my brethren dear,
  Our heavenly home discerning;
  Our absent Lord has left us word,
  Let every lamp be burning.
    For now we stand, &c.

3 Should coming days be cold and dark,
  We need not cease our singing;
  That perfect rest naught can molest
  Where golden harps are ringing.
    For now we stand, &c.

4 Let sorrow's rudest tempest blow,
  Each chord on earth to sever,
  Our King says come, and there's our home,
  Forever! Oh, forever!
    For now we stand, &c.

51. *Baptism; Christ, our Example.* (142)

1 This rite our blest Redeemer gave
  To all in him believing;
  He bids us seek this hallowed grave,
  To his example cleaving.
    I'll follow then my glorious Lord,
    Whate'er the ties I sever,
    He saved my soul, and left his word
    To guide me now and ever.

2 For me the cross and shame to bear,
  Dear Saviour, thou wast willing:
  Nor would I shrink thy yoke to wear,
  All righteousness fulfilling.
    I'll follow, &c.

3 Jesus, to thee I yield my all;
  In thy kind arms enfold me:
  My heart is fixed; no fears appal;
  Thy gracious power shall hold me.
    I'll follow, &c.   S. D. Phelps.

THE GARDEN HYMN. C. P. M. 23

52. *The Gracious Visit.* (14)

1 THE Lord into his garden comes,
   The spices yield their rich perfumes,
   The lilies grow and thrive;
   Refreshing showers of grace divine
   From Jesus flow to every vine,
   Which make the dead revive.

2 O, that this dry and barren ground
   In springs of water may abound,
   A fruitful soil become:
   The desert blossoms as the rose,
   While Jesus conquers all his foes,
   And makes his people one.

3 The glorious time is rolling on,
   The gracious work is now begun,
   My soul a witness is:
   I taste and see the pardon free
   For all mankind as well as me,
   Who come to Christ may live.

4 Amen, amen, my soul replies,
   I'm bound to meet you in the skies,
   And claim my mansion there;
   Now here's my heart, and here's my hand,
   To meet you in that heavenly land,
   Where we shall part no more.

53. *Awakened Sinner.*
   Tune MERIBAH, page 38. (111)

1 AWAKED by Sinai's awful sound,
   My soul in bonds of guilt I found,
   And knew not where to go;
   Eternal truth did loud proclaim,
   "The sinner must be born again,
   Or sink to endless wo."

2 Amazed I stood, but could not tell
   Which way to shun the gates of hell,
   For death and hell drew near;
   I strove, indeed, but strove in vain;
   "The sinner must be born again,"
   Still sounded in my ear.

3 When to the law I trembling fled,
   It poured its curses on my head;
   I no relief could find.
   This fearful truth increased my pain;
   "The sinner must be born again,"
   O'erwhelmed my tortured mind.

4 The saints I heard with rapture tell
   How Jesus conquered death and hell,
   And broke the fowler's snare;
   Yet when I found this truth remain,
   "The sinner must be born again,"
   I sunk in deep despair.

5 But while I thus in anguish lay,
   The gracious Saviour passed this way,
   And felt his pity move;
   The sinner, by his justice slain,
   Now by his grace is born again,
   And sings redeeming love.
                              OCCUM.

ARLINGTON. C. M.

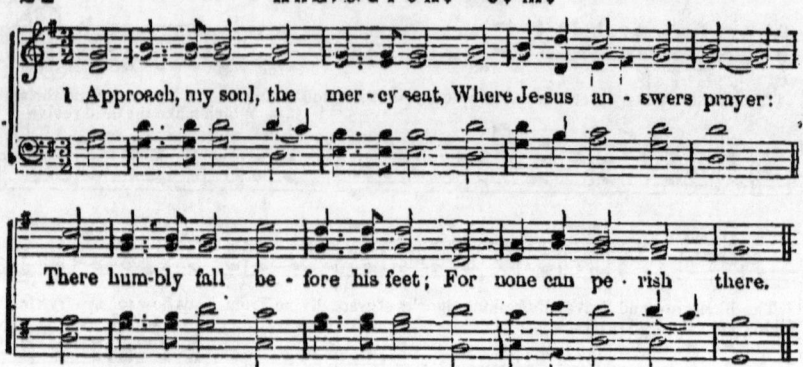

1. Approach, my soul, the mercy seat, Where Jesus answers prayer: There humbly fall before his feet; For none can perish there.

54. *Pleading the Promise.* (410)

2 Thy promise is my only plea;
  With this I venture nigh;
Thou callest burdened souls to thee
  And such, O Lord, am I.

3 Bowed down beneath a load of sin,
  By Satan sorely pressed,
By wars without, and fears within,
  I come to thee for rest.

4 Be thou my shield and hiding-place,
  That, sheltered near thy side,
I may my fierce accuser face,
  And tell him thou hast died.

5 Oh, wondrous love!—to bleed and die,
  To bear the cross and shame,
That guilty sinners, such as I,
  Might plead his gracious name!
    NEWTON.

55. *Desiring Evidence of Adoption.* (187)

1 THOU Lord of all the worlds on high,
  Allow my humble claim;
Nor, while a child would raise its cry,
  Disdain a Father's name.

2 My Father, God, how sweet the sound!
  How tender and how dear!
Not all the melody of heaven
  Could so delight the ear.

3 Come, sacred Spirit, seal the name
  On my believing heart,
And show that in Jehovah's grace
  I share a filial part.

4 By such a heavenly signal cheered,
  Unwavering I believe,
And, Abba, Father, humbly cry;
  Nor can the sign deceive.

5 On wings of everlasting love
  The Comforter is come;
All terrors at his voice disperse,
  And endless pleasures bloom.
    DODDRIDGE.

56. *Necessity of Sanctification.* (351)

1 NOR eye has seen, nor ear has heard,
  Nor sense nor reason known.
What joys the Father has prepared
  For those that love the Son.

2 But the good Spirit of the Lord
  Reveals a heaven to come;
The beams of glory in his word
  Allure and guide us home.

3 Pure are the joys above the sky,
  And all the region peace;
No wanton lips nor envious eye,
  Can see or taste the bliss.

4 Those holy gates for ever bar
  Pollution, sin and shame;
None shall obtain admittance there
  But followers of the Lamb.

5 He keeps the Father's book of life,
  There all their names are found;
The hypocrite in vain shall strive
  To tread the heavenly ground.
    WATTS.

HYMNS. 25

57. *Preciousness of the Bible.* (491)

1 How precious is the book divine,
By inspiration given!
Bright as a lamp its doctrines shine,
To guide our souls to heaven.

2 It sweetly cheers our drooping hearts
In this dark vale of tears;
Life, light and joy, it still imparts,
And quells our rising fears.

3 This lamp, through all the tedious night
Of life shall guide our way,
Till we behold the clearer light
Of an eternal day. FAWCETT.

58. *The Body and Blood of Christ.* (154)

1 HERE at thy table, Lord, we meet,
To feed on food divine;
Thy body is the bread we eat,
Thy precious blood the wine.

2 He that prepares this rich repast,
Himself comes down and dies;
And then invites us thus to feast
Upon the sacrifice.

3 Here peace and pardon sweetly flow;
Oh, what delightful food!
We eat the bread and drink the wine,
But think on nobler good.

4 Sure there was never love so free,
Dear Saviour, so divine;
Well thou mayst claim that heart of me,
Which owes so much to thine.
S. STENNETT.

59. *Living Waters.* (67)

1 OH! what amazing words of grace
Are in the gospel found!
Suited to every sinner's case,
Who hears the joyful sound.

2 Come, then, with all your wants and wounds;
Your every burden bring;
Here love, unchanging love, abounds,
A deep, celestial spring.

3 This spring with living water flows,
And heavenly joy imparts;
Come, thirsty souls, your wants disclose,
And drink with thankful hearts.

4 A host of sinners, vile as you,
Have here found life and peace;
Come, then, and prove its virtues too,
And drink, adore, and bless.
MEDLEY.

60. *Yet there is Room.* (60)

1 YE wretched, hungry, starving poor,
Behold a royal feast,
Where mercy spreads her bounteous store
For every humble guest.

2 There Jesus stands with open arms;
He calls—he bids you come:
Though guilt restrains, and fear alarms,
Behold, there yet is room.

3 O, come, and with his children taste
The blessings of his love;
While hope expects the sweet repast
Of nobler joys above.

4 There, with united heart and voice,
Before th' eternal throne,
Ten thousand thousand souls rejoice,
In songs on earth unknown.

5 And yet ten thousand thousand more
Are welcome still to come!
Ye longing souls, the grace adore
And enter while there's room.
STEELE.

61. *Filial Submission.* (355)

1 AND can my heart aspire so high
To say, "My Father," God?
Lord, at thy feet I fain would lie,
And learn to kiss the rod.

2 I would submit to all thy will,
For thou art good and wise;
Let each rebellious thought be still
Nor one faint murmur rise.

3 Thy love can cheer the darkest gloom
And bid me wait serene,
Till hopes and joys immortal bloom,
And brighten all the scene.

4 "My Father, God," permit my heart
To plead her humble claim,
And ask the bliss those words impart,
In my Redeemer's name.
STEELE.

LOTTIE. S. M.

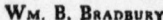

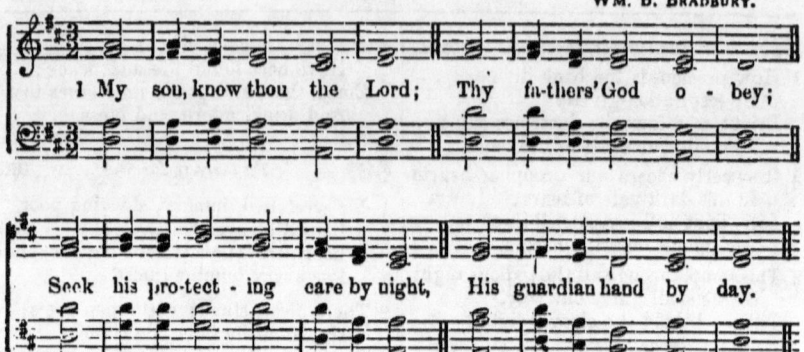

62. *Seek the Lord while He may be Found.* (421)

1 My son, know thou the Lord;
Thy fathers' God obey;
Seek his protecting care by night,
His guardian hand by day.

2 Call while he may be found;
O, seek him while he's near;
Serve him with all thy heart and mind,
And worship him with fear.

3 If thou wilt seek his face,
His ear will hear thy cry;
Then shalt thou find his mercy sure,
His grace forever nigh.

4 But if thou leave thy God,
Nor choose the path to heaven,
Then shalt thou perish in thy sins,
And never be forgiven.

63. *"O Lord, Revive thy Work."* (13)

1 O LORD, thy work revive
In Zion's gloomy hour,
And let our dying graces live
By thy restoring power.

2 O, let thy chosen few
Awake to earnest prayer;
Their sacred vows again renew,
And walk in filial fear.

3 Thy Spirit then will speak
Through lips of feeble clay,
Till hearts of adamant shall break,
Till rebels shall obey.

4 Now lend thy gracious ear;
Now listen to our cry;
O, come and bring salvation near;
Our souls on thee rely.

64. *Responsibility.* (319)

1 A CHARGE to keep I have,
The Lord to glorify,
Who died my ruined soul to save,
And fit it for the sky.

2 Let all my powers engage,
This calling to fulfill;
To serve and bless the present age,
And do my Master's will.

3 Arm me with jealous care,
As in thy sight to live;
And thus thy servant, Lord, prepare,
A strict account to give!

4 Help me to watch and pray,
And on thy grace rely;
O, let me ne'er my trust betray
But faithful live and die.

C. WESLEY.

DOYLE. S. M. 27

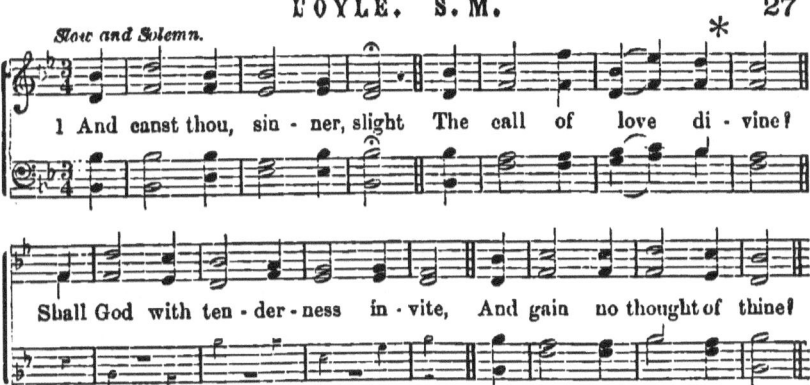

Slow and Solemn.

1 And canst thou, sin-ner, slight The call of love di-vine?
Shall God with ten-der-ness in-vite, And gain no thought of thine?

65. *Danger of Neglect.* (19)

1 AND canst thou, sinner, slight
The call of love divine?
Shall God with tenderness invite,
And gain no thought of thine?

2 Wilt thou not cease to grieve
The Spirit from thy breast,
Till he thy wretched soul shall leave
With all thy sins oppressed?

3 To-day, a pardoning God
Will hear the suppliant pray;
To-day, a Saviour's cleansing blood
Will wash thy guilt away.

4 But grace so dearly bought,
If yet thou wilt despise,
Thy fearful doom, with sorrow fraught,
Will fill thee with surprise.
HYDE.

66. *Trembling Solicitude.* (97)

1 MY former hopes are fled;
My terror now begins;
I feel, alas! that I am dead
In trespasses and sins.

2 Ah, whither shall I fly?
I hear the thunder roar;
The law proclaims destruction nigh,
And vengeance at the door.

3 When I review my ways,
I dread impending doom;
But, hark! a friendly whisper says,
"Flee from the wrath to come."

4 I see, or think I see,
A glimmering from afar,
A beam of day that shines for me,
To save me from despair.

5 Forerunner of the sun,
It marks the pilgrim's way,
I'll gaze upon it while I run,
And watch the rising day.
COWPER.

67. *Ark of Safety.* (515)

1 O, CEASE, my wandering soul,
On restless wing to roam;
All this wide world, to either pole,
Has not for thee a home.

2 Behold the ark of God;
Behold the open door;
O, haste to gain that dear abode,
And rove, my soul, no more.

3 There safe thou shalt abide,
There sweet shall be thy rest,
And every longing satisfied,
With full salvation blest.

MARCHING ALONG. 11s.

1 The people are gath'ring from near and from far, The trumpet is sounding the call for the war, The conflict is raging, 'twill be fearful and long, We'll gird on our armor, and be marching along.

CHORUS.

Marching along, we are marching along, Gird on the armor and be marching along, The conflict is raging, 'twill be fearful and long, Then gird on the armor and be marching along.

68.   *Christian Warfare.*   (325,

1 THE people are gath'ring from near and from far,
The trumpet is sounding the call for the war,
The conflict is raging, 'twill be fearful and long,
We'll gird on our armor, and be marching along.
Marching along, we are marching along,
Gird on the armor, and be marching along.
The conflict is raging, 'twill be fearful and long,
Then gird on the armor and be marching along.

2 The foe is before us in battle array,
But let us not waver nor turn from the way,
The Lord is our strength, be this ever our song,
With courage and faith we are marching along.—*Cho.*

3 We've enlisted for life, and will camp on the field,
With Christ as our Captain we never will yield;
The "sword of the Spirit," both trusty and strong,
We'll hold in our hands as we're marching along.—*Cho.*

4 Through conflicts and trials our crowns we must win,
For here we contend 'gainst temptation and sin;
But one thing assures us,—we can not go wrong,
If trusting our Saviour, while marching along.—*Cho.*

WILL YOU GO? 8s & 3s.
Western Melody.

1. We're trav'ling home to heaven above, Will you go? will you go?
To sing the Saviour's dy-ing love; Will you go? will you go?
D. C. And mil-lions more are on the road; Will you go? will you go?

Millions have reached that blest a-bode, A-noint-ed kings and priests to God;

69. *Will you Go?* (445)

2 We're going to walk the plains of light;
Will you go?
Far, far from curse and death and night;
Will you go?
The crown of life we then shall wear,
The conqueror's palm we then shall bear,
And all the joys of heaven we'll share;
Will you go?

3 The way to heaven is straight and plain;
Will you go?
Repent, believe, be born again;
Will you go?

The Saviour cries aloud to thee,
"Take up your cross and follow me,
And thou shalt my salvation see."
Will you go?

4 O, could I hear some sinner say,
" I will go;"
O, could I hear him humbly pray
" Make me go;"
And all his old companions tell,
" I will not go with you to hell,
I long with Jesus Christ to dwell;
Let me go."

UXBRIDGE. L. M.
Dr. Lowell Mason.

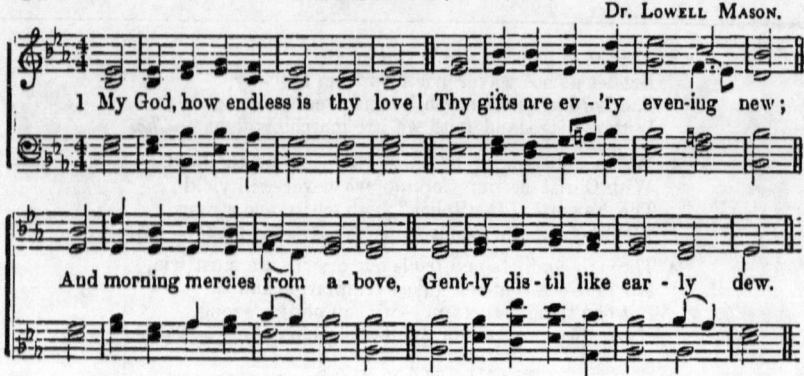

1 My God, how endless is thy love! Thy gifts are ev-'ry even-ing new; And morning mercies from a-bove, Gent-ly dis-til like ear-ly dew.

70. *A Song for Morning and Evening.* (391)

1 My God, how endless is thy love!
Thy gifts are every evening new;
And morning mercies from above,
Gently distil like early dew.

2 Thou sprend'st the curtains of the night,
Great Guardian of my sleeping hours;
Thy sovereign word restores the light,
And quickens all my drowsy powers.

3 I yield my powers to thy command;
To thee I consecrate my days;
Perpetual blessings from thine hand.
Demand perpetual songs of praise.
                                    Watts.

71. *Communion with Christ in Worship.* (5)

1 Far from my thoughts, vain world, begone!
Let my religious hours alone:
Fain would mine eyes my Saviour see,
I wait a visit, Lord, from thee.

|: My heart grows warm with holy fire,
And kindles with a pure desire:
Come, my dear Jesus! from above,
And feed my soul with heavenly love.

Blest Saviour! what delicious fare,
How sweet thine entertainments are!
Never did angels taste above,
Redeeming grace and dying love.
                                    Watts.

72. *The Gracious Promise.* (398)

1 Where two or three, with sweet accord,
Obedient to their sovereign Lord,
Meet to recount his acts of grace,
And offer solemn prayer and praise,

2 "There," says the Saviour, "will I be,
Amid this little company;
To them unvail my smiling face,
And shed my glories round the place."

3 We meet at thy command, dear Lord,
Relying on thy faithful word!
Now send thy Spirit from above,
And fill our hearts with heavenly love.
                                    Stennett.

73. *Religion Nothing without Love.* (357)

1 Had I the tongues of Greeks and Jews,
And nobler speech than angels use,
If love be absent, I am found,
Like tinkling brass, an empty sound.

2 Were I inspired to preach and tell
All that is done in heaven or hell,
Or could my fate the world remove,
Still am I nothing without love.

3 Should I distribute all my store,
To feed the hungry, clothe the poor—
Or give my body to the flame,
To gain a martyr's glorious name—

4 If love to God and love to men
Be absent, all my hopes are vain;
Nor tongues, nor gifts, nor fiery zeal,
The work of love can e'er fulfill.
                                    Watts.

BLOOMFIELD CHANT. L. M. 31

From the "Shawm."

1 Stand up, my soul, shake off thy fears, And gird the gospel armor on; March to the gates of endless joy, Where Jesus, thy great Captain's, gone, Where Jesus, thy great Captain's, gone.

* May end here.

74.   *The March.*   (324)

1 STAND up, my soul, shake off thy fears,
And gird the gospel armor on;
March to the gates of endless joy,
Where Jesus, thy great Captain's, gone.

2 Hell and thy sins resist thy course;
But hell and sin are vanquished foes;
Thy Saviour nailed them to the cross,
And sung the triumph when he rose.

3 Then let my soul march boldly on,—
Press forward to the heavenly gate;
There peace and joy eternal reign,
And glittering robes for conquerors wait.

4 There shall I wear a starry crown,
And triumph in almighty grace;
While all the armies of the skies
Join in my glorious Leader's praise.
WATTS.

75.   *Divine Power Supplicated.*   (524)

1 ARM of the Lord, awake, awake;
Put on thy strength, the nations shake;
Now, let the world, adoring, see
Triumphs of mercy wrought by thee.

2 Say to the heathen, from thy throne,
"I am Jehovah, God alone:"
Thy voice their idols shall confound,
And cast their altars to the ground.

3 Let Zion's time of favor come;
O, bring the tribes of Israel home;
Soon may our wandering eyes behold
Gentiles and Jews in Jesus' fold.

4 Almighty God, thy grace proclaim
Through every clime, of every name;
Let adverse powers before thee fall,
And crown the Saviour Lord of all.
C. WESLEY.

76.   *The Christian Race.*   (331)

1 AWAKE, our souls; away, our fears;
Let every trembling thought be gone;
Awake, and run the heavenly race,
And put a cheerful courage on.

2 True, 'tis a strait and thorny road,
And mortal spirits tire and faint;
But they forget the mighty God,
Who feeds the strength of every saint.

3 From thee the overflowing spring,
Our souls shall drink a full supply;
While those who trust their native strength
Shall melt away, and droop, and die.

4 Swift as an eagle cuts the air,
We'll mount aloft to thine abode;
On wings of love our souls shall fly,
Nor tire amid the heavenly road.
WATTS

PENITENCE. S. M.

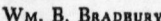
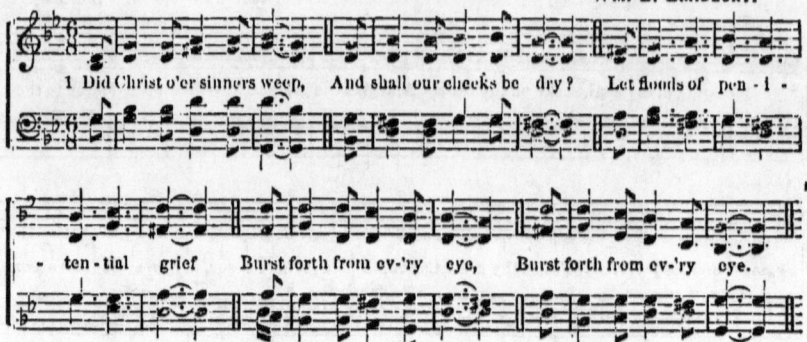

77. *Repentance in View of Christ's Compassion.* (9)

1 DID Christ o'er sinners weep,
  And shall our cheeks be dry?
Let floods of penitential grief
  Burst forth from every eye.

2 The Son of God in tears
  The wondering angels see;
Be thou astonished, O my soul;
  He shed those tears for thee.

3 He wept that we might weep;
  Each sin demands a tear:
In heaven alone no sin is found,
  And there's no weeping there.
              BEDDOME.

78. *Hope from the Gospel only.* (84)

1 GOD's holy law, transgressed,
  Speaks nothing but despair;
Burden'd with guilt, with grief oppress'd,
  We find no comfort there.

2 Not all our groans and tears,
  Nor works which we have done,
Nor vows, nor promises, nor prayers,
  Can e'er for sin atone.

3 Relief alone is found
  In Jesus' precious blood:
'Tis this that heals the mortal wound,
  And reconciles to God.

4 High lifted on the cross,
  The spotless Victim dies:
This is salvation's only source;
  And hence our hopes arise.
              BEDDOME.

79. *The Solemn Question.* (583)

1 WAKED by the trumpet's sound,
  I from the grave must rise,
And see the Judge with glory crowned,
  And see the flaming skies.

2 How shall I leave my tomb?—
  With triumph, or regret?—
A fearful or a joyful doom,
  A curse or blessing, meet?

3 I must from God be driven,
  Or with my Saviour dwell;
Must come, at his command to heaven,
  Or else depart—to hell.

4 O Thou, that wouldst not have
  One wretched sinner die,—
Who diedst thyself, my soul to save
  From endless misery;

5 Show me the way to shun
  Thy dreadful wrath severe,
That, when thou comest on thy throne,
  I may with joy appear.

DOVER. S. M.   33

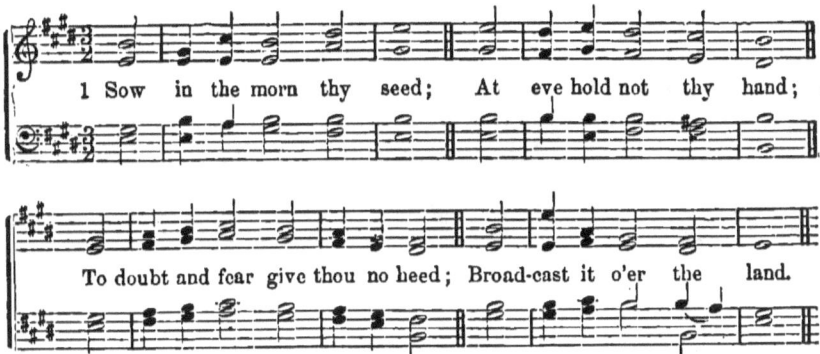

80.   *Sowing Ever.*   (342)
1 Sow in the morn thy seed;
　At eve hold not thy hand;
　To doubt and fear give thou no heed;
　Broadcast it o'er the land.

2 And duly shall appear,
　In verdure, beauty, strength,
　The tender blade, the stalk, the ear,
　And the full corn at length.

3 Thou canst not toil in vain;
　Cold, heat, and moist and dry,
　Shall foster and mature the grain
　For garners in the sky.

4 Thence, when the glorious end,
　The day of God, shall come,
　The angel reapers shall descend,
　And heaven cry, "Harvest Home!"
　　　　　　　　MONTGOMERY.

81.   *Hope of the Resurrection.*   (585)
1 AND must this body die?
　This mortal frame decay?
　And must these active limbs of mine
　Lie mouldering in the clay?

2 God, my Redeemer, lives,
　And often, from the skies
　Looks down, and watches all my dust,
　Till he shall bid it rise.
　　　3

3 Arrayed in glorious grace,
　Shall these vile bodies shine;
　And every shape, and every face,
　Look heavenly and divine.

4 These lively hopes we owe
　To Jesus' dying love;
　We would adore his grace below,
　And sing his power above.
　　　　　　　　　WATTS.

82.   *The Colporteur's Work.*   (487)
1 Now mercy's light-winged page,
　Swift messenger of love,
　Comes to the home of lonely age,
　To guide his thoughts above.

2 The way-side beggar hears
　Its ministry divine;
　And want's pale children dry their tears
　To trace its radiant line.

3 On, on, ye faithful band,
　Your precious bounty shed;
　With single hearts and tireless hand,
　The joyful tidings spread.

4 "The Lord our righteousness"
　Still on your banner write;
　Nor stay your toil until he bless
　The world with saving light.
　　　　　　　L. H. SIGOURNEY.

HEBER. C. M.

Geo. Kingsley.

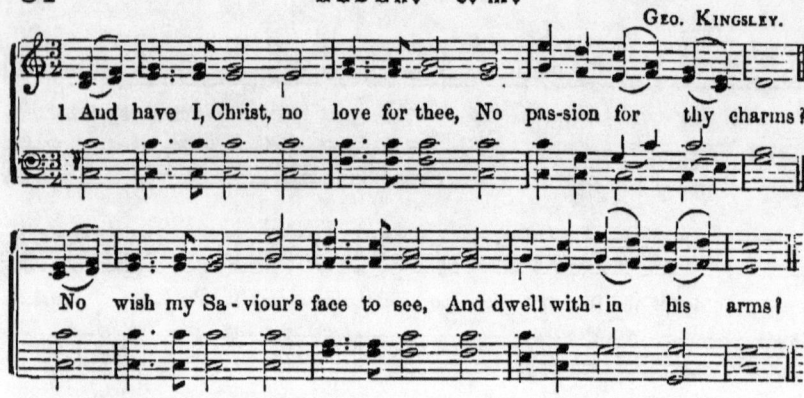

1 And have I, Christ, no love for thee, No passion for thy charms?
No wish my Saviour's face to see, And dwell within his arms?

83. *Profession of Love to Christ.* (241)

2 Is there no spark of gratitude,
   In this cold heart of mine,
   To Him whose generous bosom glowed
   With friendship all divine?

3 Can I pronounce his charming name,
   His acts of kindness tell,
   And, while I dwell upon the theme,
   No sweet emotion feel?

4 Such base ingratitude as this
   What heart but must detest?
   Sure Christ deserves the noblest place
   In every human breast.

5 A very wretch, Lord, I should prove,
   Had I no love for thee;
   Rather than not my Saviour love,
   O, may I cease to be.
                         S. Stennett.

84. *Reflections at the End of the Year.* (560)

1 And now, my soul, another year
   Of thy short life has past;
   I cannot long continue here,
   And this may be my last.

2 Much of my hasty life is gone,
   Nor will return again;
   And swift my passing moments run—
   The few that yet remain.

3 Awake, my soul, with utmost care
   Thy true condition learn:

   What are thy hopes? how sure? how fair?
   What is thy great concern?

4 Behold, another year begins;
   Set out afresh for heaven;
   Seek pardon for thy former sins,
   In Christ so freely given.

5 Devoutly yield thyself to God,
   And on his grace depend;
   With zeal pursue the heavenly road,
   Nor doubt a happy end.

85. *An Afterthought of the Afflicted.* (3½℃)

1 I cannot call affliction sweet;
   And yet 'twas good to bear:
   Affliction brought me to thy feet,
   And I found comfort there.

2 No balm that earthly plants distil
   Can soothe the mourner's smart;
   No mortal hand, with lenient skill,
   Bind up the broken heart.

3 But one alone, who reigns above,
   Our woe to joy can turn,
   And light the lamp of joy and love,
   That long has ceased to burn.

4 Then, O, my soul, to Jesus flee;
   To him thy woes reveal;
   His eye alone thy wounds can see,
   His hand alone can heal.
                         Montgomery.

86. *Preparation for Death.* (578)
1 IF I must die, O, let me die
With hope in Jesus' blood—
The blood that saves from sin and guilt,
And reconciles to God.

2 If I must die, O, let me die
In peace with all mankind,
And change these fleeting joys below
For pleasures more refined.

3 If I must die,—and die I must,—
Let some kind seraph come,
And bear me on his friendly wing
To my celestial home.

4 Of Canaan's land, from Pisgah's top,
May I but have a view,
Tho' Jordan should o'erflow its banks,
I'll boldly venture through.
BEDDOME.

87. *Pardon Implored.* (369)
1 How oft, alas! this wretched heart
Has wandered from the Lord!
How oft my roving thoughts depart,
Forgetful of his word!

2 Yet sovereign mercy calls, "Return;"
Dear Lord, and may I come?
My vile ingratitude I mourn;
O, take the wanderer home.

3 And canst thou, wilt thou, yet forgive,
And bid my crimes remove?
And shall a pardoned rebel live
To speak thy wondrous love?

4 Thy pardoning love, so free, so sweet,
Dear Saviour, I adore;
O keep me at thy sacred feet,
And let me rove no more.
STEELE.

88. *Self-Denial for Christ.* (258)
1 AND must I part with all I have,
My dearest Lord, for thee?
It is but right, since thou hast done
Much more than this for me.

2 Yes, let it go! one look from thee
Will more than make amends
For all the losses I sustain
Of honor, riches, friends.

3 Ten thousand worlds, ten thousand lives,
How worthless they appear,
Compared with thee, supremely good,
Divinely bright and fair!

4 Saviour of souls, could I from thee
A single smile obtain,
The loss of all things I could bear,
And glory in my gain.
BEDDOME.

89. *The Day Approaches.* (588)
1 THE day approaches, O, my soul,—
The great, decisive day,—
Which from the verge of mortal life
Shall bear thee far away.

2 Another day more awful dawns,
And, lo! the Judge appears:
Ye heavens, retire before his face;
And sink, ye darkened stars.

3 Yet does one short, preparing hour—
One precious hour—remain:
Rouse, then, my soul, with all thy power,
Nor let it pass in vain.
DODDRIDGE.

90. *Church Covenant.* (155)
1 PLANTED in Christ, the living vine,
This day, with one accord,
Ourselves, with humble faith and joy,
We yield to thee, O Lord.

2 Joined in one body may we be;
One inward life partake;
One be our heart; one heavenly hope
In every bosom wake.

3 In prayer, in effort, tears, and toils,
One wisdom be our guide;
Taught by one Spirit from above,
In thee may we abide.

4 Complete in us, whom grace hath called,
Thy glorious work begun,
O Thou, in whom the church on earth
And church in heaven are one.

5 Then, when, among the saints in light,
Our joyful spirits shine,
Shall anthems of immortal praise,
O Lamb of God, be thine.
S. F. SMITH.

LOOKING HOME. 7s & 6s.
Wm. B. Bradbury.

91. "*Looking Home.*" (457)

1 Ah! this heart is void and chill,
'Mid earth's noisy throngings;
For my Father's mansions still
Earnestly is longing.
Looking home, looking home,
Towards the heavenly mansions
Jesus hath prepared for me,
In his Father's kingdom.

2 Soon the glorious day will dawn,
Heavenly pleasures bringing;
Night will be exchanged for morn,
Sighs give place to singing.
Looking home, &c.

3 Oh! to be at home again,
All for which we're sighing,
From all earthly want and pain
To be swiftly flying.
Looking home, &c.

4 Blessed home! Oh, blessed home!
All for which we're sighing,

Soon our Lord will bid us come
To our Father's kingdom.
Looking home, &c.

92 *God is Love.* (213)
. Tune Melody, page 5.

1 Come, ye that know and fear the Lord!
And raise your souls above;
Let every heart and voice accord,
To sing that—God is love.

2 This precious truth his word declares,
And all his mercies prove;
While Christ, th' atoning Lamb, appears,
To show that—God is love.

3 Behold, his loving-kindness waits
For those who from him rove,
And calls for mercy reach their hearts,
To teach them—God is love.

4 O, may we all, while here below,
This best of blessings prove;
Till warmer hearts, in brighter world
Shall shout that—God is love.
G. Burder.

OH, HOW HE LOVES! 8s & 4s. 37
Arranged.

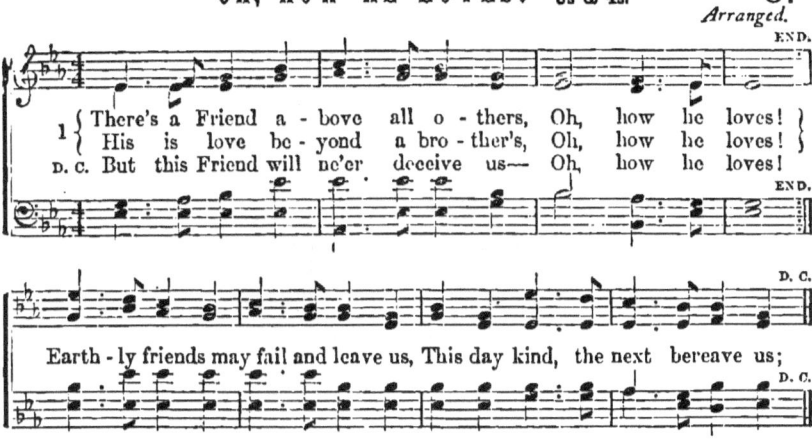

1. There's a Friend above all others, Oh, how he loves!
His is love beyond a brother's, Oh, how he loves!
Earthly friends may fail and leave us, This day kind, the next bereave us;
But this Friend will ne'er deceive us— Oh, how he loves!

93. *Jesus, a Loving Friend.* (240)

2 Blessed Jesus! wouldst thou know him,
  Oh, how he loves!
Give thyself e'en this day to him,
  Oh, how he loves!
Is it sin that pains and grieves thee?
Doubts and trials do they tease thee?
Jesus can from all release thee—
  Oh, how he loves!

3 Pause, my soul! adore and wonder,
  Oh, how he loves!
Nought can cleave this love asunder;
  Oh, how he loves!
Neither trial, nor temptation,
Doubt, nor fear, nor tribulation,
Can bereave us of salvation—
  Oh, how he loves!

4 Let us still this love be viewing,
  Oh, how he loves!
And, though faint, keep on pursuing,
  Oh, how he loves!
He will strengthen each endeavor,
And when passed o'er Jordan's river,
This shall be our song forever—
  Oh, how he loves!

94. *The Warning Voice.* (37)
Tune MERIBAH, page 38.

1 That warning voice, O, sinner, hear,
  And while salvation lingers near,
    The heav'nly call obey;
  Flee from destruction's downward path,
  Flee from the threat'ning storm of wrath,
    That rises o'er thy way.

2 Soon night comes on with thick'ning shade,
  The tempest hovers o'er thy head,
    The winds their fury pour:
  The lightnings rend the earth and skies,
  The thunders roar, the flames arise;
    What terrors fill that hour.

3 That warning voice, O, sinner, hear,
  Whose accents linger on thine ear;
    Thy footsteps now retrace;
  Renounce thy sins and be forgiv'n,
  Believe, become an heir of heav'n,
    And sing redeeming grace.

4 Then, while a voice of pardon speaks.
  The storm is hush'd, the morning breaks,
    The heavens are all serene;
  Fresh verdure clothes the beauteous fields,
  Joy echoes on the distant hills,
    New wonders fill the scene.

T. HASTINGS.

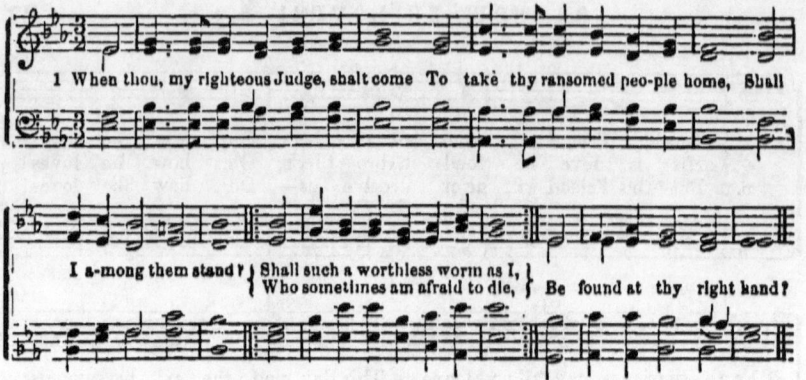

95. *Pleading for Acceptance.* (368)

1 When thou, my righteous Judge, shalt come
   To take thy ransomed people home,
   Shall I among them stand?
   Shall such a worthless worm as I,
   Who sometimes am afraid to die,
   Be found at thy right hand?

2 I love to meet among them now,
   Before thy gracious feet to bow,
   Though vilest of them all:
   But—can I bear the piercing thought?—
   What if my name should be left out,
   When thou for them shalt call?

3 Prevent, prevent it by thy grace;
   Be thou, dear Lord, my hiding-place,
   In this, th' accepted day;
   Thy pardoning voice, O, let me hear,
   To still my unbelieving fear,
   Nor let me fall, I pray.

4 Let me among thy saints be found
   Whene'er the archangel's trump shall
      sound,
   To see thy smiling face;
   Then loudest of the crowd I'll sing,
   While heaven's resounding mansions ring
   With shouts of sovereign grace.

96. *Trusting in Christ for Pardon.* (103)

1 O thou that hear'st the prayer of faith,
   Wilt thou not save a soul from death,
      That casts itself on thee?
   I have no refuge of my own,
   But fly to what my Lord hath done
      And suffered once for me.

2 Slain in the guilty sinner's stead,
   His spotless righteousness I plead,
      And his availing blood;
   That righteousness my robe shall be,
   That merit shall atone for me,
      And bring me near to God.

3 Then save me from eternal death,
   The spirit of adoption breathe,
      His consolations send;
   By him some word of life impart,
   And sweetly whisper to my heart,
      "Thy Maker is thy friend."

4 The king of terrors then would be
   A welcome messenger to me,
      To bid me come away;
   Unclogged by earth, or earthly things,
   I'd mount, I'd fly, with eager wings,
      To everlasting day.
                                TOPLADY.

BREMEN. C. P. M.

Manhattan Coll.

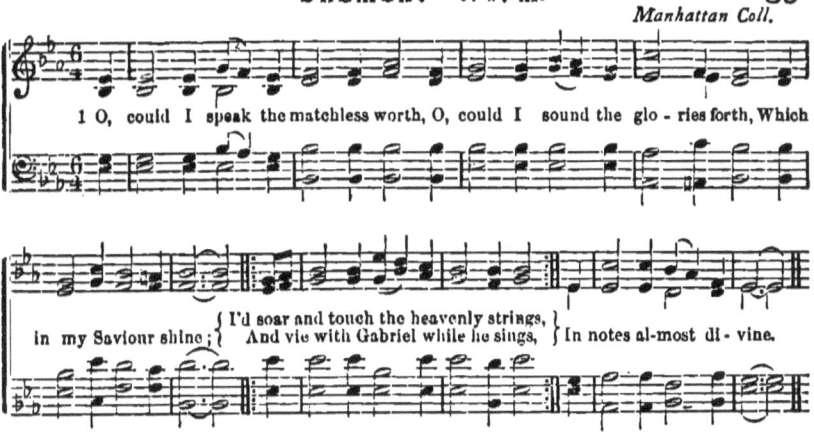

1 O, could I speak the matchless worth, O, could I sound the glories forth, Which in my Saviour shine; I'd soar and touch the heavenly strings, And vie with Gabriel while he sings, In notes almost divine.

97. "*The unsearchable riches of Christ.*" (276)

1 O, could I speak the matchless worth,
O, could I sound the glories forth
Which in my Saviour shine!
I'd soar, and touch the heavenly strings,
And vie with Gabriel, while he sings,
In notes almost divine.

2 I'd sing the precious blood he spilt,
My ransom from the dreadful guilt
Of sin and wrath divine:
I'd sing his glorious righteousness,
In which all perfect, heavenly dress
My soul shall ever shine.

3 I'd sing the characters he bears,
And all the forms of love he wears,
Exalted on his throne:
In loftiest songs of sweetest praise,
I would to everlasting days
Make all his glories known.

4 Well, the delightful day will come
When my dear Lord will bring me home,
And I shall see his face;
Then with my Saviour, Brother, Friend,
A blest eternity I'll spend,
Triumphant in his grace.
MEDLEY.

98. *Eternity Contemplated.* (34)
Tune MERIBAH, page 38.

1 Lo! on a narrow neck of land,
'Twixt two unbounded seas I stand,
Yet how insensible!
A point of time, a moment's space,
Removes me to yon heavenly place,
Or shuts me up in hell.

2 O God, my inmost soul convert,
And deeply on my thoughtless heart,
Eternal things impress;
Give me to feel their solemn weight,
And save me ere it be too late;
Wake me to righteousness.

3 Be this my one great business here,
With holy trembling, holy fear,
To make my calling sure;
Thine utmost counsel to fulfill,
And suffer all thy righteous will,
And to the end endure.

4 Then Saviour, then my soul receive,
Transported from this vale, to live
And reign with thee above;
Where faith is sweetly lost in sight,
And hope, in full, supreme delight,
And everlasting love
C. WESLEY

BROWN. C. M.

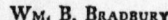

1 The Saviour! Oh, what endless charms Dwell in that blissful sound! Its influence ev'ry fear disarms, And spreads delight around.

99. *Condescension of Christ.* (227)

2 Here pardon, life and joy divine,
In rich profusion flow,
For guilty rebels, lost in sin,
And doomed to endless woe.

3 The mighty former of the skies
Descends to our abode,
While angels view with wondering eyes,
And hail the incarnate God.

4 How rich the depths of love divine!
Of bliss, a boundless store!
Dear Saviour, let me call thee mine;
I cannot wish for more.

5 On thee alone my hope relies;
Beneath thy cross I fall,
My Lord, my life, my sacrifice,
My Saviour and my all.
STEELE.

100. *Sanctuary Blessing.* (162)

1 Dear Shepherd of thy people, here
Thy presence now display;
As thou hast given a place for prayer,
So give us hearts to pray.

2 Within these walls let holy peace,
And love and concord dwell;
Here give the troubled conscience ease,
The wounded spirit heal.

3 The feeling heart, the melting eye,
The humble mind bestow;
And shine upon us from on high,
To make our graces grow!

4 May we in faith receive the word,
In faith present our prayers;
And in the presence of our Lord
Unbosom all our cares.

5 And may the gospel's joyful sound,
Enforced by mighty grace,
Awaken many sinners round,
To come and fill the place.
NEWTON.

101. *The Harvest.* (16)

1 The Lord can clear the darkest skies,
Can give us day for night;
Make drops of sacred sorrow rise
To rivers of delight.

2 Let those that sow in sadness wait
Till the fair harvest come,
They shall confess their sheaves are great,
And shout the blessings home.

3 Though seed lie buried long in dust,
It shan't deceive their hope;
The precious grain can ne'er be lost,
For grace insures the crop. WATTS.

102. *"We are more than Conquerors."* (242)

1 Oh, who can part our ransomed souls
From Jesus and his love!
Or break the sacred chain that binds
The earth to heaven above?

2 Let troubles rise, and terrors frown,
And days of darkness fall;—
Through him all dangers we'll defy,
And more than conquer all.

HYMNS.

3 Nor death, nor life, nor earth, nor hell,
Nor time's destroying sway
Can e'er efface us from his heart,
Or make his love decay.

4 Each coming period he will bless,
As he hath blessed the past ;
He loved us from the first of time,—
He loves us to the last.

103. *Care for the Poor.* (503)

1 LORD, lead the way the Saviour went,
By lane and cell obscure,
And let our treasures still be spent,
Like his, upon the poor.

2 Like him, thro' scenes of deep distress,
Who bore the world's sad weight,
We, in their gloomy loneliness,
Would seek the desolate.

3 For thou hast placed us side by side,
In this wide world of ill ;
And that thy followers may be tried,
The poor are with us still.

4 Small are the offerings we can make ;
Yet thou hast taught us, Lord,
If given for the Saviour's sake,
They lose not their reward.
CROSWELL.

104. *The Saviour's Invitation.* (75)

1 THE Saviour calls ; let every ear
Attend the heavenly sound ;
Ye doubting souls, dismiss your fear ;
Hope smiles reviving round.

2 For every thirsty, longing heart,
Here streams of bounty flow ;
And life, and health, and bliss impart,
To banish mortal woe.

3 Ye sinners, come ; 'tis mercy's voice ;
That gracious voice obey ;
'Tis Jesus calls to heavenly joys ;
And can you yet delay ?

4 Dear Saviour, draw reluctant hearts ;
To thee let sinners fly,
And take the bliss thy love imparts,
And drink, and never die.
STEELE.

105. *Happy Child of Grace.* (422)

1 How happy every child of grace,
Who knows his sins forgiven ;
This earth, he says, is not my place,
I seek my home in heaven.
Oh ! heaven, dear heaven, sweet
land of rest,
When shall my soul be there,
To dwell forever with the blest,
Eternal joys to share.

2 A country far from mortal sight ;
Yet, Oh ! by faith I see
The land of rest, the saints' delight,
The heaven prepared for me.

3 Oh, what a blessed hope is ours !
While here on earth we stay,
We more than taste the heav'nly powers,
And antedate that day.

4 We feel the resurrection near,
Our life in Christ concealed,
And with his glorious presence here
Our earthen vessels filled.

5 O, would he more of heaven bestow ;
And let the vessel break ;
And let our ransomed spirits go,
To grasp the God we seek ?

6 In rapturous awe on him to gaze,
Who bought the sight for me,
And shout and wonder at his grace
Through all eternity.
C. WESLEY.

106. *The Great Change.* (118)

1 WHEN God revealed his gracious name,
And changed my mournful state,
My rapture seemed a pleasing dream,
The grace appeared so great.

2 The world beheld the glorious change,
And did thy hand confess ;
My tongue broke out in unknown strains,
And sung surprising grace.

3 "Great is the work," my neighbors cried,
And owned thy power divine ;
" Great is the work," my heart replied,
" And be the glory thine."
WATTS.

SWEET REST IN HEAVEN.

Wm. B. Bradbury.

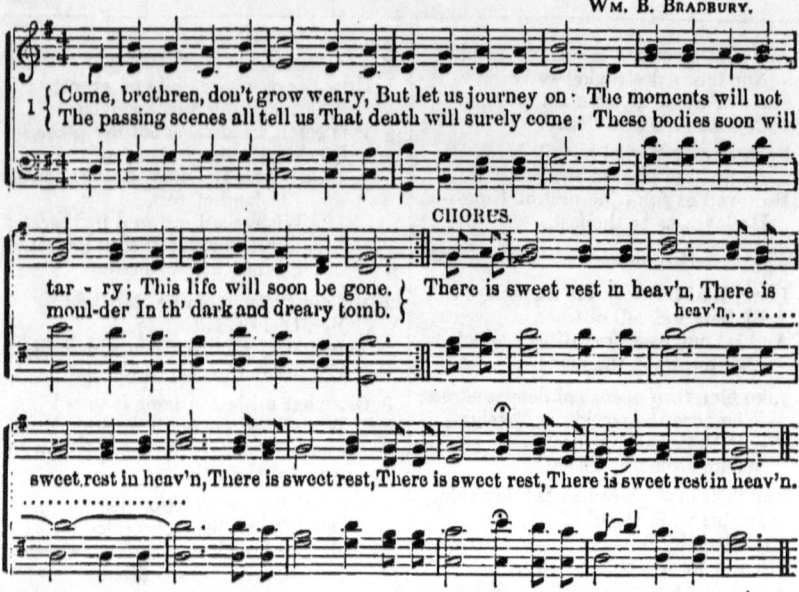

107. *Sweet Rest in Heaven.* (300)

1 Come, brethren, don't grow weary,
  But let us journey on:
The moments will not tarry;
  This life will soon be gone.
The passing scenes all tell us
  That death will surely come;
These bodies soon will moulder
  In th' dark and dreary tomb.
    There is sweet rest in heaven,
    There is sweet rest in heaven,
      There is sweet rest,
      There is sweet rest,
    There is sweet rest in heaven.

2 Loved ones have gone before us,
  They beckon us away,
O'er aerial plains they're soaring,
  Blest in eternal day;
But we are in the army,
  And dare not leave our post;
We'll fight until we conquer
  The foe's most mighty host.

3 Our Captain's gone before us,
  He kindly calls us home
To yonder world of glory,
  And sweetly bids us come.
The world, the flesh, and Satan,
  Will strive to hedge our way,
But we'll o'ercome these powers—
  We'll hourly watch and pray.

108. *Sabbath Peace.* (177)
Tune Ward, page 64.

1 My opening eyes with rapture see
  The dawn of thy returning day;
My thoughts, O God, ascend to thee,
  While thus my early vows I pay.

2 O, bid this trifling world retire,
  And drive each carnal thought away;
Nor let me feel one vain desire—
  One sinful thought through all the day.

3 Then, to thy courts when I repair,
  My soul shall rise on joyful wing,
The wonders of thy love declare,
  And join the strains which angels sing.
        J. Hutton.

109. *The Sinner's Friend.* (283)

1 WHATEVER cross the world may bring
Of poverty and shame,
To Jesus' hand we still can cling—
He always is the same.
He who was the sinner's Friend
Will be with us to the end,
Noting every smile and tear:
Our blessed Saviour's ever near.

2 In sorrow's hour his love can cheer,
And bid our fears depart;
He makes our happiness more dear,
And fills with peace our heart.
He who was the sinner's Friend, &c.

3 Dear Saviour, make us truly thine,
And all our sins forgive,
Conform us to thy will divine,
And bless us while we live.
He who was the sinner's Friend, &c.

4 And in the world beyond the sky,
With thee we'll gladly dwell;
No more to weep, no more to die,
No more to say farewell.
He who was the sinner's Friend, &c.

KATE CAMERON.

110. *Prayer for Revival.*
Tune GREENVILLE, page 89. (11)

1 SAVIOUR, visit thy plantation,
Grant us, Lord, a gracious rain;
All will come to desolation,
Unless thou return again.
Lord, revive us;
All our help must come from thee.

2 Keep no longer at a distance,
Shine upon us from on high,
Lest for want of thine assistance,
Every plant should droop and die.
Lord, revive us, &c

3 Let our mutual love be fervent,
Make us prevalent in prayers;
Let each one esteemed thy servant,
Shun the world's bewitching snares.
Lord, revive us, &c.

4 Break the tempter's fatal power
Turn the stony heart to flesh;
And begin, from this good hour,
To revive thy work afresh.
Lord, revive us, &c.

NEWTON.

ORTONVILLE. C. M.

T. Hastings.

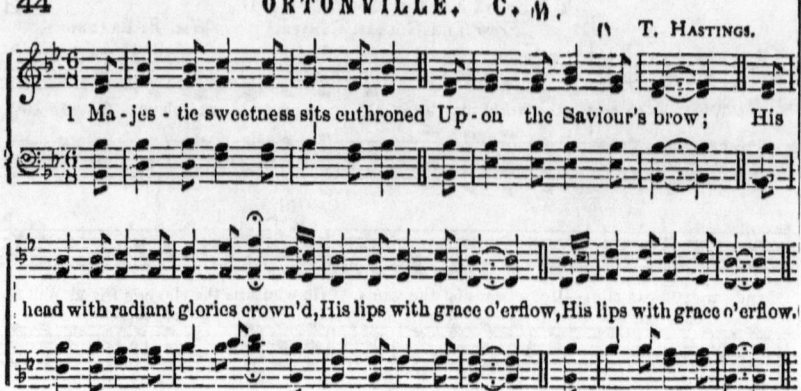

1 Majestic sweetness sits enthroned
Upon the Saviour's brow;
His head with radiant glories crown'd,
His lips with grace o'erflow, His lips with grace o'erflow.

111. *Indebtedness to Christ.* (246)

2 No mortal can with him compare
Among the sons of men;
Fairer is he than all the fair
Who fill the heavenly train.

3 He saw me plunged in deep distress,
And flew to my relief;
For me he bore the shameful cross,
And carried all my grief.

4 To him I owe my life and breath,
And all the joys I have;
He makes me triumph over death,
And saves me from the grave.

5 To heaven, the place of his abode,
He brings my weary feet,
Shows me the glories of my God,
And makes my joys complete.

6 Since from his bounty I receive
Such proofs of love divine,
Had I a thousand hearts to give,
Lord, they should all be thine.
S. Stennett.

112. *Divine Blessings Solicited.* (164)

1 To thee this temple we devote,
Our Father and our God;
Accept it thine, and seal it now
Thy Spirit's blest abode.

2 Here may the prayer of faith ascend,
The voice of praise arise;
O, may each lowly service prove
Accepted sacrifice.

3 Here may the sinner learn his guilt,
And weep before his Lord;
Here, pardoned, sing a Saviour's love,
And here his vows record.

4 Peace be within these sacred walls;
Prosperity be here;
Long smile upon thy people, Lord,
And evermore be near.
J. R. Scott.

113. *Parting with all for Christ.* (260)

1 Ye glittering toys of earth, adieu;
A nobler choice be mine;
A heavenly prize attracts my view,
A treasure all divine.

2 Jesus, to multitudes unknown,—
Oh, name divinely sweet!—
Jesus, in thee, in thee alone,
True wealth and honor meet.

3 Should earth's vain treasures all depart,
Of this dear gift possessed,
I'd clasp it to my joyful heart,
And be forever blest.

4 Dear portion of my soul's desires,
Thy love is bliss divine;
Accept the wish that love inspires
And let me call thee mine.
Steele.

114. *Desires for Holiness.* (350)

1 O, could I find from day to day,
A nearness to my God,
Then would my hours glide sweet away,
While leaning on his word.

2 Lord, I desire with thee to live
Anew from day to day,
In joys the world can never give
Nor ever take away.

3 Blest Jesus, come, and rule my heart,
And make me wholly thine,
That I may never more depart,
Nor grieve thy love divine.

4 Thus, till my last, expiring breath,
Thy goodness I'll adore;
And when my frame dissolves in death
My soul shall love thee more.

115. *The Bible full of Christ.* (476)

1 Thou lovely source of true delight,
Unseen, whom I adore,
Unvail thy beauties to my sight,
That I may love thee more.

2 Thy glory o'er creation shines;
But in thy sacred word
I read, in fairer, brighter lines,
My bleeding, dying Lord.

3 'Tis here, whene'er my comforts droop,
And sins and sorrows rise,
Thy love, with cheerful beams of hope,
My fainting heart supplies.

4 Jesus, my Lord, my life, my light,
O, come with blissful ray!
Break, radiant thro' the shades of night,
And chase my fears away.

5 Then shall my soul with rapture trace
The wonders of thy love;
Then shall I see thy glorious face,
In endless joy above. STEELE.

116. *The Bible the Light of the World.* (439)

1 What glory gilds the sacred page!
Majestic, like the sun,
It gives a light to every age:
It gives, but borrows none.

2 The power that gave it still supplies
The gracious light and heat:
Its truths upon the nations rise;
They rise, but never set.

3 Let everlasting thanks be thine
For such a bright display
As makes a world of darkness shine
With beams of heavenly day.

4 My soul rejoices to pursue
The steps of Him I love,
Till glory breaks upon my view
In brighter worlds above. COWPER.

117. *Sincere Devotion.* (380)

1 Prayer is the soul's sincere desire,
Unuttered or expressed,
The motion of a hidden fire,
That trembles in the breast.

2 Prayer is the burden of a sigh,
The falling of a tear,
The upward glancing of an eye,
When none but God is near.

3 Prayer is the simplest form of speech
That infant lips can try;
Prayer, the sublimest strains that reach
The Majesty on high.

4 Prayer is the Christian's vital breath,
The Christian's native air,
His watchword at the gates of death;
He enters heaven with prayer. MONTGOMERY.

118. *Prayer for Assurance.* (304)

1 Why should the children of a King
Go mourning all their days?
Great Comforter! descend and bring
Some tokens of thy grace.

2 Dost thou not dwell in all the saints,
And seal the heirs of heaven?
When wilt thou banish my complaints,
And show my sins forgiven?

3 Assure my conscience of her part
In the Redeemer's blood;
And bear thy witness with my heart,
That I am born of God.

4 Thou art the earnest of his love,
The pledge of joys to come,
And thy soft wings, celestial Dove,
Will safe convey me home. WATTS.

ZEPHYR. L. M.

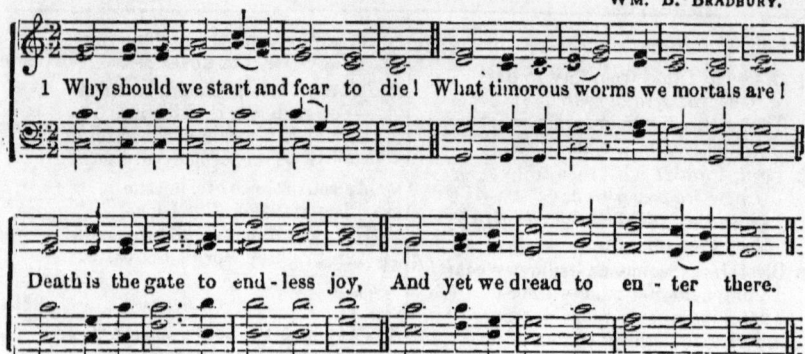

Wm. B. Bradbury.

1 Why should we start and fear to die! What timorous worms we mortals are! Death is the gate to endless joy, And yet we dread to enter there.

119. *Death Disarmed.* (569)

2 O, if my Lord would come and meet,
　My soul should stretch her wings in haste,
Fly fearless through death's iron gate,
　Nor feel the terrors as she passed!

3 Jesus can make a dying bed
　Feel soft as downy pillows are,
While on his breast I lean my head,
　And breathe my life out sweetly there.
　　　　　　　　WATTS.

120. *Past Joys Remembered.* (366)

1 O, WHERE is now that glowing love,
　That marked our union with the Lord?
Our hearts were fixed on things above,
　Nor could the world a joy afford.

2 Where is the zeal that led us then
　To make our Saviour's glory known?
That freed us from the fear of men,
　And kept our eye on him alone?

3 Where are the happy seasons spent
　In fellowship with him we loved?
The sacred joy, the sweet content,
　The blessedness that then we proved!

4 Behold! again we turn to thee;
　O, cast us not away, though vile!
No peace we have, no joy we see,
　O, Lord, our God! but in thy smile!

121. *Blessedness of the Righteous in Death.* (573)

1 How blest the righteous when he dies,
　When sinks a weary soul to rest!
How mildly beam the closing eyes!
　How gently heaves th'expiring breast!

2 So fades a summer cloud away;
　So sinks the gale when storms are o'er,
So gently shuts the eye of day;
　So dies a wave along the shore.

3 A holy quiet reigns around,
　A calm which life nor death destroys,
And nought disturbs that peace profound,
　Which his unfettered soul enjoys.

4 Life's labor done, as sinks the clay,
　Light from its load the spirit flies,
While heaven and earth combine to say,
　"How blest the righteous when he dies."
　　　　　　　　BARBAULD.

122. *The Spirit Enlightening and Renewing.* (306)

1 ETERNAL Spirit, we confess
　And sing the wonders of thy grace;
Thy power conveys our blessings down
　From God the Father, and the Son.

2 Enlightened by thine heavenly ray,
　Our shades and darkness turn to day;
Thine inward teachings make us know,
　Our danger and our refuge too

3 Thy power and glory work within,
And break the chains of reigning sin ;
Our wild, imperious lusts subdue,
And form our wretched hearts anew.
WATTS.

123. *The Season of Mercy Short.* (26)

1 WHILE life prolongs its precious light,
Mercy is found, and peace is given ;
But soon, ah, soon, approaching night
Shall blot out every hope of heaven.
2 Soon borne on time's most rapid wing,
Shall death command you to the grave,
Before his bar your spirits bring,
And none be found to hear or save.
3 In that lone land of deep despair,
No Sabbath's heavenly light shall rise,
No God regard your bitter prayer,
No Saviour call you to the skies.
4 While God invites, how blest the day !
How sweet the gospel's charming sound !
Come, sinners, haste, O, haste away,
While yet a pardoning God is found.
DWIGHT.

124. *The Voice Within.* (32)

1 SAY, sinner, hath a voice within,
Oft whispered to thy secret soul,
Urged thee to leave the ways of sin,
And yield thy heart to God's control?

2 Sinner, it was a heav'nly voice;
It was the Saviour's gracious call ;
It bade thee make the better choice,
And haste to seek in Christ thine all.

3 Spurn not the call to life and light ;
Regard in time the warning kind ;
That call thou mayst not always slight,
And yet the gate of mercy find.

4 Sinner, perhaps this very day
Thy last accepted time may be ;
O, shouldst thou grieve him now away,
Then hope may never beam on thee.
HYDE.

125. *The Sufferings of Christ.* (222)

DEEP in our hearts let us record
The deeper sorrows of our Lord
Behold the rising billows roll,
To overwhelm his holy soul !

2 Yet, gracious God ! thy power and love
Have made the curse a blessing prove ;
These dreadful sufferings of thy Son
Atoned for sins that we had done.

3 The pangs of our expiring Lord
The honors of thy law restored ;
His sorrows made thy justice known,
And paid for follies not his own.

4 O, for his sake, our guilt forgive,
And let the mourning sinner live ;
The Lord will hear us in his name,
Nor shall our hope be turned to shame.
WATTS.

126. *Sense of Sin.* (281)

1 JESUS demands this heart of mine,
Demands my love, my joy, my care ;
But, ah ! how dead to things divine,
How cold, my best affections are !

2 'Tis sin, alas ! with dreadful power,
Divides my Saviour from my sight ;
O, for one happy, shining hour
Of sacred freedom, sweet delight !

3 Come, gracious Lord, thy love can raise
My captive powers from sin and death,
And fill my heart with life and praise,
And tune my last expiring breath.
STEELE.

127. *Renouncing Earthly Joys.* (316)

1 I SEND the joys of earth away ;
Away, ye tempters of the mind !
False as the smooth, deceitful sea,
And empty as the whistling wind.

2 Your streams were floating me along
Down to the gulf of black despair ;
And while I listened to your song,
Your streams had e'en conveyed me there.

3 Lord, I adore thy matchless grace,
That warned me of that dark abyss,
That drew me from those treacherous seas,
And bade me seek superior bliss.

4 Now to the shiny realms above
I stretch my hands, and glance mine eyes
O, for the pinions of a dove,
To bear me to the upper skies !
WATTS.

BRADEN. S. M.

Wm. B. Bradbury.

1 The swift de-clin-ing day, How fast its moments fly,

While eve-ning's broad and gloom-y shade Gains on the western sky!

128. *"Work while it is Day."* (47)

1 The swift-declining day,
  How fast its moments fly,
While evening's broad and gloomy shade
  Gains on the western sky!

2 Ye mortals, mark its pace,
  And use the hours of light;
For know, its Maker can command
  An instant, endless night.

3 Give glory to the Lord,
  Who rules the rolling sphere;
Submissive, at his footstool bow,
  And seek salvation there.

4 Then shall new lustre break
  Through all the heavy gloom,
And lead you to unchanging light,
  In your celestial home.
                        Doddridge.

129. *The Christian Never Dies.* (571)

1 It is not death to die,
  To leave this weary road,
And 'midst the brotherhood on high,
  To be at home with God.

2 It is not death to close
  The eye long dimmed by tears,
And wake in glorious repose,
  To spend eternal years.

3 It is not death to fling
  Aside this sinful dust,
And rise, on strong, exulting wing,
  To live among the just.

4 Jesus, thou Prince of Life!
  Thy chosen cannot die;
Like thee, they conquer in the strife,
  To reign with thee on high.
                    G. W. Bethune.

130. *God Working in the Soul.* (312)

1 'Tis God the Spirit leads
  In paths before unknown;
The work to be performed is ours;
  The strength is all his own.

2 Supported by his grace,
  We still pursue our way,
And hope at last to reach the prize,
  Secure in endless day.

3 'Tis he that works to will;
  'Tis he that works to do;
The power by which we act is his,
  And his the glory too.
                        Montgomery

Doxology.

To God, the Father, Son,
  And Spirit, glory be,
As was, and is, and shall rem in
  Through all eternity!

HOW BEAUTEOUS ARE THEIR FEET.

Dr. L. Mason.

131. *Ministers the Bearers of Good Tidings.* (160)

1 How beauteous are their feet
   Who stand on Zion's hill;
   Who bring salvation on their tongues,
   And words of peace reveal!

2 How charming is their voice!
   How sweet their tidings are!—
   "Zion, behold thy Saviour King;
   He reigns and triumphs here."

3 How happy are our ears,
   That hear this joyful sound!

Which kings and prophets waited for,
   And sought, but never found.

4 How blessed are our eyes,
   That see this heavenly light!
   Prophets and kings desired it long,
   But died without the sight.

5 The Lord makes bare his arm
   Through all the earth abroad;
   Let every nation now behold
   Their Saviour and their God. WATTS.

50   EDEN. 8s.

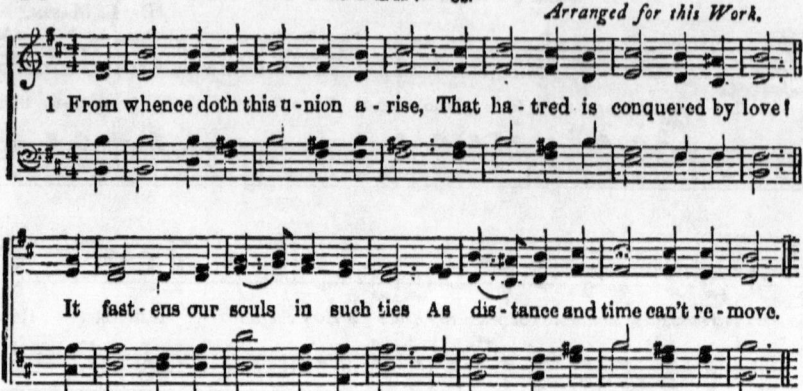

Arranged for this Work.

1 From whence doth this u-nion a-rise, That ha-tred is conquered by love! It fast-ens our souls in such ties As dis-tance and time can't re-move.

132.   *The Union of Saints.*   (359)

1 From whence doth this union arise,
   That hatred is conquered by love?
It fastens our souls in such ties
   As distance and time can't remove.

2 It cannot in Eden be found,
   Nor yet in a Paradise lost;
It grows on Immanuel's ground,
   And Jesus' dear blood it did cost.

3 My brethren are dear unto me,
   Our hearts all united in love;
Where Jesus is gone we shall be,
   In yonder blest mansions above.

4 Why, then, so unwilling to part,
   Since there we shall all meet again?
Engraved on Immanuel's heart,
   At a distance we cannot remain.

Oh, when shall we see that bright day,
   And join with the angels above,
Set free from these prisons of clay,
   United in Jesus's love?

5 With Jesus we ever shall reign,
   And all his bright glories shall see,
And sing, Hallelujah! amen!
   Amen! even so let it be.   BALDWIN.

133.   *Longing for Heaven.*   (432)

1 Ye angels, who stand round the throne,
   And view my Immanuel's face,
In rapturous songs make him known;
   Tune, tune your soft harps to his praise.

2 Ye saints, who stand nearer than they,
   And cast your bright crowns at his feet,
His grace and his glory display,
   And all his rich mercy repeat.

3 He snatch'd you from hell and the grave;
   He ransomed from death and despair;
For you he was mighty to save,
   Almighty to bring you safe there.

4 O, when will the moment appear
   When I shall unite in your song?
I'm weary of lingering here,
   And I to your Saviour belong!

5 I'm fettered and chained here in clay;
   I struggle and pant to be free;
I long to be soaring away,
   My God and Redeemer to see!

6 I want, O, I want to be there,
   Where sorrow and sin never come;
Your joy and your friendship to share,
   And dwell with my Saviour at home!   M. DE FLEURY.

DE FLEURY. 8s. Double. 51

1 How tedious and tasteless the hours When Jesus no longer I see!
D.C. But when I am happy in him, December's as pleasant as May.
Sweet prospects, sweet birds, and sweet flow'rs Have lost all their sweetness with me:
The midsummer sun shines but dim; The fields strive in vain to look gay;

134. *The Presence of Christ Desired.* (263)

1 How tedious and tastcless the hours
   When Jesus no longer I see!
Sweet prospects, sweet birds, and sweet flowers
   Have lost all their sweetness with me:
The midsummer sun shines but dim;
   The fields strive in vain to look gay;
But when I am happy in him,
   December's as pleasant as May.

2 His name yields the richest perfume,
   And sweeter than music his voice;
His presence disperses my gloom,
   And makes all within me rejoice:
I should, were he always so nigh,
   Have nothing to wish or to fear;
No mortal so happy as I;
   My summer would last all the year.

3 Content with beholding his face,
   My all to his pleasure resigned,
No changes of season or place
   Would make any change in my mind:
While blest with a sense of his love,
   A palace a toy would appear;
And prisons would palaces prove,
   If Jesus would dwell with me there.

4 Dear Lord, if indeed, I am thine,
   If thou art my sun and my song,
Say, why do I languish and pine?
   And why are my winters so long?
O, drive these dark clouds from my sky;
   Thy soul-cheering presence restore;
Or take me unto thee on high,
   Where winter and clouds are no more.
                                    NEWTON.

THE SOLID ROCK. L. M. 6 lines.

Wm. B. Bradbury.

135. *The Solid Rock.* (296)

1 My hope is built on nothing less
Than Jesus' blood and righteousness;
I dare not trust the sweetest frame,
But wholly lean on Jesus' name:
   On Christ, the solid rock, I stand;
   All other ground is sinking sand.

2 When darkness seems to vail his face,
I rest on his unchanging grace;
In every high and stormy gale,
My anchor holds within the vail:
   On Christ, the solid rock, I stand
   All other ground is sinking sand.

3 His oath, his covenant, and blood,
Support me in the whelming flood:
When all around my soul gives way,
He then is all my hope and stay:
   On Christ, the solid rock, I stand;
   All other ground is sinking sand.

136. *Conflicting Feelings.* (378)

1 Strange and mysterious is my life.
What opposites I feel within!
A stable peace, a constant strife;
The rule of grace, the power of sin:
Too often I am captive led,
Yet daily triumph in my Head.

2 I prize the privilege of prayer,
But oh! what backwardness to pray!
Though on the Lord I cast my care,
I feel its burden every day;
I seek his will in all I do,
Yet find my own is working too.

3 I call the promises my own,
And prize them more than mines of gold;
Yet though their sweetness I have known,
They leave me unimpressed and cold
One hour upon the truth I feed,
The next I know not what I read.

4 While on my Saviour I rely,
  I know my foes shall lose their aim,
And therefore dare their power defy,
  Assured of conquest through his name,
But soon my confidence is slain,
And all my fears return again.

5 Thus different powers within me strive,
  And grace and sin by turns prevail;
I grieve, rejoice, decline, revive,
  And victory hangs in doubtful scale:
But Jesus has his promise passed,
That grace shall overcome at last.
NEWTON.

LATTER DAY. 8s & 7s.

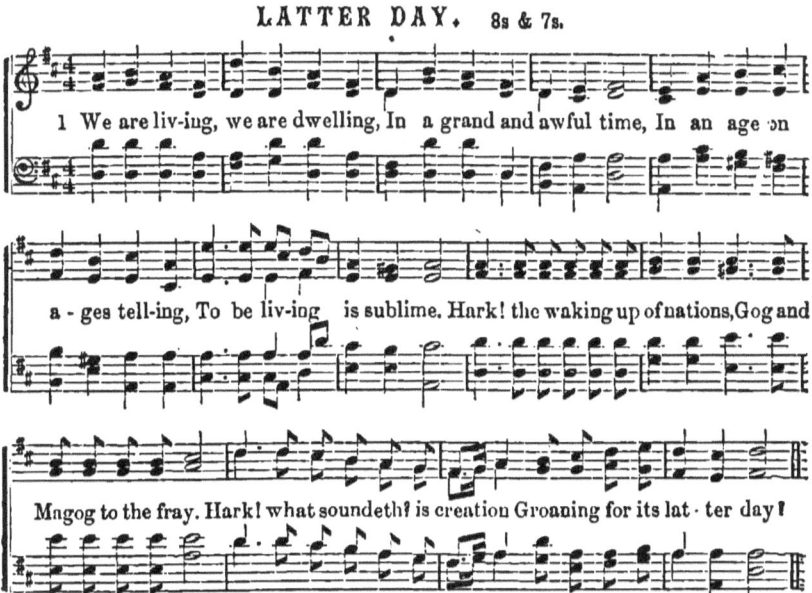

1 We are liv-ing, we are dwelling, In a grand and awful time, In an age on a-ges tell-ing, To be liv-ing is sublime. Hark! the waking up of nations, Gog and Magog to the fray. Hark! what soundeth? is creation Groaning for its lat-ter day!

137. *We are living in the Latter day.* (341)

1 WE are living, we are dwelling,
    In a grand and awful time,
  In an age on ages telling,
    To be living is sublime.
  Hark! the waking up of nations,
    Gog and Magog to the fray.
  Hark! what soundeth? is creation
    Groaning for its latter day?

2 Will ye play, then, will ye dally,
    With your music and your wine?
  Up! it is Jehovah's rally!
    God's own arm hath need of thine

Hark! the onset! will ye fold your
    Faith-clad arms in lazy lock?
  Up, O up, thou drowsy soldier;
    Worlds are charging to the shock.

3 Worlds are charging—heaven beholding,
    Thou hast but an hour to fight;
  Now the blazoned cross unfolding,
    On—right onward, for the right
  On! let all the soul within you
    For the truth's sake go abroad!
  Strike! let every nerve and sinew
    Tell on ages—tell for God!
A. C. COXE.

NOTHING BUT LEAVES.

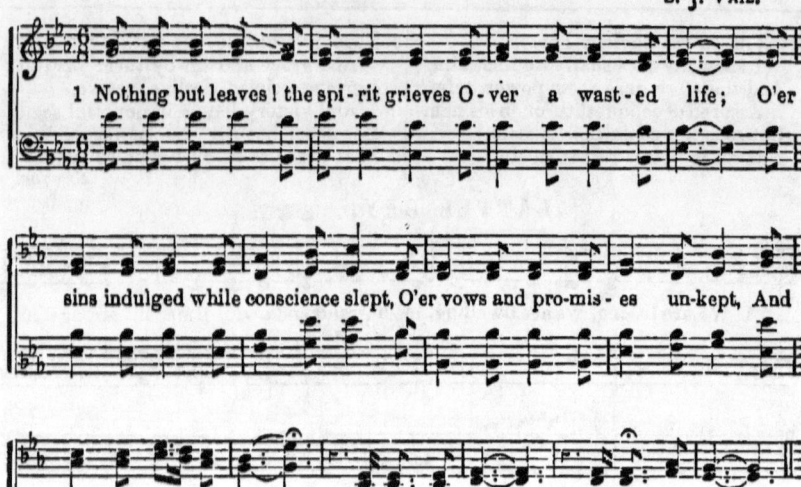

138. *Nothing but Leaves.* (320)

1 NOTHING but leaves! the spirit grieves
  Over a wasted life;
  O'er sins indulged while conscience slept,
  O'er vows and promises unkept,
    And reap from years of strife—
      Nothing but leaves.

2 Nothing but leaves! no gathered sheaves
  Of life's fair ripening grain;
  We sow our seeds, lo! tares and weeds,
  Words, idle words for earnest deeds,
    We reap with toil and pain—
      Nothing but leaves.

3 Nothing but leaves! sad memory weaves
  No vail to hide the past;
  And as we trace our weary way,
  Counting each lost and misspent day,
    Sadly we find at last—
      Nothing but leaves.

4 Ah! who shall thus the Master meet,
    Bearing but withered leaves!
  Ah! who shall at the Saviour's feet,
  Before the awful judgment-seat,
    Lay down, for golden sheaves,
      Nothing but leaves!

139. *The Sinner Invited and Warned.* (73)
  Tune HOWELL, page 21.

1 HEAR, O sinner! Mercy hails you;
  Now with sweetest voice she calls;
  Bids you haste to seek the Saviour,
  Ere the hand of justice falls:
    Trust in Jesus;
  'Tis the voice of Mercy calls.

2 Haste, O sinner, to the Saviour;
  Seek his mercy while you may;
  Soon the day of grace is over;
  Soon your life will pass away·
    Haste to Jesus;
  You must perish if you stay.

REED.

THERE WILL BE NO PARTING THERE. 55

140. *No Parting in Heaven.* (470)

1 We are going, we are going,
To a home beyond the skies,
Where the fields are robed in beauty,
And the sunlight never dies;
Where the fount of joy is flowing
In the valley green and fair,
We shall dwell in love together,
There will be no parting there.

2 We are going, we are going,
And the music we have heard,
Like the echo of the woodland,
Or the carol of a bird;
With the rosy light of morning
On the calm and fragrant air,
Still it murmurs, softly murmurs
There will be no parting there.

3 We are going, we are going,
When the day of life is o'er;
To that pure and happy region
Where our friends have gone before;

They are singing with the angels
In that land so bright and fair,
We shall dwell with them forever,
There will be no parting there.
FANNY CROSBY.

Blest Hour.

141. *Tune* ROLLAND, page 208. (176)

1 BLEST hour when earthly cares resign
Their empire o'er the anxious breast,
While all around the calm divine
Proclaims the holy day of rest.

2 Blest hour when God himself draws nigh,
Well pleased his people's voice to hear,
To hush the penitential sigh,
And wipe away the mourner's tear.

3 Blest hour, for where the Lord resorts—
Foretastes of future bliss are given,
And mortals find his earthly courts
The house of God, the gate of Heaven.
RAFFLES.

LA MIRA. C. M.

Chanting style.

1 Re-member thy Cre-a-tor now, In these, thy youthful days;
He will ac-cept thy ear-liest vow, And lis-ten to thy praise.

142. *"Remember now thy Creator in the days of thy Youth."* (416)

1 REMEMBER thy Creator now,
  In these thy youthful days;
  He will accept thy earliest vow,
  And listen to thy praise.

2 Remember thy Creator now,
  And seek him while he's near;
  For evil days will come, when thou
  Shalt find no comfort near.

3 Remember thy Creator now;
  His willing servant be:
  Then, when thy head in death shall bow,
  He will remember thee.

4 Almighty God! our hearts incline
  Thy heavenly voice to hear;
  Let all our future days be thine,
  Devoted to thy fear.

143. *God Omnipresent.* (180)

1 IN all my vast concerns with thee,
  In vain my soul would try
  To shun thy presence, Lord, or flee
  The notice of thine eye.

2 Thine all-surrounding sight surveys
  My rising and my rest;
  My public walks, my private ways,
  And secrets of my breast.

3 Oh! wondrous knowledge deep and high!
  Where can a creature hide?
  Within thy circling arms I lie,
  Enclosed on every side.

4 So let thy grace surround me still
  And like a bulwark prove,
  To guard my soul from every ill,
  Secured by sovereign love.
  WATTS.

144. *The Gospel a Savor of Life or Death.* (264)

1 CHRIST and his cross are all our theme;
  The mysteries that we speak
  Are scandal in the Jews' esteem,
  And folly to the Greek.

2 But souls enlightened from above
  With joy receive the word;
  They see what wisdom, power, and love
  Shine in their dying Lord.

3 The vital savor of his name
  Restores their fainting breath;
  But unbelief perverts the same
  To guilt, despair, and death.

4 Till God diffuse his graces down,
  Like showers of heavenly rain,
  In vain Apollos sows the ground,
  And Paul may plant in vain.
  WATTS

WIRTH. C. M.

WM. B. BRADBURY

1 How sweet, how heavenly is the sight, When those who love the Lord, In one an-other's peace de-light,.... And so ful-fill his word.

145. *"Love as Brethren."* (363)

1 How sweet, how heavenly is the sight,
When those who love the Lord
In one another's peace delight,
And so fulfill his word!

2 When each can feel his brother's sigh,
And with him bear a part;
When sorrow flows from eye to eye,
And joy from heart to heart!

3 When, free from envy, scorn, and pride,
Our wishes all above,
Each can his brother's failings hide,
And show a brother's love!

4 Let love, in one delightful stream,
Through every bosom flow,
And union sweet, and dear esteem
In every action glow.

5 Love is the golden chain that binds
The happy souls above;
And he's an heir of heaven who finds
His bosom glow with love.
SWAIN.

146. *Surprising Grace.* (374)

1 AND will the Lord thus condescend
To visit sinful worms?
Thus at the door shall mercy stand,
In all her winning forms?

2 Surprising grace?—and shall my heart
Unmoved and cold remain?
Has it no soft, no tender part?
Must Mercy plead in vain?

3 Shall Jesus for admission sue,
His charming voice unheard?
And shall my heart, his rightful due,
Remain forever barred?

4 O Lord, exert thy conquering grace;
Thy mighty power display;
One beam of glory from thy face
Can melt my sin away. STEELE.

147. *Morning Praise.* (392)

1 LORD of my life, oh, may thy praise
Employ my noblest powers,
Whose goodness lengthens out my days,
And fills the circling hours.

2 Preserved by thine almighty arm,
I passed the shades of night,
Secure and safe from every harm,
And see returning light.

3 Oh let the same almighty care
My waking hours attend;
From every danger, every snare,
My heedless steps defend.

4 Smile on my minutes as they roll,
And guide my future days;
And let thy goodness fill my soul
With gratitude and praise.
STEELE.

HAMBURG. L. M.
Arranged by Dr. Lowell Mason.

1 Who can describe the joys that rise, Thro' all the courts of Par-a-dise,

To see a pen-i-tent re-turn,— To see an heir of glo-ry born!

148. *Heaven Rejoicing over the Penitent.* (124)

2 With joy the Father does approve
The fruit of his eternal love;
The Son with joy looks down, and sees
The purchase of his agonies.

3 The Spirit takes delight to view
The holy soul he formed anew;
And saints and angels join to sing
The growing empire of their King.
WATTS.

149. *Glorying in the Cross.* (298)

1 WHEN I survey the wondrous cross,
On which the Prince of Glory died,
My richest gain I count but loss,
And pour contempt on all my pride.

2 Forbid it, Lord, that I should boast,
Save in the death of Christ, my God;
All the vain things that charm me most,
I sacrifice them to his blood.

3 See from his head, his hands, his feet,
Sorrow and love flow mingled down;
Did e'er such love and sorrow meet,
Or thorns compose so rich a crown?

4 Were all the realm of nature mine,
That were a present far too small;
Love so amazing, so divine,
Demands my soul, my life, my all.
WATTS.

150. *National Gratitude.* (555)

1 LORD, may thy goodness cause our land,
Preserved by thine almighty hand,
The tribute of its love to bring
To thee, our Saviour and our King.

2 So shall each public temple raise
A song of triumph to thy praise;
And every peaceful private home
To thee a temple shall become

3 Still be it our supreme delight
To walk as in thine awful sight;
And in thy precepts and thy fear,
Till life's last hour, to persevere.
DODDRIDGE.

151. *Object of Christ's Mission.* (94)

1 NOT to condemn the sons of men,
Did Christ, the Son of God, appear;
No weapons in his hands are seen,
No flaming sword nor thunder there.

2 Such was the pity of our God,
He loved the race of man so well,
He sent his Son to bear our load
Of sins, and save our souls from hell.

3 Sinners, believe the Saviour's word;
Trust in his mighty name, and live;
A thousand joys his lips afford,
His hands a thousand b'essings give.
WATTS.

LOVING KINDNESS. L. M. 59

1 Awake, my soul, in joyful lays, And sing thy great Redeemer's praise; He justly claims a song from me: His loving kindness, Oh, how free! His loving kindness, loving kindness, His loving kindness, Oh, how free!

152. *Christ's Loving Kindness.* (252)

1 AWAKE, my soul, in joyful lays,
And sing thy great Redeemer's praise;
He justly claims a song from me;
His loving kindness, Oh, how free!

2 He saw me ruined by the fall,
Yet loved me, notwithstanding all;
He saved me from my lost estate:
His loving kindness, Oh, how great!

3 Though numerous hosts of mighty foes,
Though earth and hell my way oppose,
He safely leads my soul along:
His loving kindness, Oh, how strong!

4 I often feel my sinful heart
Prone from my Saviour to depart;
But though I oft have him forgot,
His loving kindness changes not.

5 Soon shall I pass the gloomy vale;
Soon all my mortal powers must fail;
O, may my last, expiring breath
His loving kindness sing in death.

6 Then let me mount and soar away
To the bright world of endless day
And sing with rapture and surprise,
His loving kindness in the skies.

MEDLEY.

153. *Prayer for the Conversion of Seamen.* (512)
Tune HAMBURG.

1 GRANT the abundance of the sea
May be converted, Lord, to thee,
And every sailor on the shore
Return to God, to roam no more.

2 The nations, then, with joy shall hail
The Bethel flag in every sail;
And every ship that ploughs the sea
A gospel messenger shall be.

3 Hasten, O Lord, that glorious day
When seamen shall thy word obey,
And safe from port to port be driven
To point a ruined world to heaven.

154. *The Saviour's Call.* (65)

1 YE dying sons of men,—
 Sunk deep in guilt and woe,
 The gracious call attend,
  Which Jesus sends to you;
 Ye perishing and helpless, come;
 In Jesus' arms there yet is room.

2 No longer now delay,
  Nor vain excuses frame:
 He bids you come to-day,
  Though poor, and blind, and lame:
 All things are ready: sinners, come;
 For every trembling soul there's room.

3 Believe the heavenly word
  His messengers proclaim;
 He is a gracious Lord,
  And faithful is his name.
 Backsliding souls, return and come;
 Cast off despair; there yet is room.

4 Compelled by bleeding love,
  Ye wandering sheep, draw near;
 Christ calls you from above;
  His charming accents hear:
 Let whosoever will now come:
 In mercy's breast there still is room.
                              BODEN.

155. *The Voice of Free Grace.* (270)

1 THE voice of Free Grace, cries, escape
  to the mountain,
 For all that believe, Christ has opened
  a fountain;
 For sin, and uncleanness, and every
  transgression,
 His blood flows most freely in streams
  of salvation.
  Hallelujah to the Lamb, who hath
   purchased our pardon:
  We'll praise him again, when we pass
   over Jordan.

2 Ye souls that are wounded, haste, haste
  to the Saviour;
 He calls you in mercy—O, slight not
  his favor:
 Your sins, that have risen as high as a
  mountain,
 Shall find full remission, in this precious
  fountain.
  Hallelujah to the Lamb, &c.

3 O Jesus, our King, all blessed and
  glorious!
 O'er sin, death, and hell, thine arm is
  victorious;
 With shouting proclaim it, in th' great
  congregation:
 Let angels and men raise the song of
  salvation.
  Hallelujah to the Lamb, &c.

4 And when thou shalt bring us to thy
  heavenly dwelling,
 To gaze on thy glory, all glory excelling,
 We'll sound forth thy honors, with harps
  that cease never,
 And sing thy salvation for ever and ever.
  Hallelujah to the Lamb, &c.
                              THORNDY

LISCHER. H. M. 61
Dr. Lowell Mason.

1 { Welcome, delightful morn! Sweet day of sa-cred rest; / I hail thy kind return; Lord, make these moments blest: } From low desires and fleeting toys

I soar to reach im-mor-tal joys, I soar.... to reach.......... im-mor-tal joys.
CHORUS.

156. *Lord's Day Morning.* (170)

1 WELCOME, delightful morn;
Sweet day of sacred rest,
I hail thy kind return;
Lord, make these moments blest:
From low desires and fleeting toys,
I soar to reach immortal joys.

2 Now may the King descend,
And fill his throne of grace;
Thy sceptre, Lord, extend,
While saints address thy face:
Let sinners feel thy quickening word,
And learn to know and fear the Lord.

3 Descend, celestial Dove,
With all thy quickening powers;
Disclose a Saviour's love,
And bless the sacred hours:
Then shall my soul new life obtain,
Nor Sabbaths be enjoyed in vain.
HAYWARD.

157. *Election.* (113)
Tune HOWELL, page 21.

1 SONS we are through God's election,
Who in Jesus Christ believe;
By eternal destination,
Sovereign grace we here receive
Lord, thy mercy
Doth both grace and glory give.

2 Every fallen soul, by sinning,
Merits everlasting pain;
But thy love, without beginning,
Has restored thy sons again;
Countless millions
Shall in life through Jesus reign.

3 Since that love had no beginning,
And shall never, never cease;
Keep, O, keep me, Lord, from sinning;
Guide me in the way of peace!
Make me walk in
All the paths of holiness.

4 When I quit this feeble mansion,
And my soul returns to thee;
Let the power of thy salvation
Manifest itself in me;
Through thy spirit,
Give the final victory!

158. *Dismission.* (601)
Tune AUTUMN, page 82.

1 LORD, dismiss us with thy blessing;
Bid us now depart in peace;
Still on heavenly manna feeding,
Let our faith in thee increase.

2 Fill each breast with consolation;
Up to thee our hearts we raise;
When we reach our blissful station,
Then we'll give thee nobler praise.

159. *Dwelling with God.* (485)

3 My Father's house on high—
   Home of my soul—how near,
At times, to faith's foreseeing eye
   Thy golden gates appear!

4 "Forever with the Lord!"
   Father, if 'tis thy will,
The promise of that faithful word
   E'en here to me fulfill.

5 So when my latest breath
   Shall rend the vail in twain,
 By death I shall escape from death,
   And life eternal gain.

6 That resurrection word!
   That shout of victory
 Once more—"Forever with the Lord!"
   Amen, so let it be!
                                MONTGOMERY.

SWEET LAND OF REST. S. M.
WM. B. BRADBURY.

1 Sweet land of rest, for thee I sigh; When will the moment come? When I shall lay my ar-mor by, And dwell with Christ at home.

REFRAIN.
Home, home, sweet, sweet home; And dwell with Christ at home. home.

160. *Sweet Land of Rest.* (460)

2 No tranquil joys on earth I know,
   No peaceful sheltering home;
 This world's a wilderness of woe,
   This world is not my home.
     Home, home, &c.

3 To Jesus Christ I sought for rest,
   He bade me cease to roam,
 But fly for succor to his breast,
   And he'd conduct me home.
     Home, home, &c.

4 When, by affliction sharply tried,
   I viewed the gaping tomb,
 Although I dread death's chilling tide,
   Yet still I sighed for home.
     Home, home, &c.

5 Weary of wandering round and round
   This vale of sin and gloom,
 I long to leave th' unhallowed ground,
   And dwell with Christ at home.
     Home, home, &c.

WARD. L. M.
Arranged by Dr. L. Mason.

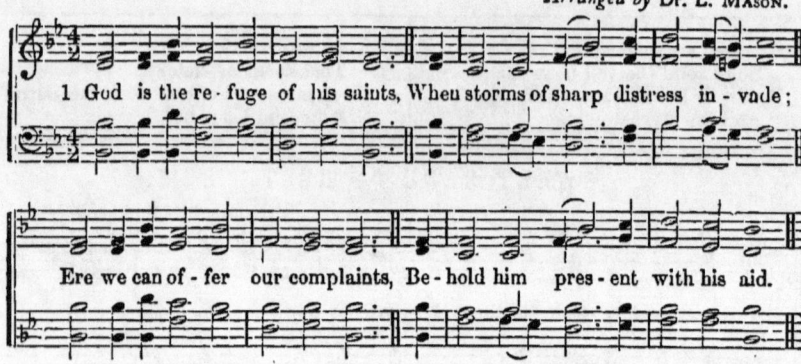

1 God is the re-fuge of his saints, When storms of sharp distress in-vade;
Ere we can of-fer our complaints, Be-hold him pres-ent with his aid.

161. *God the Refuge and Portion of his People.* (195)

2 Loud may the troubled ocean roar;
In sacred peace our souls abide;
While every nation, every shore,
Trembles, and dreads the swelling tide.

3 There is a stream whose gentle flow
Supplies the city of our God;
Life, love, and joy still gliding through,
And watering our divine abode.

4 That sacred stream, thine holy word,
Supports our faith, our fear controls;
Sweet peace thy promises afford,
And give new strength to fainting souls.

5 Zion enjoys her Monarch's love,
Secure against a threatening hour;
Nor can her firm foundation move,
Built on his truth, and armed with power.
WATTS.

162. *Rest for the Weary Penitent.* (71)

1 COME, weary souls, with sin distressed,
Come, and accept the promised rest;
The Saviour's gracious call obey,
And cast your gloomy fears away.

2 Oppressed with sin, a painful load,
Oh, come, and spread your woes abroad;
Divine compassion, mighty love,
Will all the painful load remove.

3 Here mercy's boundless ocean flows,
To cleanse your guilt and heal your woes;
Pardon, and life, and endless peace;
How rich the gift! how free the grace!

4 Lord, we accept, with thankful heart,
The hope thy gracious words impart;
We come with trembling, yet rejoice,
And bless the kind, inviting voice.

5 Dear Saviour, let thy wondrous love
Confirm our faith, our fears remove;
O, sweetly influence every breast,
And guide us to eternal rest.
STEELE.

163. *National Praise.* (557)

1 WE bless thy name, Almighty God,
For all the kindness thou hast shown
To this fair land our fathers trod,
This land we fondly call our own.

2 Here freedom spreads her banner wide,
And casts her soft and hallowed ray;
For thou our country's arms didst guide
And lead them on their conquering way.

3 We praise thee, that the gospel light
Through all our land its radiance sheds;
Scatters the shades of error's night,
And heavenly blessings round us spreads.

HYMNS. 65

4 When foes without, and foes within,
With threatening ills our land have pressed,
Thou hast our nation's bulwark been,
And, smiling, sent us peaceful rest.

5 O God, preserve us in thy fear,
In troublous times our helper be;
Diffuse thy truth's bright precepts here,
And may we worship only thee!

GOING HOME. L. M.

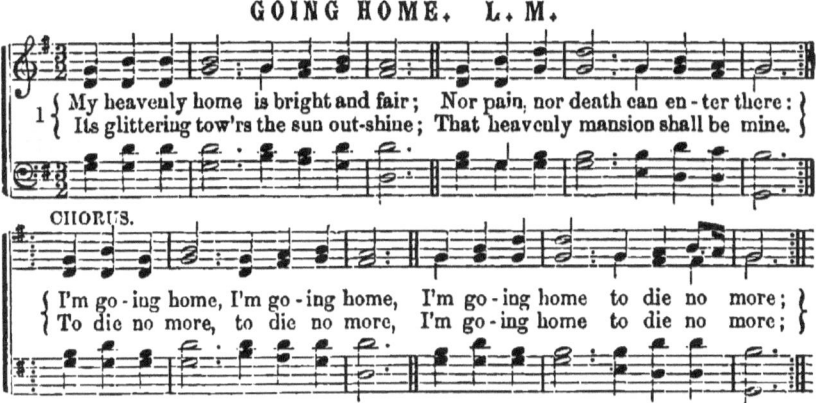

1 { My heavenly home is bright and fair; Nor pain, nor death can en-ter there: }
  { Its glittering tow'rs the sun out-shine; That heavenly mansion shall be mine. }

CHORUS.

{ I'm go-ing home, I'm go-ing home, I'm go-ing home to die no more; }
{ To die no more, to die no more, I'm go-ing home to die no more; }

164. *The Heavenly Home.* (430)

1 My heavenly home is bright and fair;
Nor pain, nor death can enter there;
Its glitt'ring towers the sun outshine;
That heav'nly mansion shall be mine.
I'm going home, &c.

2 My Father's house is built on high,
Far, far above the starry sky:
When from this earthy prison free,
That heavenly mansion mine shall be.
I'm going home, &c.

3 Let others seek a home below,
Which flames devour, or waves o'erflow;
Be mine a happier lot to own
A heavenly mansion near the throne.
I'm going home, &c.

165. *Christ the Hiding-Place.*
Tune WARD, page 64. (126)

1 HAIL, sovereign love, that first began
The scheme to rescue fallen man!
Hail, matchless, free, eternal grace,
That gave my soul a hiding-place.

2 Against the God that rules the sky,
I fought with hands uplifted high;
Despised the offers of his grace,
Too proud to seek a hiding-place.

3 But thus th' eternal counsel ran—
"Almighty love—arrest the man;"
I felt the arrows of distress,
And found I had no hiding-place.

4 Vindictive Justice stood in view;
To Sinai's fiery mount I flew,
But Justice cried, with frowning face—
"This mountain is no hiding-place."

5 But lo, a heavenly voice I heard—
And mercy's angel soon appeared;
Who led me on, a pleasing pace,
To Jesus Christ, my hiding-place.

6 On him almighty vengeance fell,
Which he must have sunk a world to hell,
He bore it for his chosen race,
And now he is my hiding-place.
BREWER.

166.
Our Fathers Long Ago. (559)

1 WHEN across the ocean wide,
  Where the heaving waters flow,
 Came the Mayflower o'er the tide,
  With our fathers, long ago ;
 When they neared the rocky strand,
  And their chorus rent the air,
 Children in that pilgrim band
  Clasped their little hands in prayer.

2 Sweetly rang their evening hymn
  O'er that region vast and wide,
 Through the forest dark and dim,
  And the rocking pines replied.
 'Twas a cold December night,
  And the earth was robed in snow,
 But the stars with mellow light
  Blessed our fathers long ago.

* From "THE GOLDEN CENSER."

3 When the early buds were seen,
   And the robin's song was heard,
  Children frolicked on the green,
   Happy as the woodland bird;
  Culled the daisy young and fair,
  Watched the brooklet's quiet flow,
  Banished every cloud of care
   From our fathers long ago.

4 When our country's banner bright
   Told her deeds of noble worth,
  Children hailed its radiant light,
   Hailed the land that gave them birth,
  Children now rejoice to hear,
  All their youthful hearts can know,
  And the precepts still revere
   Of their fathers long ago.
                     FANNY CROSBY.

THE ANGELS SING. S. M.

1 Come, we that love the Lord, And let our joys be known; Join in a song with sweet ac-cord, And thus surround the throne. The an-gels sing in their happy home, The home..... angels sing in their happy home, The angels sing in their happy home, And we will join them here.

167. *Heavenly Joy on Earth.* (435)

1 COME, we that love the Lord,
   And let our joys be known;
  Join in a song with sweet accord,
   And thus surround the throne.
     The angels sing, &c.

  The sorrows of the mind
   Be banished from the place;
  Religion never was designed
   To make our pleasures less.
     The angels sing, &c.

3 Let those refuse to sing,
   That never knew our God;

But favorites of the heavenly King
 May speak their joys abroad.
   The angels sing, &c.

4 The hill of Zion yields
   A thousand sacred sweets,
  Before we reach the heavenly fields,
   Or walk the golden streets.
     The angels sing, &c.

5 Then let our songs abound,
   And every tear be dry:
  We're marching thro' Immanuel's ground,
   To fairer worlds on high.
     The angels sing, &c.   WATTS.

ELTHAM. 7s, Double.

Dr. Lowell Mason.

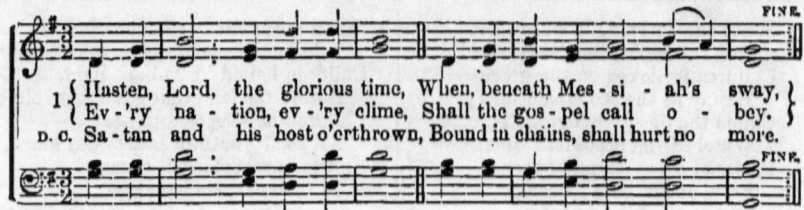

1. Hasten, Lord, the glorious time, When, beneath Mes-si-ah's sway,
Ev-'ry na-tion, ev-'ry clime, Shall the gos-pel call o - bey.
D.C. Sa-tan and his host o'erthrown, Bound in chains, shall hurt no more.

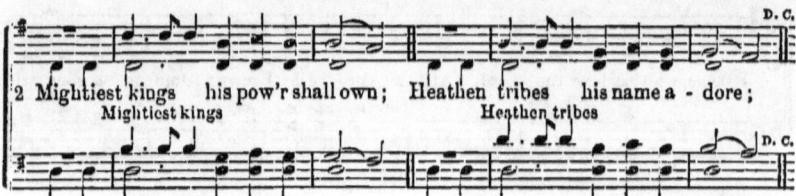

2 Mightiest kings his pow'r shall own; Heathen tribes his name a-dore;

168. *Christ's Universal Reign.* (529)

3 Then shall wars and tumults cease;
  Then be banished grief and pain;
  Righteousness, and joy, and peace,
  Undisturbed shall ever reign.

4 Bless we, then, our gracious Lord;
  Ever praise his glorious name;
  All his mighty acts record—
  All his wondrous works proclaim.

169. *Thanksgiving.* (553)

1 Swell the anthem, raise the song,
  Praises to our God belong;
  Saints and angels join to sing
  Praises to the heavenly King.

2 Blessings from his liberal hand
  Flow around this happy land:
  Kept by him, no foes annoy;
  Peace and freedom we enjoy.

3 Here, beneath a virtuous sway,
  May we cheerfully obey,—
  Never feel oppression's rod,—
  Ever own and worship God.

4 Hark! the voice of nature sings
  Praises to the King of kings;
  Let us join the choral song,
  And the grateful notes prolong.

170. *What of the Night?* (528)

1 Watchman! tell us of the night,
  What its signs of promise are.
  Traveler! o'er yon mountain's height,
  See that glory-beaming star.

2 Watchman! does its beauteous ray
  Aught of hope or joy foretell?
  Traveler! yes; it brings the day,
  Promised day of Israel.

3 Watchman! tell us of the night;
  Higher yet that star ascends.
  Traveler! blessedness and light,
  Peace and truth its course portends.

4 Watchman! will its beams alone
  Gild the spot that gave them birth?
  Traveler! ages are its own;
  See, it bursts o'er all the earth.

5 Watchman! tell us of the night,
  For the morning seems to dawn.
  Traveler! darkness takes its flight;
  Doubt and terror are withdrawn.

6 Watchman! let thy wanderings cease;
  Hie thee to thy quiet home.
  Traveler! lo! the Prince of Peace,
  Lo! the Son of God, is come.
                Bowring.

171. *Uncertainty of Life.* (565)

1 While, with ceaseless course, the sun,
  Hasted through the former year,
  Many souls their race have run,
  Never more to meet us here:
  Fixed in an eternal state,
  They have done with all below:
  We a little longer wait,
  But how little none can know.

2 As the wingèd arrow flies,
  Speedily the mark to find;
  As the lightning from the skies
  Darts, and leaves no trace behind;
  Swiftly thus our fleeting days
  Bear us down life's rapid stream:
  Upward, Lord, our spirits raise;
  All below is but a dream.

3 Thanks for mercies past receive;
  Pardon of our sins renew;
  Teach us, henceforth, how to live,
  With eternity in view;
  Bless thy word to young and old,
  Fill us with a Saviour's love;
  And when life's short tale is told,
  May we dwell with thee above!
  NEWTON.

172. *The New Year.* (567)

1 See! another year is gone!
  Quickly have the seasons passed!
  This we enter now upon
  May to many prove their last.

2 Mercy hitherto has spared:
  But have mercies been improved?
  Let us ask, "Am I prepared
  Should I be this year removed?"

3 Some we now no longer see,
  Who their mortal race have run,
  Seemed as fair for life as we,
  When the former year begun.

4 Some, but who God only knows,
  Who are here assembled now,
  Ere the present year shall close,
  To the stroke of death must bow.

5 If from guilt and sin set free
  By the knowledge of thy grace,
  Welcome, then, the call will be
  To depart and see thy face.

6 To thy saints, while here below,
  With new years, new mercies come;
  But the happiest year they know
  Is their last, which leads them home.
  NEWTON.

173. *Seeking Admission to the Church.* (135)

1 People of the living God,
  I have sought the world around,
  Paths of sin and sorrow trod,
  Peace and comfort nowhere found.

2 Now to you my spirit turns—
  Turns, a fugitive unblest;
  Brethren, where your altar burns,
  O, receive me into rest.

3 Lonely I no longer roam,
  Like the cloud, the wind, the wave;
  Where you dwell shall be my home,
  Where you die shall be my grave.

4 Mine the God whom you adore;
  Your Redeemer shall be mine;
  Earth can fill my soul no more;
  Every idol I resign.
  MONTGOMERY.

174. *Singing on the Way.* (454)

1 Children of the heavenly King,
  As ye journey, sweetly sing;
  Sing your Saviour's worthy praise,
  Glorious in his works and ways.

2 We are traveling home to God,
  In the way the fathers trod;
  They are happy now; and we
  Soon their happiness shall see.

3 Shout, ye little flock, and blest;
  You on Jesus' throne shall rest;
  There your seat is now prepared,
  There your kingdom and reward.

4 Lord, obediently we go,
  Gladly leaving all below;
  Only thou our Leader be,
  And we still will follow thee.
  CENNICK.

AZMON. C. M.

From GLAZER.

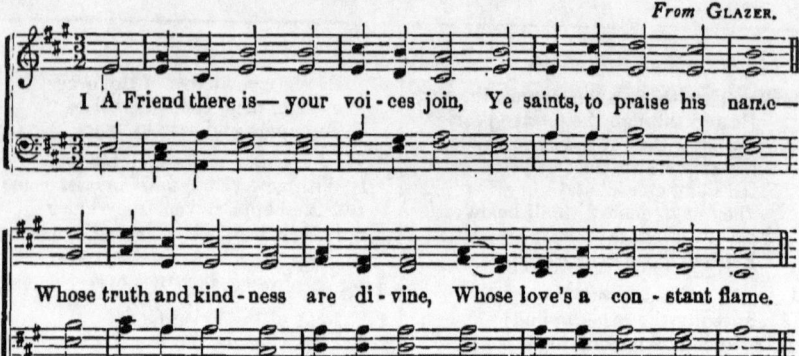

1 A Friend there is— your voi-ces join, Ye saints, to praise his name— Whose truth and kind-ness are di-vine, Whose love's a con-stant flame.

175.   *Christ a Friend.*   (273)

2 When most we need his helping hand,
  This Friend is always near;
  With heaven and earth at his command,
  He waits to answer prayer.

3 When frowns appear to vail his face,
  And clouds surround his throne,
  He hides the purpose of his grace,
  To make it better known.

4 And if our dearest comforts fall
  Before his sovereign will,
  He never takes away our all;
  Himself he gives us still.

5 Our sorrows in the scale he weighs,
  And measures out our pains;
  The wildest storm his word obeys;
  His word its rage restrains.
    SWAIN.

176.   *The Answer.*   (244)

1 Do not I love thee, O, my Lord?
  Behold my heart and see;
  And turn each hated idol out,
  That dares to rival thee.

2 Do not I love thee from my soul
  Then let me nothing love;
  Dead be my heart to every joy,
  When Jesus cannot move.

3 Is not thy name melodious still
  To my attentive ear?
  Doth not each pulse with pleasure bound,
  My Saviour's voice to hear?

4 Thou know'st I love thee, dearest Lord;
  But, O, I long to soar
  Far from the sphere of mortal joys,
  And learn to love thee more.
    DODDRIDGE.

177.   *The Healing Leaves.*   (488)

1 Go forth on wings of faith and prayer,
  Ye pages, bright with love;
  Though mute, the joyful tidings bear—
  Salvation from above.

2 Go, tell the sinful, careless soul
  The warning God has given;
  Go, make the wounded spirit whole,
  With healing balm from heaven.

3 Go to the rude, the dark, the poor,
  That live estranged from God;—
  Bid them the pearl of price secure,
  Bought with a Saviour's blood.

4 O Jesus, Friend of dying men,
  Thy presence we implore;
  Without thy blessing all is vain;
  Be with us evermore.
    HASTINGS.

178. *Purity of Heart.* (349)

1 O, for a heart to praise my God!
  A heart from sin set free!
  A heart that's sprinkled with the blood
  So freely shed for me!

2 O, for a heart submissive, meek,
  My great Redeemer's throne,
  Where only Christ is heard to speak,
  Where Jesus reigns alone!

3 O, for an humble, contrite heart,
  Believing, true, and clean,
  Which neither life nor death can part
  From him that dwells within!

4 Thy temper, gracious Lord, impart;
  Come quickly from above;
  O, write thy name upon my heart;
  Thy name, O God, is love.
  C. WESLEY.

179. *Access to God by a Mediator.* (235)

1 COME, let us lift our joyful eyes
  Up to the courts above,
  And smile to see our Father there,
  Upon a throne of love.

2 Come, let us bow before his feet,
  And venture near the Lord;
  No fiery cherub guards his seat,
  Nor double-flaming sword.

3 The peaceful gates of heavenly bliss
  Are opened by the Son;
  High let us raise our notes of praise,
  And reach th' almighty throne.

4 To thee ten thousand thanks we bring,
  Great Advocate on high,
  And glory to th' eternal King
  Who lays his anger by. WATTS.

180. *Lord, Teach us how to Pray.* (383)

1 PRAYER is the contrite sinner's voice,
  Returning from his ways,
  While angels in their songs rejoice,
  And cry, "Behold, he prays."

2 The saints in prayer appear as one
  In word, and deed, and mind,
  While with the Father and the Son
  Sweet fellowship they find.

3 Nor prayer is made on earth alone;
  The Holy Spirit pleads,
  And Jesus, on th' eternal throne,
  For sinners intercedes.

4 O, thou, by whom we come to God—
  The life, the truth, the way—
  The path of prayer thyself hast trod;
  Lord, teach us how to pray.
  MONTGOMERY.

181. *Yet there is Room.* (63)

1 COME, sinner, to the gospel feast;
  O, come without delay;
  For there is room in Jesus' breast
  For all who will obey.

2 There's room in God's eternal love
  To save thy precious soul;
  Room in the Spirit's grace above
  To heal and make thee whole.

3 There's room within the church, redeemed
  With blood of Christ divine;
  Room in the white-robed throng conven'd,
  For that dear soul of thine.

4 There's room in heaven among the choir,
  And harps and crowns of gold,
  And glorious palms of victory there,
  And joys that ne'er were told.

5 There's room around thy Father's board
  For thee and thousands more:
  O, come and welcome to the Lord;
  Yea, come this very hour.

182. *The Lost Found.* (116)

1 O! how divine, how sweet the joy,
  When but one sinner turns,
  And, with an humble, broken heart,
  His sins and errors mourns!

2 Pleased with the news, the saints below
  In songs their tongues employ;
  Beyond the skies the tidings go,
  And heaven is filled with joy.

3 Well pleased the Father sees and hears
  The conscious sinner's moan:
  Jesus receives him in his arms,
  And claims him for his own.
  NEEDHAM.

O, WHEN SHALL I SEE JESUS? 7s & 6s.
From Vestry Harp.

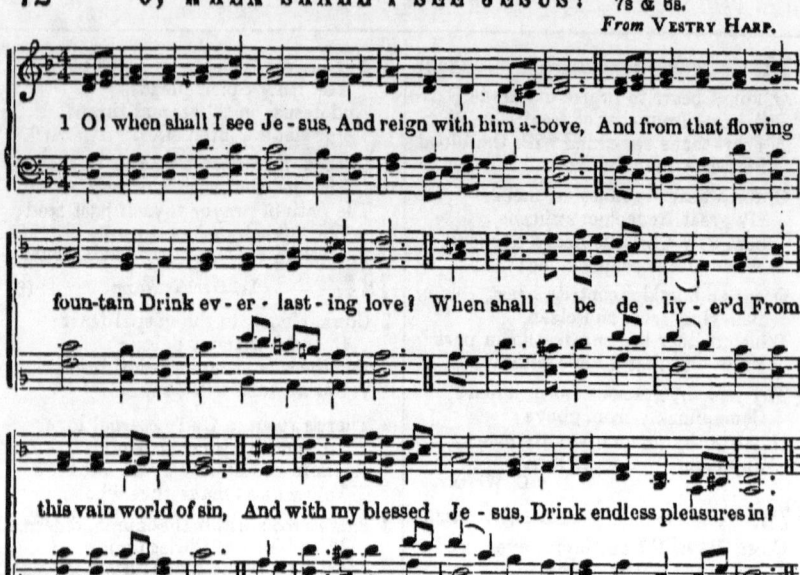

1 O! when shall I see Je-sus, And reign with him a-bove, And from that flowing foun-tain Drink ev-er-last-ing love? When shall I be de-liv-er'd From this vain world of sin, And with my blessed Je-sus, Drink endless pleasures in?

183.   *Longing to see Jesus.*   (427)

2 But now I am a soldier;
  My Captain's gone before;
  He's given me my orders,
  And bid me not give o'er;
  His faithful word has promised
  A righteous crown to give;
  And all his valiant soldiers
  Eternal life shall have.

3 Through grace, I am determined
  To conquer, though I die,
  And then away to Jesus
  On wings of love to fly.
  Farewell to sin and sorrow—
  I bid you all adieu;
  And O, my friends, prove faithful,
  And on your way pursue!

4 And if you meet with troubles
  And trials on your way,
  Then cast your care on Jesus,
  And don't forget to pray.

  Gird on the heavenly armor
  Of faith, and hope, and love;
  Then, when the combat's ended,
  He'll carry you above.

184.   *Cast thy Burden on the Lord.*   (294)

1 I LAY my sins on Jesus,
  The spotless Lamb of God;
  He bears them all, and frees us
  From the accursed load.

2 I bring my guilt to Jesus,
  To wash my crimson stains
  White in his blood most precious,
  Till not a spot remains.

3 I lay my wants on Jesus,
  All fullness dwells in him;
  He healeth my diseases,
  He doth my soul redeem.

4 I lay my griefs on Jesus,
  My burdens and my cares;
  He from them all releases,
  He all my sorrows shares.

5 I long to be like Jesus,
  Meek, loving, lowly, mild;
  I long to be like Jesus,
  The Father's holy child.

6 I long to be with Jesus,
  Amid the heavenly throng,
  To sing with saints his praises,
  And learn the angels' song.
                              BONAR.

185. *Christ the Great Physician.* (114)

1 How lost was my condition,
  Till Jesus made me whole!
  There is but one Physician
  Can cure a sin-sick soul.
  Next door to death he found me,
  And snatched me from the grave,
  To tell to all around me
  His wondrous power to save.

2 From men great skill professing,
  I thought a cure to gain;
  But this proved more distressing,
  And added to my pain.
  Some said that nothing ailed me;
  Some gave me up for lost;
  Thus every refuge failed me,
  And all my hopes were crossed.

3 At length this great Physician—
  How matchless is his grace!
  Accepted my petition,
  And undertook my case;
  First gave me sight to view him—
  For sin my eyes had sealed,—
  Then bade me look unto him;
  I looked, and I was healed.

4 A dying, risen Jesus,
  Seen by the eye of faith,
  At once from danger frees us,
  And saves the soul from death.
  Come, then, to this Physician;
  His help he'll freely give;
  He makes no hard condition;
  'Tis only, Look and live.
                              NEWTON.

186. *Evangelization of our Country.* (509)
       Tune MISSIONARY HYMN, page 195.

1 OUR country's voice is pleading,
  Ye men of God, arise!
  His providence is leading,
  The land before you lies;
  Day-gleams are o'er it brightening,
  And promise clothes the soil;
  Wide fields for harvest whitening,
  Invite the reaper's toil.

2 Go where the waves are breaking
  On California's shore,
  Christ's precious gospel taking,
  More rich than golden ore;
  On Alleghany's mountains,
  Through all the western vale,
  Beside Missouri's fountains,
  Rehearse the wondrous tale.

3 The love of Christ unfolding,
  Speed on from east to west,
  Till all, his cross beholding,
  In him are fully blest.
  Great Author of salvation,
  Haste, haste the glorious day,
  When we, a ransomed nation,
  Thy sceptre shall obey.
                       MRS. G. W. ANDERSON.

187. *Universal Hallelujah.* (525)
       Tune WEBB, page 194.

1 WHEN shall the voice of singing
  Flow joyfully along?
  When hill and valley, ringing
  With one triumphant song,
  Proclaim the contest ended,
  And Him, who once was slain,
  Again to earth descended,
  In righteousness to reign?

2 Then from the craggy mountains
  The sacred shout shall fly,
  And shady vales and fountains
  Shall echo the reply:
  High tower and lowly dwelling
  Shall send the chorus round,
  The hallelujah swelling
  In one eternal sound.

EVEN ME. 8s, 7s & 3s.

WM. B. BRADBURY.

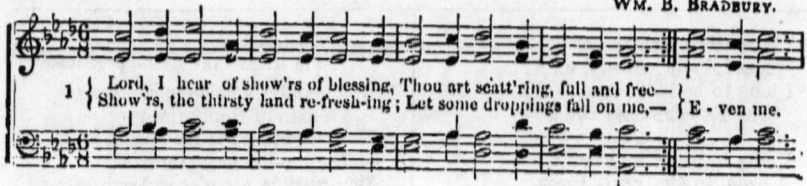

1 Lord, I hear of show'rs of blessing, Thou art scatt'ring, full and free—
Show'rs, the thirsty land re-fresh-ing; Let some droppings fall on me,—
E - ven me.

E- ven me, Let some droppings fall on me.

188. *Longing for Divine Favor.* (105)

2 Pass me not, O God, our Father!
   Sinful though my heart may be;
   Thou might'st leave me, but the rather
   Let thy mercy light on me!—
        Even me.

3 Pass me not, O gracious Saviour!
   Let me live and cling to thee;
   For I'm longing for thy favor;
   Whilst thou art calling, O! call me—
        Even me.

4 Pass me not, O mighty Spirit!
   Thou can'st make the blind to see;
   Witnesser of Jesus' merit!
   Speak some word of power to me—
        Even me.

5 Have I long in sin been sleeping—
   Long been slighting, grieving thee?
   Has the world my heart been keeping?
   Oh! forgive, and rescue me!—
        Even me.

6 Love of God—so pure and changeless;
   Blood of Christ—so rich, so free;
   Grace of God—so strong and boundless,
   Magnify it all in me!—
        Even me.

AMOY. 6s & 4s.

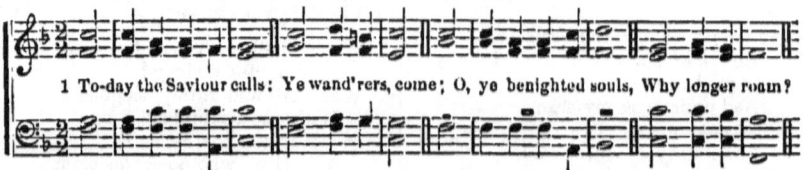

1 To-day the Saviour calls: Ye wand'rers, come; O, ye benighted souls, Why longer roam?

189. *The Saviour Calls.* (59)

1 To-DAY the Saviour calls,
   Ye wanderers, come;
   O ye benighted souls,
   Why longer roam?

2 To-day the Saviour calls:
   Oh, hear him now;
   Within these sacred walls
   To Jesus bow.

3 To-day the Saviour calls:
   For refuge fly;
   The storm of justice falls,
   And death is nigh.

4 The Spirit calls to-day:
   Yield to his power;
   O, grieve him not away;
   'Tis mercy's hour.

THE SWEETEST NAME. 75
WM. B. BRADBURY.

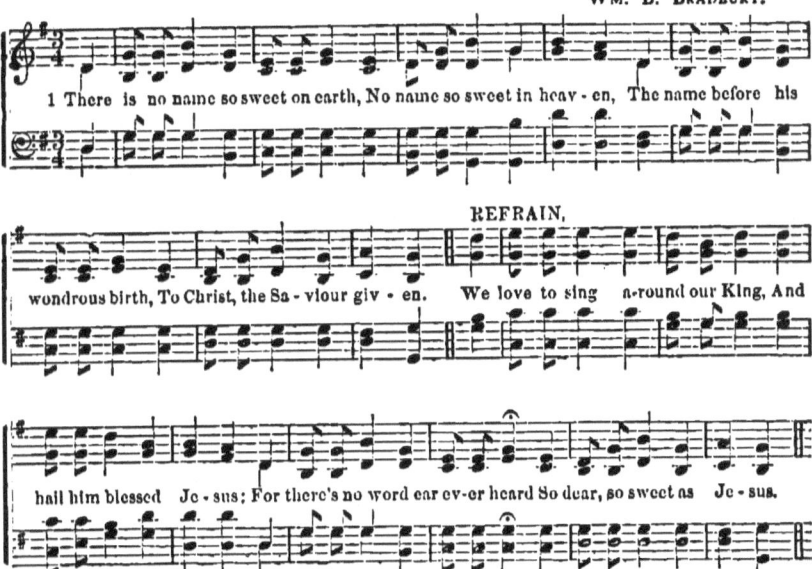

190. *The Name of Jesus.* (262)

1 THERE is no name so sweet on earth,
No name so sweet in heaven,—
The name before his wondrous birth
To Christ the Saviour given.
We love to sing around our King,
And hail him blessed Jesus;
For there's no word ear ever heard
So dear, so sweet, as Jesus.

2 And when he hung upon the tree,
They wrote this name above him,
That all might see the reason we
Forevermore must love him.
We love to sing, &c.

3 So now, upon his Father's throne,
Almighty to release us
From sin and pains, he ever reigns,
The Prince and Saviour Jesus.
We love to sing, &c.

4 O Jesus, by that matchless name,
Thy grace shall fail us never;

To-day as yesterday the same,
Thou art the same forever.
Then let us sing, around our King,
The faithful, precious Jesus, &c.

191. *Sowing and Reaping.* (339)
Tune NETTLETON, page 83.

1 HE that goeth forth with weeping,
Bearing precious seed in love,
Never tiring, never sleeping,
Findeth mercy from above:
Soft descend the dews of Heaven,
Bright the rays celestial shine;
Precious fruits will thus be given,
Through an influence all divine.

2 Sow thy seed, be never weary,
Let no fears thy soul annoy;
Be the prospect ne'er so dreary,
Thou shalt reap the fruits of joy,
Lo. the scene of verdure brightening!
See the rising grain appear;
Look, again! the fields are whitening,
For the harvest time is near.

BALERMA. C. M.

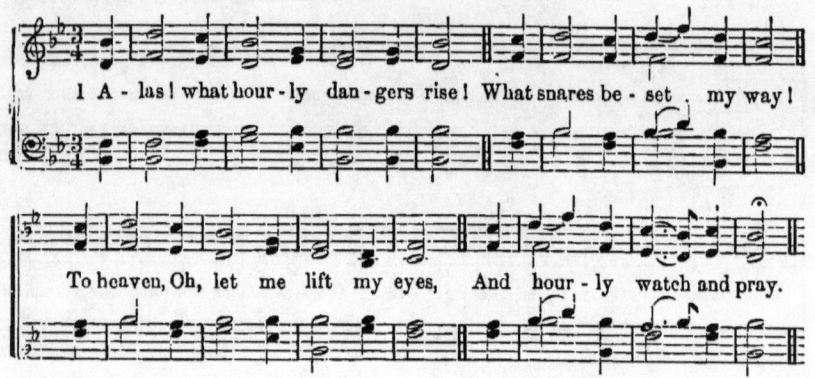

1. A-las! what hour-ly dan-gers rise! What snares be-set my way! To heaven, Oh, let me lift my eyes, And hour-ly watch and pray.

192. *The Watcher Strengthened.* (334)

1 Alas! what hourly dangers rise!
  What snares beset my way!
  To heaven, O, let me lift my eyes,
  And hourly watch and pray.

2 O gracious God, in whom I live,
  My feeble efforts aid;
  Help me to watch, and pray, and strive,
  Though trembling and afraid.

3 Increase my faith, increase my hope,
  When foes and fears prevail;
  And bear my fainting spirit up,
  Or soon my strength will fail.

4 Oh, keep me in thy heavenly way,
  And bid the tempter flee;
  And let me never, never stray
  From happiness and thee.
                                STEELE.

193. *Exhortation to Christian Activity.* (328)

1 My drowsy powers, why sleep ye so?
  Awake, my sluggish soul!
  Nothing has half thy work to do,
  Yet nothing's half so dull.

2 The little ants, for one poor grain,
  Labor, and tug, and strive;
  Yet we, who have a heaven t' obtain,
  How negligent we live!

3 We, for whose sake all nature stands,
  And stars their courses move;
  We, for whose guard the angel bands
  Come flying from above;—

4 We, for whom God the Son came down,
  And labored for our good,
  How careless to secure that crown
  He purchased with his blood!

5 Lord, shall we lie so sluggish still,
  And never act our parts?
  Come, holy Dove, from th' heavenly hill,
  And sit, and warm our hearts.

6 Then shall our active spirits move,
  Upward our souls shall rise;
  With hands of faith, and wings of love,
  We'll fly and take the prize.
                                WATTS.

194. *Prayer for Seamen.* (513)

1 We come, O Lord, before thy throne,
  And, with united pleas,
  We meet and pray for those who roam
  Far off upon the seas.

2 Oh, may the Holy Spirit bow
  The sailor's heart to thee,
  Till tears of deep repentance flow
  Like rain-drops in the sea.

3 Then may a Saviour's dying love
  Pour peace into his breast,
  And waft him to the port above
  Of everlasting rest.

195. *The Blood of Jesus the Ground of Pardon.* (102)

1 In vain we seek for peace with God
By methods of our own:
Blest Saviour, nothing but thy blood
Can bring us near the throne.

2 The threatenings of thy broken law
Impress the soul with dread:
If God his sword of justice draw,
It strikes the spirit dead.

3 But thy atoning sacrifice
Hath answered all demands;
And peace and pardon from the skies
Are blessings from thy hands.

4 'Tis by thy death we live, O Lord;
'Tis on thy cross we rest:
Forever be thy love adored,
Thy name forever blest.

196. *Youthful Piety.* (420)

1 Bestow, O Lord, upon our youth
The gift of saving grace,
And let the seed of sacred truth
Fall in a fruitful place.

2 Grace is a plant, where'er it grows,
Of pure and heavenly root,
But fairest in the youngest shows,
And yields the sweetest fruit.

3 Ye careless ones, O, hear betimes
The voice of sovereign love;
Your youth is stained with many crimes,
But mercy reigns above.

4 For you the public prayer is made;
O, join the public prayer!
For you the secret tear is shed;
O, shed yourselves a tear!

5 We pray that you may early prove
The Spirit's power to teach;
You cannot be too young to love
That Jesus whom we preach.
Cowper.

197. *A Welcome to Fellowship.* (146)

1 Come in, thou blessed of the Lord:
Stranger nor foe art thou:
We welcome thee with warm accord,
Our friend, our brother now.

2 The hand of fellowship, the heart
Of love, we offer thee;
Leaving the world, thou dost but part
From lies and vanity.

3 The cup of blessing which we bless,
The heavenly bread we break,—
Our Saviour's blood and righteousness,
Freely with us partake.

4 In weal or woe, in joy or care,
Thy portion shall be ours;
Christians their mutual burdens bear;
They lend their mutual powers.

5 Come with us; we will do thee good,
As God to us hath done;
Stand but in him, as those have stood
Whose faith the victory won.

6 And when, by turns, we pass away,
As star by star grows dim,
May each, translated into day,
Be lost, and found in him.
Montgomery.

198. *Prayer for Repentance.* (87)

1 O, for that tenderness of heart,
Which bows before the Lord!
That owns how just and good thou art,
And trembles at thy word!

2 O, for those humble, contrite tears
Which from repentance flow!
That sense of guilt, which trembling fears
The long-suspended blow!

3 Saviour, to me in pity give
For sin the deep distress,
The pledge thou wilt at last receive,
And bid me die in peace.

4 O, fill my soul with faith and love,
And strength to do thy will;
Raise my desires and hopes above;
Thyself to me reveal.
C. Wesley.

199. *After Hearing Converts.* (137)

1 Dear Saviour, we rejoice to hear
Poor sinners sweetly tell,
How thou art pleased to save from sin,
From sorrow, death, and hell.

2 Lord, we unite to praise thy name
For grace so freely given;
Still may we keep in Zion's road.
And dwell at last in heaven.

DUKE STREET. L. M.

JOHN HATTON.

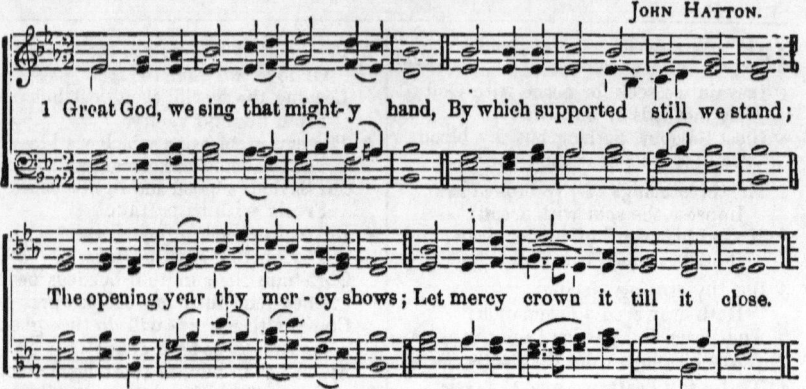

1 Great God, we sing that mighty hand, By which supported still we stand;
The opening year thy mercy shows; Let mercy crown it till it close.

200. *A Song for the Opening Year.* (563)

2 By day, by night, at home, abroad,
Still, we are guarded by our God;
By his incessant bounty fed,
By his unerring counsel led.

3 With grateful hearts the past we own
The future—all to us unknown—
We to thy guardian care commit,
And peaceful leave before thy feet.

4 In scenes exalted or depressed,
Be thou our joy, and thou our rest;
Thy goodness all our hopes shall raise,
Adored through all our changing days.
DODDRIDGE.

201. *The Promised Reign of Christ.* (532)

1 JESUS shall reign where'er the sun
Does his successive journeys run;
His kingdom stretch from shore to shore,
Till moons shall wax and wane no more.

2 For him shall endless prayer be made,
And endless praises crown his head;
His name, like sweet perfume, shall rise
With every morning sacrifice.

3 People and realms of every tongue
Dwell on his love with sweetest song;
And infant voices shall proclaim
Their early blessings on his name.

4 Blessings abound where'er he reigns;
The joyful prisoner bursts his chains;
The weary find eternal rest,
And all the sons of want are blest.
WATTS.

202. *Song of Gratitude and Praise.* (207)

1 GOD of my life, through all my days
I'll tune the grateful notes of praise;
The song shall wake with opening light,
And warble to the silent night.

2 When anxious care would break my rest
And grief would tear my throbbing breast,
The notes of praise, ascending high,
Shall check the murmur and the sigh.

3 When death o'er nature shall prevail,
And all the powers of language fail,
Joy through my swimming eyes shall break,
And mean the thanks I cannot speak.

4 But, oh! when that last conflict's o'er,
And I am chained to earth no more,
With what glad accents shall I rise,
To join the music of the skies!

5 Then shall I learn the exalted strains
That echo through the heavenly plains,
And emulate, with joy unknown,
The glowing seraphs round thy throne.
DODDRIDGE.

DUANE STREET. L. M. 79
Rev. G. Coles.

1. Je-sus, my all, to heaven is gone,—He, whom I fix my hopes up-on;
His track I see, and I'll pur-sue The nar-row way, till him I view
D. S. The King's highway of ho-li-ness—I'll go, for all the paths are peace.

2. The way the ho-ly prophets went—The way that leads from ba-nishment—

---

203. *I am the Way.* (117)

3 This is the way I long have sought,
And mourned because I found it not;
My grief, my burden long have been,
Because I could not cease from sin.

4 The more I strove against its power,
I sinned and stumbled but the more;
Till late I heard my Saviour say,
"Come hither, soul, I am the way."

5 Lo! glad I come! and thou, dear Lamb
Shalt take me to thee as I am!
My sinful self to thee I give:
Nothing but love shall I receive.

Then will I tell to sinners round
What a dear Saviour I have found
I'll point to thy redeeming blood,
And say—Behold the way to God!
CENNICK.

204. *Deity, Humiliation, and Exaltation of Christ.* (217)
Tune, DUKE STREET.

1 Now for a tune of lofty praise
To great Jehovah's equal Son:
Awake, my voice, in heavenly lays,
And tell the wonders he hath done.

2 Sing how he left the worlds of light,
And those bright robes he wore above;
How swift and joyful was his flight,
On wings of everlasting love!

3 Deep in the shades of gloomy death,
Th' almighty Captive prisoner lay;
Th' almighty Captive left the earth.
And rose to everlasting day

4 Among a thousand harps and songs,
Jesus, the God, exalted reigns:
His sacred name fills all their tongues.
And echoes through the heavenly plains.
WATTS.

MARTYN. 7s.

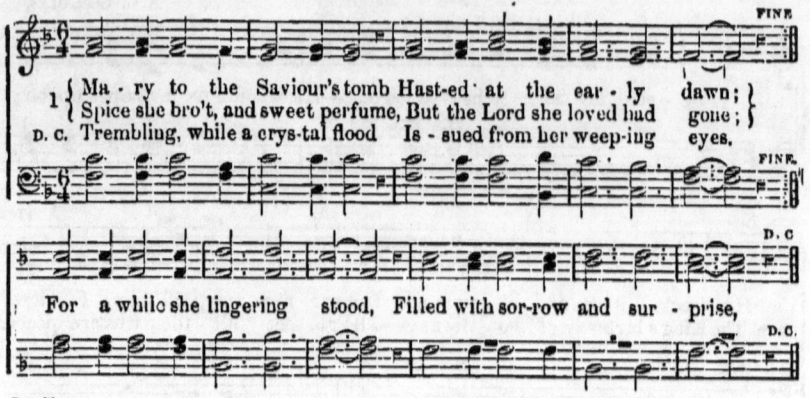

1. Mary to the Saviour's tomb Hast-ed at the ear-ly dawn;
Spice she bro't, and sweet perfume, But the Lord she loved had gone;
D. C. Trembling, while a crys-tal flood Is-sued from her weep-ing eyes.

For a while she lingering stood, Filled with sor-row and sur-prise,

205. *Mary at the Saviour's Tomb.* (436)

2 But her sorrows quickly fled
 When she heard his welcome voice:
Christ had risen from the dead;
 Now he bids her heart rejoice:
What a change his word can make,
 Turning darkness into day!
Ye who weep for Jesus' sake,
 He will wipe your tears away.
 NEWTON.

206 *Sinners Entreated.* (33)

1 SINNERS, turn; why will ye die?
 God, your Maker, asks you why;
God, who did your being give,
 Made you with himself to live.

2 Sinners, turn; why will ye die?
 God, your Saviour, asks you why:
Will ye not in him believe?
 He has died that ye might live.

3 Will ye let him die in vain?
 Crucify your Lord again?
Why, unpardoned sinners, why
 Will ye slight his grace, and die?

4 Sinners, turn; why will ye die;
 God, the Spirit, asks you why—
Often with you has he strove,
 Wooed you to embrace his love.

5 Will ye not his grace receive?
 Will ye still refuse to live?
O, ye dying sinners, why,
 Why will ye forever die?
 J. WESLEY.

207. *Christ the only Refuge.* (280)

1 JESUS! lover of my soul,
 Let me to thy bosom fly,
While the raging billows roll,
 While the tempest still is high;
Hide me, O, my Saviour! hide,
 Till the storm of life is past;
Safe into the haven guide;
 O, receive my soul at last!

2 Other refuge have I none,—
 Hangs my helpless soul on thee!
Leave, ah! leave me not alone!
 Still support and comfort me;
All my trust on thee is stayed;
 All my help from thee I bring;
Cover my defenseless head
 With the shadow of thy wing.

3 Thou, O, Christ, art all I want;
 All and all in thee I find;
Raise the fallen, cheer the faint,
 Heal the sick, and lead the blind;
Just and holy is thy name,
 I am all unrighteousness,
Vile, and full of sin I am,
 Thou art full of truth and grace.
 C. WESLEY.

208. *Saved by Grace.* (115)

1 SAVED by grace, I live to tell
What the love of Christ hath done,
He redeemed my soul from hell,
Of a rebel made a son;
Oh! I tremble still to think,
How secure I lived in sin;
Sporting on destruction's brink,
Yet preserved from falling in.

2 In his own appointed hour,
To my heart the Saviour spoke;
Touched me by his Spirit's power,
And my dangerous slumber broke.
Then I saw and owned my guilt;
Soon my gracious Lord replied,
"Fear not, I my blood have spilt,
'Twas for such as thee I died."

3 Shame and wonder, joy and love,
All at once possessed my heart;
Can I hope thy grace to prove
After acting such a part?
"Thou hast greatly sinned," he said,
"But I freely all forgive;
I myself thy debt have paid
Now I bid thee rise and live."

4 Come, my fellow-sinners, try,
Jesus' heart is full of love!
O, that you, as well as I,
May his wondrous mercy prove!
He has sent me to declare,
All is ready, all is free:
Why should any soul despair,
When he saved a wretch like me?
NEWTON.

209. *We shall soon be at Home.* (337)

1 BRETHREN, while we sojourn here,
Fight we must, but should not fear;
Foes we have, but we've a friend,
One that loves us to the end;
Forward, then, with courage go,
Long we shall not dwell below;
Soon the joyful news will come,
"Child, your Father calls, come home."

2 In our way, a thousand snares
Lie to take us unawares;
Satan with malicious art,
Watches each unguarded heart;

But from Satan's malice free,
Saints shall soon in glory be;
Soon the joyful news will come,
"Child, your Father calls, come home."

3 But of all the foes we meet,
None so oft mislead our feet
None betray us into sin,
Like the foes that dwell within;
Yet, let nothing spoil your peace,
Christ shall also conquer these;
Then the joyful news will come,
"Child, your Father calls, come home."
SWAIN.

210. *"Hasten, Lord, the promised Hour."* (499)

1 SEE the ransomed millions stand —
Palms of conquest in their hands!
This before the throne their strain:
"Hell is vanquished, Death is slain!

2 "Blessing, honor, glory, might,
Are the Conqueror's native right;
Thrones and powers before him fall—
Lamb of God, and Lord of all!"

3 Lo! thy sun goes down no more,
God himself will be thy light;
All that caused thee grief before
Buried lies in endless night.

4 Zion, now arise and shine!
Lo! thy light from heaven is come:
These that crowd from far are thine;
Give thy sons and daughters room.

211. *The Heathen Crying for Help.* (521)
Tune BARTIMEUS, page 94.

1 HARK! what mean those lamentations
Rolling sadly through the sky?
'Tis the cry of heathen nations—
"Come and help us, or we die!"

2 Hear the heathen's sad complaining,
Christians! hear their dying cry;
And, the love of Christ constraining,
Haste to help them, ere they die.
CAWOOD.

AUTUMN. 8s & 7s. Double.

Spanish.

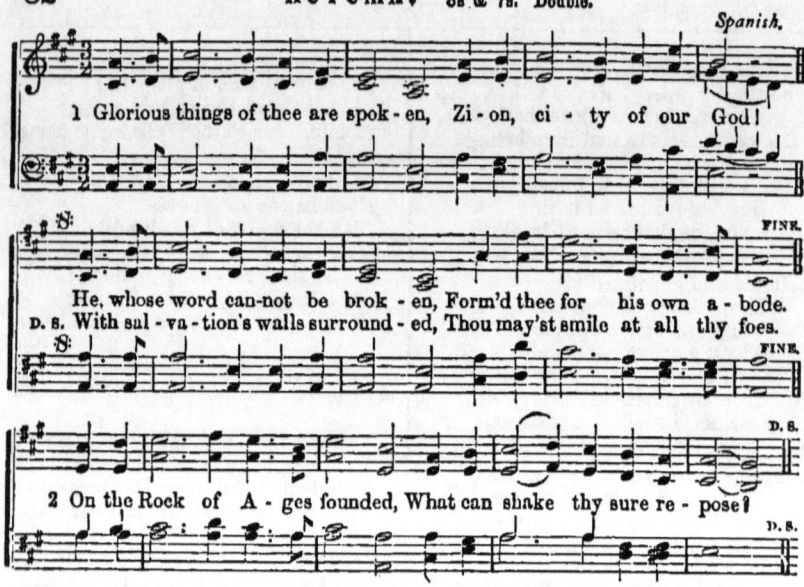

1 Glorious things of thee are spoken, Zion, city of our God!
He, whose word cannot be broken, Form'd thee for his own abode.
With salvation's walls surrounded, Thou may'st smile at all thy foes.

2 On the Rock of Ages founded, What can shake thy sure repose?

212. *Glory of the Church.* (535)

1 GLORIOUS things of thee are spoken,
  Zion, city of our God!
He, whose word cannot be broken,
  Form'd thee for his own abode.

2 On the Rock of Ages founded,
  What can shake thy sure repose?
With salvation's walls surrounded,
  Thou may'st smile at all thy foes.

3 See! the streams of living waters
  Springing from eternal love;
Well supply thy sons and daughters,
  And all fear of want remove.

4 Who can faint while such a river
  Ever flows their thirst t' assuage;
Grace, which, like the Lord, the giver,
  Never fails from age to age?

5 Saviour, if of Zion's city
  I through grace a member am;
Let the world deride or pity,
  I will glory in thy name.

6 Fading is the worldling's pleasure,
  All his boasted pomp and show;
Solid joys and lasting treasure,
  None but Zion's children know.
                                NEWTON.

213. *Christ with us.* (293)
Tune BARTIMEUS, page 94.

1 ALWAYS with us, always with us—
  Words of cheer and words of love;
Thus the risen Saviour whispers,
  From his dwelling-place above.

2 With us when we toil in sadness,
  Sowing much and reaping none;
Telling us that in the future
  Golden harvests shall be won.

3 With us when the storm is sweeping
  O'er our pathway dark and drear;
Waking hope within our bosoms,
  Stilling every anxious fear.

4 With us in the lonely valley,
  When we cross the chilling stream;
Lighting up the steps to glory,
  With salvation's radiant beam.
                                BONAR.

NETTLETON. 8s & 7s. Double. 83

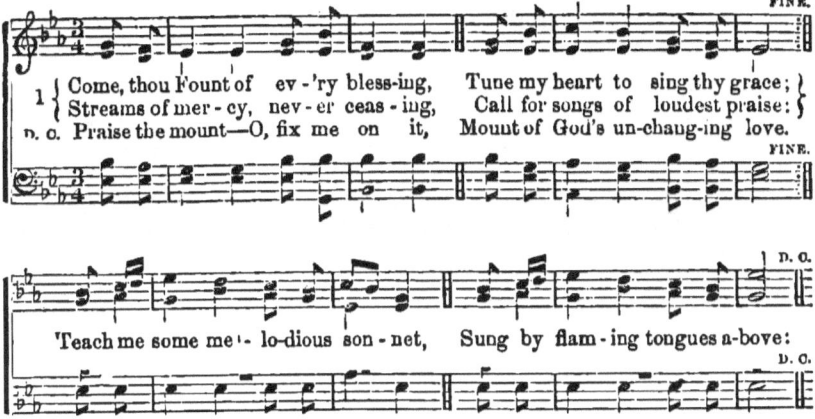

1. Come, thou Fount of ev-'ry bless-ing, Tune my heart to sing thy grace;
Streams of mer-cy, nev-er ceas-ing, Call for songs of loudest praise:
D.C. Praise the mount—O, fix me on it, Mount of God's un-chang-ing love.
Teach me some me-lo-dious son-net, Sung by flam-ing tongues a-bove:

---

214. *The Fount of Blessing.* (286)

2 Here I raise my Ebenezer;
Hither, by thy help I'm come;
And I hope, by thy good pleasure,
Safely to arrive at home:
Jesus sought me when a stranger,
Wandering from the fold of God;
He, to save my soul from danger,
Interposed his precious blood.

3 Oh! to grace how great a debtor
Daily I'm constrained to be!
Let that grace, Lord, like a fetter,
Bind my wandering heart to thee.
Prone to wander, Lord, I feel it;
Prone to leave the God I love;
Here's my heart; Lord, take and seal it;
Seal it from thy courts above.
ROBINSON.

215. *"From Grace to Glory."* (253)

1 KNOW, my soul, thy full salvation;
Rise o'er sin, and fear, and care;
Joy to find in every station
Something still to do or bear;
Think what Spirit dwells within thee:
Think what Father's smiles are thine;
Think that Jesus died to win thee:
Child of heaven, canst thou repine?

2 Haste thee on from grace to glory,
Armed by faith, and winged by prayer;
Heaven's eternal day before thee—
God's own hand shall guide thee there.
Soon shall close thine earthly mission,
Soon shall pass thy pilgrim days;
Hope shall change to glad fruition,
Faith to sight, and prayer to praise.
HENRY F. LYTE.

216. *The Spirit Invoked.* (308)

1 HOLY source of consolation,
Light and life thy grace imparts;
Visit us in thy compassion;
Guide our minds, and fill our hearts.

2 Heavenly blessings, without measure,
Thou canst bring us from above;
Lord, we ask that heavenly treasure,
Wisdom, holiness, and love.

3 Dwell within us, blessed Spirit;
Where thou art no ill can come;
Bless us now, through Jesus' merit;
Reign in every heart and home

4 Saviour, lead us to adore thee,
While thou dost prolong our days;
Then, with angel hosts before thee,
May we worship, love, and praise.

SHIRLAND. S. M.

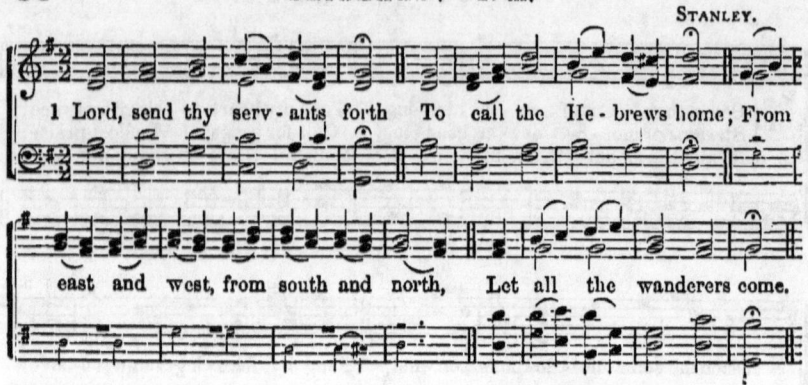

STANLEY.

1 Lord, send thy serv-ants forth To call the He-brews home; From east and west, from south and north, Let all the wanderers come.

217. *Prayer for Israel.* (542)

1 Lord, send thy servants forth
  To call the Hebrews home;
From east and west, from south and north,
  Let all the wanderers come.

2 Where'er in lands unknown,
  The fugitives remain,
Bid every creature help them on,
  Thy holy mount to gain.

3 An offering to the Lord,
  There let them all be seen,
And washed with water and with blood,
  In soul and body clean.

4 With Israel's myriads sealed,
  Let all the nations meet,
And show the promises fulfilled—
  Thy family complete.
            C. Wesley.

218. *Love the Spring of True Obedience.* (353)

1 Love is the fountain whence
  All true obedience flows;
The Christian serves the God he loves,
  And loves the God he knows.

2 He treads the heavenly road,
  And neither faints nor tires;
That generous love which warms his breast,
  With fortitude inspires.

3 No burden seems so great,
  No task so hard appears,
But this he cheerfully performs,
  And that he meekly bears.

4 May love,—that shining grace,
  O'er all my powers preside;
Direct my thoughts, suggest my words,
  And every action guide!
            Beddome.

219. *Love to the Church.* (156)

1 I love thy kingdom, Lord,
  The house of thine abode,
The church our blest Redeemer saved
  With his own precious blood.

2 I love thy church, O God;
  Her walls before thee stand,
Dear as the apple of thine eye,
  And graven on thy hand.

3 For her my tears shall fall;
  For her my prayers ascend;
To her my cares and toils be given,
  Till toils and cares shall end.

4 Beyond my highest joy
  I prize her heavenly ways,
Her sweet communion, solemn vows,
  Her hymns of love and praise.

HYMNS. 85

5 Jesus, thou Friend divine,
  Our Saviour and our King,
Thy hand, from every snare and foe
Shall great deliverance bring.

6 Sure as thy truth shall last,
  To Zion shall be given
The brightest glories earth can yield,
And brighter bliss of heaven.
                        DWIGHT.

ST. THOMAS. S. M.
HANDEL.

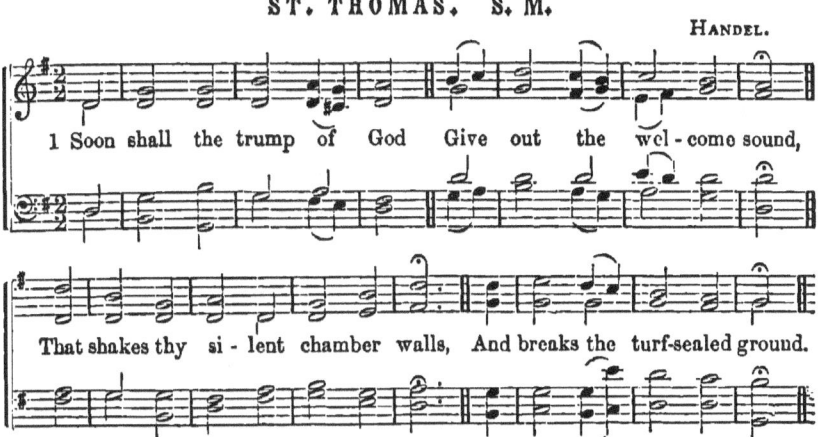

1 Soon shall the trump of God Give out the welcome sound,
That shakes thy silent chamber walls, And breaks the turf-sealed ground.

220. *The Trumpet Shall Sound.* (582)

2 Ye dwellers in the dust,
  Awake, come forth and sing;
Sharp has your frost of winter been,
But bright shall be your spring.

3 'Twas sown in weakness here;
  'Twill then be raised in power;
That which was sown an earthly seed,
Shall rise a heavenly flower.
                        BONAR.

221. *The Soldier Armed.* (326)

1 SOLDIERS of Christ, arise,
  And gird your armor on,
Strong in the strength which God supplies
Through his eternal Son.

2 Strong in the Lord of hosts,
  And in his mighty power,
The man who in the Saviour trusts
Is more than conqueror.

3 Stand, then, in his great might,
  With all his strength endued,
And take, to arm you for the fight,
The panoply of God.
                        C. WESLEY.

222. *Mercy of God.* (202)

1 MY soul, repeat his praise,
  Whose mercies are so great,
Whose anger is so slow to rise,
  So ready to abate.

2 His power subdues our sins,
  And his forgiving love,
Far as the east is from the west,
  Doth all our guilt remove.

3 High as the heavens are raised
  Above the ground we tread,
So far the riches of his grace
  Our highest thoughts exceed.
                        WATTS.

BLESSED BIBLE. 8s & 7s, Double.

WM. B. BRADBURY.

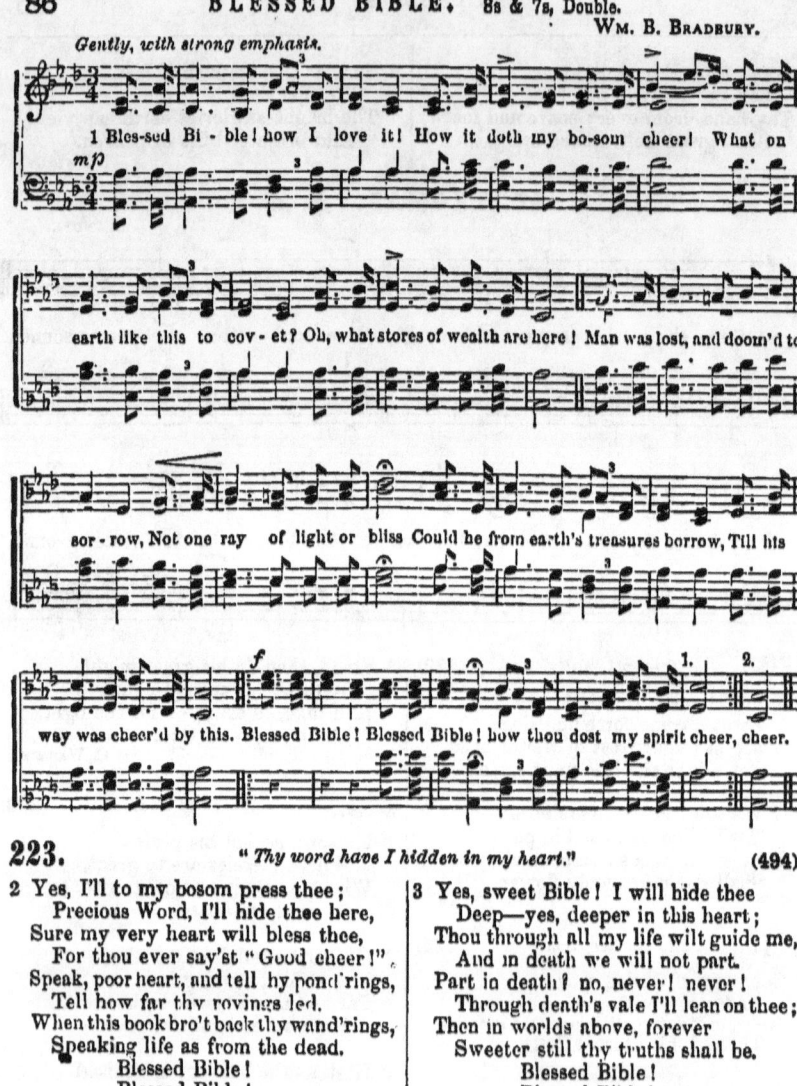

1 Bles-sed Bi-ble! how I love it! How it doth my bo-som cheer! What on earth like this to cov-et? Oh, what stores of wealth are here! Man was lost, and doom'd to sor-row, Not one ray of light or bliss Could he from earth's treasures borrow, Till his way was cheer'd by this. Blessed Bible! Blessed Bible! how thou dost my spirit cheer, cheer.

223.   *" Thy word have I hidden in my heart."*   (494)

2 Yes, I'll to my bosom press thee;
   Precious Word, I'll hide thee here,
   Sure my very heart will bless thee,
   For thou ever say'st "Good cheer!"
Speak, poor heart, and tell hy pond'rings,
   Tell how far thy rovings led.
When this book bro't back thy wand'rings,
   Speaking life as from the dead.
      Blessed Bible!
      Blessed Bible!
   How thou dost my spirit cheer.

3 Yes, sweet Bible! I will hide thee
   Deep—yes, deeper in this heart;
   Thou through all my life wilt guide me,
   And in death we will not part.
Part in death? no, never! never!
   Through death's vale I'll lean on thee;
Then in worlds above, forever
   Sweeter still thy truths shall be.
      Blessed Bible!
      Blessed Bible!
   How thou dost my spirit cheer.
          MRS. PHEBE PALMER.

YOUNG PILGRIMS.
WM. B. BRADBURY.

224. *Young Pilgrims.* (464)

2 With cheerful steps we'll hasten,
Nor list the tempter's charms:
But to the Spirit listen
That calls to Jesus' arms.
Twill make life's burden lighter
To feel God's gracious love:
And every precept brighter
That points to realms above.
We are going to fields Elysian,
Far, far beyond the sky,
The golden gates of heaven
Will open by-and-by, &c.

3 His holy book will ever
Our onward footsteps guide,
Until we reach our Saviour,
And anchor near his side.
And when we meet our Jesus,
And tears are wiped away,
We'll take the harp he gives us,
And shout and sing for aye,
We've reached the fields Elysian
The Eden of the blest,
With angels now in heaven.
The pilgrims are at rest.
MRS. LYDIA BAXTER.

HARWELL. 8s & 7s, Double.

Dr. L. Mason.

1 { Je-sus, I my cross have tak-en, All to leave and fol-low thee:
   { Nak-ed, poor, despised, for-sak-en, Thou, from hence, my all shalt be;
D.C. Yet how rich is my con-di-tion! God and heaven are still my own.

Per-ish ev-'ry fond am-bition, All I've sought, or hoped, or known;

225. *"Jesus, I my Cross have taken."* (269)

2 Let the world despise and leave me,
  They have left my Saviour, too;
  Human hearts and looks deceive me;
  Thou art not, like them, untrue:
  And while thou shalt smile upon me,
  God of wisdom, love, and might,
  Foes may hate, and friends may scorn me;
  Show thy face, and all is bright.

3 Man may trouble and distress me,
  'T will but drive me to thy breast:
  Life with trials hard may press me,
  Heaven will bring me sweeter rest.
  Oh! 'tis not in grief to harm me,
  While thy love is left to me;
  Oh! 't were not in joy to charm me,
  Were that joy unmixed with thee.
                          HENRY F. LYTE.

226. *God is Love.* (181)

1 GOD is love; his mercy brightens
  All the path in which we rove;
  Bliss he wakes, and woe he lightens,
  God is wisdom, God is love.

2 Chance and change are busy ever;
  Man decays, and ages move;
  But his mercy waneth never;
  God is wisdom, God is love.

3 E'en the hour that darkest seemeth
  Will his changeless goodness prove;
  From the gloom his brightness streameth:
  God is wisdom, God is love.

4 He with earthly cares entwineth
  Hope and comfort from above:
  Everywhere his glory shineth;
  God is wisdom, God is love.
                          BOWRING.

227. *Joy at the Cross.* (228)

1 SWEET the moments, rich in blessing,
  Which before the cross I spend;
  Life, and health, and peace possessing,
  From the sinner's dying friend.

2 Love and grief, my heart dividing,
  With my tears his feet I'll bathe;
  Constant still, in faith abiding,
  Life deriving from his death.

3 Truly blessed is this station,
  Low before his cross to lie;
  While I see divine compassion
  Beaming in his gracious eye.

4 Here I'll sit, for ever viewing
  Mercy streaming in his blood;
  Precious drops my soul bedewing,
  Plead, and claim my peace with God.
                          BATTY.

GREENVILLE. 8s & 7s, Double.

J. J. Rousseau.

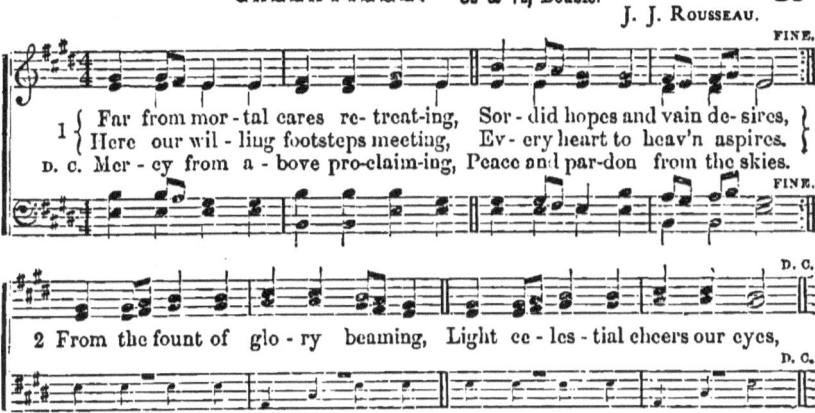

1 Far from mor-tal cares re-treat-ing, Sor-did hopes and vain de-sires,
  Here our wil-ling footsteps meeting, Ev-ery heart to heav'n aspires.
D. C. Mer-cy from a-bove pro-claim-ing, Peace and par-don from the skies.

2 From the fount of glo-ry beaming, Light ce-les-tial cheers our eyes,

---

228. *The Fount of Blessing.* (455)

3 Who may share this great salvation?
  Every pure and humble mind,
Every kindred, tongue, and nation,
  From the stains of guilt refined.

4 Blessings all around bestowing,
  God withholds his care from none,
Grace and mercy ever flowing
  From the fountain of his throne.
                                J. Taylor.

229. *Watchful Providence.* (390)

1 Saviour, breathe an evening blessing,
  Ere repose our spirits seal;
Sin and want we come confessing,—
  Thou canst save, and thou canst heal.
Though destruction walk around us,
  Though the arrow past us fly,
Angel-guards from thee surround us;
  We are safe, if thou art nigh.

2 Though the night be dark and dreary,
  Darkness cannot hide from thee;
Thou art he who, never weary,
  Watchest where thy people be;
Should swift death this night o'ertake us,
  And our couch become our tomb;
May the morn in heaven awake us,
  Clad in light and deathless bloom.
                                Edmeston.

230. *Declension Lamented.* (10)

1 Once, O Lord, thy garden flourished,
  Every part looked gay and green;
Then thy word our spirits nourished,
  Happy seasons we have seen!

2 But a drought has since succeeded,
  And a sad decline we see;
Lord, thy help is greatly needed,
  Help can only come from thee.

3 Some, in whom we once delighted,
  We shall meet no more below;
Some, alas! we fear are blighted,—
  Scarce a single leaf they show.

4 Dearest Saviour, hasten hither,
  Thou canst make them bloom again;
O, permit them not to wither,
  Let not all our hopes be vain!
                                Newton.

231. *Christ Victorious.* (538)

1 Zion's King shall reign victorious;
  All the earth shall own his sway;
His dominion shall be glorious,
  Nor shall ever pass away,

2 Mighty King, thy love revealing,
  Now thy holy cause maintain;
Bring the nations, humbly kneeling,
  Now to own thy blessed reign.

EVAN. C. M.

Dr. LOWELL MASON.

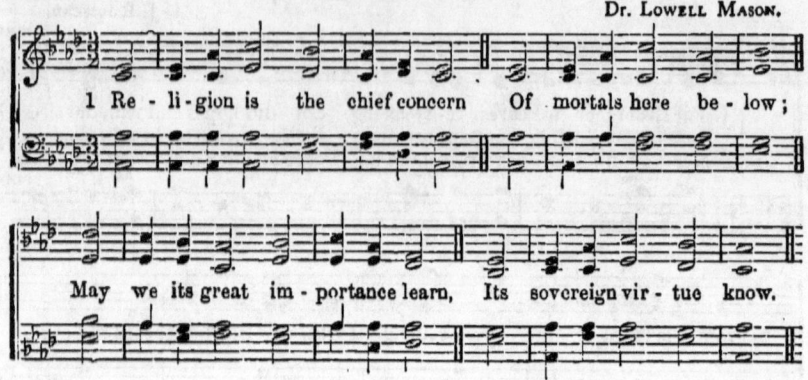

1 Religion is the chief concern Of mortals here below;
May we its great importance learn, Its sovereign virtue know.

232. *Importance of Religion.* (21)

2 Religion should our thoughts engage
   Amidst our youthful bloom;
'Twill fit us for declining age,
   And for the solemn tomb.

3 O, may our hearts, by grace renewed,
   Be our Redeemer's throne;
And be our stubborn wills subdued,
   His government to own.

4 Let deep repentance, faith, and love
   Be joined with godly fear,
And all our conversation prove
   Our hearts to be sincere.

5 Let lively hope our souls inspire;
   Let warm affections rise;
And may we wait with strong desire
   To mount above the skies.
                              FAWCETT.

233. *Imitation of Christ.* (247)

1 In duties and in sufferings too,
   Thy path, my Lord, I'd trace;
As thou hast done, so would I do,
   Depending on thy grace.

2 Inflamed with zeal, 'twas thy delight
   To do thy Father's will;
O, may that zeal my soul excite
   Thy precepts to fulfill.

3 Unsullied meekness, truth, and love,
   Through all thy conduct shine;
O, may my whole deportment prove
   A copy, Lord, of thine.
                              BEDDOME.

234. *Repentance Commanded.* (18)

1 "REPENT!" the voice celestial cries;
   No longer dare delay:
The soul that scorns the mandate dies,
   And meets a fiery day.

2 No more the sovereign eye of God
   O'erlooks the crimes of men;
His heralds now are sent abroad
   To warn the world of sin.

3 O, sinners, in his presence bow,
   And all your guilt confess;
Accept the offered Saviour now,
   Nor trifle with his grace.

4 Soon will the awful trumpet sound,
   And call you to his bar;
His mercy knows th' appointed bound,
   And yields to justice there.

5 Amazing love, that yet will call,
   And yet prolong our days!
Our hearts, subdued by goodness, fall
   And weep, and love, and praise.
                              DODDRIDGE.

235. *There is a Time.* (17)

1 THERE is a time we know not when,
   A point we know not where,
That marks the destiny of men,
   To glory or despair.

2 There is a line, by us unseen,
   That crosses every path;
The hidden boundary between
   God's patience and his wrath.

3 To pass that limit is to die—
   To die as if by stealth;
It does not quench the beaming eye,
   Or pall the glow of health.

4 The conscience may be still at ease,
   The spirit, light and gay,
That which is pleasing, still may please,
   And care be thrust away.

5 Oh! where is this mysterious bourne,
   By which our path is crossed;
Beyond which, God himself hath sworn,
   That he who goes is lost?

6 How far may we go on in sin?
   How long will God forbear?
Where does hope end? and where begin
   The confines of despair?

7 An answer from the skies is sent:
   "Ye that from God depart!
While it is called to-day, repent!
   And harden not your heart."

236. *God our Support.* (452)

1 How can I sink with such a prop
   As my eternal God,
Who bears the earth's huge pillars up,
   And spreads the heavens abroad?

2 How can I die, while Jesus lives,
   Who rose and left the dead?
Pardon and grace my soul receives
   From my exalted Head.

3 All that I am, and all I have,
   Shall be for ever thine;
Whate'er my duty bids me give,
   My cheerful hands resign.

4 Yet, if I might make some reserve,
   And duty did not call,
I love my God with zeal so great,
   That I should give him all.
                          WATTS.

237. *Weep for the Lost.* (8)

1 WEEP for the lost! Thy Saviour wept
   O'er Salem's hapless doom;
He wept, to think their day was past,
   And come their night of gloom.

2 Weep for the lost! The prophets wept
   O'er Israel's gloomy fate,
When Vengeance had unsheathed her sword
   Repentance came too late.

3 Weep for the lost! Apostles wept,
   That men should error choose;
That dying men should Christ reject,
   And endless life refuse.

4 Weep for the lost! The lost will weep,
   In that long night of woe,
On which no star of hope will rise,
   And tears in vain will flow.

5 Weep for the lost! Lord make us weep,
   And toil, with ceaseless care,
To save our friends, ere yet they pass
   That point of deep despair.
                          COLVER.

238. *The Fruitless Fig-Tree.* (42)

1 SEE how the fruitless fig-tree stands
   Beneath the owner's frown;
The axe is lifted in his hands,
   To cut the cumberer down.

2 "Year after year, I come," he cries,
   "And still no fruit is shown;
I see but empty leaves arise;
   Then cut the cumberer down."

3 "The axe of death, at one sharp stroke,
   Shall make my justice known;
Each bough shall tremble at the shock
   Which cuts the cumberer down."

4 Sinner, beware!—the axe of death
   Is raised, and aimed at thee:
A while thy Maker spares thy breath;
   Beware, O, barren tree!
                          HARMOTTLE.

EVENING HYMN. L. M.
TALLIS.

1 Glory to thee, my God, this night, For all the blessings of the light
Keep me, O keep me, King of kings, Beneath the shadow of thy wings.

239. *Trusting God.* (387)

1 GLORY to thee, my God, this night,
For all the blessings of the light;
Keep me, O, keep me, King of kings,
Beneath the shadow of thy wings.

2 Forgive me, Lord, for thy dear Son,
The ills which I this day have done:
That with the world, myself, and thee,
I, ere I sleep, at peace may be.

3 Teach me to live that I may dread
The grave as little as my bed;
Teach me to die that so I may
With joy behold the judgment day.

4 Be thou my Guardian while I sleep;
Thy watchful station near me keep;
My heart with love celestial fill,
And guard me from the approach of ill.

5 Lord, let my heart for ever share
The bliss of thy paternal care:
'Tis heaven on earth, 'tis heaven above,
To see thy face and sing thy love.
KENNY.

240. *The Good Old Way.* (74)

1 INQUIRING souls, who long to find
Pardon of sin, and peace of mind;
Attend the voice of God to-day,
Who bids you seek the good old way.

2 The righteousness, th' atoning blood
Of Jesus, is the way to God;
Oh, may you then no longer stray,
But walk in Christ, the good old way

3 The prophets and th' apostles too,
Pursued this way, while here below;
Then let not fear your souls dismay,
But come to Christ, the good old way
DOBELL.

241. *The Guiding Spirit.* (30?)

1 COME, gracious Spirit, heavenly Dove,
With light and comfort from above;
Be thou our guardian, thou our guide;
O'er every thought and step preside.

2 To us the light of truth display,
And make us know and choose thy way
Plant holy fear in every heart,
That we from God may ne'er depart.

3 Lead us to holiness—the road
Which we must take to dwell with God
Lead us to Christ—the living way;
Nor let us from his pastures stray.

4 Lead us to God,—our final rest,—
To be with him for ever blest;
Lead us to heaven, its bliss to share—
Fullness of joy for ever there.
BROWNE.

MEROE. L. M. 93
WM. B. BRADBURY.

1 Je-sus, and shall it ev - er be— A mortal man ashamed of thee!
Ashamed of thee, whom angels praise, Whose glories shine through endless days.

242. *Not Ashamed of Christ.* (245)

1 JESUS, and shall it ever be—
A mortal man ashamed of thee!
Ashamed of thee, whom angels praise,
Whose glories shine through endless days!

2 Ashamed of Jesus!—that dear Friend
On whom my hopes of heaven depend!
No!—when I blush, be this my shame—
That I no more revere his name.

3 Ashamed of Jesus!—yes, I may,
When I've no guilt to wash away,
No tear to wipe, no good to crave,
No fears to quell, no soul to save.

4 Till then—nor is my boasting vain—
Till then, I boast a Saviour slain;
And, O, may this my glory be—
That Christ is not ashamed of me.
GRIGG.

243. *Christ the Physician of the Soul.* (96)

1 DEEP are the wounds which sin has made;
Where shall the sinner find a cure?
In vain, alas! is nature's aid;
The work exceeds her utmost power.

2 But can no sovereign balm be found?
And is no kind physician nigh,
To ease the pain, and heal the wound,
Ere life and hope for ever fly?

3 There is a great Physician near;
Look up, oh, fainting soul, and live;
See, in his heavenly smiles appear
Such help as nature cannot give.

4 See, in the Saviour's dying blood,
Life, health, and bliss abundant flow:
'Tis only that dear, sacred flood
Can ease thy pain, and heal thy woe
STEELE.

244. *National Judgments Deprecated.* (547)

1 O RIGHTEOUS God, thou Judge supreme
We tremble at thy dreadful name!
And all our crying guilt we own,
In dust and tears, before thy throne.

2 Justly might this polluted land
Prove all the vengeance of thy hand:
And, bathed in heaven, the sword might come,
To drink our blood, and seal our doom.

3 Yet hast thou not a remnant here,
Whose souls are filled with pious fear?
O bring thy wonted mercy nigh,
While prostrate at thy feet they lie!

4 Behold their tears, attend their moan,
Nor turn away their secret groan;
With these we join our humble prayer;
Our nation shield, our country spare.
DODDRIDGE

BARTIMEUS. 8s & 7s.

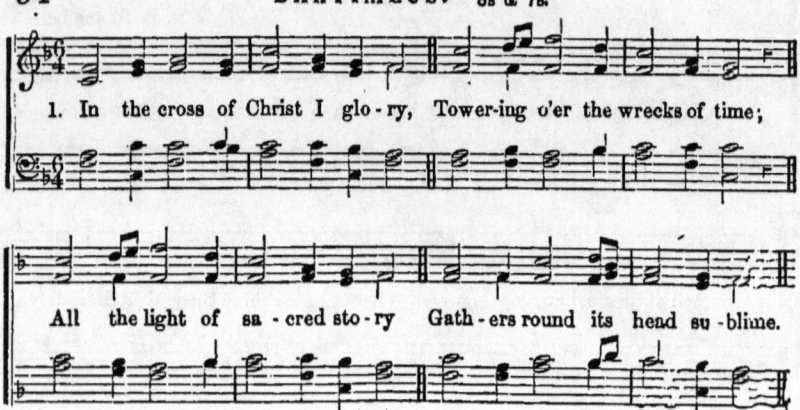

1. In the cross of Christ I glory, Towering o'er the wrecks of time;
All the light of sacred story Gathers round its head sublime.

245. *Glorying in the Cross.* (225)

2 When the woes of life o'ertake me,
  Hopes deceive and fears annoy,
Never shall the cross forsake me;
  Lo! it glows with peace and joy.

3 When the sun of bliss is beaming
  Light and love upon my way,
From the cross the radiance streaming
  Adds new lustre to the day.

4 Bane and blessing, pain and pleasure,
  By the cross are sanctified;
Peace is there that knows no measure,
  Joys that through all time abide.

5 In the cross of Christ I glory,
  Towering o'er the wrecks of time;
All the light of sacred story
  Gathers round its head sublime.
  BOWRING.

246. *Spiritual Blindness Removed.* (132)

. "Mercy, O thou Son of David!"
  Thus blind Bartimeus prayed;
"Others by thy word are saved,
  Now to me afford thine aid."

2 Many for his crying chid him,
  But he called the louder still;
Till the gracious Saviour bid him—
  "Come, and ask me what you will."

3 "Lord, remove this grievous blindness,
  Let my eyes behold the day"—
Straight he saw, and won by kindness,
  Followed Jesus in the way.

4 O, methinks I hear him praising,
  Publishing to all around—
"Friends, is not my case amazing?
  What a Saviour I have found!

5 "O that all the blind but knew him,
  And would be advised by me;
Surely they would hasten to him,
  He would cause them all to see."
  NEWTON.

DOXOLOGY.

1 Praise the God of our salvation,
  Praise the Father's boundless love;
Praise the Lamb, our expiation;
  Praise the Spirit from above;

2 Praise the Fountain of salvation,
  Him by whom our spirits live;
Undivided adoration
  To the one Jehovah give!

DOXOLOGY.

Praise the Father, earth and heaven,
Praise the Son, the Spirit praise,
As it was, and is, be given,
Glory through eternal days.

PLEADING SAVIOUR. 8s & 7s. 95

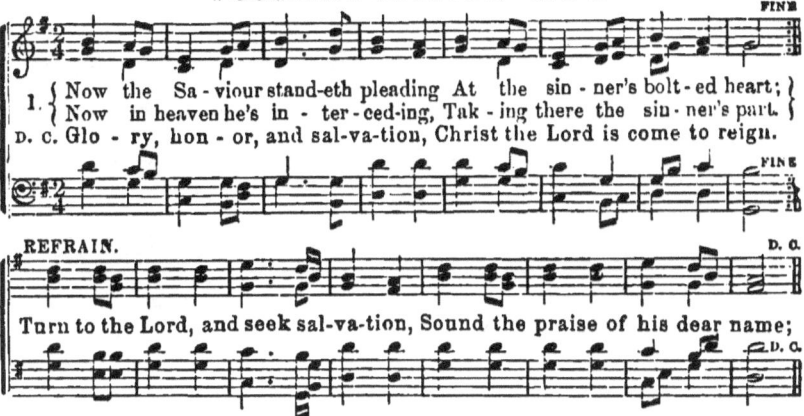

1. Now the Saviour stand-eth pleading At the sin-ner's bolt-ed heart;
   Now in heaven he's in-ter-ced-ing, Tak-ing there the sin-ner's part.
D. C. Glo-ry, hon-or, and sal-va-tion, Christ the Lord is come to reign.

REFRAIN.
Turn to the Lord, and seek sal-va-tion, Sound the praise of his dear name;

247.
2 Sinner! hear your God and Saviour,
  Hear his gracious voice to-day,
  Turn from all your vain behavior,
  O repent, return and pray!
  Turn to the Lord, &c.

3 Now he's waiting to be gracious,
  Now he stands and looks on thee;
  See what kindness, love, and pity,
  Shine around on you and me.
  Turn to the Lord, &c.

4 Come, for all things now are ready,
  Yet there's room for many more:
  O ye blind, ye lame and needy,
  Come to wisdom's boundless store!
  Turn to the Lord, &c.

248. Christ the best Friend. (249)
1 ONE there is, above all others,
  Well deserves the name of Friend;
  His is love beyond a brother's,
  Costly, free, and knows no end!
  Sinner, can you hate the Saviour?
  Can you thrust him from your arms?
  Once he died for your behavior,
  Now he calls you by his charms.

Which of all our friends, to save us,
  Could, or would, have shed his blood?
But our Jesus died to have us
  Reconciled, in him, to God.
    Sinner, can you hate, &c.

(22) 3 When he lived on earth abasèd,
       Friend of Sinners was his name;
       Now, above all glory raised,
       He rejoices in the same.
         Sinner, can you hate, &c.

4 O for grace our hearts to soften!
  Teach us, Lord, at length to love;
  We, alas! forget too often;
  What a Friend we have above.
    Sinner, can you hate, &c.
                                NEWTON.

249. Pardon implored for National Sins.
        Tune BARTIMEUS. (551)
1 DREAD Jehovah! God of nations!
  From thy temple in the skies,
  Hear thy people's supplications,
  Now for their deliverance rise.

2 Though our sins, our hearts confounding,
  Long and loud for vengeance call,
  Thou hast mercy more abounding;
  Jesus' blood can cleanse them all.

3 Let that love vail our transgression:
  Let that blood our guilt efface·
  Save thy people from oppression;
  Save from spoil thy holy place

4 Lo! with deep contrition turning,
  Humbly at thy feet we bend;
  Hear us, fasting, praying, mourning;
  Hear us, spare us, and defend.

STEPHENS. C. M.

JONES.

1 To our Redeemer's glorious name A-wake the sacred song
O, may his love—immortal flame— Tune ev-'ry heart and tongue.

250. *Love of Christ Celebrated.* (278)

2 His love what mortal thought can reach!
  What mortal tongue display!
  Imagination's utmost stretch
  In wonder dies away.

3 Dear Lord, while we, adoring, pay
  Our humble thanks to thee,
  May every heart with rapture say,
  "The Saviour died for me."

4 O, may the sweet, the blissful theme
  Fill every heart and tongue,
  Till strangers love thy charming name,
  And join the sacred song.   STEELE.

251. *Providence Dark but Gracious.* (201)

1 GOD moves in a mysterious way
  His wonders to perform;
  He plants his footsteps in the sea,
  And rides upon the storm.

2 Deep in unfathomable mines
  Of never-failing skill,
  He treasures up his vast designs,
  And works his sovereign will.

3 Ye fearful saints, fresh courage take;
  The clouds ye so much dread
  Are big with mercy, and will break
  In blessings on your head.

4 Judge not the Lord by feeble sense,
  But trust him for his grace;
  Behind a frowning providence
  He hides a smiling face.

5 His purposes will ripen fast,
  Unfolding every hour;
  The bud may have a bitter taste,
  But sweet will be the flower.

6 Blind unbelief is sure to err,
  And scan his work in vain;
  God is his own interpreter,
  And he will make it plain.
                              COWPER.

252. *Encouragement to Young Persons to Seek Christ.* (498)

1 YE hearts with youthful vigor warm,
  In smiling crowds draw near,
  And turn from every mortal charm,
  A Saviour's voice to hear.

2 He, Lord of all the worlds on high,
  Stoops to converse with you;
  And lays his radiant glories by,
  Your friendship to pursue.

3 "The soul that longs to see my face,
  Is sure my love to gain;
  And those that early seek my grace,
  Shall never seek in vain."
                              DODDRIDGE.

HYMNS.

253. *Supporting Grace.* (429)
1 How happy is the Christian's state!
  His sins are all forgiven;
  A cheering ray confirms the grace,
  And lifts his hopes to heaven.

2 Though, in the rugged path of life,
  He heaves the pensive sigh,
  Yet, trusting in the Lord, he finds
  Supporting grace is nigh.

3 If, to prevent his wandering steps,
  He feels the chastening rod,
  The gentle stroke shall bring him back
  To his forgiving God.

4 And when the welcome message comes,
  To call his soul away,
  His soul in raptures will ascend
  To everlasting day. HUDSON.

254. *Prayer for our Country.* (550)
1 LORD, while for all mankind we pray,
  Of every clime and coast,
  O, hear us for our native land—
  The land we love the most.

2 O, guard our shores from every foe,
  With peace our borders bless,
  With prosperous times our cities crown,
  Our fields with plenteousness.

3 Unite us in the sacred love
  Of knowledge, truth and thee;
  And let our hills and valleys shout
  The songs of liberty.

4 Lord of the nations, thus to thee
  Our country we commend;
  Be thou her refuge and her trust,
  Her everlasting friend. WREFORD.

255. *Confidence in God.* (193)
1 SOON as I heard my Father say,
  "Ye children, seek my grace,"
  My heart replied, without delay,
  "I'll seek my Father's face."

2 Let not thy face be hid from me,
  Nor frown my soul away;
  God of my life, I fly to thee
  In each distressing day.

3 Should friends and kindred, near and dear,
  Leave me to want, or die,
  My God will make my life his care,
  And all my need supply.

4 Wait on the Lord, ye trembling saints,
  And keep your courage up;
  He'll raise your spirit when it faints,
  And far exceed your hope. WATTS.

256. *Prayer Divinely Inspired.* (379)
1 PRAYER is the breath of God in man,
  Returning whence it came;
  Love is the sacred fire within,
  And prayer the rising flame.

2 It gives the burdened spirit ease,
  And soothes the troubled breast;
  Yields comfort to the mourners here,
  And to the weary rest.

3 When God inclines the heart to pray,
  He hath an ear to hear;
  To him there's music in a groan,
  And beauty in a tear.

4 The humble suppliant cannot fail
  To have his wants supplied,
  Since he for sinners intercedes,
  Who once for sinners died. BEDDOME.

257. *Will Ye also Go Away?* (367)
1 WHEN any turn from Zion's way,
  Alas! what numbers do!
  Methinks I hear my Saviour say,
  "Wilt thou forsake me too?"

2 Ah, Lord! with such a heart as mine,
  Unless thou hold me fast,
  I feel I must, I shall decline,
  And prove like them at last.

3 Yet, thou alone hast power, I know,
  To save a wretch like me;
  To whom, or whither could I go,
  If I should turn from thee?

4 No voice but thine can give me rest,
  And bid my fears depart;
  No love but thine can make me blest,
  And satisfy my heart.

5 What anguish has that question stirred,
  If I will also go?
  Yet, Lord, relying on thy word,
  I humbly answer—No! NEWTON.

JOYFULLY.

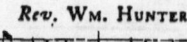

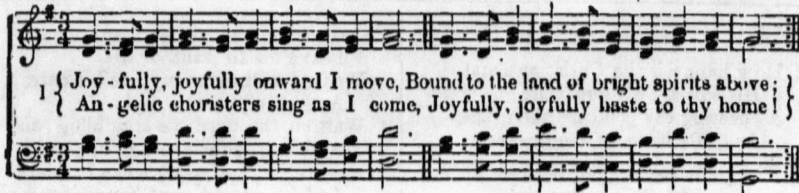

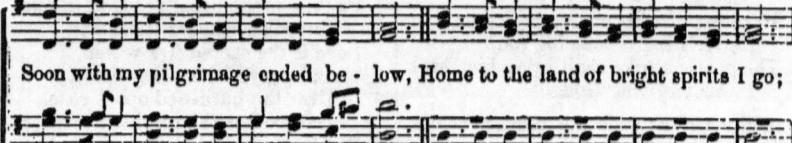

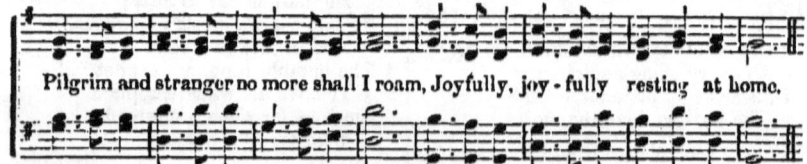

Joyfully Onward.

2 Friends, fondly cherished, have passed on before;
Waiting, they watch me approaching the shore;
Singing to cheer me through death's chilling gloom,
Joyfully, joyfully haste to thy home.
Sounds of sweet melody fall on my ear;
Harps of the blessed, your voices I hear
Rings with the harmony heaven's high dome,—
Joyfully, joyfully haste to thy home.

3 Death, with thy weapons of war lay me low,
Strike, king of terrors, I fear not the blow;
Jesus hath broken the bars of the tomb!
Joyfully, joyfully will I go home.
Bright will the morn of eternity dawn,
Death shall be banished, his sceptre be gone:
Joyfully, then, shall I witness his doom,
Joyfully, joyfully, safely at home.

THE GOLDEN SHORE.

WM. B. BRADBURY.

259. *A Home Beyond the Tide.* (441)

1 We are out on the ocean sailing,
　Homeward bound we sweetly glide;
　We are out on the ocean sailing,
　To a home beyond the tide.
　　All the storms, &c.

Millions now are safely landed,
　Over on the golden shore;
Millions more are on the journey,
　Yet there's room for millions more.
　　All the storms, &c.

3 Spread your sails while heavenly breezes
　Gently waft our vessel on;
　All on board are sweetly singing—
　Free salvation is the song.
　　All the storms, &c.

4 When we all are safely anchored,
　We will shout—our trials o'er;
　We will walk about the city,
　And we'll sing for evermore.
　　All the storms, &c.

HEBRON. L. M.

Dr. Lowell Mason.

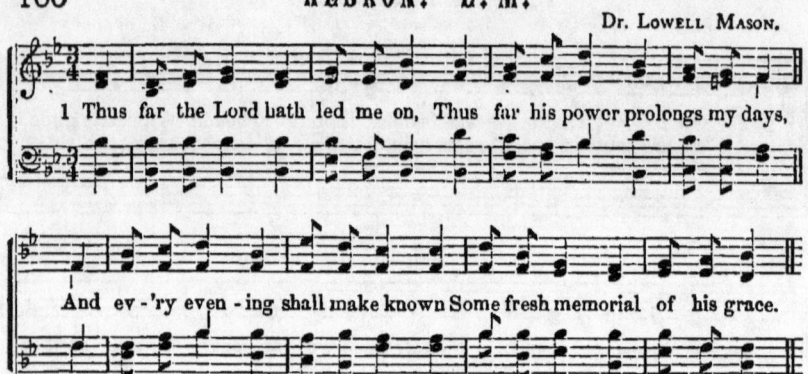

1 Thus far the Lord hath led me on, Thus far his power prolongs my days, And ev-'ry even-ing shall make known Some fresh memorial of his grace.

260. *Evening Meditation.* (388)

2 Much of my time has run to waste,
  And I perhaps am near my home;
  But he forgives my follies past,
  He gives me strength for days to come.

3 I lay my body down to sleep;
  Peace is the pillow for my head;
  While well-appointed angels keep
  Their watchful stations round my bed.

4 Thus when the night of death shall come,
  My flesh shall rest beneath the ground,
  And wait thy voice to rend my tomb,
  With sweet salvation in the sound.
                                    Watts.

261. *Providence Wise.* (200)

1 Wait, oh, my soul, thy Maker's will;
  Tumultuous passions, all be still!
  Nor let a murmuring thought arise;
  His ways are just, his counsels wise.

2 He in the thickest darkness dwells,
  Performs his work, the cause conceals;
  But, though his methods are unknown,
  Judgment and truth support his throne.

3 In heaven, and earth, and air, and seas,
  He executes his firm decrees;
  And by his saints it stands confessed,
  That what he does is ever best.

4 Wait then, my soul, submissive wait,
  Prostrate before his awful seat;
  And, 'midst the terrors of his rod,
  Trust in a wise and gracious God.
                                    Beddome.

262. *Welcome to Fellowship.* (148)

1 Kindred in Christ, for his dear sake,
  A hearty welcome here receive;
  May we together now partake
  The joys which only he can give.

2 To you and us by grace 'tis given
  To know the Saviour's precious name;
  And shortly we shall meet in heaven,
  Our hope, our way, our end the same.
                                    Newton.

263. *Not Lost, but Gone Before.* (570)

1 Say, why should friendship grieve for those
  Who safe arrive on Canaan's shore?
  Released from all their hurtful foes.
  They are not lost but gone before.

2 How many painful days on earth
  Their fainting spirits numbered o'er!
  Now they enjoy a heavenly birth;
  They are not lost—but gone before.

3 Dear is the spot where Christians sleep,
  And sweet the strain which angels pour;
  O why should we in anguish weep?
  They are not lost but gone before.

264. *Preserve us from National Foes.* (546)

1 HEAR us, O Lord, in time of need,
  And let thy name our cause defend;
  Grant that our efforts may succeed,
  And victory on our steps attend.

2 On horse and chariot some rely,
  And some in numbers make their boast;
  Our trust is in the Lord Most High;
  His favor is itself a host.

3 In his salvation we rejoice,
  And lift our banners in his name;
  Lord, hear our supplicating voice,
  And put our haughty foes to shame.

4 Spread over us thy shelt'ring wing,
  And bless with peace our favor'd land;
  That we may still thy glory sing,
  By whose protecting care we stand.

265. *Christ the Lamb Slain.* (98)

1 BEHOLD the sin-atoning Lamb,
  With wonder, gratitude and love,
  To take away our guilt and shame,
  See him descending from above!

2 Our sins and griefs on him were laid;
  He meekly bore the mighty load;
  Our ransom-price he fully paid,
  In groans and tears, in sweat and blood.

3 To save a guilty world, he dies;
  Sinners, behold the bleeding Lamb!
  To him lift up your longing eyes,
  And hope for mercy in his name.

4 Pardon and peace through him abound:
  He can the richest blessings give;
  Salvation in his name is found,
  He bids the dying sinner live.

5 Jesus, my Lord, I look to thee;
  Where else can helpless sinners go?
  Thy boundless love shall set me free
  From all my wretchedness and woe.
  FAWCETT.

266. *The Gospel Originating in Sovereign Mercy.* (493)

1 GOD, in the Gospel of his son,
  Makes his eternal counsels known;
  Here love in all its glory shines,
  And truth is drawn in fairest lines.

2 Here sinners, of an humble frame,
  May taste his grace, and learn his name;
  May read, in characters of blood,
  The wisdom, power, and grace of God.

3 Here faith reveals to mortal eyes
  A brighter world beyond the skies:
  Here shines the light which guides our way
  From earth to realms of endless day.

4 O, grant us grace, almighty Lord,
  To read and mark thy holy word,
  Its truths with meekness to receive,
  And by its holy precepts live.
  BEDDOME.

267. *Exemplifying the Gospel.* (329)

1 So let our lips and lives express
  The holy gospel we profess;
  So let our works and virtues shine,
  To prove the doctrine all divine.

2 Thus shall we best proclaim abroad
  The honors of our Saviour God,
  When his salvation reigns within,
  And grace subdues the power of sin.

3 Religion bears our spirits up,
  While we expect that blessed hope,
  The bright appearance of the Lord,
  And faith stands leaning on his word.
  WATTS.

268. *Missionary Meeting.* (518)

1 ASSEMBLED at thy great command,
  Before thy face, dread king, we stand;
  The voice that marshaled every star
  Has called thy people from afar.

2 We meet through distant lands to spread
  The truth for which the martyrs bled;
  Along the line—to either pole—
  The anthem of thy praise to roll.

3 Our prayers assist; accept our praise;
  Our hopes revive; our courage raise;
  Our counsels aid; to each impart
  The single eye, the faithful heart.

4 Forth with thy chosen heralds come;
  Recall the wandering spirits home:
  From Zion's mount send forth the sound,
  To spread the spacious earth around.
  COLLYER.

102   BRIGHT CROWN. C. M.

Wm. B. Bradbury.
CHORUS.

1 { Ye val-iant sol-diers of the cross, Ye hap-py, pray-ing band, }
    { Tho' in this world you suf-fer loss, You'll reach fair Canaan's land; } Let us never mind the scoffs nor the frowns of the world, For we all have the cross to bear, It will only make the crown the brighter to shine, When we have the crown to wear.

269.   *Forsaking Earthly Pleasures.*   (335)

1 YE valiant soldiers of the cross,
   Ye happy, praying band,
Though in this world you suffer loss,
   You'll reach fair Canaan's land.
     Let us never mind the scoffs nor the
       frowns of the world,
     For we all have the cross to bear,
     It will only make the crown the
       brighter to shine,
     When we have the crown to wear.

2 All earthly pleasures we'll forsake,
   When heaven appears in view,
In Jesus' strength we'll undertake
   To fight our passage through.
     Let us never mind the scoffs, &c.

3 Oh, what a glorious shout there'll be,
   When we arrive at home!
Our friends and Jesus we shall see,
   And God shall say "Well done."
     Let us never mind the scoffs, &c.

270.   *Christian Soldier.*   (315)

1 AM I a soldier of the cross,
   A follower of the Lamb;
And shall I fear to own his cause,
   Or blush to speak his name?
     Let us never mind the scoffs nor the
       frowns of the world,
     For we've all got the cross to bear,
     It will only make the crown the
       brighter to shine,
     When we have the crown to wear.

2 Must I be carried to the skies,
   On flowery beds of ease,
While others fought to win the prize,
   And sailed through bloody seas?
     Let us never mind the scoffs, &c.

3 Are there no foes for me to face?
   Must I not stem the flood?
Is this vile world a friend to grace,
   To help me on to God?
     Let us never mind the scoffs, &c.
                           WATTS.

I DO BELIEVE. C. M.

Arranged for this work.

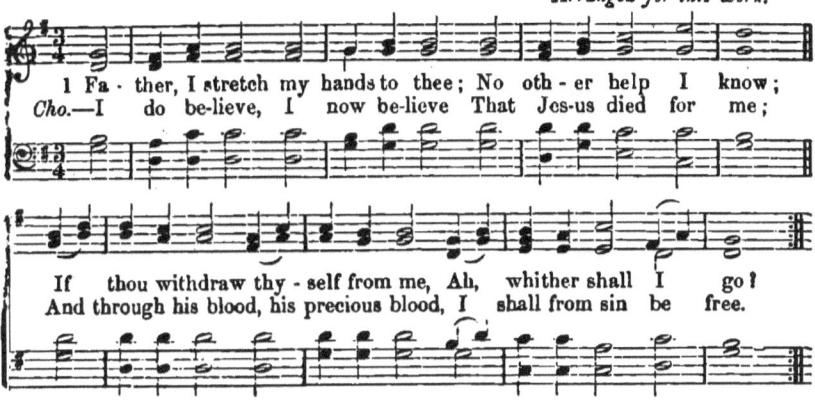

1 Fa-ther, I stretch my hands to thee; No oth-er help I know;
Cho.—I do be-lieve, I now be-lieve That Jes-us died for me;

If thou withdraw thy-self from me, Ah, whither shall I go?
And through his blood, his precious blood, I shall from sin be free.

---

271. *Faith the Gift of God.* (100)

1 FATHER, I stretch my hands to thee;
No other help I know;
If thou withdraw thyself from me,
Ah, whither shall I go?

2 What did thine only Son endure
Before I drew my breath!
What pain, what labor, to secure
My soul from endless death!

3 Author of faith, to thee I lift
My weary, longing eyes;
O, may I now receive that gift;
My soul, without it, dies.
C. WESLEY.

272. *"There is a Fountain filled with Blood."* (77)
[ORIGINAL FORM.]

1 THERE is a fountain filled with blood,
Drawn from Immanuel's veins;
And sinners, plunged beneath that flood,
Lose all their guilty stains.
I do believe, I now believe,
That Jesus died for me;
And through his blood, his precious blood,
I shall from sin be free.

2 The dying thief rejoiced to see
That fountain in his day;
And there have I, as vile as he,
Washed all my sins away.

3 Dear, dying Lamb! Thy precious blood
Shall never lose its power,
Till all the ransomed church of God
Be saved, to sin no more.

4 E'er since, by faith, I saw the stream
Thy flowing wounds supply,
Redeeming love has been my theme,
And shall be till I die.

5 Then, in a nobler, sweeter song,
I'll sing thy power to save,
When this poor, lisping, stammering tongue
Lies silent in the grave.

6 Lord, I believe thou hast prepared,
Unworthy though I be,
For me a blood-bought, free reward,
A golden harp for me!

7 'Tis strung and tuned for endless years;
And formed by power divine,
To sound in God the Father's ears
No other name but thine. COWPER.

DOXOLOGY. L. M.

ETERNAL Father! throned above,
Thou fountain of redeeming love!
Eternal Word! who left thy throne
For man's rebellion to atone;
Eternal Spirit, who dost give
That grace whereby our spirits live;
Thou God of our salvation, be
Eternal praises paid to thee!

104 THE EVERGREEN SHORE.
WM. B. BRADBURY.

273. *The Evergreen Shore.* (480)

1 WE are joyously voyaging over the main,
    Bound for the evergreen shore,
  Whose inhabitants never of sickness complain,
    And never see death any more.
      Then let the hurricane roar, &c.

2 We have nothing to fear from the wind and the wave,
    Under our Saviour's command;
  And our hearts in the midst of the dangers are brave,
    For Jesus will bring us to land.
      Then let the hurricane roar, &c.

HYMNS.

3 Both the winds and the waves our Commander controls;
Nothing can baffle his skill:
And his voice, when the thundering hurricane rolls,
Can make the loud tempest be still.
Then let the hurricane roar, &c.

4 Let the vessel be wrecked on the rock or the shoal,
Sink to be seen never more,
He will bear, none the less, every passenger soul,
Safe, safe to the evergreen shore.
Then let the hurricane roar, &c.

ALL WILL BE WELL.
From THE GOLDEN CHAIN.

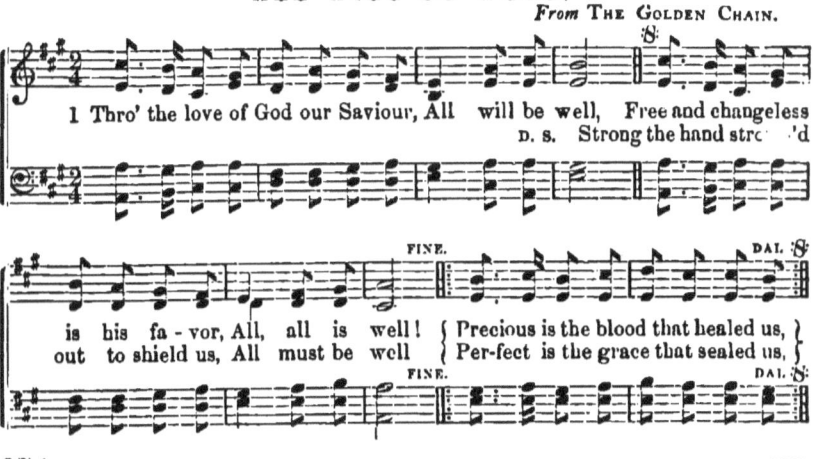

274. *All will be Well.* (434)

1 THROUGH the love of God our Saviour,
All will be well,
Free and changeless is his favor,
All, all is well!
Precious is the blood that healed us,
Perfect is the grace that sealed us,
Strong the hand stretch'd out to shield us,
All must be well!

2 Though we pass through tribulation,
All will be well;
Ours is such a full salvation,
All, all is well!

Happy still in God confiding,
Fruitful if in Christ abiding,
Holy through the Spirit's guiding,
All must be well.

3 We expect a bright to-morrow,
All will be well;
Faith can sing through days of sorrow,
All, all is well!
On our Father's love relying,
Jesus every need supplying,
Or in living or in dying,
All must be well!

MARY BOWLEY.

DUNLAP'S CREEK. C. M.

Western Melody.

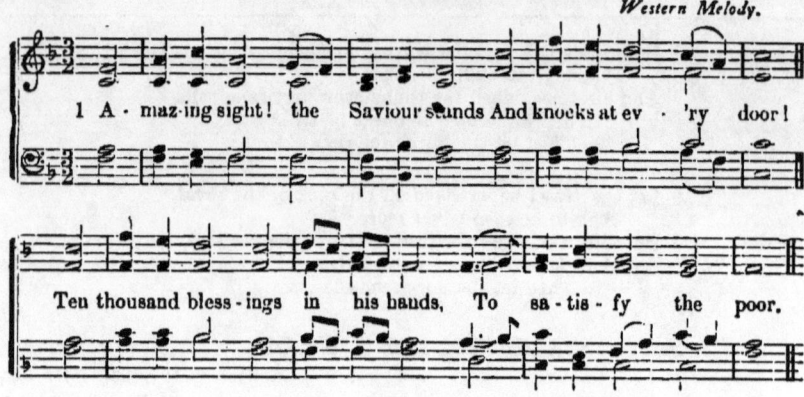

1 Amazing sight! the Saviour stands And knocks at ev'ry door! Ten thousand bless-ings in his hands, To sa-tis-fy the poor.

275. *The Saviour at the Door.* (69)

1 Amazing sight! the Saviour stands
  And knocks at every door!
  Ten thousand blessings in his hands,
  To satisfy the poor.

2 "Behold," he saith, "I bleed and die,
  To bring you to my rest:
  Hear, sinners, while I'm passing by,
  And be forever blest.

3 "Will you despise my bleeding love,
  And choose the way to hell?
  Or in the glorious realms above,
  With me for ever dwell?

4 "Say, will you hear my gracious voice,
  And have your sins forgiven?
  Or will you make that wretched choice,
  And bar yourselves from heaven?"

276. *Justification through Faith.* (81)

1 Vain are the hopes the sons of men
  On their own works have built;
  Their hearts by nature all unclean,
  And all their actions guilt.

2 Let Jew and Gentile silent bow,
  Without a murmuring word;
  Let all the race of man confess
  Their guilt before the Lord.

3 In vain we ask God's righteous law
  To justify us now;
  Since to convince and to condemn
  Is all the law can do.

4 Jesus, how glorious is thy grace!
  When in thy name we trust,
  Our faith receives a righteousness
  That makes the sinner just.
  WATTS.

277. *"The Time is Short."* (36)

1 The time is short! sinners beware,
  Nor trifle time away;
  The word of great salvation hear,
  While it is called to-day.

2 The time is short! O sinners, now
  To Christ, the Lord, submit;
  To mercy's golden sceptre bow,
  And fall at Jesus' feet.

3 The time is short! ye saints, rejoice—
  The Lord will quickly come;
  Soon shall you hear the Bridegroom's voice,
  To call you to your home.

4 The time is short! the moment near,
  When we shall dwell above,
  And be forever happy there,
  With Jesus, whom we love.
  HOSKINS.

BURFORD. C. M.
PURCELL.

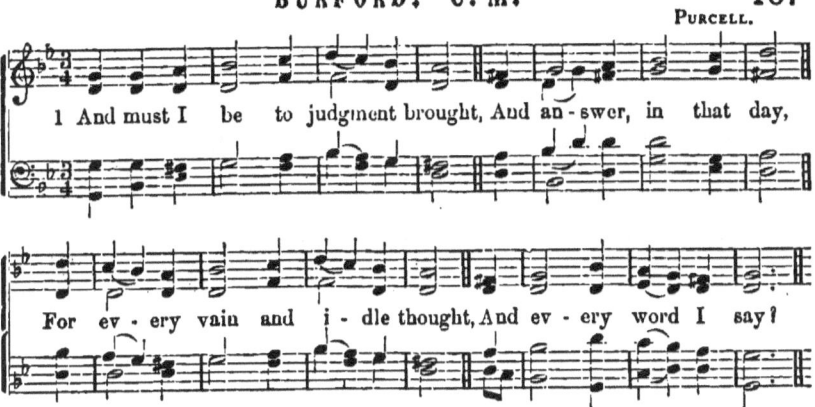

1 And must I be to judgment brought, And an-swer, in that day, For ev-ery vain and i-dle thought, And ev-ery word I say?

278. *I Must Go to the Judgment.* (586)

2 Yes, every secret of my heart
Shall shortly be made known,
And I receive my just desert
For all that I have done.

3 How careful, then, ought I to live;
With what religious fear;
Who such a strict account must give
For my behaviour here!

4 Thou mighty Judge of quick and dead,
The watchful power bestow;
So shall I to my ways take heed,
In all I speak or do.

279. *A Voice from the Tomb.* (572)

1 Hark! from the tombs a doleful sound;
My ears attend the cry,—
"Ye living men, come view the ground
Where you must shortly lie.

2 "Princes, this clay must be your bed,
In spite of all your towers:
The tall, the wise, the reverend head,
Must lie as low as ours."

3 Great God, is this our certain doom?
And are we still secure?—
Still walking downward to the tomb,
And yet prepare no more?

4 Grant us the power of quickening grace,
To fit our souls to fly;
Then, when we drop this dying flesh,
We'll rise above the sky. WATTS.

280. *Time the Period to Prepare for Eternity.* (564)

1 Thee we adore, Eternal Name,
And humbly own to thee
How feeble is our mortal frame,
What dying worms are we.

2 The year rolls round, and steals away
The breath that first it gave;
Whate'er we do, where'er we be,
We're traveling to the grave.

3 Great God, on what a slender thread
Hang everlasting things!—
The final state of all the dead
Upon life's feeble strings!

4 Eternal joy, or endless woe,
Attends on every breath;
And yet how unconcerned we go
Upon the brink of death!

5 Awake, O Lord, our drowsy sense,
To walk this dangerous road;
And if our souls are hurried hence,
May they be found with God.
WATTS.

IOWA. S. M.

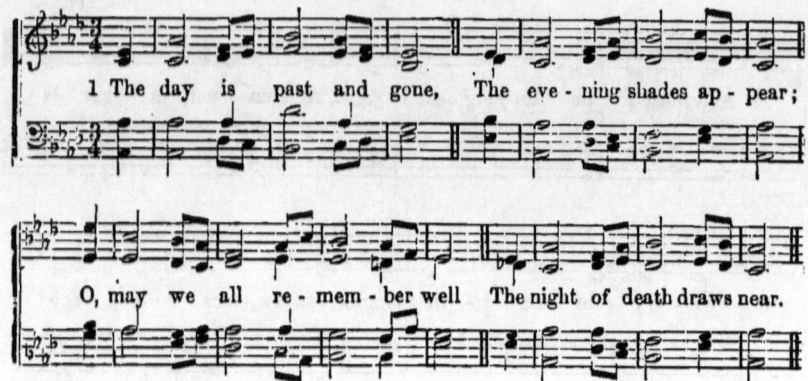

1 The day is past and gone, The evening shades appear;
O, may we all remember well The night of death draws near.

281. *Evening Hymn.* (389)

2 We lay our garments by,
   Upon our beds to rest;
So death will soon disrobe us all
   Of what we here possess.

3 Lord, keep us safe this night,
   Secure from all our fears;
May angels guard us while we sleep,
   Till morning light appears.

4 And if we early rise,
   And view th' unwearied sun,
May we set out to win the prize,
   And after glory run.

5 And when our days are past,
   And we from time remove,
O, may we in thy bosom rest—
   The bosom of thy love!

282. *Praying for Repentance.* (93)

1 O, THAT I could repent,
   With all my idols part,
And to thy gracious eye present
   An humble, contrite heart.

2 A heart with grief oppressed,
   For having grieved my God:
A troubled heart, that cannot rest
   Till sprinkled with thy blood.

3 Jesus, on me bestow
   The penitent desire;
With true sincerity of woe
   My aching breast inspire.

4 With soft'ning pity look,
   And melt my hardness down:
Strike with thy love's resistless stroke
   And break this heart of stone.
                                C. WESLEY.

283. *The Accepted Time.* (41

1 Now is th' accepted time;
   Now is the day of grace;
Now, sinners, come, without delay,
   And seek the Saviour's face.

2 Now is th' accepted time;
   The Saviour calls to-day;
To-morrow it may be too late;
   Then why should you delay?

3 Now is th' accepted time;
   The gospel bids you come,
And every promise in his word
   Declares there yet is room.

4 Lord, draw reluctant souls,
   And feast them with thy love·
Then will the angels swiftly fly
   To bear the news above.
                                DOBELL.

STATE STREET. S. M. 109
J. C. WOODMAN.

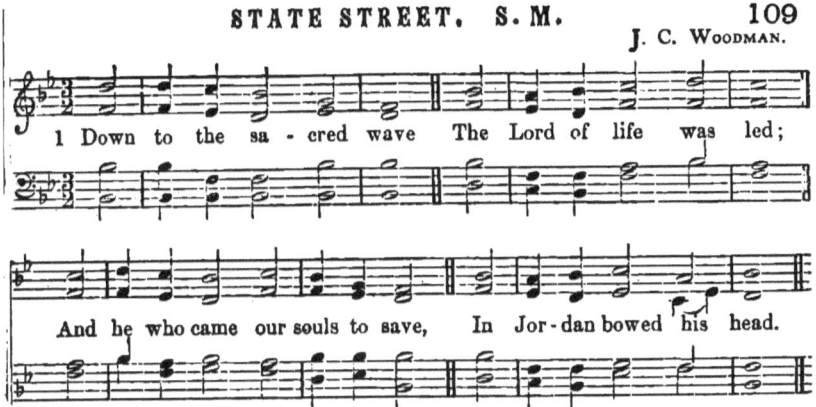

1 Down to the sa-cred wave The Lord of life was led;
And he who came our souls to save, In Jor-dan bowed his head.

284. *The Baptism of Christ.* (145)

1 DOWN to the sacred wave
The Lord of life was led;
And he who came our souls to save
In Jordan bowed his head.

2 He taught the solemn way;
He fixed the holy rite;
He bade his ransomed ones obey,
And keep the path of light.

3 Blest Saviour, we will tread
In thy appointed way;
Let glory o'er these scenes be shed,
And smile on us to-day.
S. F. SMITH.

285. *The Grace of Christ.* (290)

1 WE sing the Saviour's love,
Who pitied wretched man,
Delighting in the thought of peace,
Ere time and worlds began.

2 We see its smiling beams,
Forthshining at his birth,
And trace its lustre day by day,
While he sojourned on earth.

3 But, in his closing hour,
How infinite his grace,
When, bowed beneath the curse, he died
To save the chosen race!

4 Ten thousand thousand songs,
With high, seraphic flame,
Fall far below the boundless praise
Of our Immanuel's name.

286. *The Spirit Inviting.* (76)

1 THE Spirit, in our hearts,
Is whispering, "Sinner, come;"
The bride, the church of Christ, proclaims
To all his children, "come!"

2 Let him that heareth say
To all about him, "come;"
Let him that thirsts for righteousness,
To Christ, the fountain, come.

3 Yes, whosoever will,
O, let him freely come,
And freely drink the stream of life;
'Tis Jesus bids him come.
H. U. ONDERDONK.

287. *Danger of Delay.* (23)

1 ALL yesterday is gone;
To-morrow's not our own;
O, sinner, come, without delay,
To bow before the throne.

2 O, hear his voice to-day,
And harden not your heart;
To-morrow, with a frown, he may
Pronounce the word—"Depart."

FOREST. L. M.

CHAPIN

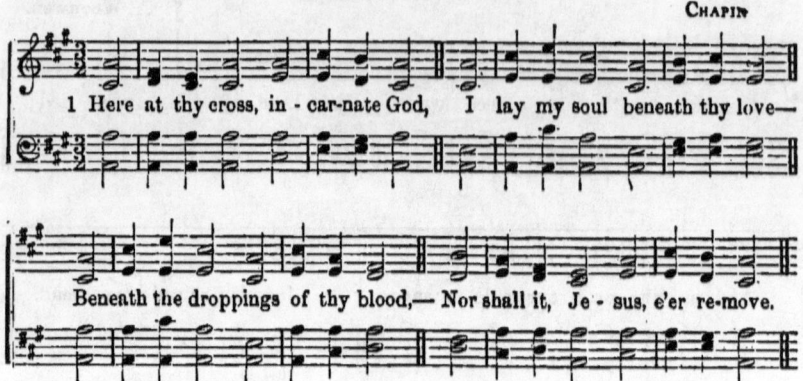

1 Here at thy cross, in-car-nate God, I lay my soul beneath thy love— Beneath the droppings of thy blood,— Nor shall it, Je-sus, e'er re-move.

288.   *Security in the Cross.*   (224)

2 Should worlds conspire to drive me thence
Unmoved and firm this heart should lie;
Resolved,—for that's my last defense,—
If I must perish, there to die.

3 But speak, my Lord, and calm my fear;
Am I not safe beneath thy shade?
Thy justice will not strike me here,
Nor Satan dare my soul invade.

4 Yes, I'm secure beneath thy blood,
And all my foes shall lose their aim:
Hosanna to my Saviour God,
And my best honors to his name.
WATTS.

289.   *A Remedy for Sin found in the Gospel.*   (82)

1 WHAT shall the dying sinner do,
Who seeks relief for all his woe?
Where shall the guilty sufferer find
A balm to soothe his anguished mind?

2 In vain we search, in vain we try,
Till Jesus brings his gospel nigh;
'Tis there we find a sure relief,
A soothing balm for inward grief.

3 Be this the pillar of our hope;
This bears the fainting spirit up;
We read the grace, we trust the word,
And find salvation in the Lord.

4 Then let his name, who shed his blood
To bring the guilty nigh to God,
Be great in all the earth, and sung
In every land, by every tongue.
WATTS.

290.   *The Burden of Sin.*   (88)

1 O, THAT my load of sin were gone!
O, that I could at last submit,
At Jesus' feet to lay me down,
To lay my soul at Jesus' feet!

2 Rest for my soul I long to find;
Fountain of rest, thou, Saviour, art,
Give me thy meek and lowly mind,
And stamp thine image on my heart.

3 Fain would I learn of thee, my God,
Thy light and easy burden prove;
The cross, all stained with hallowed blood,
The labor of thy dying love.

4 I would; but thou must give the power
My heart from every sin release;
Bring near, bring near the joyful hour,
And fill my soul with heavenly peace.

5 Come, Lord, the drooping sinner cheer,
Nor let thy chariot wheels delay;
Appear, in my poor heart, appear;
My God, my Saviour come away.
C. WESLEY.

CAPTIVITY. L. M.

1 A broken heart, my God! my king!
Is all the sacrifice I bring;
The God of grace will ne'er despise
A broken heart for sacrifice.

291. *Returning to God.* (372)

2 My soul lies humbled in the dust,
And owns thy dreadful sentence just;
Look down, O Lord! with pitying eye,
And save the soul condemned to die.

3 Then will I teach the world thy ways;
Sinners shall learn thy sovereign grace;
I'll lead them to my Saviour's blood,
And they shall praise the pardoning God.

4 O, may thy love inspire my tongue;
Salvation shall be all my song;
And all my powers shall join to bless
The Lord, my strength, my righteousness.
WATTS.

292. *Holy Aspirations.* (393)

1 My God, permit me not to be
A stranger to myself and thee:
Amid a thousand thoughts I rove,
Forgetful of my highest love.

2 Why should my passions mix with earth,
And thus debase my heavenly birth?
Why should I cleave to things below,
And let my God, my Saviour go?

3 Call me away from flesh and sense:
One sovereign word can draw me thence:
I would obey the voice divine,
And all inferior joys resign.

4 Be earth, with all her scenes, withdrawn;
Let noise and vanity be gone:
In secret silence of the mind,
My heaven, and there my God, I find.
WATTS.

293. *Delight in Christ.* (277)

1 JESUS, thou joy of loving hearts!
Thou fount of life! thou light of men!
From the best bliss that earth imparts,
We turn unfilled to thee again.

2 Thy truth unchanged hath ever stood;
Thou savest those that on thee call;
To them that seek thee, thou art good,
To them that find thee—all in all!

3 We taste thee, O, thou living bread,
And long to feast upon thee still;
We drink of thee, the fountain head,
And thirst our souls from thee to fill.

4 Our restless spirits yearn for thee,
Where'er our changeful lot is cast;
Glad, when thy gracious smile we see,
Blest, when our faith can hold thee fast.

5 O, Jesus, ever with us stay!
Make all our moments calm and bright;
Chase the dark night of sin away—
Shed o'er the world thy holy light!

112. WELCOME HOME.

Rev. R. Lowry.

294. (597)

1 THERE is a realm where Jesus reigns,
   A home of grace and love,
   Where angels wait with sweetest strains,
   To greet the saints above.
      They'll sing their welcome, &c.

2 There sons of earth will join to bless
   The precious Saviour's name,
   Clothed in his perfect righteousness,
   And saved from sin and shame.
      They'll sing their welcome, &c.

3 Yet all, alas! may not be there,
   For some will slight his grace,
   Tho' now he calls, they do not care
   To turn and seek his face.
      They'll sing their welcome, &c.

4 He speaks so kindly, "Come to me,
   And I will give you rest;"
   The angels wait their melody,
   To greet you with the blest.
      They'll sing their welcome, &c.

IVES. 7s. E. Ives, Jr.   113

295. *The Redeemed in Heaven.* (594)

1 Who are these in bright array,
  This exulting, happy throng,
  Round the altar night and day,
  Hymning one triumphant song?—
  "Worthy is the Lamb, once slain,
  Blessing, honor, glory, power,
  Wisdom, riches, to obtain,
  New dominion every hour."

2 These through fiery trials trod;
  These from great affliction came;
  Now, before the throne of God,
  Sealed with his almighty name:
  Clad in raiment pure and white,
  Victor-palms in every hand.
  Through their great Redeemer's might,
  More than conquerors they stand.

3 Hunger, thirst, disease, unknown,
  On immortal fruits they feed;
  Them the Lamb, amidst the throne,
  Shall to living fountains lead;
  Joy and gladness banish sighs:
  Perfect love dispels all fears;
  And forever from their eyes
  God shall wipe away their tears.
                              MONTGOMERY.

296. *Invitation to the Mercy Seat.* (407)
       Tune COME YE DISCONSOLATE.

1 Come, ye disconsolate, where'er ye languish,
  Come to the mercy seat, fervently kneel:
  Here bring your wounded heart, here tell your anguish;
  Earth has no sorrows that heaven cannot heal.

2 Joy of the desolate, light of the straying,
  Hope of the penitent, fadeless and pure,
  Here speaks the Comforter, tenderly saying,
  Earth has no sorrow that heaven cannot cure.   MOORE.

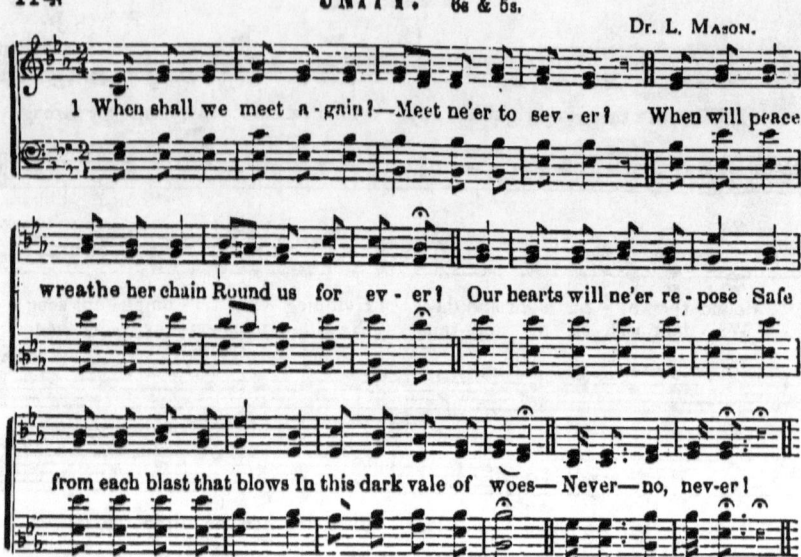

297. *Reunion in Heaven.* (596)

1 When shall we meet again?—
  Meet ne'er to sever?
 When will peace wreathe her chain
  Round us for ever?
 Our hearts will ne'er repose
 Safe from each blast that blows
 In this dark vale of woes—
  Never—no, never!

2 When shall love freely flow
  Pure as life's river?
 When shall sweet friendship glow
  Changeless for ever?
 Where joys celestial thrill,
 Where bliss each heart shall fill,
 And fears of parting chill
  Never—no, never!

3 Up to that world of light
  Take us, dear Saviour;
 May we all there unite,
  Happy forever:
 Where kindred spirits dwell
 There may our music swell,
 And time our joys dispel,
  Never—no, never!

298. *The Sinner at the Judgment* (29)
  Tune PLEYEL, *page* 150.

1 When thy mortal life is fled,
 When the death-shades o'er thee spread,
 When is finished thy career,
 Sinner, where wilt thou appear?

2 When the world has passed away,
 When draws near the judgment-day,
 When the awful trump shall sound,
 Say, O where wilt thou be found?

2 When the Judge descends in light,
 Clothed in majesty and might,
 When the wicked quail with fear,
 Where, O where wilt thou appear?

4 While the Holy Ghost is nigh,
 Quickly to the Saviour fly;
 Then shall peace thy spirit cheer;
 Then in heaven shalt thou appear.

S. F. SMITH.

LANESBOROUGH. C. M. 115

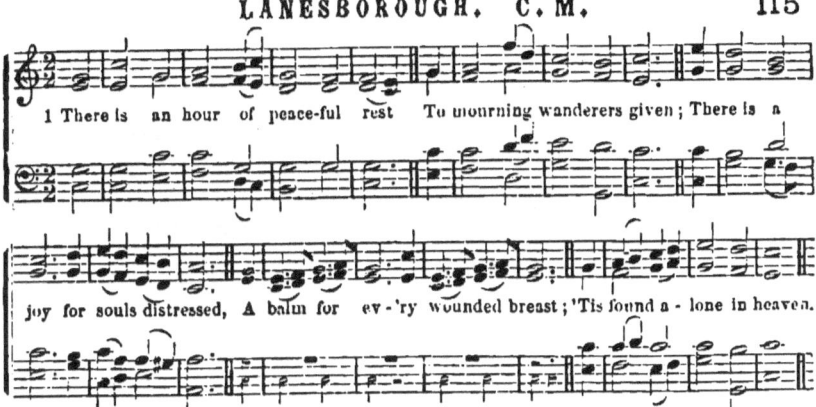

1 There is an hour of peace-ful rest To mourning wanderers given; There is a joy for souls distressed, A balm for ev-'ry wounded breast; 'Tis found a-lone in heaven.

299. *Rest in Heaven.* (591)

2 There is a home for weary souls,
By sins and sorrows driven,
When tossed on life's tempestuous shoals,
Where storms arise and ocean rolls,
And all is drear but heaven.

3 There faith lifts up the tearless eye,—
The heart no longer riven,—
And views the tempest passing by,
Sees evening shadows quickly fly,
And all serene in heaven.

4 There fragrant flowers immortal bloom,
And joys supreme are given;
There rays divine disperse the gloom;
Beyond the dark and narrow tomb
Appears the dawn of heaven.
TAPPAN.

300. *The Colporteur.* (488)

1 WHAT courteous stranger at the door,
Bowed with his burden, stands?
He brings, perchance, a precious store,
Of gems, or pearls, or golden ore,
Or tidings from far land.

2 His gems are books, and fervent prayers,
Warnings and counsels kind:
Letters from his dear Lord, he bears,
And news from heaven of high affairs,
For man's great good designed.

3 Hark! for the stranger's voice is heard,
Waking the slumbering mind:

Tears fall like rain-drops at his word,
And listening hearts like leaves are stirred,
When breathes the sweet south wind.

4 He speaks, in accents soft and low,
Of Christ and all his love:
His bitter cup of shame and wo,
The pangs he bore for man below,
The throne he fills above.

5. On! on! thy holy light impart;
Sow thick the golden seed;
Through every door, on every heart
The sunbeam of the gospel dart:
Speed with thy jewels, speed!

301. *Christian Courage.* (487)
Tune SALZBURGH, page 177.

1 HASTENING on to death's dark river,
Daily nearer to the shore
Where our warfare ceased forever,
We shall meet the foe no more.
Cheer you, then, my brethren dear,
Falter not while battling here.

2 Soon we'll see that blissful region,
Where the Prince of Peace doth reign;
Blessed thought! no hostile legion
Enters there with grief or pain.
Cheer you, then, &c.

3 Clothed with bodies pure and glorious,
God's free grace we there shall own,
In the Saviour's strength victorious
Cast before him every crown.
Cheer you, then, &c.
RICHARD S. JAMES.

HAPPY DAY. L. M.

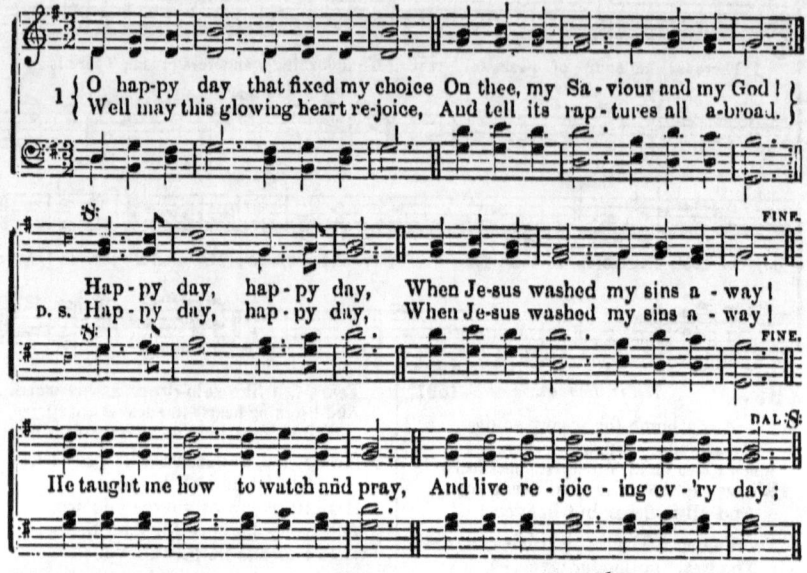

1. O happy day that fixed my choice On thee, my Saviour and my God! Well may this glowing heart rejoice, And tell its raptures all abroad.

D.S. Happy day, happy day, When Jesus washed my sins away! Happy day, happy day, When Jesus washed my sins away!

He taught me how to watch and pray, And live rejoicing ev'ry day;

302. *The Baptismal Vow.* (122)

1 Oh, happy day, that fixed my choice
On thee, my Saviour, and my God;
Well may this glowing heart rejoice,
And tell its raptures all abroad.
Happy day, happy day, &c.

2 'Tis done—the great transaction's done;
I am my Lord's, and he is mine;
He drew me, and I followed on,
Rejoiced to own the call divine.
Happy day, happy day, &c.

3 Now rest—my long-divided heart—
Fixed on this blissful centre, rest—
Here have I found a nobler part,
Here heavenly pleasures fill my breast;
Happy day, happy day, &c.

4 High heaven that hears the solemn vow,
That vow renewed shall daily hear;
Till in life's latest hour I bow,
And bless in death a bond so dear.
Happy day, happy day, &c.
DODDRIDGE.

303. *"Amid the Joyous Scenes of Earth."* (428)

1 Amid the joyous scenes of earth,
When hope's bright visions round us play,
There still remains an hour most dear:
The mem'ry of that happy day.
Happy day, happy day, &c.

2 Should all the joys of earth grow dim,
And melt like fancy's dreams away,
There lingers deep within the heart,
Fond mem'ries of that happy day.
Happy day, &c.

3 When sorrow's clouds around us lower,
Amid the gloom a cheering ray
Comes gently stealing o'er the soul,
It is the memory of that day,
Happy day, &c.

4 When death's dark shadows gather round;
When nature's noblest pow'rs decay
A spirit's whispering voice recalls
The blessed mem'ries of that day,
Happy day, &c.
JOHN M. EVANS.

SWEET HOUR OF PRAYER. Wm. B. Bradbury. 117

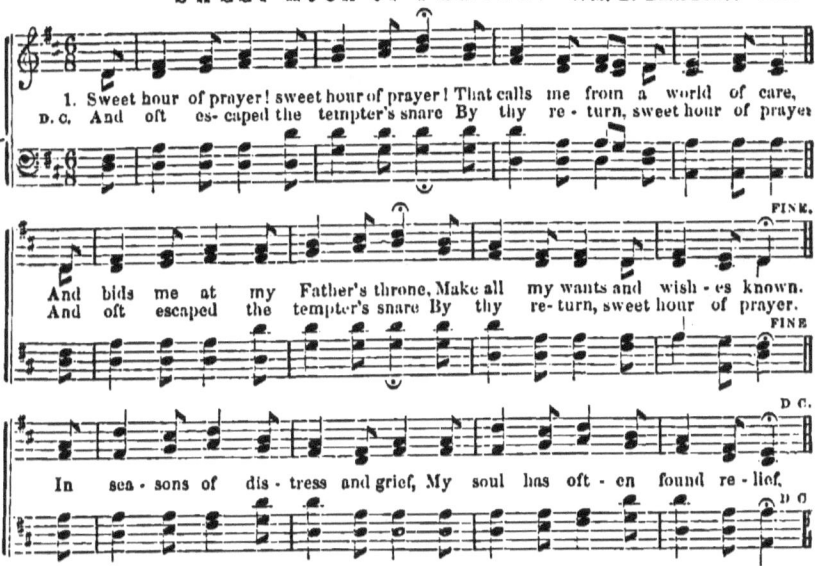

304. *Sweet Hour of Prayer.* (399)

1 Sweet hour of prayer! sweet hour of prayer!
That calls me from a world of care,
And bids me at my Father's throne,
Make all my wants and wishes known.
In seasons of distress and grief,
My soul has often found relief,
And oft escaped the tempter's snare
By thy return, sweet hour of prayer.

2 Sweet hour of prayer! sweet hour of prayer!
Thy wings shall my petition bear,
To him whose truth and faithfulness,
Engage the waiting soul to bless;
And since he bids me seek his face,
Believe his word, and trust his grace,
I'll cast on him my every care,
And wait for thee. sweet hour of prayer.

3 Sweet hour of prayer! sweet hour of prayer!
May I thy consolation share;
Till from Mount Pisgah's lofty height,
I view my home, and take my flight:
This robe of flesh I'll drop, and rise
To seize the everlasting prize;
And shout, while passing through the air.
Farewell, farewell, sweet hour of prayer.

305. *The Altar and the School.* (496)
Tune Old Hundred, page 6.

1 When driven by oppression's rod,
  Our fathers fled beyond the sea,
Their care was first to honor God,
  And next to leave their children free.

2 Above the forest's gloomy shade,
  The altar and the school appeared;
On that the gifts of faith were laid,
  On this their precious hopes were reared.

3 The altar and the school still stand,
  The sacred pillars of our trust;
And freedom's sons shall fill the land,
  While we are sleeping in the dust.

4 Before thine altar, Lord, we bend,
  With grateful song and fervent prayer;
For thou, who wast our fathers' Friend,
  Wilt make their offspring still thy care.

SILOAM. C. M.

I. B. Woodburn.

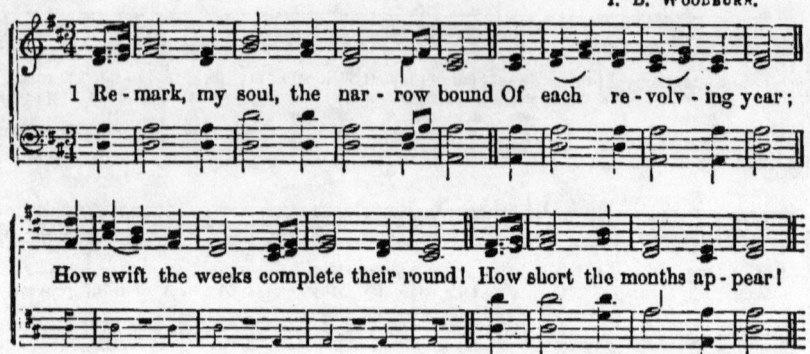

1 Remark, my soul, the narrow bound Of each revolving year; How swift the weeks complete their round! How short the months appear!

306. *Swiftness of Time.* (562)

2 So fast eternity comes on,
  And that important day
When all that mortal life hath done
  God's judgment shall survey.

3 Awake, O God, my careless heart,
  Its great concerns to see,
That I may act the Christian part,
  And give the year to thee.

4 So shall their course more grateful roll,
  If future years arise;
Or this shall bear my waiting soul
  To joy beyond the skies.
    Doddridge.

307. *Gratitude.* (209)

1 When all thy mercies, O my God,
  My rising soul surveys,
Transported with the view, I'm lost
  In wonder, love, and praise.

2 Unnumbered comforts on my soul
  Thy tender care bestowed,
Before my infant heart conceived
  From whom those comforts flowed.

3 When in the slippery paths of youth
  With heedless steps I ran,
Thine arm, unseen, conveyed me safe,
  And led me up to man.

4 Ten thousand thousand precious gifts
  My daily thanks employ;
Nor is the least a cheerful heart,
  That tastes those gifts with joy.

5 Through every period of my life,
  Thy goodness I'll pursue;
And after death, in distant worlds,
  The glorious theme renew.

6 Through all eternity, to thee
  A grateful song I'll raise;
But, oh! eternity's too short
  To utter all thy praise!
    Addison.

308. *True Happiness to be found only in God.* (189)

1 In vain I trace creation o'er
  In search of solid rest;
The whole creation is too poor
  To make me truly blest.

2 Let earth and all her charms depart
  Unworthy of the mind;
In God alone this restless heart
  Enduring bliss can find.

3 Thy favor, Lord, is all I want:
  Here would my spirit rest:
O, seal the rich, the boundless grant,
  And make me fully blest.
    Steele.

CHINA. C. M.

SWAN.

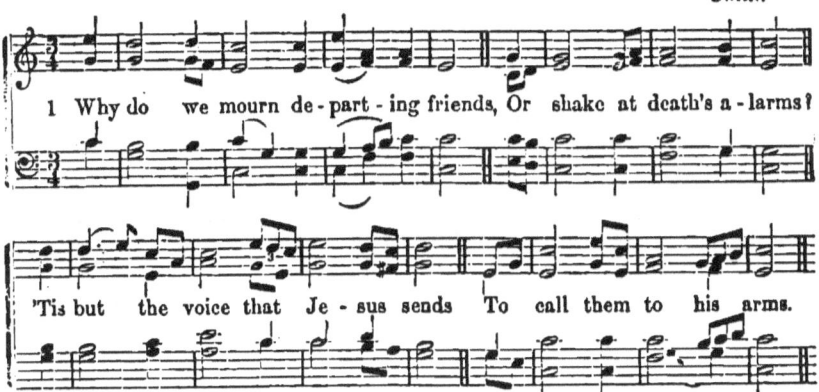

1 Why do we mourn de-part-ing friends, Or shake at death's a-larms? 'Tis but the voice that Je-sus sends To call them to his arms.

309. *Mourn not the Departed.* (579)

2 Why should we tremble to convey
  Their bodies to the tomb!
There the dear flesh of Jesus lay,
  And left a long perfume.

3 The graves of all his saints he blest,
  And softened every bed:
Where should the dying members rest,
  But with the dying Head?

4 Thence he arose, ascending high,
  And showed our feet the way:
Up to the Lord our flesh shall fly
  At the great rising day. WATTS.

310. *Dependence on the Spirit.* (303)

1 How helpless guilty nature lies,
  Unconscious of its load!
The heart, unchanged, can never rise
  To happiness and God.

2 Can aught beneath a power divine,
  The stubborn will subdue?
'Tis thine, eternal Spirit, thine
  To form the heart anew.

3 'Tis thine the passions to recall,
  And upward bid them rise,
And make the scales of error fall
  From reason's darkened eyes.

4 To chase the shades of death away,
  And bid the sinner live,
A beam of heaven, a vital ray,
  'Tis thine alone to give. STEELE.

311. *Everlasting Absence of God Intolerable.* (587)

1 THAT awful day will surely come,—
  Th' appointed hour makes haste,—
When I must stand before my Judge,
  And pass the solemn test.

2 Thou lovely Chief of all my joys,
  Thou Sovereign of my heart,
How could I bear to hear thy voice
  Pronounce the sound, "Depart!"

3 Oh! wretched state of deep despair,
  To see my God remove,
And fix my dreadful station where
  I must not taste his love!

4 Jesus, I throw my arms around,
  And hang upon thy breast;
Without one gracious smile from thee,
  My spirit cannot rest.

5 O, tell me that my worthless name
  Is graven on thy hands;
Show me some promise in thy book,
  Where my salvation stands. WATTS.

A LIGHT IN THE WINDOW.

WM. B. BRADBURY.

1 There's a light in the window for thee, brother, There's a light in the window for thee;
A dear one has moved to the mansions a-bove, There's a light in the window for thee.

CHORUS.
A mansion in heav-en we see, And a light in the window for thee,
A mansion in heav-en we see, And a light in the window for thee.

312. *A Light in the Window.* (473)

2 There's a crown, and a robe, and a palm, brother,
When from toil and from care you are free;
The Saviour has gone to prepare you a home,
With a light in the window for thee.—*Cho.*

3 O watch, and be faithful, and pray, brother,
All your journey o'er life's troubled sea,
Though afflictions assail you, and storms beat severe,
There's a light in the window for thee.—*Cho.*

4 Then on, perseveringly on, brother,
Till from conflict and suffering free,
Bright angels now beckon you over the stream,
There's a light in the window for thee.—*Cho.*

SAY, BROTHERS, WILL YOU MEET US? 121

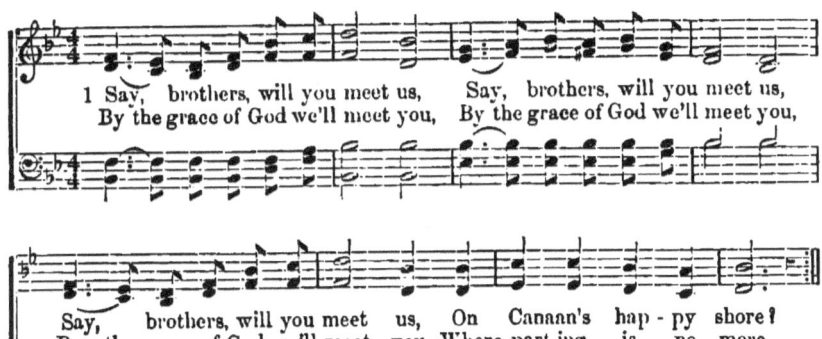

313.   *"Will you Meet us."*   (443)

1 Say, brothers, will you meet us,
   On Canaan's happy shore?
By the grace of God we'll meet you,
   Where parting is no more.

2 Jesus lives and reigns forever,
   On Canaan's happy shore!
Glory, glory, hallelujah!
   For ever, evermore!

314.   *Delight in the Lord's House.*
            Tune MARCHING ALONG, page 28.   (483)

1 We come to his courts, where so often we prove
   The truth of his promise, the depth of his love,—
How blissful the moment as, in sweetest accord,
We visit his temple, and rejoice in the Lord!
   Rejoice in the Lord, rejoice in the Lord,
   Visit his Temple, and rejoice in the Lord;
How blissful the moment as, in sweetest accord,
We visit his Temple, and rejoice in the Lord!

2 How matchless the Grace that redeemed us with blood,
That cleanses from guilt in this life-giving flood;
Forever, unwearied, our glad anthems shall ring,
Ascribing salvation to our Saviour and King!—*Cho.*

3 We enter thy courts, ever open and free,
O, grant us, dear Saviour, thy beauty to see;
And ere we depart, may each worshiper prove
The truth of thy promise, all the depths of thy love!—*Cho.*

                                                         S. Dyer.

122 LABAN. S. M.

Dr. Lowell Mason.

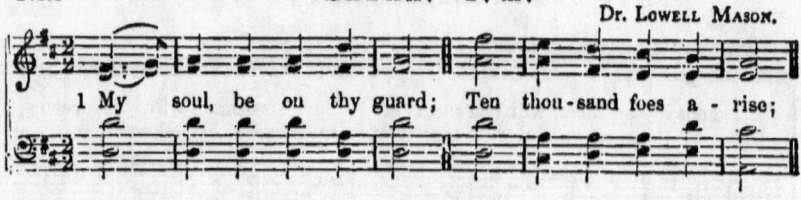

1 My soul, be on thy guard; Ten thou-sand foes a-rise;

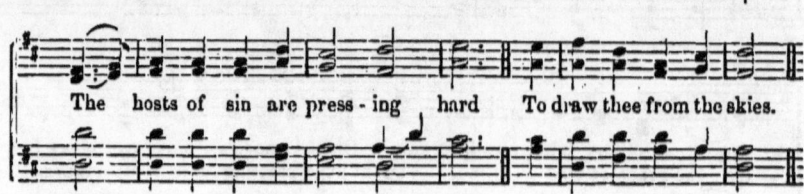

The hosts of sin are press-ing hard To draw thee from the skies.

315. *The Soldier on his Guard.* (327)

2 O, watch, and fight, and pray,
  The battle ne'er give o'er;
  Renew it boldly every day,
  And help divine implore.

3 Ne'er think the victory won,
  Nor lay thine armor down;
  Thy arduous work will not be done
  Till thou obtain thy crown.

4 Fight on, my soul, till death
  Shall bring thee to thy God;
  He'll take thee at thy parting breath,
  To his divine abode.   Heath.

316. *The Charming Place.* (174)

1 How charming is the place
  Where my Redeemer, God,
  Unvails the beauties of his face
  And sheds his love abroad!

2 Here, on the mercy seat,
  With radiant glory crowned,
  Our joyful eyes behold him sit,
  And smile on all around.

3 Give me, O Lord, a place
  Within thy blest abode,
  Among the children of thy grace,
  The servants of my God.   Watts.

317. *Redemption Completed.* (230)

1 "The Lord is risen indeed;"
  He lives to die no more;
  He lives the sinner's cause to plead,
  Whose curse and shame he bore.

2 "The Lord is risen indeed;"
  Then hell has lost its prey;
  With him is risen the ransomed seed,
  To reign in endless day.

3 "The Lord is risen indeed;"
  Attending angels, hear;
  Up to the courts of heaven, with speed,
  The joyful tidings bear.

4 Then wake your golden lyres,
  And strike each cheerful chord;
  Join, all ye bright, celestial choirs,
  To sing our risen Lord.   Kelly.

Doxology.

1 Thy name, almighty Lord,
  Shall sound through distant lands;
  Great is thy grace, and sure thy word;
  Thy truth for ever stands.

2 Far be thine honor spread,
  And long thy praise endure,
  Till morning light and evening shade
  Shall be exchanged no more.

SILVER STREET. S. M. 123
I. SMITH.

1 Come, sound his praise a-broad, And hymns of glo-ry sing;
Je-ho-vah is the sovereign God, The u-ni-ver-sal King.

118. *Exhortation to Praise.* (205)

Come, worship at his throne;
 Come, bow before the Lord;
We are his work, and not our own;
 He formed us by his word.

To-day attend his voice,
 Nor dare provoke his rod;
Come, like the people of his choice,
 And own your gracious God.
　　　　　　　　WATTS.

119. *Redemption by Grace.* (453)

GRACE! 'tis a charming sound;
 Harmonious to the ear;
Heaven with the echo shall resound,
 And all the earth shall hear.

Grace first contrived the way
 To save rebellious man;
And all the steps that grace display,
 Which drew the wondrous plan.

Grace led my roving feet
 To tread the heavenly road;
And new supplies each hour I meet,
 While pressing on to God.

Grace all the work shall crown,
 Through everlasting days;
It lays in heaven the topmost stone,
 And well deserves the praise.
　　　　　　　　DODDRIDGE.

320. *Song of Moses and the Lamb.* (248)

1 AWAKE, and sing the song
 Of Moses and the Lamb;
Wake every heart, and every tongue,
 To praise the Saviour's name.

2 Sing of his dying love;
 Sing of his rising power;
Sing how he intercedes above
 For us, whose sins he bore.

3 Sing, till we feel our heart
 Ascending with our tongue;
Sing, till the love of sin depart,
 And grace inspire our song.

4 Sing on your heavenly way,
 Ye ransomed sinners, sing;
Sing on, rejoicing every day
 In Christ, th' eternal King.

5 Soon shall we hear him say,
 "Ye blessed children, come!"
Soon will he call us hence away,
 To our eternal home.　　HAMMOND.

DOXOLOGY.

To God, the Father, Son,
 And Spirit, glory be,
As was, and is, and shall remain
 Through all eternity!

CADDO. C. M.

WM. B. BRADBURY.

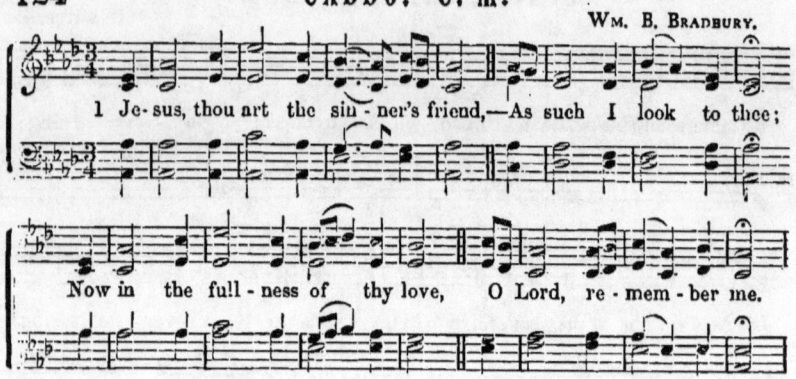

1 Jesus, thou art the sinner's friend,—As such I look to thee;
Now in the fullness of thy love, O Lord, remember me.

321. *"Lord, Remember Me."* (95)

2 Remember thy pure word of grace,
Remember Calvary;
Remember all thy dying groans,
And then remember me.

3 Thou wondrous advocate with God,
I yield myself to thee,
While thou art sitting on thy throne
Dear Lord, remember me.

4 I own I'm guilty, own I'm vile,
Yet thy salvation's free;
Then in thy all-abounding grace,
Dear Lord, remember me.

5 Howe'er forsaken or distressed,
Howe'er oppressed I be,
Howe'er afflicted here on earth,
Do thou remember me.

6 And when I close my eyes in death,
And creature helps all flee,
Then, O, my dear Redeemer, God,
I pray remember me.
BURNHAM.

322. *Behold the Lamb of God.* (255)

1 BEHOLD the Lamb of God, who bore
Thy guilt upon the tree,
And paid in blood the dreadful score,
The ransom due for thee.

2 Behold him till the sight endears
The Saviour to thy heart;
His pierced feet bedew with tears,
Nor from his cross depart.

3 Behold him till his dying love
Thy every thought control;
Its vast, constraining influence prove
O'er body, spirit, soul.

4 Behold him, as the race you run,
Your never-failing Friend;
He will complete the work begun,
And grace in glory end.

323. *Judgment for National Sins Deprecated.* (54)

1 ALMIGHTY Lord, before thy throne
Thy mourning people bend;
'Tis on thy pardoning grace alone
Our dying hopes depend.

2 Dark judgments, from thy heavy hand
Thy dreadful power display;
Yet mercy spares our guilty land,
And still we live to pray.

3 O, turn us, turn us, mighty Lord;
Convert us by thy grace;
Then shall our hearts obey thy word
And see again thy face.

4. Then should oppressing foes invade
We will not yield to fear,
Secure of all-sufficient aid,
When thou, O God, art near.
STEELE.

24. *The Importance and Influence of Love.* (352)

Happy the heart where graces reign,
  Where love inspires the breast:
Love is the brightest of the train,
  And strengthens all the rest.

Knowledge, alas! 'tis all in vain,
  And all in vain our fear:
Our stubborn sins will fight and reign,
  If love be absent there.

'Tis love that makes our cheerful feet
  In swift obedience move ;
The devils know, and tremble too;
  But they can never love.

This is the grace that lives and sings
  When faith and hope shall cease ;
'Tis this shall strike our joyful strings
  In brightest realms of bliss.
  WATTS.

25. *Love Strong as Death.*
  Tune La Mira, page 56. (238)

Plunged in a gulf of dark despair,
  We wretched sinners lay,
Without one cheerful beam of hope,
  Or spark of glimmering day.

With pitying eyes the Prince of grace
  Beheld our helpless grief;
He saw, and oh! amazing love!—
  He flew to our relief.

Down from the shining seats above,
  With joyful haste he fled,
Entered the grave in mortal flesh,
  And dwelt among the dead.

Oh! for this love, let rocks and hills
  Their lasting silence break,
And all harmonious human tongues
  The Saviour's praises speak.

Angels, assist our mighty joys;
  Strike all your harps of gold;
But when you raise your highest notes,
  His love can ne'er be told.
  WATTS.

326. *Self-Admonition.* (333)

1 Awake, my drowsy soul, awake!
  And view the threatening scene ;
See, how thy foes encamp around,
  And treason lurks within.

2 'Tis not this mortal life alone
  These hostile powers assail:
How canst thou hope for future bliss,
  If their attempts prevail ?

3 Then to the work of God awake ;
  Behold thy Master near ;
The various, arduous task pursue
  With vigor and with fear.

4 The awful register goes on ;
  Th' account will surely come ;
And opening day, or closing night,
  May bear me to my doom.

5 Tremendous thought! how deep it strikes!
  Yet like a dream it flies,
Till God's own voice the slumbers chase
  From these deluded eyes.
  DODDRIDGE.

327. *Christ Precious.* (268)

1 Jesus! delightful, charming name!
  It spreads a fragrance round ;
Justice and mercy, truth and peace,
  In union here are found.

2 He is our life, our joy, our strength ;
  In him all glories meet ;
He is a shade above our heads,
  A light to guide our feet.

3 The thickest clouds are soon dispersed,
  If Jesus shows his face ;
To weary, heavy-laden souls
  He is the resting-place.

4 When storms arise and tempests blow,
  He speaks the stilling word ;
The threatening billows cease to flow,
  The winds obey their Lord.

5 Through every age he's still the same ;
  But we ungrateful prove,
Forget the savor of his name,
  The sweetness of his love.
  BEDDOME.

JESUS PAID IT ALL.

Wm. B. Bradbury.

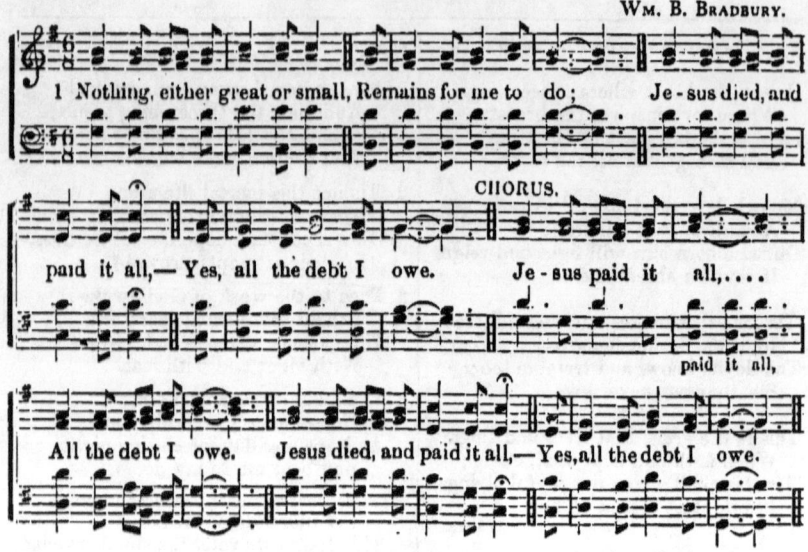

328. *Jesus Paid it all.* (468)

1 Nothing, either great or small,
   Remains for me to do;
   Jesus died, and paid it all,—
   Yes, all the debt I owe.
      Jesus paid it all, &c.

2 When he from his lofty throne,
   Stooped down to do and die,
   Every thing was fully done;
   Yes, "finished!" was his cry.
      Jesus paid it all, &c.

3 Weary, working, plodding one!
   O, wherefore toil you so?
   Cease your "doing;" all was done
   Yes, ages long ago.
      Jesus paid it all, &c.

   Till to Jesus' work you cling,
   Alone by simple faith,
   "Doing" is a deadly thing,
   All "doing" ends in death.
      Jesus paid it all, &c.

5 Cast your deadly "doing" down,
   Down, all at Jesus' feet;
   Stand in him, in him alone,
   All glorious and complete.
      Jesus paid it all, &c.

329. *Pagan Darkness.* (527
Tune Zion, page 130.

1 O'er the gloomy hills of darkness,
   Look, my soul, be still and gaze;
   See the promises advancing
   To a glorious day of grace:
      Blessed jubilee,
   Let thy glorious morning dawn.

2 Kingdoms wide, that sit in darkness,
   Grant them, Lord, the glorious light
   Now, from eastern coast to western,
   May the morning chase the night:
      Let redemption,
   Freely purchased, win the day.

3 Fly abroad, thou mighty gospel:
   Win and conquer—never cease
   May thy lasting, wide dominions
   Multiply, and still increase;
      Sway thy sceptre,
   Saviour, all the world around.
                        Williams

ZION'S PILGRIM. 127
From The Golden Chain.

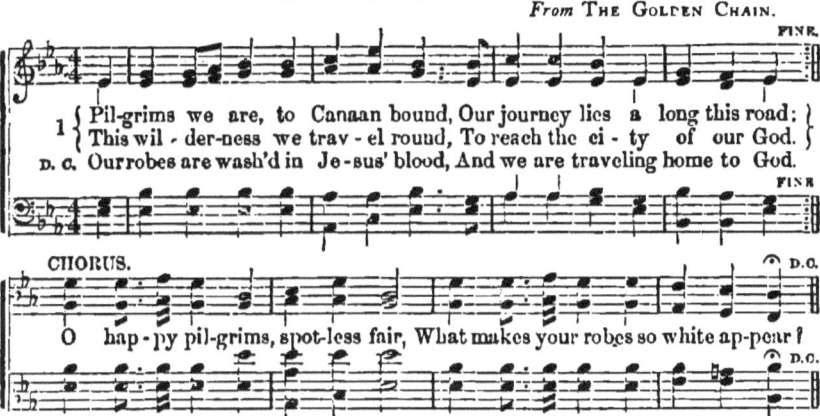

1. Pil-grims we are, to Canaan bound, Our journey lies a long this road;
This wil - der-ness we trav - el round, To reach the ci - ty of our God.
D.C. Our robes are wash'd in Je-sus' blood, And we are traveling home to God.

CHORUS.
O hap-py pil-grims, spot-less fair, What makes your robes so white ap-pear?

330. *Zion's Pilgrim.* (439)

2 A few more days, or weeks, or years,
In this dark desert to complain;
A few more sighs, a few more tears,
And we shall bid adieu to pain.
Oh happy pilgrims, &c.

3 Oh blessed land! Oh happy land!
When shall we reach thy golden shore?
And one redeemed, unbroken band
United be forevermore.
Oh happy pilgrims, &c.

4 And if our robes are pure and white,
May we all reach that blest abode?
Oh yes! they all shall dwell in light
Whose robes are washed in Jesus' blood.
Oh happy pilgrims, &c.

5 We all shall reach that golden shore
If here we watch, and fight, and pray;
Strait is the way, and strait the door,
And none but pilgrims find the way.
Oh happy pilgrims, &c.

6 Oh may we meet at last above
Amid the holy blood-washed throng,
And sing for ever Jesus' love,
While saints and angels join the song.
Oh happy pilgrims, &c.

331. *Bound for the Mansions of Glory.*
Tune Marching Along, page 28. (481)

1 'Tis sweet in the trials of conflict and sin,
Temptation without and temptation within,
To know through the journey of life as I roam,
I am bound for the mansions of glory at home.
Of glory at home, of glory at home,
I am bound for the mansions of glory at home.

2 'Tis sweet in the gloom of earth's sorrow or fears,
My eyes overflowing with penitent tears,
To know, though the billows around me may foam,
I am bound for the mansions of glory at home.

3 I ask not to hasten from duty or care,
The troubles of life let me patiently bear,
If only I know as I look through the gloom,
I am bound for the mansions of glory at home.

4 When all earthly conflicts and trials are o'er,
When sin and temptation beset me no more,
Still trusting in Jesus, I'll welcome the tomb,
For I am bound for the mansions of glory at home.
J. Wheaton Smith.

NUREMBURG. 7s.

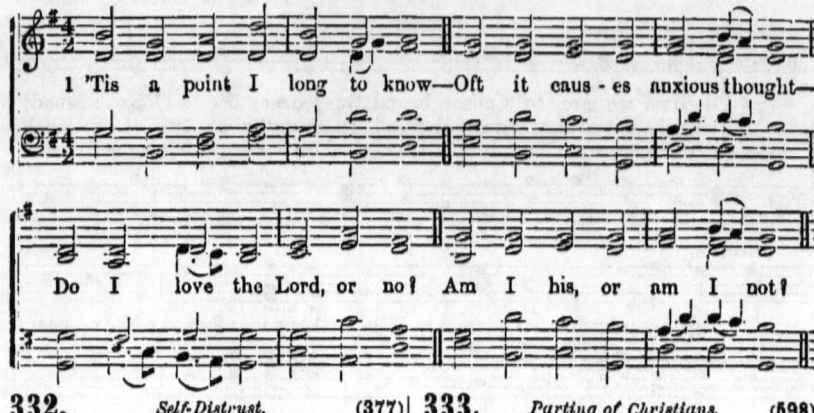

1 'Tis a point I long to know—Oft it caus-es anxious thought—
Do I love the Lord, or no? Am I his, or am I not?

332. *Self-Distrust.* (377)

2 If I love, why am I thus?
 Why this dull and lifeless frame?
 Hardly, sure, can they be worse,
 Who have never heard his name.

3 When I turn my eyes within,
 All is dark, and vain, and wild;
 Filled with unbelief and sin,
 Can I deem myself a child?

4 If I pray, or hear, or read,
 Sin is mixed with all I do;
 You that love the Lord indeed,
 Tell me, is it thus with you?

5 Yet I mourn my stubborn will,
 Find my sin a grief and thrall;
 Should I grieve for what I feel,
 If I did not love at all?

6 Lord, decide the doubtful case;
 Thou, who art thy people's sun,
 Shine upon thy work of grace,
 If it be indeed begun.

7 Let me love thee more and more,
 If I love at all, I pray;
 If I have not loved before,
 Help me to begin to-day.
   NEWTON.

333. *Parting of Christians.* (598)

1 For a season called to part,
 Let us now ourselves commend
 To the gracious eye and heart
 Of our ever present Friend.

2 Jesus! hear our humble prayer;
 Tender Shepherd of thy sheep!
 Let thy mercy and thy care
 All our souls in safety keep.

3 In thy strength may we be strong,
 Sweeten every cross and pain;
 Grant, that, if we live, ere long
 We may meet in peace again.

4 Then, if thou thy help afford,
 Joyful songs to thee shall rise,
 And our souls shall praise the Lord,
 Who regards our humble cries.
   NEWTON.

334. *Jubilee Song.* (508)

1 WAKE the song of Jubilee!
 Let it echo o'er the sea!
 Now is come the promised hour,
 Jesus reigns with glorious power.

2 All the nations join and sing,
 Praise your Saviour, praise your King;
 Let it sound from shore to shore,—
 "Jesus reigns forevermore!"
   L. BACON.

SABBATH. 7s, 6 lines.

Dr. L. MASON.

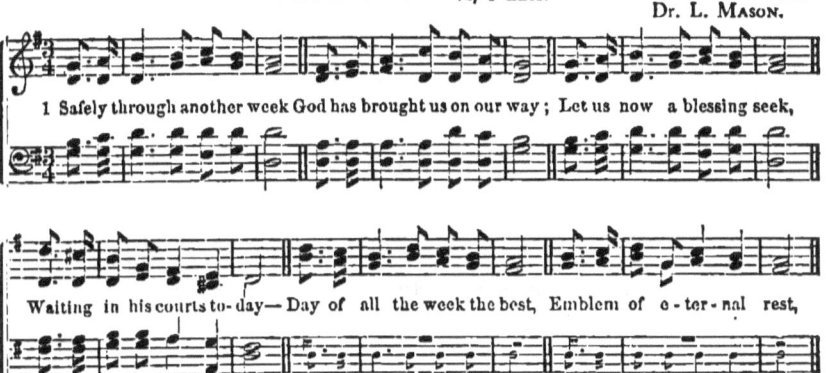

1 Safely through another week God has brought us on our way; Let us now a blessing seek, Waiting in his courts to-day— Day of all the week the best, Emblem of e-ter-nal rest,

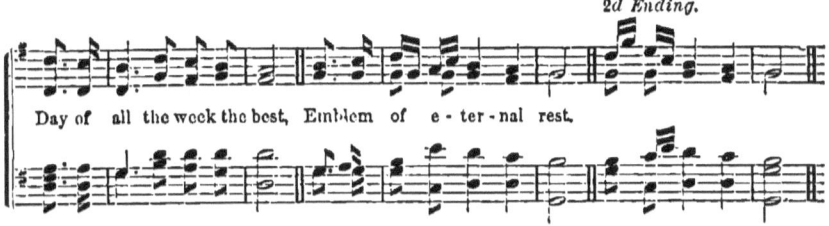

Day of all the week the best, Emblem of e-ter-nal rest.

335. *Lord's Day in the Sanctuary.* (165)

2 While we seek supplies of grace,
  Through the dear Redeemer's name,
Show thy reconciling face,
  Take away our sin and shame:
From our worldly cares set free,
May we rest, this day, in thee.

3 Here we come thy name to praise;
  Let us feel thy presence near;
May thy glory meet our eyes,
  While we in thy house appear:
Here afford us, Lord, a taste
Of our everlasting feast.

4 May the gospel's joyful sound
  Conquer sinners, comfort saints,
Make the fruits of grace abound,
  Bring relief from all complaints:
Thus let all our Sabbaths prove,
Till we join the church above.

NEWTON.

336. *The Sanctifier.* (307)

1 HOLY GHOST, with light divine,
  Shine upon this heart of mine;
Chase the shades of night away;
  Turn the darkness into day.

2 Holy Ghost, with power divine,
  Cleanse this guilty heart of mine:
Long has sin, without control,
  Held dominion o'er my soul.

3 Holy Ghost, with joy divine,
  Cheer this saddened heart of mine;
Bid my many woes depart;
  Heal my wounded, bleeding heart.

4 Holy Spirit, all divine,
  Dwell within this heart of mine;
Cast down every idol throne;
  Reign supreme, and reign alone.

REED.

ZION. 8s, 7s & 4s.

Dr. HASTINGS.

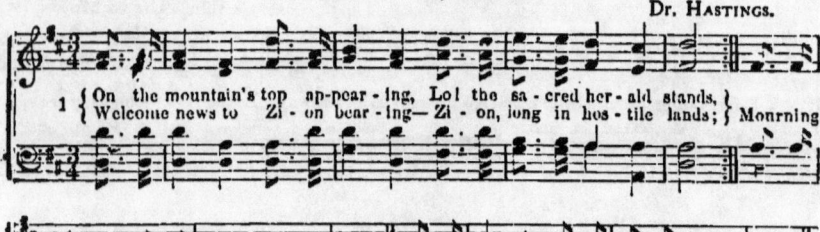

337. *Zion Encouraged.* (540)

2 Has thy night been long and mournful?
 Have thy friends unfaithful proved?
 Have thy foes been proud and scornful,
  By thy sighs and tears unmoved?
   Cease thy mourning;
  Zion still is well beloved.

3 God, thy God, will now restore thee;
 He himself appears thy Friend;
 All thy foes shall flee before thee;
  Here their boasts and triumphs end:
   Great deliverance
  Zion's King will surely send.

4 Enemies no more shall trouble,
 All thy wrongs shall be redress'd;
 For thy shame thou shalt have double,
  In thy Maker's favor bless'd;
   All thy conflicts
  End in everlasting rest. KELLY.

338. *God the Defence of Zion.* (157)

1 ZION stands with hills surrounded—
 Zion, kept by power divine:
 All her foes shall be confounded,
  Though the world in arms combine:
   Happy Zion,
  What a favored lot is thine!

2 Every human tie may perish;
 Friend to friend unfaithful prove;
 Mothers cease their own to cherish;

Heaven and earth at last remove;
 But no changes
Can attend Jehovah's love.

3 In the furnace God may prove thee,
 Thence to bring thee forth more bright,
 But can never cease to love thee;
  Thou art precious in his sight:
   God is with thee—
  God, thine everlasting light. KELLY.

339. *Atonement Finished.* (279)

1 HARK! the voice of love and mercy,
 Sounds aloud from Calvary;
 See! it rends the rocks asunder,
  Shakes the earth and vails the sky:
   "It is finished!"
  Hear the dying Saviour cry.

2 "It is finished!"—Oh, what pleasure
 Do these charming words afford!
 Heavenly blessings without measure,
  Flow to us through Christ the Lord;
   "It is finished!"
  Saints, the dying words record.

3 Tune your harps anew, ye seraphs
 Join to sing the pleasing theme;
 All in earth and heaven uniting,
  Join to praise Immanuel's name;
   Hallelujah!
  Glory to the bleeding Lamb.
   J. EVANS

THAT BEAUTIFUL LAND.

131

Wm. B. Bradbury.

1 A beau-ti-ful land by faith I see, A land of rest, from sor-row free, The

CHORUS.

home of the ransomed, bright and fair, And beautiful angels, too, are there. Will you go? Will you go?

May be repeated at pleasure, pp

Go to that beautiful land with me? Will you go? Will you go? Go to that beautiful land?

340. *That Beautiful Land.* (595)

1 A BEAUTIFUL land by faith I see,
A land of rest, from sorrow free,
The home of the ransomed, bright, and fair,
And beautiful angels too, are there.
    Will you go? Will you go? &c.

2 That beautiful land, the city of light,
It ne'er has known the shades of night;
The glory of God, the light of day,
Hath driven the darkness far away.
    Will you go? Will you go? &c.

3 In vision I see its streets of gold,
Its beautiful gates I, too, behold,
The river of life, the crystal sea,
The ambrosial fruit of life's fair tree.
    Will you go? Will you go? &c.

The heavenly throng arrayed in white
In rapture range the plains of light;
And in one harmonious choir they praise
Their glorious Saviour's matchless grace.
    Will you go? Will you go? &c.

341. *Prayer for the Heathen.* (526)
Tune ZION, page 130.

1 O'ER the realms of pagan darkness,
    Let the eye of pity gaze;
See the kindreds of the people
    Lost in sin's bewildering maze;
        Darkness brooding
    O'er the face of all the earth.

2 Light of them that sit in darkness,
    Rise and shine, thy blessings bring;
Light, to lighten all the Gentiles,
    Rise with healing in thy wing
        To thy brightness
    Let all kings and nations come.

3 May the heathen, now adoring
    Idol gods of wood and stone,
Come, and, worshiping before him,
    Serve the living God alone:
        Let thy glory
    Fill the earth as floods the sea.

T. COTTERILL.

CANAAN. C.M.

Arranged for this work.

342. *Fellowship of Love.* (361)

1 How pleasant thus to dwell below,
  In fellowship of love!
And, though we part, 'tis bliss to know
  The good shall meet above.
    Oh, that will be joyful, joyful, joyful!
  Oh, that will be joyful
    To meet to part no more,
  To meet to part no more,
    On Canaan's happy shore,
  And sing the everlasting song
  With those who've gone before!

2 Yes, happy thought! when we are free
  From earthly grief and pain,
In heaven we shall each other see
  And never part again.
    Oh, that will be joyful, &c.

3 Then let us each, in strength divine,
  Still walk in wisdom's ways,
That we with those we love may join
  In never-ending praise.
    Oh, that will be joyful, &c.

CORONATION. C. M.

Oliver Holden.

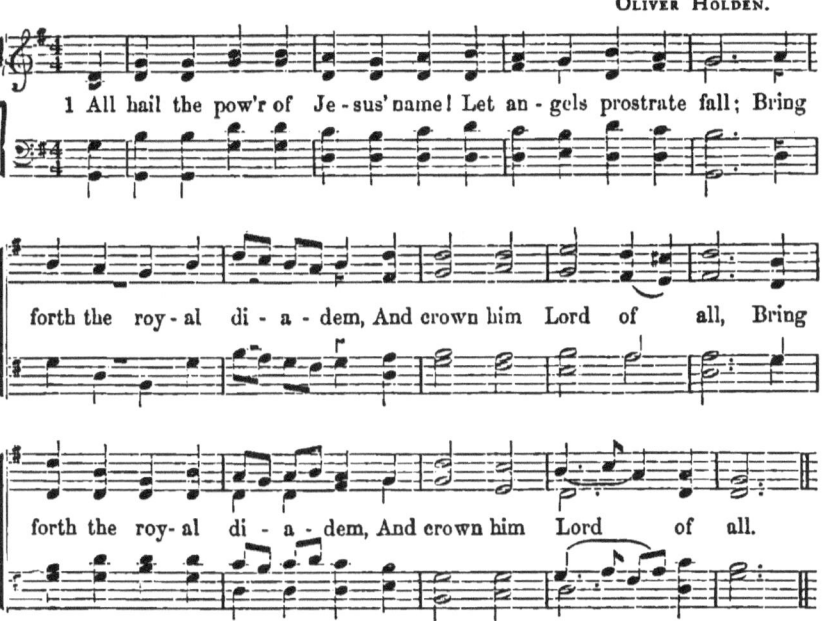

1 All hail the pow'r of Jesus' name! Let angels prostrate fall; Bring forth the royal diadem, And crown him Lord of all, Bring forth the royal diadem, And crown him Lord of all.

343. *The Mediator Crowned.* (237)

2 Ye chosen seed of Israel's race,—
A remnant weak and small,—
Hail him, who saves you by his grace,
And crown him Lord of all.

3 Ye gentile sinners, ne'er forget
The wormwood and the gall;
Go, spread your trophies at his feet,
And crown him Lord of all.

4 Let every kindred, every tribe,
On this terrestrial ball,
To him all majesty ascribe,
And crown him Lord of all.

5 O, that, with yonder sacred throng,
We at his feet may fall!
We'll join the everlasting song,
And crown him Lord of all.
     Edward Perronet.

344. *The Hope of Heaven.* (475)
Tune Canaan, page 132.

1 When I can read my title clear
To mansions in the skies,
I bid farewell to every fear,
And wipe my weeping eyes.

2 Should earth against my soul engage,
And fiery darts be hurled,
Then I can smile at Satan's rage,
And face a frowning world.

3 Let cares, like a wild deluge, come,
And storms of sorrow fall!
May I but safely reach my home,
My God, my heaven, my all.

4 There shall I bathe my weary soul
In seas of heavenly rest,
And not a wave of trouble roll
Across my peaceful breast.
     Watts.

134   OBERLIN. L. M.

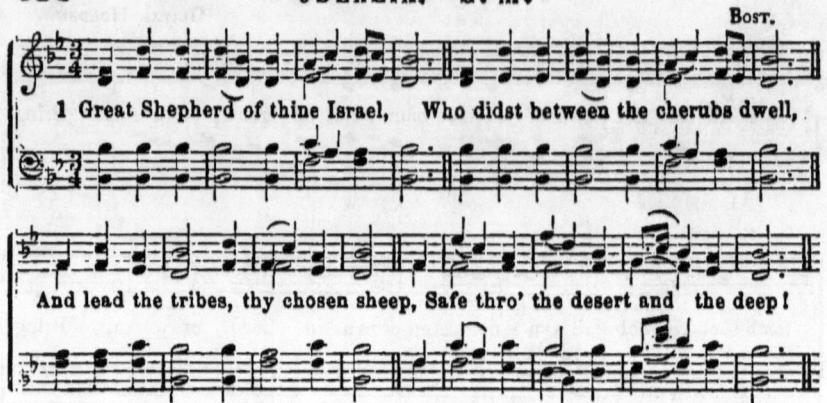

Bost.

1 Great Shepherd of thine Israel, Who didst between the cherubs dwell, And lead the tribes, thy chosen sheep, Safe thro' the desert and the deep!

345. *Prayer of the Church in Time* (500)
of Desertion.

2 Thy church is in the desert now:
Shine from on high, and guide us thro';
Turn us to thee, thy love restore:
We shall be saved, and sigh no more.

3 Hast thou not planted with thy hand
A lovely vine in this our land?
Did not thy power defend it round,
And heavenly dew enrich the ground?

4 How did the spreading branches shoot,
And bless the nations with their fruit?
But now, O Lord, look down and see
Thy mourning vine, that lovely tree.

5 Return, Almighty God, return!
Nor let thy bleeding vineyard mourn:
Turn us to thee, thy love restore;
We shall be saved, and sigh no more!

346.   *Remembering Christ.*   (257)

1 O, thou, my soul, forget no more
The Friend who all thy sorrows bore;
Let every idol be forgot;
But, O, my soul, forget him not.

2 Renounce thy works and ways, with grief,
And fly to this divine relief;
Nor Him forget, who left his throne,
And for thy life gave up his own.

3 Eternal truth and mercy shine,
In him, and he himself is thine:
And canst thou, then, with sin beset,
Such charms, such matchless charms, forget!

4 O, no! till life itself depart,
His name shall cheer and warm my heart;
And lisping this, from earth I'll rise,
And join the chorus of the skies.
                          Krishna Pal.

347. *Trusting Christ, the only Refuge.* (292)

1 Thou only Sovereign of my heart,
My refuge, my almighty friend,
And can my soul from thee depart,
On whom alone my hopes depend!

2 Whither, ah, whither shall I go,
A wretched wanderer from my Lord!
Can this dark world of sin and woe
One glimpse of happiness afford?

3 Let earth's alluring joys combine;
While thou art near, in vain they call;
One smile, one blissful smile, of thine,
My gracious Lord, outweighs them all.

4 Low at thy feet my soul would lie;
Here safety dwells, and peace divine;
Still let me live beneath thine eye,
For life, eternal life, is thine.
                          Steele.

STAR OF BETHLEHEM. L. M.

1. When, marshalled on the night-ly plain, The glittering host be-stud the sky,
One star a-lone of all the train, Can fix the sin-ner's wand'ring eye,
D. S. But one a-lone the Saviour speaks—It is the Star of Beth-le-hem!
Hark! hark! to God the cho-rus breaks, From ev-'ry host, from ev-'ry gem,

348. *The Star of Bethlehem.* (442)

2 Once on the raging seas I rode;
 The storm was loud, the night was dark;
The ocean yawned, and rudely blowed
 The wind that tossed my foundering bark.
Deep horror then my vitals froze;
 Death-struck, I ceased the tide to stem;
When suddenly a star arose—
 It was the Star of Bethlehem!

3 It was my guide, my light, my all;
 It bade my dark forebodings cease;
And, thro' the storm and danger's thrall,
 It led me to the port of peace.
Now, safely moored, my perils o'er,
 I'll sing, first in night's diadem,
For ever, and forever more,
 The Star—the Star of Bethlehem!
  H. K. WHITE.

349. *The Christian's Prospect.* (431)
 Tune OBERLIN.

1 WHAT sinners value I resign;
 Lord, 'tis enough that thou art mine;
I shall behold thy blissful face,
 And stand complete in righteousness.

2 This life's a dream—an empty show;
 But that bright world to which I go
Hath joys substantial and sincere:
 When shall I wake and find me there?

3 Oh, glorious hour! Oh, blest abode!
 I shall be near and like my God!
And flesh and sin no more control
 The sacred pleasures of my soul.

4 My flesh shall slumber in the ground
 Till the last trumpet's joyful sound,
Then burst the chains with glad surprise,
 And in my Saviour's image rise. WATTS.

GOSHEN. 11s.

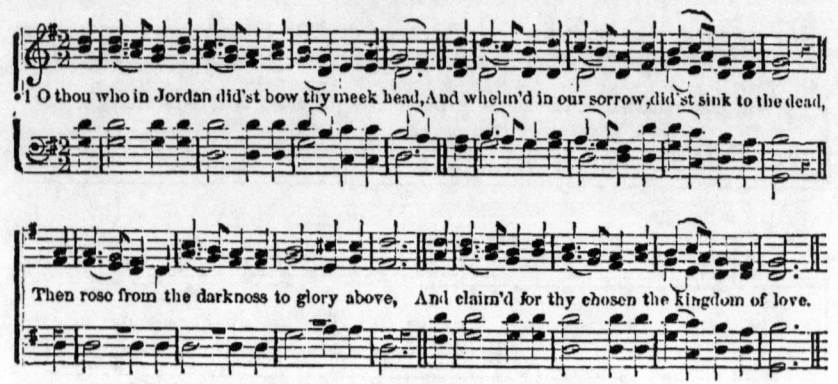

1 O thou who in Jordan did'st bow thy meek head, And whelm'd in our sorrow, did'st sink to the dead, Then rose from the darkness to glory above, And claim'd for thy chosen the kingdom of love.

350. *Baptism, a Symbol of Regeneration.* (141)

1 O thou who in Jordan did'st bow thy meek head,
And whelmed in our sorrow, did'st sink to the dead,
Then rose from the darkness to glory above,
And claimed for thy chosen the kingdom of love.

2 Thy footsteps we follow, to bow in the tide,
And are buried with thee in the death thou hast died,
Then wake with thy likeness to walk in the way
That brightens and brightens to shadowless day.

3 O Jesus, our Saviour, O Jesus, our Lord!
By the life of thy passion, the grace of thy word,
Accept us, redeem us, dwell ever within,
To keep, by thy Spirit, our spirits from sin.

4 Till crowned with thy glory, and waving the palm,
Our garments all white from the blood of the Lamb,
We join the bright millions of saints gone before,
And bless thee, and wonder, and praise evermore.

351. *Rejoicing in Jesus.* (125)

1 How loving is Jesus, who came from the sky,
In tenderest pity for sinners to die!
His hands and his feet were nail'd to the tree,
And all this he suffer'd for you and for me.

2 How gladly does Jesus free pardon impart
To all who receive him by faith in their heart;
No evil befalls them, their home is above,
And Jesus throws round them the arms of his love.

3 How precious is Jesus to all who believe,
  And out of his fullness what grace they receive!
  When weak, he supports them; when erring, he guides;
  And every thing needful he kindly provides.

4 O, give then to Jesus your earliest days,
  They only are blessed who walk in his ways,
  In life and in death he will still be your friend,
  For whom Jesus loves, he loves to the end.

352. *The Firm Foundation.* (456)

1 How firm a foundation, ye saints of the Lord,
  Is laid for your faith in his excellent word!
  What more can he say than to you he hath said—
  You who unto Jesus for refuge have fled?

2 In every condition—in sickness, in health,
  In poverty's vale, or abounding in wealth,
  At home and abroad, on the land, on the sea,—
  As thy day may demand, shall thy strength ever be.

3 E'en down to old age, all my people shall prove
  My sovereign, eternal, unchangeable love;
  And when hoary hairs shall their temples adorn,
  Like lambs they shall still in my bosom be borne.

4 The soul that on Jesus hath leaned for repose,
  I will not, I will not, desert to its foes;
  That soul, though all hell should endeavor to shake,
  I'll never, no, never, no, never, forsake!   KIRKHAM.

353. *Unbelief Banished.* (341)

1 BEGONE, unbelief! my Saviour is near;
  And for my relief will surely appear:
  By prayer let me wrestle, and he will perform;
  With Christ in the vessel, I smile at the storm.

2 Determined to save, he watched o'er my path,
  When Satan's blind slave, I sported with death;
  And can he have taught me to trust in his name,
  And thus far have brought me to put me to shame?

3 Though dark be my way, since he is my guide,
  'Tis mine to obey, 'tis his to provide;
  His way was much rougher and darker than mine;
  Did Jesus thus suffer, and shall I repine?

4 His love, in time past, forbids me to think,
  He'll leave me at last in trouble to sink;
  Though painful at present, 'twill cease before long,
  And then, oh, how pleasant the conqueror's song!   NEWTON.

EXPOSTULATION. 11s.

1 O turn ye, O turn ye, for why will ye die, When God in great mer-cy is com-ing so nigh? Now Je-sus in-vites you, the Spirit says, Come, And an-gels are waiting to welcome you home.

354.   *Turn Ye.*   (62)

2 How vain the delusion, that while you delay,
Your hearts may grow better; your chains melt away;
Come guilty, come wretched, come just as you are;
All helpless and dying, to Jesus repair.

3 The contrite in heart he will freely receive,
O, why will you not the glad message believe?
If sin be your burden, why will you not come?
'Tis you he makes welcome; he bids you come home.

4 Come, give us your hand, and the Saviour your heart;
In him once united, we never shall part;
O, how can we leave you? why will you not come?
We'll journey together, and soon be at home.

355.   *Slumbering Professors Exhorted.*   (340)

1 Why sleep we, my brethren! come, let us arise;
O, why should we slumber in sight of the prize?
Salvation is nearer, our days are far spent;
O, let us be active; awake! and repent.

2 O, how can we slumber! the Master is come,
And calling on sinners to seek them a home;
The Spirit and Bride now in concert unite,
The weary they welcome, the careless invite.

3 O, how can we slumber! when so much was done,
To purchase salvation, by Jesus, the Son?
Now mercy is proffered, and justice displayed,
Now God can be honored, and sinners be saved!

Hopkins.

WE ARE COMING, BLESSED SAVIOUR.

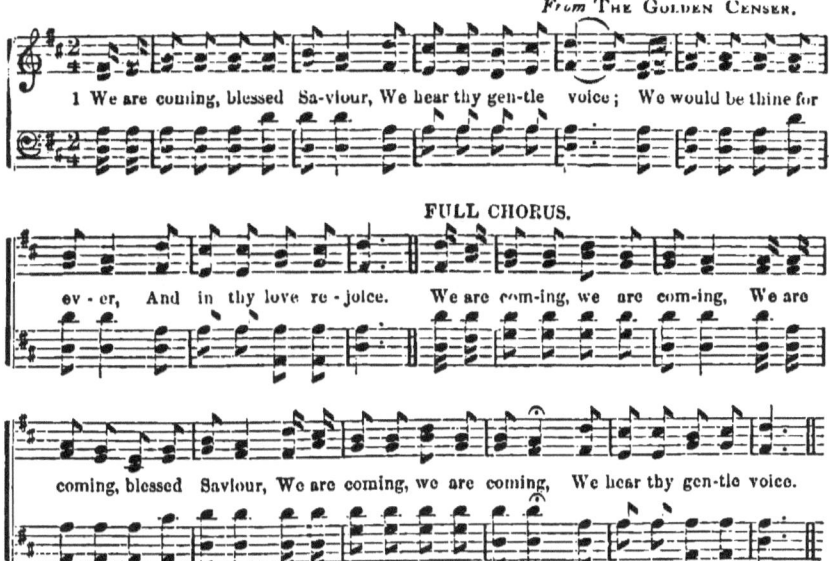

From THE GOLDEN CENSER.

1. We are coming, blessed Saviour, We hear thy gentle voice; We would be thine forever, And in thy love rejoice.

FULL CHORUS. We are coming, we are coming, We are coming, blessed Saviour, We are coming, we are coming, We hear thy gentle voice.

356. "We are Coming, blessed Saviour." (465)

1 WE are coming, blessed Saviour,
We hear thy gentle voice;
We would be thine for ever,
And in thy love rejoice.
We are coming, &c.
We hear thy gentle voice.

2 We are coming, blessed Saviour,
To meet that happy band,
And sing with them for ever,
And in thy presence stand.
We are coming, &c.
To meet that happy band.

3 We are coming, blessed Saviour,
Our Father's house we see—
A glorious mansion ever
For those that trust in thee.
We are coming, &c.
Our Father's house we see.

4 We are coming, blessed Saviour,
That happy home is ours;
If here we gain thy favor
We'll reach those fragrant bowers.
We are coming, &c.
That happy home is ours.

5 We are coming, blessed Saviour,
To crown our Jesus King,
And then with angels ever
His praises we will sing.
We are coming, &c.
To crown our Jesus King.
LYDIA BAXTER.

357. *Dismission.* (599)
Tune OLD HUNDRED, page 6.

1 DISMISS us with thy blessing, Lord;
Help us to feed upon thy word;
All that has been amiss, forgive,
And let thy truth within us live.

2 Though we are guilty, thou art good;
Wash all our works in Jesus' blood;
Give every burdened soul release,
And bid us all depart in peace.
HART.

WOODSTOCK. C. M.

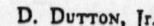

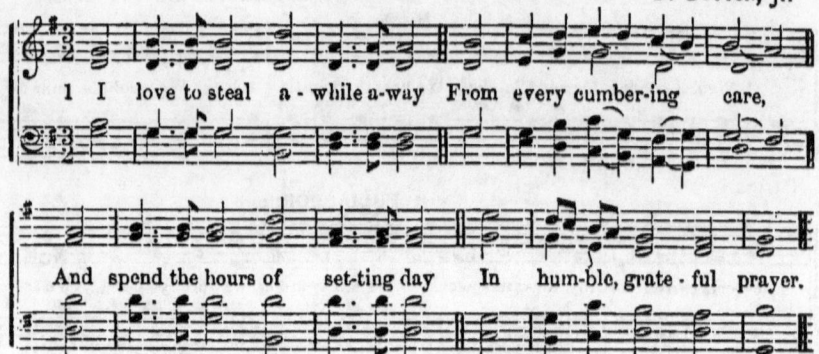

358.   *Evening Devotion.*   (382)

1 I love to steal awhile away
   From every cumbering care,
And spend the hours of setting day
   In humble, grateful prayer.

2 I love in solitude to shed
   The penitential tear,
And all his promises to plead,
   Where none but God can hear.

3 I love to think on mercies past
   And future good implore,
And all my cares and sorrows cast,
   On him whom I adore.

4 I love by faith to take a view
   Of brighter scenes in heaven;
The prospect doth my strength renew,
   While here by tempests driven.

5 Thus when life's toilsome day is o'er,
   May its departing ray,
Be calm as this impressive hour,
   And lead to endless day.
                          Mrs. Brown.

359. *Joy in the Conversion of Sinners.* (129)

1 O, how the hearts of those revive,
   Who fear and love the Lord,
When sinners dead are made alive,
   By his all-quickening word.

2 The church of God their praises join,
   And of salvation sing;
They glorify the grace divine,
   Of their victorious King.

3 But greater joy must they possess,
   Who feel this glorious change;
Their laboring tongues can but express
   How true, and yet how strange!
                          Hoskins.

360.   *Comfort in God.*   (192)

1 Dear Refuge of my weary soul,
   On thee, when sorrows rise,
On thee, when waves of trouble roll,
   My fainting hope relies.

2 To thee I tell each rising grief,
   For thou alone canst heal;
Thy word can bring a sweet relief
   For every pain I feel.

3 But, O, when gloomy doubts prevail,
   I fear to call thee mine;
The springs of comfort seem to fail,
   And all my hopes decline.

4 Yet, gracious God, where shall I flee?
   Thou art my only trust;
And still my soul would cleave to thee,
   Though prostrate in the dust.
                          Steele.

Doxology.

To God the Father glory be,
   And to his only Son;
The same, O Holy Ghost! to thee,
   While ceaseless ages run.

BANKS OF JORDAN. C. M.

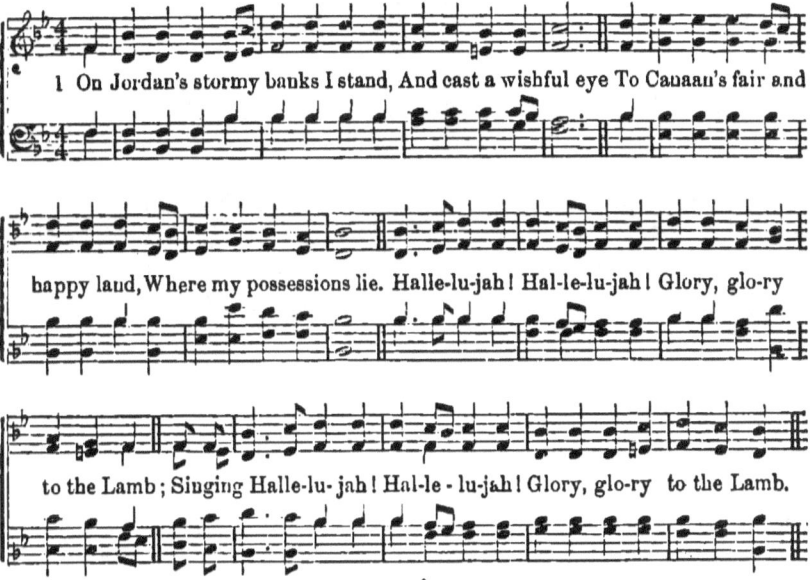

1 On Jordan's stormy banks I stand, And cast a wishful eye To Canaan's fair and happy land, Where my possessions lie. Halle-lu-jah! Hal-le-lu-jah! Glory, glo-ry to the Lamb; Singing Halle-lu-jah! Hal-le-lu-jah! Glory, glo-ry to the Lamb.

361. *The Banks of Jordan.* (438)

1 On Jordan's stormy banks I stand,
  And cast a wishful eye
To Canaan's fair and happy land,
  Where my possessions lie.
    Hallelujah, &c.

2 Oh! the transporting, rapturous scene,
  That rises to my sight!—
Sweet fields, arrayed in living green,
  And rivers of delight.
    Hallelujah, &c.

3 O'er all those wide-extended plains
  Shines one eternal day;
There God the Son forever reigns,
  And scatters night away.
    Hallelujah, &c.

4 When shall I reach that happy place,
  And be for ever blest?
When shall I see my Father's face,
  And in his bosom rest!
    Hallelujah, &c.

5 Filled with delight, my raptured soul
  Would here no longer stay;
Though Jordan's waves around me roll,
  I'd fearless launch away.
    Hallelujah, &c.
        S. STENNETT.

362. *The Saviour Welcome.* (261)
Tune WOODSTOCK, page 140.

1 WELCOME, O Saviour! to my heart;
  Possess thine humble throne;
Bid every rival hence depart,
  And claim me for thine own.

2 The world and Satan I forsake—
  To thee, I all resign;
My longing heart, O Jesus! take,
  And fill with love divine.

3 O, may I never turn aside,
  Nor from thy bosom flee,
Let nothing here my heart divide—
  I give it all to thee.

142   GOLDEN HILL. S. M.   *A Western Tune.*

363.   *The Blessed Bond.*   (362)
1 BLEST be the tie that binds
    Our hearts in Christian love;
    The fellowship of kindred minds
    Is like to that above.

2 Before our Father's throne
    We pour our ardent prayers;
    Our fears, our hopes, our aims are one,
    Our comforts and our cares.

3 We share our mutual woes,
    Our mutual burdens bear;
    And often for each other flows
    The sympathizing tear.

4 When we asunder part,
    It gives us inward pain;
    But we shall still be joined in heart,
    And hope to meet again.

5 This glorious hope revives
    Our courage by the way;
    While each in expectation lives,
    And longs to see the day.
                      FAWCETT.

364.   *Faith in Christ's Sacrifice.*   (123)
1 NOT all the blood of beasts,
    On Jewish altars slain,
    Could give the guilty conscience peace,
    Or wash away the stain.

2 But Christ, the heavenly Lamb,
    Takes all our sins away;
    A sacrifice of nobler name,
    And richer blood, than they.

3 My faith would lay her hand
    On that dear head of thine,
    While like a penitent I stand,
    And there confess my sin.

4 My soul looks back, to see
    The burdens thou didst bear,
    When hanging on the cursed tree,
    And hopes her guilt was there.

5 Believing, we rejoice
    To see the curse remove;
    We bless the Lamb with cheerful voice,
    And sing his bleeding love.
                      WATTS.

365.   *The Sacrifice of Gratitude.*   (554)
1 THY bounties, gracious Lord,
    With gratitude we own;
    We praise thy providential care,
    That showers its blessings down.

2 With joy thy people bring
    Their offerings round thy throne;
    With thankful souls, behold, we pay
    A tribute of thine own.

3 O, may this sacrifice,
    While at thy feet we bend,
    An odor of a sweet perfume
    To thee, the Lord, ascend.

4 Well pleased our God will view
    The products of his grace;
    With endless life will he fulfill
    His kindest promises.
                      E. SCOTT.

366. *Salvation only through the blood of Christ.* (109)

1 NOT what I feel or do
  Can give me peace with God;
  Not all my prayers, and sighs, and tears,
  Can bear my awful load.

  Thy work alone, O Christ,
  Can case this weight of sin;
  Thy blood alone, O Lamb of God,
  Can give me peace within.

3 Thy love to me, O God,
  Not mine, O Lord, to thee,
  Can rid me of this dark unrest,
  And set my spirit free.

4 'Tis Christ who saveth me,
  And freely pardon gives;
  I love because he loveth me,
  I live because he lives.
  BONAR.

367. *Prayer for all Lands.* (531)

1 O GOD of sovereign grace,
  We bow before thy throne,
  And plead, for all the human race,
  The merits of thy Son.

2 Spread through the earth, O Lord,
  The knowledge of thy ways,
  And let all lands with joy record
  The great Redeemer's praise.

368. *Praise for Mercies.* (204)

1 O, BLESS the Lord, my soul;
  His grace to thee proclaim;
  And all that is within me, join
  To bless his holy name.

2 O, bless the Lord, my soul;
  His mercies bear in mind;
  Forget not all his benefits;
  The Lord to thee is kind.

  He will not always chide;
  He will with patience wait;
  His wrath is ever slow to rise,
  And ready to abate.

4 The Lord forgives thy sins,
  Prolongs thy feeble breath;
  He healeth thine infirmities,
  And ransoms thee from death.

5 He clothes thee with his love,
  Upholds thee with his truth,
  And like the eagle he renews
  The vigor of thy youth.

6 Then bless his holy name
  Whose grace hath made thee whole,
  Whose loving kindness crowns thy days;
  O, bless the Lord, my soul.
  MONTGOMERY.

369. *Providence Gracious.* (193)

1 To God, the only wise,
  Our Saviour and our King,
  Let all the saints below the skies,
  Their humble praises bring.

2 'Tis his almighty love,
  His counsel and his care,
  Preserves us safe from sin and death,
  And every hurtful snare.

3 He will present our souls
  Unblemished and complete,
  Before the glory of his face,
  With joys divinely great.

4 Then all the chosen seed
  Shall meet around the throne;
  Shall bless the conduct of his grace,
  And make his wonders known.
  WATTS.

370. *Blessings sought in Prayer.* (403)

1 BEHOLD the throne of grace!
  The promise calls me near;
  There Jesus shows a smiling face,
  And waits to answer prayer.

2 Thine image, Lord, bestow,
  Thy presence and thy love;
  I ask to serve thee here below,
  And reign with thee above.

3 Teach me to live by faith;
  Conform my will to thine,
  Let me victorious be in death,
  And then in glory shine.

144 GRATITUDE. L. M.
Bost.

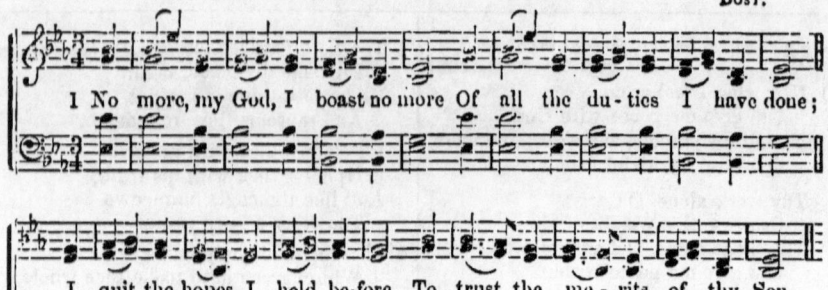

1 No more, my God, I boast no more Of all the du-ties I have done;
I quit the hopes I held be-fore, To trust the me-rits of thy Son.

371. *Depending on Christ's Right-eousness.* (134)

1 No more, my God, I boast no more
   Of all the duties I have done;
   I quit the hopes I held before,
     To trust the merits of thy Son.

2 Now, for the love I bear his name,
   What was my gain I count my loss;
   My former pride I call my shame,
     And nail my glory to his cross.

3 Yes, and I must and will esteem
   All things but loss for Jesus' sake;
   O, may my soul be found in him,
     And of his righteousness partake.

4 The best obedience of my hands
   Dares not appear before thy throne;
   But faith can answer thy demands,
     By pleading what my Lord has done.
                     WATTS.

372. *Church Union.* (360)

1 How blest the sacred tie that binds
   In sweet communion kindred minds:
   How swift the heavenly course they run,
     Whose hearts, whose faith, whose hopes
        are one!

2 To each the soul of each how dear!
   What tender love, what holy fear,
   How does the generous flame within
     Refine from earth, and cleanse from sin!

3 Their streaming eyes together flow
   For human guilt and human wo!
   Their ardent prayers together rise,
     Like mingling flames in sacrifice.

4 Nor shall the glowing flame expire,
   When dimly burns frail nature's fire
   Then shall they meet in realms above—
     A heaven of joy—a heaven of love.
                     BARBAULD.

373. *Seaman's Prayer.* (511

1 BESET with snares on every hand,
   In life's uncertain path I stand;
   Saviour divine! diffuse thy light
     To guide my doubtful footsteps right.

2 Engage this roving, treacherous heart,
   Great God, to choose the better part;
   To scorn the trifles of a day,
     For joys that none can take away.

3 Then let the wildest storms arise;
   Let tempests mingle earth and skies;
   No fatal shipwreck shall I fear,
     But all my treasures with me bear.

4 If thou, my Jesus, still art nigh,
   Cheerful I live, and cheerful die:
   Secure, when mortal comforts flee
     To find ten thousand worlds in thee.
                     DODDRIDGE.

OLIVES' BROW. L. M.
WM. B. BRADBURY.

1 The billows swell; the winds are high; Clouds over-cast my wintry sky: Out of the depths to thee I call; My fears are great, my strength is small.

374. *Temptation Compared to a Storm.* (514)

2 O Lord, the pilot's part perform,
And guide and guard me through the storm!
Defend me from each threatening ill;
Control the waves; say, "Peace! be still."

3 Amidst the roaring of the sea,
My soul still hangs her hope on thee;
Thy constant love, thy faithful care,
Is all that saves me from despair.

4 Dangers of every shape and name
Attend the followers of the Lamb,
Who leave the world's deceitful shore
And leave it to return no more.

5 Though tempest-tossed, and half a wreck,
My Saviour through the floods I seek;
Let neither winds nor stormy rain
Force back my shattered bark again.
COWPER.

375. *Enjoyment of Christ's Love.* (250)

1 JESUS, thy boundless love to me
No thought can reach, no tongue declare;
Unite my thankful heart to thee,
And reign without a rival there.

2 Thy love, how cheering is its ray!
All pain before its presence flies;
Care, anguish, sorrow, melt away
Where'er its healing beams arise.

3 O, let thy love my soul inflame,
And to thy service sweetly bind:
Transfuse it through my inmost frame,
And mould me wholly to thy mind.

4 Thy love, in sufferings, be my peace;
Thy love, in weakness, make me strong;
And, when the storms of life shall cease,
Thy love shall be in heaven my song.
C. WESLEY.

376. *Eternity Near.* (51)

1 ETERNITY is just at hand!
And shall we waste our ebbing sand,
And careless view departing day,
And throw this inch of time away?

2 For all an endless state there is
Of wo extreme, or perfect bliss;
And swift as time fulfills its round,
We to that final doom are bound.

3 What countless millions of mankind
Have left this fleeting world behind!
All gone!—but where?—ah, pause and see,
Gone to a long eternity!

4 Sinner! canst thou for ever dwell
Amid the fiery deeps of hell!
Has death no warning sound for thee?
O, turn, and to the Saviour flee.
STEELE.

THE ANGELS' WELCOME.

Rev. ROBERT LOWRY

377. "*My Rest is in Heaven.*" (482)

1 My rest is in heaven, my rest is not here;
　Then why should I murmur when trials are near?
　Be hush'd, my dark spirit, the worst that can come
　But shortens thy journey, and hastens thee home.
　　Then the angels will come, with their music will come, &c.

2 It is not for me to be seeking my bliss,
　Or building my hopes in a region like this;
　I look for a city that hands have not piled,
　I pant for a country by sin undefiled.
　　Then the angels will come, &c

3 Afflictions may press me, they cannot destroy—
  One glimpse of His love turns them all into joy;
  And the bitterest tears, if he smile but on them,
  Like dew in the sunshine, grow diamond and gem.—*Cho.*

4 Let trial and danger my progress oppose,
  They only make heaven more sweet at its close;
  Come joy, or come sorrow, whate'er may befall,
  An hour with my Saviour will make up for all.—*Cho.*

HOMEWARD BOUND.

J. W. DADMUN.

378. *Homeward Bound.* (440)

1 Out on an ocean all boundless we ride,
  We're homeward bound;
  Tossed on the waves of a rough restless tide,
  We're homeward bound;
  Far from the safe, quiet harbor we rode,
  Seeking our Father's celestial abode,
  Promise of which on us each he bestowed.
  We're homeward bound.

2 Wildly the storm sweeps us on as it roars;
  We're homeward bound;
  Look! yonder lie the bright heavenly shores,
  We're homeward bound;
  Steady! O pilot! stand firm at the wheel,
  Steady, we soon shall outweather the gale,
  Oh! how we fly 'neath the loud creaking sail,
  We're homeward bound.

3 We'll tell the world as we journey along,
  We're homeward bound;
  Try to persuade them to enter our throng,
  We're homeward bound;
  Come, trembling sinner, forlorn and oppressed,
  Join in our number, O come and be blest;
  Journey with us to the mansions of rest,
  We're homeward bound.

4 Into the harbor of heaven we now glide,
  We're home at last;
  Softly we drift on its bright silver tide,
  We're home at last;
  Glory to God! all our dangers are o'er;
  We stand secure on the glorified shore,
  Glory to God! we will shout evermore,
  We're home at last.

HENDON. 7s.

Rev. Dr. Malan.

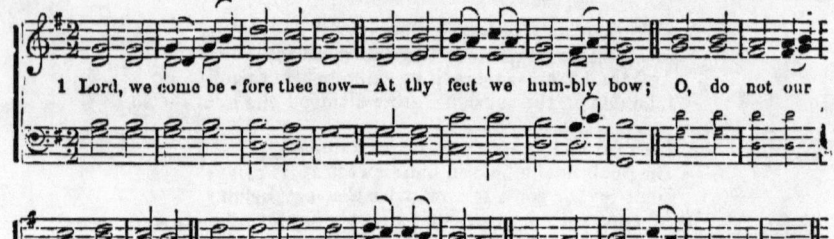

1 Lord, we come before thee now— At thy feet we humbly bow; O, do not our suit disdain! Shall we seek thee, Lord, in vain, Shall we seek thee, Lord, in vain?

379. *Blessing Sought.* (3)

1 Lord, we come before thee now—
At thy feet we humbly bow:
O, do not our suit disdain!
Shall we seek thee, Lord, in vain?

2 Lord, on thee our souls depend;
In compassion now descend;
Fill our hearts with thy rich grace,
Tune our lips to sing thy praise.

3 In thy own appointed way,
Now we seek thee, here we stay;
Lord, we know not how to go,
Till a blessing thou bestow.

4 Send some message from thy word,
That may peace and joy afford;
Let thy Spirit now impart
Full salvation to each heart.
HAMMOND.

380. *Christ the Ground of Hope.* (321)

1 Christ, of all my hopes the ground—
Christ, the spring of all my joy!
Still in thee let me be found,
Still for thee my powers employ.

2 Fountain of o'erflowing grace!
Freely from thy fullness give;
Till I close my earthly race,
Be it "Christ for me to live!"

3 Firmly trusting in thy blood,
Nothing shall my heart confound;
Safely I shall pass the flood,
Safely reach Immanuel's ground.

4 Thus—O, thus an entrance give
To the land of cloudless sky;
Having known it, "Christ to live,"
Let me know it, "gain to die."
WINDHAM.

381. *Danger of Delay.* (44)

1 Haste, O, sinner; now be wise;
Stay not for the morrow's sun;
Wisdom if you still despise,
Harder is it to be won.

2 Haste, and mercy now implore;
Stay not for the morrow's sun,
Lest thy season should be o'er,
Ere this evening's stage be run.

3 Haste, O, sinner; now return;
Stay not for the morrow's sun,
Lest thy lamp should cease to burn,
Ere salvation's work is done.

4 Haste, O, sinner; now be blest;
Stay not for the morrow's sun,
Lest perdition thee arrest,
Ere the morrow is begun.
T. SCOTT.

1 Come, my soul, thy suit prepare, Jesus loves to answer prayer; He himself hath bid thee pray, Rise and ask without delay.

382. *Encouragement to Prayer.* (406)

2 Thou art coming to a King,
Large petitions with thee bring;
For his grace and power are such,
None can ever ask too much.

3 With my burden I begin;
Lord, remove this load of sin!
Let thy blood for sinners spilt,
Set my conscience free from guilt!

4 Lord, I come to thee for rest;
Take possession of my breast;
There, thy blood-bought right maintain,
And, without a rival, reign.
NEWTON.

383. *Strength Equal to the Day.* (284)

1 WAIT, my soul, upon the Lord,
To his gracious promise flee,
Laying hold upon his word,
"As thy days, thy strength shall be."

2 If the sorrows of thy case
Seem peculiar still to thee,
God has promised needful grace,
"As thy days, thy strength shall be."

3 Days of trial, days of grief,
In succession thou may'st see;
This is still thy sweet relief,
"As thy days thy strength shall be."

4 Rock of Ages, I'm secure,
With thy promise full and free;
Faithful, positive, and sure,—
"As thy days thy strength shall be."

384. *The Sweet Communion.* (401)

1 LORD, 'tis sweet to mingle where
Christians meet for social prayer;
O, 'tis sweet with them to raise
Songs of holy joy and praise!

2 From thy gracious presence flows
Bliss that softens all our woes;
While thy Spirit's holy fire
Warms our hearts with pure desire.

3 Here we supplicate thy throne;
Here, thy pardoning grace is known;
Here, we learn thy righteous ways,
Taste thy love, and sing thy praise.

4 Thus with prayer, and hymns of joy,
We the happy hours employ;
Love, and long to love thee more,
Till from earth to heaven we soar.
TURNER

385. *What Religion Gives.* (456)

1 'TIS religion that can give
Sweetest pleasure while we live;
'Tis religion must supply
Solid comfort when we die.

2 After death its joys shall be
Lasting as eternity;
Be the living God our friend,
Then our bliss shall never end.
MASTERS.

150   PLEYEL'S HYMN. 7s.
J. PLEYEL.

1 Depth of mer-cy!—can there be Mer-cy still reserved for me?
Can my God his wrath for-bear, And the chief of sin-ners spare?

386.   *The Penitent Inquirer.*   (86)

2 I have long withstood his grace;
Long provoked him to his face;
Would not hear his gracious calls;
Grieved him by a thousand falls.

3 Jesus, answer from above:
Is not all thy nature love?
Wilt thou not the wrong forget?—
Lo, I fall before thy feet.

4 Now incline me to repent;
Let me now my fall lament;
Deeply my revolt deplore;
Weep, believe, and sin no more.
                               C. WESLEY.

387.   *Expostulation.*   (31)

1 SINNER, what has earth to show
Like the joys believers know?
Is thy path of fading flowers
Half so bright, so sweet, as ours?

2 Doth a skillful, healing friend
On thy daily path attend,
And, where thorns and stings abound,
Shed a balm on every wound?

3 When the tempest rolls on high,
Hast thou still a refuge nigh?
Can, O, can thy dying breath
Summon one more strong than death

4 Canst thou, in that awful day,
Fearless tread the gloomy way,
Plead a glorious ransom given,
Burst from earth, and soar to heaven?

388.   *Confession of Sin.*   (104)

1 GOD of mercy, God of grace,
   Hear our sad repentant songs;
O, restore thy suppliant race,
   Thou, to whom our praise belongs.

2 Deep regret for follies past,
   Talents wasted, time misspent;—
Hearts debased by worldly cares,
   Thankless for the blessings lent;—

3 Foolish fears, and fond desires,
   Vain regrets for things as vain,
Lips too seldom taught to praise,
   Oft to murmur and complain;—

4 These, and every secret fault,
   Filled with grief and shame, we own
Humbled at thy feet we lie,
   Seeking pardon from thy throne.

5 God of mercy, God of grace,
   Hear our sad repentant songs;
O, restore thy suppliant race,
   Thou, to whom our praise belongs.
                               J. TAYLOR.

FULTON. 7s. 151
WM. B. BRADBURY.

1 Hark, my soul, it is the Lord; 'Tis thy Saviour, hear his word; Jesus speaks, and speaks to thee: "Say, poor sinner, lov'st thou me?"

389. *Lovest thou Me?* (243)

2 "I delivered thee when bound,
And, when wounded, healed thy wound;
Sought thee wandering, set thee right,
Turned thy darkness into light.

3 "Can a woman's tender care
Cease toward the child she bare?
Yes, she may forgetful be,
Yet will I remember thee.

4 "Mine is an unchanging love,
Higher than the heights above;
Deeper than the depths beneath,
Free and faithful, strong as death.

5 "Thou shalt see my glory soon,
When the work of grace is done;
Partner of my throne shalt be;
Say, poor sinner, lov'st thou me?"

6 Lord, it is my chief complaint,
That my love is weak and faint;
Yet I love thee and adore,
O, for grace to love thee more.
NEWTON.

390. *The Secure Admonished.* (28)

1 SINNER, art thou still secure?
Wilt thou still refuse to pray?
Can thy heart or hand endure
In the Lord's avenging day?

2 See, his mighty arm is bared,
Awful terrors clothe his brow!
For his judgment stand prepared—
Thou must either break or bow.

3 Who his advent may abide?
You, who glory in your shame,
Will you find a place to hide,
When the world is wrapped in flame?

4 Let us now our day improve,
Listen to the gospel's voice;
Seek the things that are above;
Scorn the world's pretended joys.
NEWTON.

391. *"Awake thou that Sleepest."* (20)

1 SINNER, rouse thee from thy sleep;
Wake, and o'er thy folly weep;
Raise thy spirit, dark and dead;
Jesus waits his light to shed.

2 Wake from sleep; arise from death;
See the bright and living path;
Watchful, tread that path; be wise;
Leave thy folly; seek the skies.

3 Leave thy folly; cease from crime;
From this hour redeem thy time;
Life secure without delay;
Evil is thy mortal day.

4 O, then, rouse thee from thy sleep;
Wake, and o'er thy folly weep;
Jesus calls from death and night;
Jesus waits to shed his light.

152 SHALL WE MEET BEYOND THE RIVER?

Wm. B. Bradbury.

1 Shall we meet beyond the river, Where the surges cease to roll,
Where in all the bright forever, Sorrow ne'er shall press the soul.
D. S. Shall we meet beyond the river, Where the surges cease to roll?

CHORUS.
Shall we meet? shall we meet? Shall we meet beyond the river,

392. *Shall we Meet beyond the River.* (462)

2 Shall we meet in that blest harbor,
   When our stormy voyage is o'er?
Shall we meet and cast the anchor,
   By the fair celestial shore?

3 Shall we meet in yonder city,
   Where the towers of crystal shine,
Where the walls are all of jasper,
   Built by workmanship divine?

4 Where the music of the ransomed
   Rolls its harmony around,
And creation swells the chorus,
   With its sweet melodious sound?

5 Shall we meet with many a loved one,
   That was torn from our embrace?
Shall we listen to their voices,
   And behold them face to face?

Shall we meet with Christ our Saviour,
   When he comes to claim his own?
Shall we know his blessed favor,
   And sit down upon his throne?

393. *The Home Missionary's Example.* (510)
Tune BARTIMEUS, page 94.

1 ONWARD, herald of the gospel,
   Bear thy tidings through the land;
Preach the word, as heaven's apostle,
   Sent by Christ's divine command.

2 Jesus, once the gospel preaching,
   Through his native Judah went,
Salem's sons in mercy teaching,
   Calling Israel to repent.

3 Israel, all his deep love slighting,
   Spurning all his tenderness,
Still he followed, still inviting,
   Weeping where he could not bless.

4 Follow, then, thy Lord's example;
   Toil in hope, nor faint, nor fear,
For thy needs his grace is ample,
   At thy side he's ever near.

5 Work, until the day is ended,
   Till thy sun sinks in the West;
Then, with joy and triumph blended,
   Christ shall bring thee to his rest.

G. W. ANDERSON.

NO SORROW THERE. S. M. 153

Rev. E. W. Dunbar.

1 I love to think of heaven, Where white-robed an-gels are;
Where many a friend is gath-ered safe, From fear, and toil, and care.

Cho. There'll be no sor-row there, There'll be no sor-row there;
In heaven a-bove, where all is love, There'll be no sor-row there.

394. *I Love to Think of Heaven.* (474)

2 I love to think of heaven,
 Where my Redeemer reigns;
Where rapturous songs of triumph rise,
 In endless, joyous strains.
  There'll be no sorrow there, &c.

3 I love to think of heaven,
 The saints' eternal home;
Where palms, and robes, and crowns ne'er fade,
 And all our joys are one.
  There'll be no sorrow there, &c.

4 I love to think of heaven,
 The greetings there we'll meet;
The harps—the songs for ever ours—
 The walks—the golden streets.
  There'll be no sorrow there, &c.

5 I love to think of heaven,
 That promised land so fair;
O, how my raptured spirit longs
 To be for ever there.
  There'll be no sorrow there, &c.

395. *"Jesus Wept."* (239)

1 Did Jesus weep for me?
 And sigh o'er sinners here?
My soul that weeping Saviour see,
 And shed thyself a tear.

2 Did Jesus pray for me?
 For such a wand'rer care?
My heart subdued and broken be,
 And drawn to him in prayer.

3 Did Jesus die for me?
 Oh, depth of love divine!
I die to sin—I'll live to thee;
 O, Saviour, make me thine!
  S. D. Phelps.

396. *The Dying Saint.* (580)

1 O, sing to me of heaven,
 When I am called to die,
Sing songs of holy ecstacy,
 To waft my soul on high.—*Cho.*

2 When the last moment comes,
 O, watch my dying face,
To catch the bright seraphic gleam,
 Which o'er my features plays.—*Cho.*

3 Then to my raptured soul,
 Let one sweet song be given,
Let music cheer me last on earth,
 And greet me first in heaven.—*Cho.*

4 Then round my senseless clay,
 Assemble those I love,
And sing of heaven, delightful heaven,
 My glorious home above.—*Cho.*

TAPPAN. C. M.

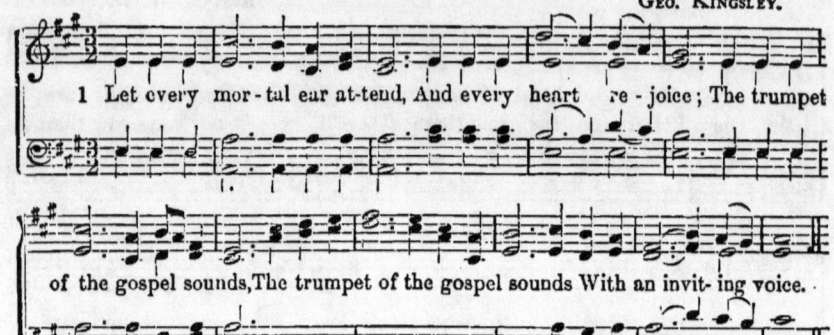

397. *The Gospel Feast.* (68)

1 LET every mortal ear attend,
  And every heart rejoice;
  The trumpet of the gospel sounds
  With an inviting voice.

2 Ho! all ye hungry, starving souls,
  That feed upon the wind,
  And vainly strive with earthly toys
  To fill an empty mind,—

3 Eternal Wisdom has prepared
  A soul-reviving feast,
  And bids your longing appetites
  The rich provision taste.

4 Ho! ye that pant for living streams,
  And pine away and die,—
  Here you may quench your raging thirst,
  With springs that never dry.
                              WATTS.

398. *King of Saints.* (275)

1 COME, ye that love the Saviour's name,
  And joy to make it known,
  The Sovereign of your hearts proclaim,
  And bow before his throne.

2 When in his earthly courts we view
  The glories of our King,
  We long to love as angels do,
  And wish like them to sing.

3 And shall we long and wish in vain?
  Lord, teach our songs to rise:
  Thy love can raise our humble strain,
  And bid it reach the skies.

4 Oh, happy period! glorious day!
  When heaven and earth shall raise,
  With all their powers, their raptured lay,
  To celebrate thy praise.
                              STEELE.

399. *Ministerial Responsibility.* (159)

1 LET Zion's watchmen all awake,
  And take the alarm they give;
  Now let them from the mouth of God
  Their solemn charge receive.

2 'Tis not a cause of small import
  The pastor's care demands;
  But what might fill an angel's heart,
  And filled a Saviour's hands.

3 They watch for souls, for which the Lord
  Did heavenly bliss forego;
  For souls which must for ever live
  In raptures or in woe.

4 May they that Jesus whom they preach,
  Their own Redeemer see;
  Lord, watch thou daily o'er their souls,
  That they may watch for thee.
                              DODDRIDGE.

DOWNS. C. M. 155
Dr. LOWELL MASON.

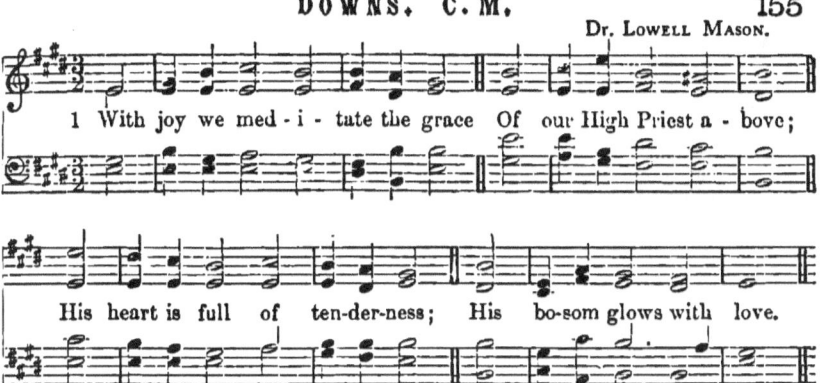

1 With joy we med-i-tate the grace Of our High Priest a-bove;
His heart is full of ten-der-ness; His bo-som glows with love.

400. *Christ a Merciful High Priest.* (234)

1 WITH joy we meditate the grace
    Of our High Priest above;
His heart is full of tenderness;
    His bosom glows with love.

2 Touched with a sympathy within,
    He knows our feeble frame;
He knows what sore temptations mean,
    For he has felt the same.

3 He, in the days of feeble flesh,
    Poured out his cries and tears,
And in his measure feels afresh
    What every member bears.

4 Then let our humble faith address
    His mercy and his power;
We shall obtain delivering grace,
    In each distressing hour.
            WATTS.

401. *Prayer for the World's Conversion.* (530)

1 PITY the nations, O our God;
    Constrain the earth to come;
Send thy victorious word abroad,
    And bring the strangers home.

2 We long to see thy churches full,
    That all the chosen race
May, with one voice, and heart, and soul,
    Sing thy redeeming grace.
            WATTS.

402. *A Name above every Name.* (267)

1 JESUS, in thy transporting name
    What glories meet our eyes!
Thou art the seraph's lofty theme,
    The wonder of the skies.

2 Well might the heavens with wonder view
    A love so strange as thine;
No thought of angels ever knew
    Compassion so divine.

3 And didst thou, Saviour, leave the sky,
    To sink beneath our woes?
Didst thou descend to bleed and die
    For thy rebellious foes?

4 O, may our willing hearts confess
    Thy sweet, thy gentle sway:
Glad captives of thy matchless grace,
    Thy righteous rule obey.
            STEELE.

403. *Christ's Inheritance.* (522)

1 GREAT God, is not thy promise pledged
    To thine exalted Son,
That through the nations of the earth
    Thy word of Life shall run?

2 From east to west, from north to south,
    Then be his name adored:
Let earth, with all its millions, shout
    Hosanna to the Lord!

404. *Security in Christ.* (287)

2 Art thou not mine, my living Lord?
  And can my hope, my comfort, die?
  'Tis fixed on thine almighty word—
    That word which built the earth and sky.

3 If my immortal Saviour lives,
    Then my immortal life is sure;
  His word a firm foundation gives;
    Here I may build and rest secure.

4 Here let my faith unshaken dwell;
    Forever sure the promise stands;
  Not all the powers of earth or hell
    Can e'er dissolve the sacred bands.

5 Here, O, my soul, thy trust repose;
    If Jesus is forever mine,
  Not death itself—that last of foes—
    Shall break a union so divine.
            STEELE.

405. *Prayer Answered by Crosses.* (396)

1 I asked the Lord, that I might grow
    In faith, and love, and every grace;
  Might more of his salvation know,
    And seek more earnestly his face.

2 I hoped that in some favored hour,
    At once he'd answer my request;
  And by his love's constraining power,
    Subdue my sins and give me rest.

3 Instead of this, he made me feel
    The hidden evils of my heart;
  And let the angry powers of hell
    Assault my soul in every part.

4 "Lord, why is this?" I, trembling, crie
  "Wilt thou pursue thy worm till death?
  "'Tis in this way," the Lord replied,
  "I answer prayer for grace and fait

5 "These inward trials I employ,
    From self and pride to set thee fre
  And break thy schemes of earthly jo
    That thou may'st seek thy all in m
            NEWTON

406. *The Cross.* (2?

1 Inscribed upon the cross we see,
    In glowing letters, "God is love;"
  He bears our sins upon the tree;
    He brings us mercy from above.

2 The cross! it takes our guilt away;
    It holds the fainting spirit up;
  It cheers with hope the gloomy day
    And sweetens every bitter cup:—

3 The balm of life, the cure of woe,
    The measure and the pledge of lo
  The sinner's refuge here below,
    The angel's theme in heaven abov
            KELL

EVENING EXPOSTULATION. L. M.

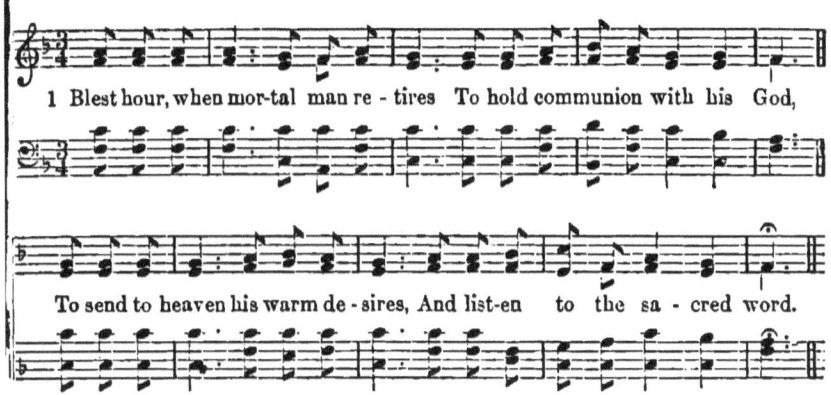

1 Blest hour, when mortal man retires To hold communion with his God, To send to heaven his warm desires, And listen to the sacred word.

407. *The Hour of Prayer.* (397)

2 Blest hour, when earthly cares resign
Their empire o'er his anxious breast,
While, all around, the calm divine
Proclaims the holy day of rest.

3 Blest hour, when God himself draws nigh,
Well pleased his people's voice to hear,
To hush the penitential sigh,
And wipe away the mourner's tear.

4 Blest hour! for, where the Lord resorts,
Foretastes of future bliss are given,
And mortals find his earthly courts
The house of God, the gate of heaven.
RAFFLES.

408. *The Teaching of Christ.* (220)

1 How sweetly flowed the gospel sound,
From lips of gentleness and grace,
When listening thousands gathered round,
And joy and gladness filled the place!

2 From heaven he came, of heaven he spoke,
To heaven he led his followers' way;
Dark clouds of gloomy night he broke,
Unvailing an immortal day.

3 "Come, wanderers, to my Father's home
Come, all ye weary ones, and rest;"
Yes, sacred Teacher, we will come,
Obey thee, love thee, and be blest.

4 Decay, then, tenements of dust;
Pillars of earthly pride, decay;
A nobler mansion waits the just,
And Jesus has prepared the way.
BOWRING.

409 *"Go, labor on."* (501)

1 Go, labor on; your hands are weak,
Your knees are faint, your soul cast down;
Yet falter not; the prize you seek
Is near,—a kingdom and a crown!

2 Go, labor on, while it is day;
The world's dark night is hastening on;
Speed, speed thy work,—cast sloth away!
It is not thus that souls are won.

3 Men die in darkness at your side,
Without a hope to cheer the tomb:
Take up the torch, and wave it wide—
The torch that lights time's thickest gloom.

4 Toil on, faint not,—keep watch, and pray!
Be wise the erring soul to win;
Go forth into the world's highway;
Compel the wanderer to come in.

ALETTA. 7s, 6 lines.

Wm. B. Bradbury.

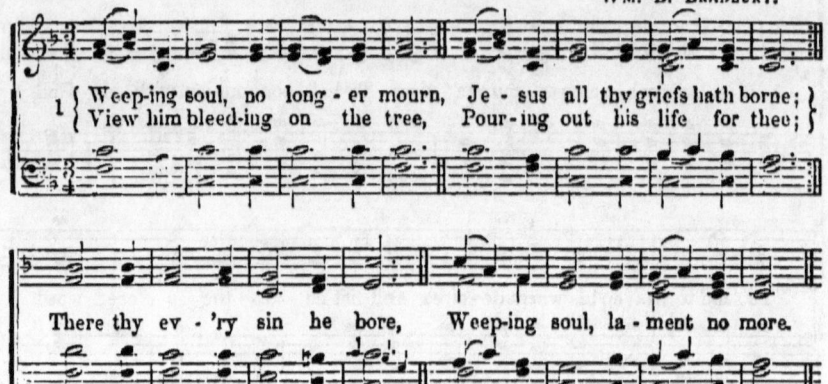

1. Weep-ing soul, no long-er mourn, Je-sus all thy griefs hath borne;
View him bleed-ing on the tree, Pour-ing out his life for thee;
There thy ev-'ry sin he bore, Weep-ing soul, la-ment no more.

---

410. *"He hath Borne our Griefs."* (110)

1 Weeping soul, no longer mourn,
Jesus all thy griefs hath borne;
View him bleeding on the tree,
Pouring out his life for thee;
There thy every sin he bore,
Weeping soul, lament no more.

2 All thy crimes on him were laid;
See upon his blameless head
Wrath its utmost vengeance pours,
Due to my offense and yours;
Weary sinner, keep thine eyes
On the atoning sacrifice.

3 Cast thy guilty soul on him,
Find him mighty to redeem;
At his feet thy burden lay,
Look thy doubts and fears away;
Now by faith the Son embrace,
Plead his promise, trust his grace.

4 Lord, thy arm must be revealed,
Ere I can by faith be healed;
Since I scarce can look to thee,
Cast a gracious eye on me;
At thy feet myself I lay,
Shine, oh, shine my sins away.
Toplady.

411. *Heart of Stone.* (92)

1 Heart of stone, relent, relent;
Break, by Jesus' cross subdued;
See his body mangled, rent,
Covered with a gore of blood;
Sinful soul, what hast thou done?
Crucified th' eternal Son.

2 Yes, thy sins have done the deed,
Driven the nails that fixed him there,
Crowned with thorns his sacred head,
Plunged into his side the spear,
Made his soul a sacrifice,
While for sinful man he dies.

3 Wilt thou let him bleed in vain?
Still to death thy Lord pursue?
Open all his wounds again?
And the shameful cross renew?
"No! with all my sins I'll part,
Saviour, take my broken heart."
C. Wesley.

412. *False Confidence.* (373)

1 Once I thought my mountain strong.
Firmly fixed no more to move;
Then my Saviour was my song,
Then my soul was filled with love
Those were happy, golden days,
Sweetly spent in prayer and praise.

HYMNS.

2 Little, then, myself I knew,
   Little thought of Satan's power;
   Now I feel my sins renew,
   Now I feel the stormy hour;
   Sin has put my joys to flight—
   Sin has turned my day to night.

3 Saviour! shine, and cheer my soul;
   Bid my dying hopes revive;
   Make my wounded spirit whole;
   Far away the tempter drive;
   Speak the word, and set me free—
   Let me live alone to Thee.
   NEWTON.

ROCK OF AGES. 7s, 6 lines.
Dr. T. HASTINGS.

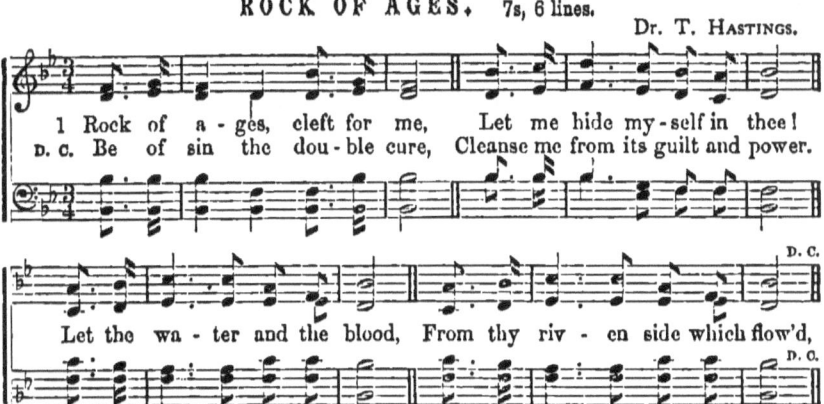

1 Rock of a-ges, cleft for me, Let me hide my-self in thee!
D. C. Be of sin the dou-ble cure, Cleanse me from its guilt and power.

Let the wa-ter and the blood, From thy riv-en side which flow'd,

413. *Rock of Ages.* (285)
[ORIGINAL FORM.]

2 Not the labors of my hands
   Can fulfill thy law's demands:
   Could my zeal no respite know,
   Could my tears forever flow,
   All for sin could not atone;
   Thou must save, and thou alone!

3 Nothing in my hand I bring;
   Simply to thy cross I cling;
   Naked, come to thee for dress;
   Helpless, look to thee for grace;
   Foul, I to thy fountain fly;
   Wash me, Saviour, or I die!

4 While I draw this fleeting breath,
   When my eyestrings break in death,
   When I soar to worlds unknown,
   See thee on thy judgment throne
   Rock of Ages, cleft for me,
   Let me hide myself in Thee.
   TOPLADY.

414. *Prayer for the Unconverted.* (12)

1 SAVED ourselves by Jesus' blood,
   Let us now draw nigh to God;
   Many round us blindly stray;
   Moved with pity, let us pray—
   Pray that they who now are blind
   Soon the way of Truth may find.

2 Lord, awaken all around,
   Let them know the joyful sound;
   Slaves to Satan heretofore,
   Let them now be slaves no more;
   Lord, we turn our eyes to thee,
   Set the captive sinner free!

3 Glorious things of thee are told,
   What thine arm has wrought of old;
   Thousands once its power confessed;
   O, for seasons like the past;
   Lord, revive the former days—
   Thine the power, and thine the praise!
   KELLY.

ROCKPORT. 7s, 6s, & 8s.

I. B. WOODBURY.

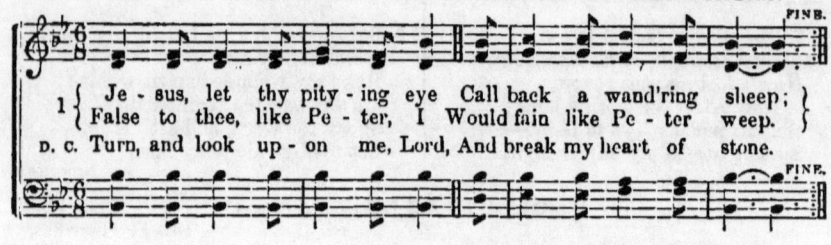

1 Jesus, let thy pitying eye Call back a wand'ring sheep;
False to thee, like Peter, I Would fain like Peter weep.
D.C. Turn, and look upon me, Lord, And break my heart of stone.

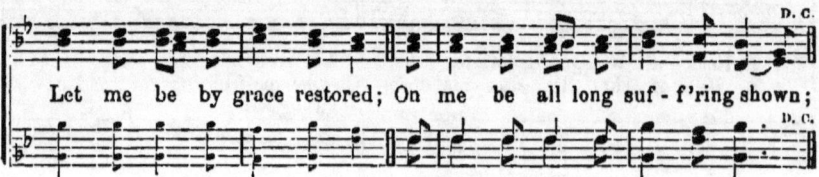

Let me be by grace restored; On me be all long suf-f'ring shown;

415. *The Backslider's Prayer.* (371)

1 JESUS, let thy pitying eye
 Call back a wand'ring sheep;
 False to thee, like Peter, I
 Would fain like Peter weep.
 Let me be by grace restored;
 On me be all long-suff'ring shown;
 Turn, and look upon me, Lord,
 And break my heart of stone.

2 Saviour, Prince, enthroned above,
 Repentance to impart,
 Give me, through thy dying love,
 The humble, contrite heart,
 This I should have long implored,
 For thou hast all my vileness known;
 Turn, and look upon me, Lord,
 And break my heart of stone.

3 See me, Saviour, from above,
 Nor suffer me to die;
 Life and happiness and love
 Smile in thy gracious eye;
 Speak the reconciling word,
 And let thy mercy melt me down;
 Turn and look upon me, Lord,
 And break my heart of stone.
 C. WESLEY.

416. *The Warning.* (40)

1 STOP, poor sinner! stop and think,
 Before you farther go!
 Will you sport upon the brink
 Of everlasting wo?
 Once again, we charge you stop!
 For, unless you warning take,
 Quick and sudden you will drop
 Into the burning lake.

2 Say, have you an arm like God,
 That you his will oppose?
 Fear you not that iron rod,
 With which he breaks his foes?
 Can you stand in that dread day,
 When he judgment shall proclaim,
 And the earth shall melt away,
 Like wax before the flame?

3 Soon relentless death will come,
 To drag you to his bar;
 Then, to hear your awful doom,
 Will fill you with despair;
 All your sins will round you crowd,
 Countless, and of crimson dye;
 Each for vengeance crying loud,
 And what can you reply?
 NEWTON.

A FRIEND THAT'S EVER NEAR. 161
Wm. B. Bradbury.

1. Tho' the days are dark with trouble, And thy heart is filled with fear, There is one that sees thee ev - er, And will hold thee near and dear.
Cheerful hearts and smiling fa - ces Oft - en make thee hap-py here; Yet no one was e'er so hap - py, But sometimes the clouds ap - pear.

REFRAIN.
There's a friend that's ev - er near, Ne - ver fear; He is ev - er near, Ne - ver, ne - ver fear,
There's a friend that's ev - er near, Ne - ver fear, He is ev - er near, Ne - ver fear.
Repeat pp

417. *A Friend that's ever Near.* (425)

2. All thy prospects will seem brighter
When the shadow leaves the heart
And the steps of time beat lighter,
When the gloomy clouds depart.
Many days have dawned serenely,
While the birds sang with delight;
But the skies were dark and gloomy
Ere the sun had reached its height.
There's a friend, &c.

3. Soon will dawn a brighter morning,
On a blessed tranquil shore;
Sighs will then give place to singing,
Tears to bliss for ever more.
Thou shalt see a world of glory,
And eternal joy and bliss;
Let not then thy soul be moaning
O'er the woes and cares of this.
There's a friend, &c.

162   HAIL TO THE BRIGHTNESS.   11s & 10.

Dr. L. Mason.

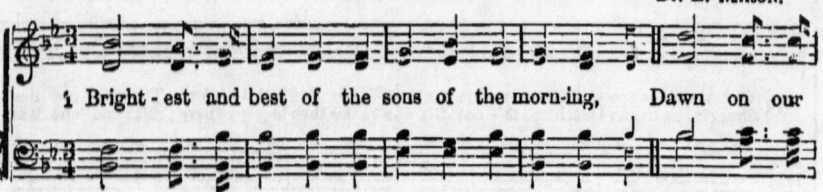
1 Bright-est and best of the sons of the morn-ing, Dawn on our

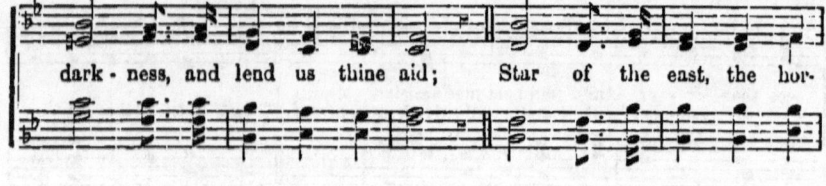
dark-ness, and lend us thine aid; Star of the east, the hor-

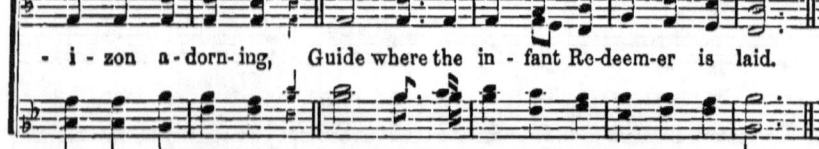
-i-zon a-dorn-ing, Guide where the in-fant Re-deem-er is laid.

418.   *The Infant Saviour.*   (216)

1 BRIGHTEST and best of the sons of the morning,
   Dawn on our darkness, and lend us thine aid;
Star of the east, the horizon adorning,
   Guide where the infant Redeemer is laid.

2 Cold, on his cradle, the dew-drops are shining;
   Low lies his bed with the beasts of the stall;
Angels adore him in slumber reclining,
   Maker, and Monarch, and Saviour of all.

3 Say, shall we yield him, in costly devotion,
   Odors of Eden and offerings divine?
Gems of the mountain, and pearls of the ocean,
   Myrrh from the forest, and gold from the mine!

4 Vainly we offer each ample oblation;
   Vainly with gifts would his favor secure:
Richer by far is the heart's adoration;
   Dearer to God are the prayers of the poor.

                                                                                      HEBER.

HYMNS.

419. *The Church Victorious.* (543)
Tune, HAIL TO THE BRIGHTNESS.

1 DAUGHTER of Zion, awake from thy sadness;
  Awake, for thy foes shall oppress thee no more;
  Bright o'er thy hills dawns the day-star of gladness;
  Arise, for the night of thy sorrow is o'er.

2 Strong were thy foes; but the arm that subdued them,
  And scattered their legions, was mightier far;
  They fled like the chaff from the scourge that pursued them,
  Vain were their steeds and their chariots of war.

3 Daughter of Zion, the power that hath saved thee
  Extolled with the harp and the timbrel should be;
  Shout, for the foe is destroyed that enslaved thee;
  Th' oppressor is vanquished, and Zion is free.

AMSTERDAM. 7s & 6s.

1 { Rise my soul and stretch thy wings; Thy better portion trace; [OMIT - - -
    Rise from trans-i-to-ry things, Towards heav'n, thy native place.
D. C. Rise, my soul, and haste a-way, To [OMIT - - - -] seats prepared a-
- bove. Sun, and moon, and stars de-cay, Time shall soon this earth re-move.

420. *Mounting Upward.* (478)

1 RISE, my soul, and stretch thy wings;
  Thy better portion trace;
  Rise from transitory things,
  Towards heaven, thy native place.
  Sun, and moon, and stars, decay;
  Time shall soon this earth remove;
  Rise, my soul, and haste away
  To seats prepared above.

2 Rivers to the ocean run,
  Nor stay in all their course;
  Fire, ascending, seeks the sun;
  Both speed them to their source:
  So a soul that's born of God
  Pants to view his glorious face,
  Upward tends to his abode,
  To rest in his embrace.

3 Cease, ye pilgrims, cease to mourn;
  Press onward to the prize;
  Soon our Saviour will return,
  Triumphant in the skies;
  Yet a season, and you know
  Happy entrance will be given,
  All our sorrows left below,
  And earth exchanged for heaven.

CENNICK.

AVON. C. M.

Scottish.

1 How sad our state by nature is! Our sin, how deep it stains!
And Satan binds our captive minds Fast in his slavish chains.

421. *The Sinner's Recovery from Ruin.* (101)

2 But there's a voice of sovereign grace
  Sounds from the sacred word;
  "Ho! ye despairing sinners, come,
  And trust upon the Lord."

3 My soul obeys the almighty call,
  And runs to this relief:
  I would believe thy promise, Lord,
  O, help my unbelief.

4 To the dear fountain of thy blood,
  Incarnate God, I fly:
  Here let me wash my spotted soul,
  From crimes of deepest dye.

5 A guilty, weak and helpless worm,
  On thy kind arms I fall:
  Be thou my strength and righteousness,
  My Jesus and my all.   WATTS.

422. *Repentance in view of God's Patience.* (85)

1 AND are we, wretches, yet alive?
  And do we yet rebel!
  'Tis boundless, 'tis amazing love,
  That bears us up from hell!

2 The burden of our weighty guilt
  Would sink us down to flames;
  And threatening terror rolls above,
  To crush our feeble frames.

3 Almighty goodness cries, "Forbear!"
  And straight the thunder stays:
  And dare we now provoke his wrath,
  And weary out his grace?

4 Lord, we have long abused thy love,
  Too long indulged our sin;
  Our aching hearts now bleed to see
  What rebels we have been.

5 No more, ye lusts, shall ye command;
  Nor more will we obey;
  Stretch out, O God, thy conquering hand,
  And drive thy foes away.   WATTS.

423. *Difficulty and Dependence.* (345)

1 STRAIT is the way, the door is strait,
  That leads to joys on high:
  'Tis but a few that find the gate,
  While crowds mistake and die.

2 Beloved self must be denied,
  The mind and will renewed,
  Passion suppressed, and patience tried,
  And vain desires subdued.

3 Lord, can a feeble, helpless worm
  Fulfill a task so hard?
  Thy grace must all the work perform,
  And give the free reward.   WATTS.

424. *The Gospel Feast.* (150)

1 How sweet and awful is the place,
   With Christ within the doors,
While everlasting love displays
   The choicest of her stores!

2 While all our hearts, and every song,
   Join to admire the feast,
Each of us cries, with thankful tongue,
   "Lord, why was I a guest?"

3 "Why was I made to hear thy voice,
   And enter while there's room,
When thousands make a wretched choice,
   And rather starve than come?"

4 'Twas the same love that spread the feast
   That sweetly forced us in;
Else we had still refused to taste,
   And perished in our sin.   WATTS.

425. *Subdued by the Cross.* (128)

1 In evil long I took delight,
   Unawed by shame or fear,
Till a new object struck my sight,
   And stopped my wild career.

2 I saw One hanging on a tree,
   In agonies and blood,
Who fixed his languid eyes on me,
   As near his cross I stood.

3 Sure, never till my latest breath,
   Can I forget that look;
It seemed to charge me with his death,
   Though not a word he spoke.

4 My conscience felt and owned the guilt,
   And plunged me in despair;
I saw my sins his blood had spilt,
   And helped to nail him there.

5 A second look he gave, which said,
   "I freely all forgive;
This blood is for thy ransom paid;
   I die that thou mayst live."

6 Thus, while his death my sin displays
   In all its blackest hue,
Such is the mystery of grace,
   It seals my pardon too.   NEWTON.

426. *A Warning from the Grave.* (568)

1 BENEATH our feet and o'er our head
   Is equal warning given;
Beneath us lie the countless dead,
   And far above is heaven.

2 Death rides on every passing breeze,
   And lurks in every flower;
Each season has its own disease,
   Its peril every hour.

3 Turn, sinner, turn: thy danger know:
   Where'er thy foot can tread,
The earth rings hollow from below,
   And warns thee of her dead.

4 Turn, Christian, turn: thy soul apply
   To truths which hourly tell
That they who underneath thee lie
   Shall live in heaven—or hell.   HEBER.

427. *Importance of the Bible to the Young.* (490)

1 How shall the young secure their hearts,
   And guard their lives from sin?
Thy word the choicest rules imparts,
   To keep the conscience clean.

2 'Tis, like the sun, a heavenly light,
   That guides us all the day,
And, through the dangers of the night,
   A lamp to lead our way.

3 Thy precepts make us truly wise:
   We hate the sinner's road;
We hate our own vain thoughts that rise,
   But love thy law, O God.

4 Thy word is everlasting truth;
   How pure is every page!
That holy book shall guide our youth,
   And well support our age.   WATTS.

PASSING AWAY.

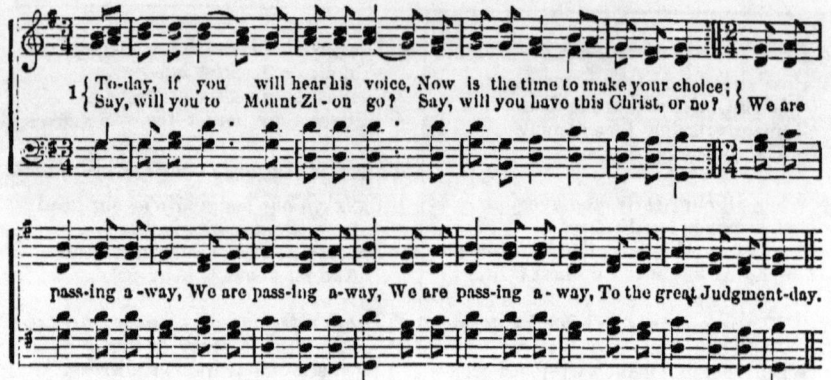

428. *We Are Passing Away.* (57)

1 To-day, if you will hear his voice,
  Now is the time to make your choice;
  Say, will you to Mount Zion go?
  Say, will you have this Christ, or no?
    We are passing away, &c.

2 Ye wandering souls, who find no rest,
  Say, will you be forever blest?
  Will you be saved from sin and hell?
  Will you with Christ in glory dwell?
    We are passing away, &c.

3 Come now, dear friends, for ruin bound,
  Obey the gospel's joyful sound;
  Come, go with us, and you shall prove
  The joy of Christ's redeeming love.
    We are passing away, &c.

4 Leave all your sports and glittering toys;
  Come, share with us eternal joys;
  Or, must we leave you bound to hell?
  Then, dearest friends, a long farewell.
    We are passing away, &c.

5 Once more, we ask you, in his name,
  For yet his love remains the same,
  Say, will you to Mount Zion go?
  Say, will you have this Christ, or no?
    We are passing away, &c.

429. *"The Heathen Perish."* (520)

1 The heathen perish; day by day,
  Thousands on thousands pass away!
  O Christians, to their rescue fly,
  Preach Jesus to them ere they die!

2 Wealth, labor, talents freely give,
  Yea, life itself, that they may live;
  What hath your Saviour done for you?
  And what for him will ye not do?

3 O, Spirit of the Lord! go forth,
  Call in the south, wake up the north;
  From every clime, from sun to sun,
  Gather God's children into one!
                    MONTGOMERY.

430. *One Thing Needful.* (25)

1 Why will ye waste on trifling cares
  That life which God's compassion spares,
  While, in the various range of thought,
  The one thing needful is forgot?
    We are passing away, &c.

2 Shall God invite you from above?
  Shall Jesus urge his dying love?
  Shall troubled conscience give you pain?
  And all these pleas unite in vain?
    We are passing away, &c.

3 Not so your eyes will always view
  Those objects which you now pursue;
  Not so will heaven and hell appear,
  When death's decisive hour is near.
    We are passing away, &c.

4 Almighty God, thy grace impart;
  Fix deep conviction on each heart;
  Nor let us waste on trifling cares
  That life which thy compassion spares.
    We are passing away, &c.
                    DODDRIDGE.

WOODWORTH. L. M.
Wm. B. Bradbury.

1 Behold, a stranger's at the door! He gently knocks—has knocked before; Has waited long—is waiting still; You treat no other friend so ill.

431. *The Waiting Saviour.* (72)

1 Behold! a stranger's at the door!
He gently knocks—has knocked before;
Has waited long—is waiting still;
You treat no other friend so ill.

2 But will he prove a friend indeed?
He will!—the very friend you need!
The Man of Nazareth!—'tis he,
With garments dyed at Calvary.

3 Oh! lovely attitude!—he stands
With melting heart, and laden hands!
Oh! matchless kindness!—and he shows
This matchless kindness to his foes.

4 Admit him, ere his anger burn—
His feet departed ne'er return;
Admit him, or the hour's at hand
When at his door denied you'll stand!
Grigg.

432. *Security of the Believer.* (297)

1 How oft have sin and Satan strove
To rend my soul from thee, my God!
But everlasting is thy love,
And Jesus seals it with his blood.

2 The oath and promise of the Lord
Join to confirm his wondrous grace;
Eternal power performs the word,
And fills all heaven with endless praise.

3 Amidst temptations sharp and long,
My soul to this dear refuge flies;
Hope is my anchor, firm and strong,
While tempests blow and billows rise.

4 The gospel bears my spirit up;
A faithful and unchanging God
Lays the foundation for my hope,
In oaths, and promises, and blood.
Watts.

433. *The Holy Spirit Invoked.* (140)

1 Come, Holy Spirit, Dove divine,
On these baptismal waters shine,
And teach our hearts, in highest strain,
To praise the Lamb, for sinners slain.

2 We love thy name, we love thy laws,
And joyfully embrace thy cause;
We love thy cross, the shame, the pain,
O Lamb of God, for sinners slain.

3 We sink beneath the mystic flood;
O, bathe us in thy cleansing blood;
We die to sin, and seek a grave,
With thee, beneath the yielding wave.

4 And as we rise, with thee to live,
O, let the Holy Spirit give
The sealing unction from above,
The breath of life, the fire of love.
Judson.

Dr. L. Mason.

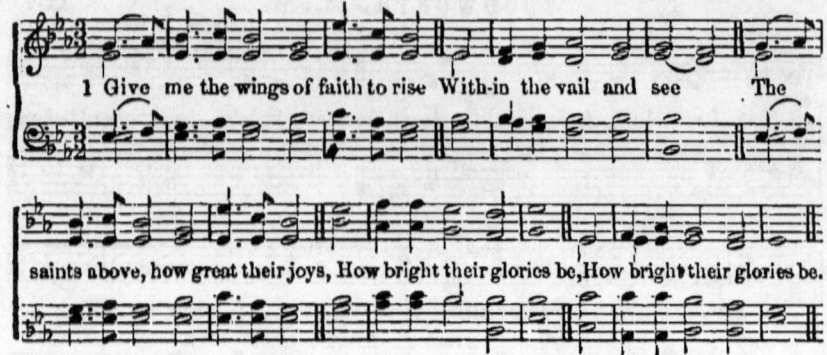

1. Give me the wings of faith to rise With-in the vail and see The saints above, how great their joys, How bright their glories be, How bright their glories be.

434. *Following Departed Worthies.* (332)

1 Give me the wings of faith to rise
  Within the vail, and see
The saints above, how great their joys,
  How bright their glories be.

2 Once they were mourning here below,
  And bathed their couch with tears;
They wrestled hard, as we do now,
  With sins, and doubts, and fears.

3 I ask them whence their victory came;
  They, with united breath,
Ascribe their conquest to the Lamb,
  Their triumph to his death.

4 They marked the footsteps that he trod,
  His zeal inspired their breast;
And, following their incarnate God,
  Possessed the promised rest.

5 Our glorious Leader claims our praise,
  For his own pattern given;
While the long cloud of witnesses
  Shows the same path to heaven.
          Watts.

435. *Praise for Salvation.* (120)

1 Salvation! Oh! the joyful sound!
  'Tis pleasure to our ears,
A sovereign balm for every wound,
  A cordial for our fears.

2 Buried in sorrow, and in sin,
  At hell's dark door we lay;
But we arise, by grace divine,
  To see a heavenly day.

3 Salvation! let the echo fly
  The spacious earth around,
While all the armies of the sky
  Conspire to raise the sound.
          Watts.

436. *God our Wisdom.* (197)

1 Since all the varying scenes of time
  God's watchful eye surveys,
Oh, who so wise to choose our lot,
  Or to appoint our ways!

3 Good when he gives,—supremely good,
  Nor less when he denies;
E'en crosses, from his sovereign hand,
  Are blessings in disguise.

3 Why should we doubt a Father's love,
  So constant and so kind?
To his unerring, gracious will
  Be every wish resigned.

4 In thy fair book of life divine,
  My God, inscribe my name;
There let it fill some humble place,
  Beneath my Lord, the Lamb.
          Hervey.

HYMNS.

437. *Sovereignty of the Spirit.* (301)

1 The blessed Spirit, like the wind,
Blows when and where he please;
How happy are the men who feel
The soul-enlivening breeze!

2 He moulds the carnal mind afresh,
Subdues the power of sin,
Transforms the heart of stone to flesh,
And plants his grace within.

3 He sheds abroad the Father's love,
Applies redeeming blood,
Bids both our guilt and fear remove,
And brings us home to God.

4 Lord, fill each dead, benighted soul
With light, and life and joy;
None can thy mighty power control,
Or shall thy work destroy.
BEDDOME.

438. *One Church.* (458)

1 Come, let us join our friends above,
Who have obtained the prize,
And on the eagle wings of love
To joy celestial rise.

2 Let saints below in concert sing
With those to glory gone;
For all the servants of our King
In heaven and earth are one.

3 One family, we dwell in him;
One church above, beneath;
Though now divided by the stream,
The narrow stream, of death.

4 One army of the living God,
To his command we bow;
Part of the host have crossed the flood,
And part are crossing now.

5 E'en now to their eternal home
Some happy spirits fly;
And we are to the margin come,
And soon expect to die.

6 O Saviour, be our constant Guide;
Then, when the word is given,
Bid Jordan's narrow stream divide,
And land us safe in heaven.
C. WESLEY.

439. *The Emblematic Dove.* (139)

1 Meekly in Jordan's holy stream
The great Redeemer bowed;
Bright was the glory's sacred beam
That hushed the wondering crowd.

2 Thus God descended to approve
The deed that Christ had done;
Thus came the emblematic Dove,
And hovered o'er the Son.

3 So, blessed Spirit, come to-day
To our baptismal scene:
Let thoughts of earth be far away,
And every mind serene.

4 This day we give to holy joy;
This day to heaven belongs:
Raised to new life, we will employ
In melody our tongues.
S. F. SMITH.

440. *Public Humiliation.* (544)

1 Lord, look on all assembled here,
Who in thy presence stand,
To offer up united prayer
For this our sinful land.

2 O, may we all, with one consent,
Fall low before thy throne,
With tears the nation's sins lament,
The church's and our own.

3 And should the dread decree be past,
And we must feel the rod—
Let faith and patience hold us fast
To our correcting God.
HART.

441. *Seeking God.* (381)

1 O, that I knew the secret place
Where I might find my God!
I'd spread my wants before his face,
And pour my woes abroad.

2 I'd tell him how my sins arise,
What sorrows I sustain;
How grace decays, and comfort dies,
And leaves my heart in pain.

3 He knows what arguments I'd take
To wrestle with my God;
I'd plead for his own mercy's sake,
And for my Saviour's blood.
WATTS.

BRIGHT CANAAN.

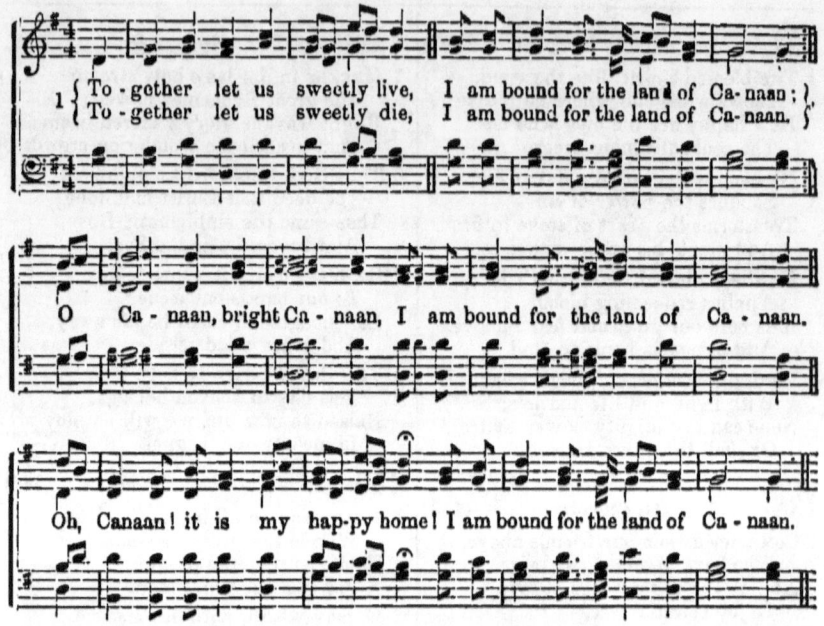

442. *I'm Bound for the Land of Canaan.* (449)

1 Together let us sweetly live,
  I am bound for the land of Canaan;
  Together let us sweetly die,
  I am bound for the land of Canaan.
  Oh, Canaan! bright Canaan!
  I am bound for the land of Canaan;
  Oh, Canaan! it is my happy home!
  I am bound for the land of Canaan.

2 If you get there before I do,
  I am bound for the land of Canaan;
  Then praise the Lord, I'm coming too,
  I am bound for the land of Canaan.
    Oh, Canaan! bright Canaan! &c.

3 Part of my friends the prize have won,
  I am bound for the land of Canaan;
  And I'm resolved to travel on,
  I am bound for the land of Canaan.
    Oh, Canaan! bright Canaan! &c.

4 Then come with me, beloved friend,
  I am bound for the land of Canaan;
  The joys of heaven shall never end,
  I am bound for the land of Canaan.
    Oh, Canaan! bright Canaan! &c.

5 Our songs of praise shall fill the skies,
  I am bound for the land of Canaan;
  While higher still our joys they rise,
  I am bound for the land of Canaan;
    Oh, Canaan! bright Canaan! &c.

No Cross, No Crown.
443. *Tune* Shining Shore, page 22. (450)

1 Come, friends, and let our hearts awake,
    To duty's call attending;
  The cross we'll take for Jesus' sake,
    Our toils and praises blending.
      For he will come and bring us home,
        Where rest and joy end never;
      The cross laid down, we'll wear the crown,
        And shout his praise forever.

HYMNS. 171

2 Gird on the heavenly armor bright,
   And standing up for Jesus,
   Watch, pray, and fight, as sons of light,
   Till from the war he frees us.
   For he will come, &c.

3 'Tis sweet to trust his glorious word,
   His name and grace confessing;
   Who serve the Lord have great reward,
   And share his richest blessing.
   For he will come, &c.

4 Let Jesus' love fill every mind,
   Our faith and hope inspiring:
   What worldlings find we leave behind,
   Immortal crowns desiring.
   For he will come, &c.

5 The painful cross for us he bore,—
   And bowed in death's cold river—
   O, for the power to love him more,
   Who did our souls deliver.
   For he will come, &c.
                                    S. D. PHELPS.

REST FOR THE WEARY.
Rev. J. W. DADMUN. *Arranged.*

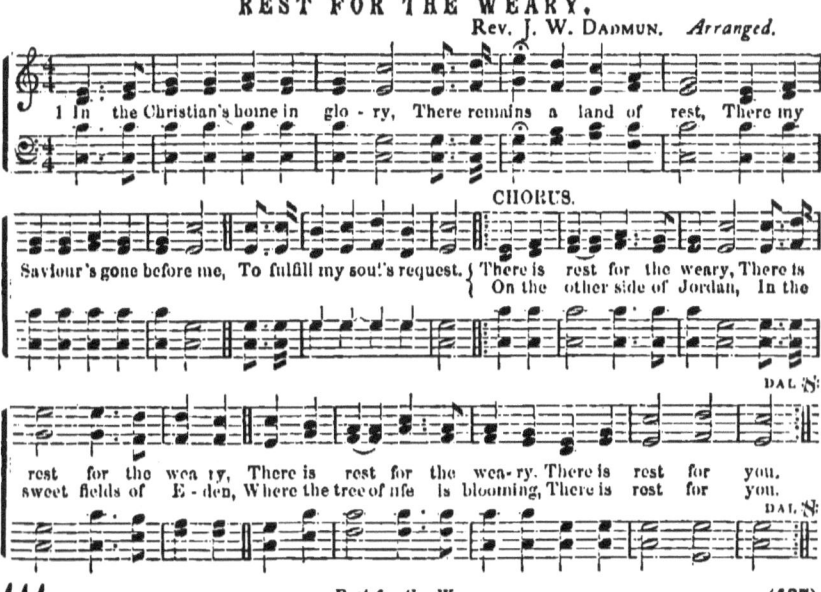

1 In the Christian's home in glo-ry, There remains a land of rest, There my Saviour's gone before me, To fulfill my soul's request. There is rest for the weary, There is rest for the weary, There is rest for the weary, There is rest for you. On the other side of Jordan, In the sweet fields of E-den, Where the tree of life is blooming, There is rest for you.

444.   *Rest for the Weary.*   (437)

2 He is fitting up my mansion,
   Which eternally shall stand,
   For my stay shall not be transient
   In that holy, happy land.
   There is rest for the weary, &c.

3 Pain nor sickness ne'er shall enter,
   Grief nor woe my lot shall share;
   But in that celestial centre,
   I a crown of life shall wear.
   There is rest for the weary, &c.

4 Death itself shall then be vanquished,
   And his sting shall be withdrawn;
   Shout for gladness, O, ye ransomed,
   Hail with joy the rising morn.
   There is rest for the weary, &c.

5 Sing, O, sing, ye heirs of glory;
   Shout your triumph as you go;
   Zion's gate will open for you,
   You shall find an entrance through.
   There is rest for the weary, &c.

FREDERICK. 11s.

Geo. Kingsley.

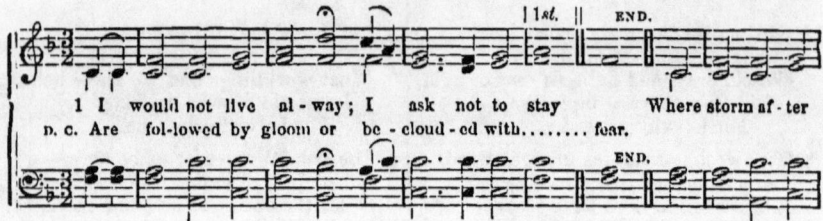

1 I would not live al-way; I ask not to stay Where storm af-ter
D. C. Are fol-lowed by gloom or be-cloud-ed with........ fear.

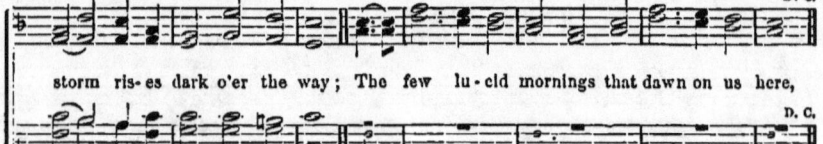

storm ris-es dark o'er the way; The few lu-cid mornings that dawn on us here,

445. *Death Welcome.* (574)

2 I would not live alway thus fettered by sin—
Temptation without and corruption within:
E'en the rapture of pardon is mingled with fears,
And the cup of thanksgiving with penitent tears.

3 I would not live alway; no—welcome the tomb;
Since Jesus hath lain there, I dread not its gloom;
There sweet be my rest till he bid me arise
To hail him in triumph descending the skies.

4 Who, who would live alway away from his God—
Away from yon heaven, that blissful abode,
Where rivers of pleasure flow bright o'er the plains,
And the noontide of glory eternally reigns?

5 There saints of all ages in harmony meet,
Their Saviour and brethren transported to greet,
While anthems of rapture unceasingly roll,
And the smile of the Lord is the feast of the soul. Muhlenberg.

446. *Delay Not.* (30)

1 Delay not, delay not; O, sinner, draw near;
The waters of life are now flowing for thee;
No price is demanded; the Saviour is here;
Redemption is purchased, salvation is free.

2 Delay not, delay not; why longer abuse
The love and compassion of Jesus thy God?
A fountain is opened; how canst thou refuse
To wash and be cleansed in his pardoning blood?

3 Delay not, delay not, O, sinner, to come,
    For Mercy still lingers, and calls thee to-day;
    Her voice is not heard in the shades of the tomb;
    Her message, unheeded, will soon pass away.

4 Delay not, delay not; the Spirit of grace,
    Long grieved and resisted, may take its sad flight,
    And leave thee in darkness to finish thy race,
    To sink in the gloom of eternity's night.

5 Delay not, delay not; the hour is at hand;
    The earth shall dissolve, and the heavens shall fade;
    The dead, small and great, in the judgment shall stand;
    What helper, then, sinner, shall lend thee his aid?

HOME. 11s.

1 When torn is the bo-som by sor-row or care,
  Be it ev - er so simple, there's nothing like.... prayer: It com-forts, it soft-ens, sub-dues, yet sustains, Bids hope rise exulting, and passion restrains; Prayer, prayer, O sweet prayer,
  D. S. Be it ever so simple, there's nothing like prayer.

447.   *Sweet Prayer.*   (413)

2 When far from the friends that are dearest we part,
    What fond recollections still cling to the heart;
    Past scenes and enjoyments live painfully there;
    And restless we languish, till peace comes in prayer;
    Prayer, prayer, O sweet prayer, &c.

3 When earthly delusions would lead us astray
    In folly's gay mazes, or sin's treacherous way,
    How strong the enchantment, how fatal the snare!
    But looking to Jesus, we conquer by prayer;
    Prayer, prayer, O sweet prayer, &c.

4 While strangers to prayer, we are strangers to bliss,
    The world has no refuge, no solace like this;
    And till we the seraph's full ecstacy share,
    Our chalice of joy must be guarded by prayer;
    Prayer, prayer, O sweet prayer, &c.

            Miss LUTTON.

DEDHAM. C. M.

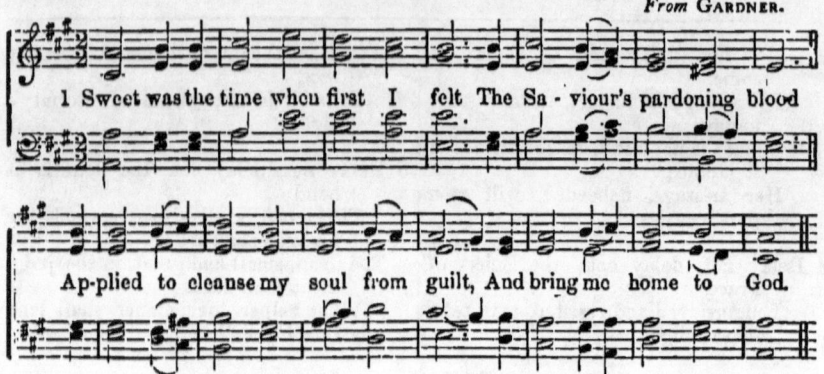

1 Sweet was the time when first I felt The Saviour's pardoning blood Applied to cleanse my soul from guilt, And bring me home to God.

448. *Mourning over Departed Comforts.* (364)

1 SWEET was the time when first I felt
　The Saviour's pardoning blood
Applied to cleanse my soul from guilt,
　And bring me home to God.

2 Soon as the morn the light revealed,
　His praises tuned my tongue;
And when the evening shades prevailed,
　His love was all my song.

3 In prayer my soul drew near the Lord,
　And saw his glory shine:
And when I read his holy word,
　I called each promise mine.

4 But now, when evening shade prevails,
　My soul in darkness mourns:
And when the morn the light reveals,
　No light to me returns.

5 Rise, Lord, and help me to prevail;
　O, make my soul thy care:
I know thy mercy cannot fail;
　Let me that mercy share.
　　　　　　　　　　NEWTON.

449. *Joy of Christ's Advent.* (214)

1 JOY to the world! the Lord is come!
　Let earth receive her King;
Let every heart prepare him room,
　And heaven and nature sing.

2 Joy to the earth! the Saviour reigns!
　Let men their songs employ;
While fields, and floods, rocks, hills and plains,
　Repeat the sounding joy.

3 No more let sins and sorrows grow,
　Nor thorns infest the ground;
He comes to make his blessings flow
　Far as the curse is found.

4 He rules the world with truth and grace,
　And makes the nations prove
The glories of his righteousness,
　And wonders of his love.
　　　　　　　　　　WATTS.

450. *Worthy the Lamb.* (274)

1 COME, let us join our cheerful songs,
　With angels round the throne:
Ten thousand thousand are their tongues,
　But all their joys are one.

2 "Worthy the Lamb that died," they cry.
　"To be exalted thus:"
"Worthy the Lamb," our lips reply,
　"For he was slain for us."

3 Jesus is worthy to receive
　Honor and power divine;
And blessings, more than we can give
　Be, Lord, for ever thine.
　　　　　　　　　　WATTS.

451. *Design of Christ's Advent.* (215)

1 Hark! the glad sound! the Saviour comes!
  The Saviour promised long!
Let every heart prepare a throne,
  And every voice a song.

2 He comes, the prisoner to release,
  In Satan's bondage held;
The gates of brass before him burst,
  The iron fetters yield.

3 He comes, from thickest films of vice
  To clear the mental ray,
And on the eyes long closed in night,
  To pour celestial day.

4 He comes, the broken heart to bind,
  The bleeding soul to cure,
And, with the treasures of his grace,
  Enrich the humble poor.

5 Our glad hosannas, Prince of Peace,
  Thy welcome shall proclaim,
And heaven's eternal arches ring
  With thy beloved name.
                                    Doddridge.

452. *Praise to the Trinity.* (313)

1 Father of glory, to thy name
  Immortal praise we give,
Who dost an act of grace proclaim,
  And bid us, rebels, live.

2 Immortal honor to the Son,
  Who makes thine anger cease;
Our lives he ransomed with his own,
  And died to make our peace.

3 To thy almighty Spirit be
  Immortal glory given,
Whose influence brings us near to thee,
  And trains us up for heaven.

4 Let men, with their united voice,
  Adore th' eternal God,
And spread his honors, and their joys,
  Through nations far abroad.

5 Let faith, and love, and duty, join
  One general song to raise;
Let saints, in earth and heaven, combine
  In harmony and praise.
                                    Watts.

453. *The Morning Worshiper.* (385)

1 Lord, in the morning thou shalt hear
  My voice ascending high;
To thee will I direct my prayer,
  To thee lift up mine eye.

2 Up to the hills where Christ is gone
  To plead for all his saints,
Presenting at his Father's throne
  Our songs and our complaints.

3 Thou art a God before whose sight
  The wicked shall not stand;
Sinners shall ne'er be thy delight,
  Nor dwell at thy right hand.

4 But to thy house will I resort,
  To taste thy mercies there;
I will frequent thine holy court,
  And worship in thy fear.

5 O, may thy Spirit guide my feet,
  In ways of righteousness,
Make every path of duty straight
  And plain before my face.
                                    Watts.

454. *The Whole Armor.* (323)

1 O, speed thee, Christian, on thy way,
  And to thy armor cling;
With girded loins the call obey
  That grace and mercy bring.

2 There is a battle to be fought,
  An upward race to run,
A crown of glory to be sought,
  A victory to be won.

3 The shield of faith repels the dart
  That Satan's hand may throw;
His arrow cannot reach thy heart,
  If Christ control the bow.

4 The glowing lamp of prayer will light
  Thee on thy anxious road;
'Twill keep the goal of heaven in sight,
  And guide thee to thy God.

5 O, faint not, Christian, for thy sighs
  Are heard before his throne;
The race must come before the prize,
  The cross before the crown.

176 THE PROMISED LAND.

WM. B. BRADBURY.

455. *The Promised Land* (448)

1 I HAVE a Father in the promised land!
   My Father calls me, I must go
   To meet him in the promised land.
   I'll away, I'll away to the promised land;
   My Father calls me, I must go
   To meet him in the promised land.

2 I have a Saviour in the promised land;
   My Saviour calls me, I must go
   To meet him in the promised land.
   I'll away, I'll away to the promised land;
   My Saviour calls me, I must go
   To meet him in the promised land.

3 I have a crown in the promised land;
   When Jesus calls me, I must go
   To wear it in the promised land.
   I'll away, I'll away to the promised land;
   When Jesus calls me, I must go
   To wear it in the promised land.

4 I hope to meet you in the promised land;
   At Jesus' feet, a joyous band,
   We'll praise him in the promised land.
   We'll away, we'll away to the promised land;
   At Jesus' feet, a joyous band,
   We'll praise him in the promised land.

SALZBURGH. 8s & 7s. 6 lines. *Arranged.* 177

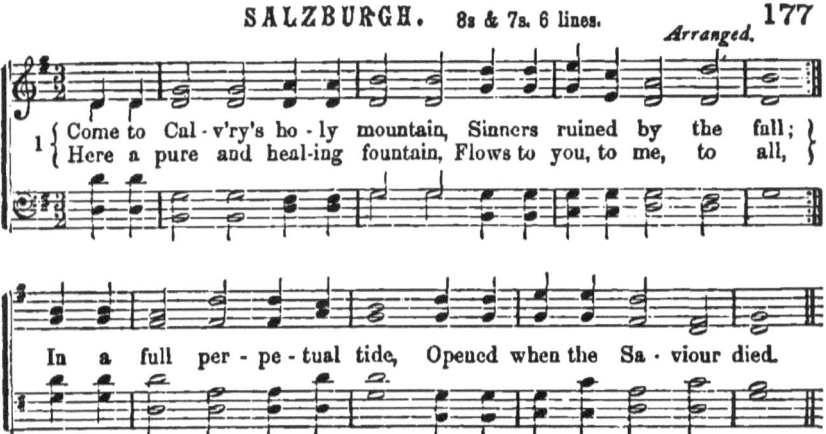

Come to Cal-v'ry's ho-ly mountain, Sinners ruined by the fall;
Here a pure and heal-ing fountain, Flows to you, to me, to all,
In a full per-pe-tual tide, Opened when the Sa-viour died.

456. *The Fountain Opened.* (56)

2 Come, in sorrow and contrition,
  Wounded, impotent, and blind
Here the guilty, free remission,
  Here the troubled, peace may find;
Health this fountain will restore;
He that drinks shall thirst no more.

3 He that drinks shall live forever:
  'Tis a soul-renewing flood:
God is faithful—God will never
  Break his covenant in blood,
Signed when our Redeemer died,
Sealed when he was glorified!
        MONTGOMERY.

457. *Precious Bible.* (492)

1 PRECIOUS Bible! what a treasure
  Does the word of God afford;
All I want for life or pleasure,
  Food and medicine, shield and sword.
Let the world account me poor,
Having this, I need no more.

2 Food to which the world's a stranger,
  Here my hungry soul enjoys;
Of excess there is no danger,
  Though it fills, it never cloys;
On a dying Christ I feed,
He is meat and drink indeed.

3 When my faith is faint and sickly,
  Or when Satan wounds my mind;
Cordials to revive me quickly,
  Healing medicines here I find;
To the promises I flee,
Each affords a remedy.

4 In the hour of dark temptation,
  Satan cannot make me yield;
For the word of consolation
  Is to me a mighty shield;
While the scripture-truths are sure,
From his malice I'm secure.
        NEWTON.

458. *Grace Triumphant.* (576)
  Tune CROSS AND CROWN, page 196.

1 DEAR as thou wast, and justly dear,
  We would not weep for thee:
One tho't shall check the starting tear,
  It is—that thou art free.

2 And thus shall faith's consoling power
  The tears of love restrain;
Oh! who that saw thy parting hour
  Could wish thee here again?

3 Gently the passing spirit fled,
  Sustained by grace divine;
O, may such grace on us be shed,
  And make our end like thine!
        DALE.

12

178   WOODLAND. C. M.

N. D. Gould.

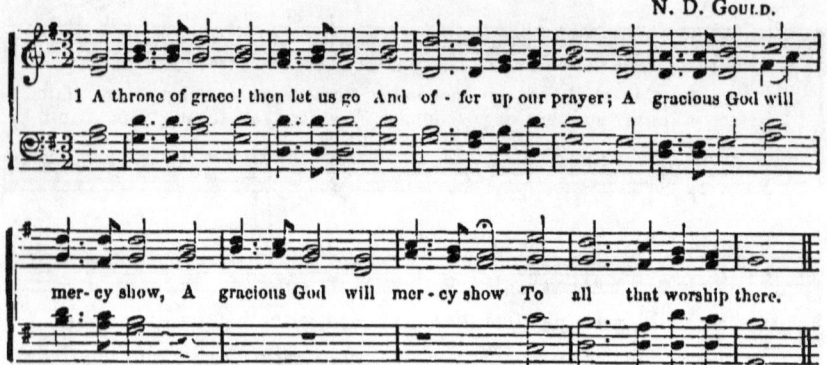

1 A throne of grace! then let us go And offer up our prayer; A gracious God will mercy show, A gracious God will mercy show To all that worship there.

459. *A Throne of Grace.* (402)

1 A THRONE of grace! then let us go
   And offer up our prayer;
  A gracious God will mercy show
   To all that worship there.

2 A throne of grace! Oh, at that throne
   Our knees have often bent:
  And God has showered his blessings down
   As often as we went.

3 A throne of grace! rejoice, ye saints;
   That throne is open still;
  To God unbosom your complaints,
   And then inquire his will.

4 A throne of grace we yet shall need
   Long as we draw our breath,
  A Saviour, too, to intercede,
   Till we are changed by death.

5 The throne of glory then shall glow
   With beams from Jesus' face,
  And we no longer want shall know,
   Nor need a throne of grace.
                        COBBIN.

460. *The Bible suited to our Wants.* (495)

1 FATHER of mercies, in thy word
   What endless glory shines!
  Forever be thy name adored,
   For these celestial lines.

2 'Tis here the tree of knowledge grows,
   And yields a free repast;
  Here purer sweets than nature knows
   Invite the longing taste.

3 'Tis here the Saviour's welcome voice
   Spreads heavenly peace around,
  And life, and everlasting joys,
   Attend the blissful sound.

4 O, may these heavenly pages be
   My ever-dear delight;
  And still new beauties may I see,
   And still increasing light.

5 Divine Instructor, gracious Lord,
   Be thou forever near;
  Teach me to love thy sacred word,
   And view my Saviour here.
                        STEELE.

461. *Praise to Christ.* (151)

1 To Him who loved the souls of men
   And washed us in his blood,
  To royal honors raised our head,
   And made us priests to God,—

2 To Him let every tongue be praise,
   And every heart be love,
  All grateful honors paid on earth,
   And nobler songs above.

462. *Security in God.* (196)
1 Through all the changing scenes of life,
In trouble and in joy,
The praises of my God shall still
My heart and tongue employ.
2 The hosts of God encamp around
The dwellings of the just;
Deliverance he affords to all
Who make his name their trust.
3 O, make but trial of his love,
Experience will decide
How blest are they, and only they,
Who in his truth confide.
4 Fear him, ye saints, and you will then
Have nothing else to fear;
Make you his service your delight,
He'll make your wants his care.
Tate & Brady.

463. *Joy in God.* (183)
1 My God, the spring of all my joys,
The life of my delights;
The glory of my brightest days,
And comfort of my nights.
2 In darkest shades, if he appear,
My dawning is begun;
He is my soul's bright morning-star,
And he my rising sun.
3 The opening heavens around me shine
With beams of sacred bliss,
While Jesus shows his love is mine,
And whispers I am his.
4 My soul would leave this heavy clay,
At that transporting word,
And run with joy the shining way,
To meet my gracious Lord.
5 Fearless of hell and ghastly death,
I'd break through every foe;
The wings of love and arms of faith
Should bear me conqueror through.
Watts.

464. *Love of Sabbath Service.* (168)
1 How sweet, upon this sacred day,
The best of all the seven,
To cast our earthly thoughts away,
And think of God and heaven!

2 How sweet to be allowed to pray
Our sins may be forgiven!
With filial confidence to say,
"Father, who art in heaven!"
3 How sweet the words of peace to hear
From Him to whom 'tis given
To wake the penitential tear,
And lead the way to heaven!
4 And if, to make our sins depart,
In vain the will has striven,
He who regards the inmost heart
Will send his grace from heaven.
5 Then hail, thou sacred, blessed day,
The best of all the seven,
When hearts unite their vows to pay
Of gratitude to Heaven!
Mrs. Follen.

465. *Acknowledgment of God's Goodness.* (210)
1 What shall I render to my God
For all his kindness shown?
My feet shall visit thine abode,
My songs address thy throne.
2 Among the saints who fill thy house
My offering shall be paid;
There shall my zeal perform the vows
My soul in anguish, made.
3 How much is mercy thy delight,
Thou ever-blessed God!
How dear thy servants in thy sight!
How precious is their blood!
4 How happy all thy servants are!
How great thy grace to me!
My life, which thou hast made thy care,
Lord, I devote to thee.
5 Now I am thine,—forever thine,—
Nor shall my purpose move;
Thy hand hath loosed my bonds of pain,
And bound me with thy love.
6 Here, in thy courts, I leave my vow,
And thy rich grace record;
Witness, ye saints, who hear me now,
If I forsake the Lord.
Watts.

WARE. L. M.

Geo. Kingsley.

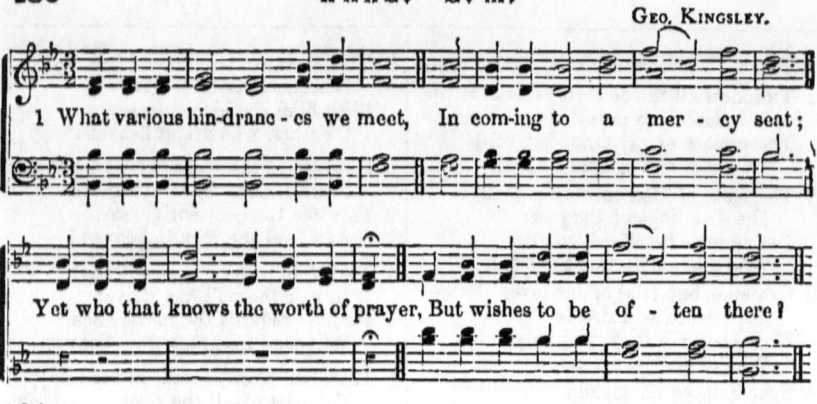

1 What various hin-dran-ces we meet, In com-ing to a mer-cy seat;
Yet who that knows the worth of prayer, But wishes to be of-ten there?

466. *Exhortation to Prayer.* (405)

1 WHAT various hindrances we meet,
In coming to a mercy seat;
Yet who that knows the worth of prayer,
But wishes to be often there?

2 Prayer makes the darkened cloud withdraw,
Prayer climbs the ladder Jacob saw,
Gives exercise to faith and love,
Brings every blessing from above.

3 Restraining prayer, we cease to fight;
Prayer makes the Christian's armor bright;
And Satan trembles when he sees
The weakest saint upon his knees.

4 Have you no words? Ah! think again,
Words flow apace when you complain,
And fill your fellow-creature's ear,
With the sad tale of all your care.

5 Were half the breath thus vainly spent,
To heaven in supplication sent,
Your cheerful song would oftener be,
"Hear what the Lord has done for me."
COWPER.

467. *The Time of Love.* (130)

1 THAT was a time of wondrous love,
When Christ my Lord was passing by;
He felt his tender pity move,
And brought his great salvation nigh.

2 Guilty and self-condemned I stood,
Nor thought his mercy was so near;

When he my stubborn heart subdued,
And planted all his graces there.

3 When on the verge of endless pain,
He gently whispered, I am thine,
I lost my fears, and dropped my chain,
And felt a transport all divine.

4 Now he supports the work begun,
Strengthens my hands and guides my ways;
To him be endless honors done,
Let heaven and earth resound his praise.
BEDDOME.

468. *Prayer Efficacious.* (409)

1 PRAYER is appointed to convey
The blessings God designs to give;
Long as they live should Christians pray,
For only while they pray they live.

2. The Christian's heart his prayer indites;
He speaks as prompted from within;
The Spirit his petition writes,
And Christ receives, and gives it in.

3 If pain afflict, or wrongs oppress,
If cares distract, or fears dismay,
If guilt deject, if sin distress,
The sweetest solace is—to pray.

4 Depend on Christ, you cannot fail;
Make all your wants and wishes known;
Fear not,—his merits must prevail—
Ask what ye will, it shall be done.
HART.

469. *Breathing after God.* (232)

1 WHERE is my God? does he retire
   Beyond the reach of humble sighs?
   Are these weak breathings of desire
   Too languid to ascend the skies?

2 He hears the breathings of desire;
   The weak petition, if sincere,
   Is not forbidden to aspire,
   And hope to reach his gracious ear.

3 Look up, my soul, with cheerful eye;
   See where the great Redeemer stands,
   The glorious advocate on high,
   With precious incense in his hands.

4 He sweetens every humble groan;
   He recommends each broken prayer;
   Recline thy hope on him alone,
   Whose power and love forbid despair.
   STEELE.

470. *Grateful Review.* (561)

1 OUR helper, God, we bless thy name,
   Whose love forever is the same;
   The tokens of thy gracious care
   Begin, and crown, and close the year.

2 Amid ten thousand snares we stand,
   Supported by thy guardian hand;
   And see, when we review our ways,
   Ten thousand monuments of praise.

3 Thus far thine arm has led us on;
   Thus far we make thy mercy known;
   And while we tread this desert land,
   New mercies shall new songs demand.

4 Our grateful souls on Jordan's shore,
   Shall raise one sacred pillar more;
   Then bear, in thy bright courts above,
   Inscriptions of immortal love.
   DODDRIDGE.

471. *Return, O, Wanderer.* (61)

1 RETURN, O, wanderer, now return,
   And seek an injured Father's face;
   Those warm desires that in thee burn,
   Were kindled by reclaiming grace.

2 Return, O, wanderer, now return,
   And seek a Father's melting heart;
   His pitying eyes thy grief discern,
   His hand shall heal thine inward smart.

3 Return, O, wanderer, now return,
   Thy Saviour bids thy spirit live;
   Go to his bleeding feet and learn
   How freely Jesus can forgive.

4 Return, O, wanderer, now return,
   And wipe away the falling tear;
   'Tis God who says, "No longer mourn,"
   'Tis mercy's voice invites thee near.
   COLLYER.

472. *Peace and Hope through Christ's Intercession.* (231)

1 HE lives! the great Redeemer lives!
   What joy the blest assurance gives!
   And now, before his Father, God,
   He pleads the merits of his blood.

2 Repeated crimes awake our fears,
   And justice, armed with frowns, appears;
   But in the Saviour's lovely face
   Sweet mercy smiles, and all is peace.

3 Great advocate, almighty friend,
   On thee our humble hopes depend;
   Our cause can never, never fail,
   For thou dost plead, and must prevail.
   STEELE.

473. *The Backslider's Supplication.* (370)

1 O THOU, that hear'st when sinners cry!
   Though all my crimes before thee lie,
   Behold them not with angry look,
   But blot their mem'ry from thy book.

2 Create my nature pure within,
   And form my soul averse to sin;
   Let thy good Spirit ne'er depart,
   Nor hide thy presence from my heart.

3 I can not live without thy light,
   Cast out and banished from thy sight;
   Thy holy joys, my God! restore,
   And guard me that I fall no more.

4 Though I have grieved thy Spirit, Lord
   His help and comfort still afford;
   And let a wretch come near thy throne
   To plead the merits of thy Son.
   WATTS.

BOYLSTON. S. M.

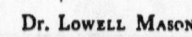
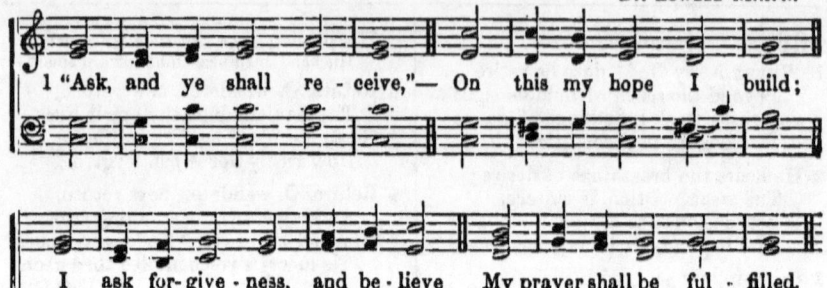

1 "Ask, and ye shall re-ceive,"— On this my hope I build;
I ask for-give-ness, and be-lieve My prayer shall be ful-filled.

474. *"Ask, and ye shall Receive."* (394)

2 Seek, and expect to find:
 Wounded to death in soul,
I seek the Saviour of mankind,
 For he can make me whole.

3 Knock, and with patience wait,
 By faith free entrance gain:
I stand, and knock at mercy's gate
 Till I thy grace obtain.

4 Shall I then ask in vain;
 Seek, and not find the Lord?
Knock, and yet no admittance gain,
 And doubt thy holy word?

5 No, Lord, thou'lt ne'er deceive;
 Thy promises are sure;
In thy good time I shall receive;
 What can I ask for more?

475. *Evils of Intemperance.* (507)

1 Mourn for the thousands slain,
 The youthful and the strong;
Mourn for the wine-cup's fearful reign,
 And the deluded throng.

2 Mourn for the ruined soul—
 Eternal life and light
Lost by the fiery, maddening bowl,
 And turned to hopeless night.

3 Mourn for the lost,—but call,
 Call to the strong, the free;
Rouse them to shun that dreadful fall,
 And to the Refuge flee.

4 Mourn for the lost—but pray,
 Pray to our God above,
To break the fell destroyer's sway,
 And show his saving love.

476. *The Peaceful Death of the Righteous.* (577)

1 O, for the death of those
 Who slumber in the Lord!
O, be like theirs my last repose,
 Like theirs my last reward!

2 Their bodies in the ground,
 In silent hope, may lie,
Till the last trumpet's joyful sound
 Shall call them to the sky.

3 Their ransomed spirits soar,
 On wings of faith and love,
To meet the Saviour they adore,
 And reign with him above.

4 With us their names shall live
 Through long-succeeding years,
Embalmed with all our hearts can give
 Our praises and our tears.

5 O, for the death of those
 Who slumber in the Lord!
O, be like theirs my last repose,
 Like theirs my last reward!

477. *The Soul Given Up to Christ.* (108)
1 AND can I yet delay
 My little all to give?—
 To tear my soul from earth away,
 And Jesus to receive?
2 Nay, but I yield, I yield!
 I can hold out no more:
 I sink, by dying love compelled,
 And own thee Conqueror.
3 Though late, I all forsake;
 My friends, my all, resign;
 Gracious Redeemer, take, O, take,
 And seal me ever thine.
4 Come, and possess me whole,
 Nor hence again remove:
 Settle and fix my wavering soul
 With all thy weight of love.
5 My one desire be this,
 Thy only love to know;
 Freely to yield all other bliss,
 All other good, below.
6 My life, my portion, thou;
 Thou all-sufficient art;
 My hope, my heavenly treasure, now
 Enter and keep my heart.
                    C. WESLEY.

478. *Soon will the Harvest Close.* (38)
1 YE sinners, fear the Lord,
 While yet 't is called to-day;
 Soon will the awful voice of death
 Command your souls away.
2 Soon will the harvest close,
 The summer soon be o'er;
 And soon your injured, angry God
 Will hear your prayers no more.
3 Then while 'tis called to-day,
 O, hear the gospel's sound!
 Come, sinners, haste, O, haste away,
 While pardon may be found!
                    DWIGHT.

479. *Kindness to our Frailty.* (186)
1 THE pity of the Lord,
 To those that fear his name,
 Is such as tender parents feel;
 He knows our feeble frame.

2 He knows we are but dust,
 Scattered with every breath;
 His anger, like a rising wind,
 Can send us swift to death.
3 Our days are as the grass,
 Or like the morning flower;
 When blasting winds sweep o'er the field,
 It withers in an hour.
4 But thy compassions, Lord,
 To endless years endure;
 And children's children ever find
 Thy words of promise sure.
                    WATTS.

480. *Drawing Nearer to Heaven.* (433)
1 YOUR harps, ye trembling saints,
 Down from the willows take;
 Loud to the praise of love divine,
 Bid every string awake.
2 Though in a foreign land,
 We are not far from home,
 And nearer to our house above,
 We every moment come.
3 His grace will, to the end,
 Stronger and brighter shine;
 Nor present things, nor things to come,
 Shall quench the spark divine.
                    TOPLADY.

481. *Preparation for the Judgment.* (43)
1 AND will the Judge descend!
 And must the dead arise?
 And not a single soul escape
 His all-discerning eyes!
2 How will my heart endure
 The terrors of that day,
 When earth and heaven, before his face,
 Astonished shrink away!
3 But, ere the trumpet shakes
 The mansions of the dead,
 Hark! from the gospel's cheering sound
 What joyful tidings spread!
4 Come, sinners, seek his grace,
 Whose wrath ye cannot bear;
 Fly to the shelter of his cross,
 And find salvation there.
                    DODDRIDGE.

DUNDEE. C. M.

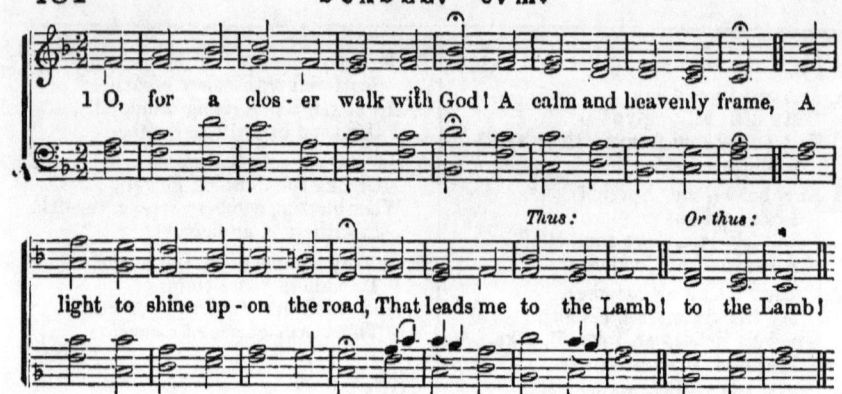

482. *Nearness to God Desired.* (348)

1 O, FOR a closer walk with God!
    A calm and heavenly frame,
A light to shine upon the road,
    That leads me to the Lamb!

2 Where is the blessedness I knew
    When first I saw the Lord?
Where is the soul-refreshing view
    Of Jesus and his word?

3 What peaceful hours I then enjoyed!
    How sweet their memory still?
But they have left an aching void,
    The world can never fill.

4 Return, O, holy Dove, return,
    Sweet messenger of rest;
I hate the sins that made thee mourn
    And drove thee from my breast.

5 The dearest idol I have known,
    Whate'er that idol be,
Help me to tear it from thy throne,
    And worship only thee.   COWPER.

483. *Praying for Strong Faith.* (344)

1 O, FOR a faith that will not shrink,
    Though pressed by every foe,
That will not tremble on the brink
    Of any earthly woe!

2 That will not murmur nor complain
    Beneath the chastening rod,
But, in the hour of grief or pain,
    Will lean upon its God;—

3 A faith that shines more bright and clear
    When tempests rage without;
That when in danger knows no fear,
    In darkness feels no doubt:—

4 A faith that keeps the narrow way
    Till life's last hour is fled,
And with a pure and heavenly ray
    Lights up a dying bed.

5 Lord, give us such a faith as this,
    And then, whate'er may come,
We'll taste, e'en here, the hallowed bliss
    Of an eternal home.
                                BATHURST.

484. *Expostulation with Sinners.* (48)

1 SINNER, the voice of God regard;
    His mercy speaks to-day;
He calls you, by his sovereign word,
    From sin's destructive way.

2 Like the rough sea, that cannot rest,
    You live devoid of peace;
A thousand stings within your breast
    Deprive your soul of ease.

3 Why will you in the crooked ways
   Of sin and folly go?
  In pain you travel all your days,
   To reap immortal wo.

4 But he who turns to God shall live,
   Through his abounding grace;
  His mercy will the guilt forgive
   Of those who seek his face.

5 Bow to the sceptre of his word,
   Renouncing every sin;
  Submit to him, your sovereign Lord,
   And learn his will divine.

6 His love exceeds your highest thoughts,
   He pardons like a God;
  He will forgive your numerous faults
   Through our Redeemer's blood.
                               FAWCETT.

AMAZING GRACE.

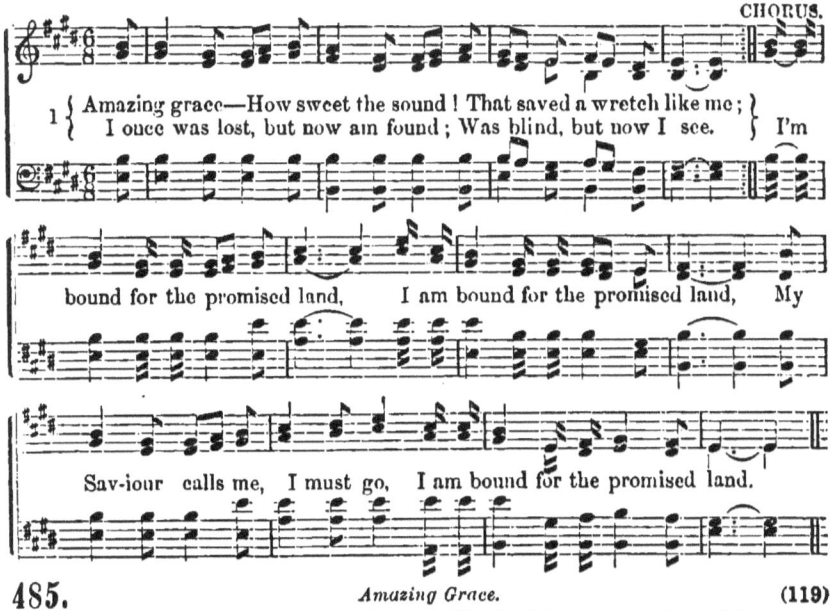

1 Amazing grace—How sweet the sound! That saved a wretch like me; I once was lost, but now am found; Was blind, but now I see. I'm bound for the promised land, I am bound for the promised land, My Sav-iour calls me, I must go, I am bound for the promised land.

485. *Amazing Grace.* (119)

2 'Twas grace that taught my heart to fear,
   And grace my fears relieved:
  How precious did that grace appear,
   The hour I first believed!
     I am bound, &c.

3 Through many dangers, toils, and snares,
   I have already come;
  'Tis grace has brought me safe thus far,
   And grace will lead me home,
     I am bound, &c.

4 The Lord has promised good to me;
   His word my hope secures;
  He will my shield and portion be,
   As long as life endures.
     I am bound, &c.

5 Yes, when this flesh and heart shall fail,
   And mortal life shall cease,
  I shall possess within the vail
   A life of joy and peace.
     I am bound, &c.
                               NEWTON.

LENOX. H. M.

Edson.

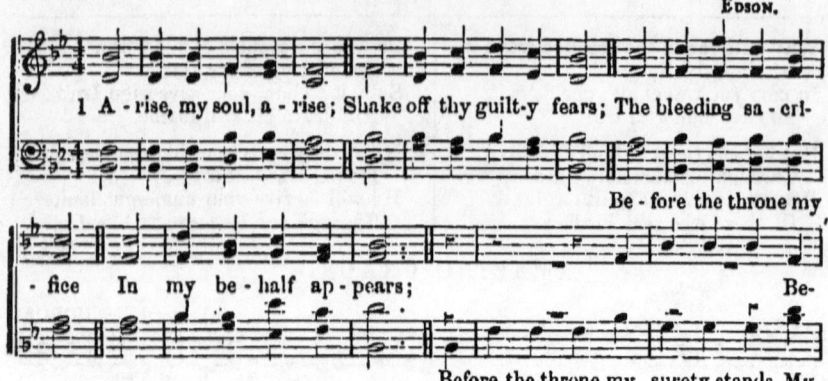

1 A-rise, my soul, a-rise; Shake off thy guilt-y fears; The bleeding sa-cri-fice In my be-half ap-pears; Be-fore the throne my surety stands, My name is written on his hands,

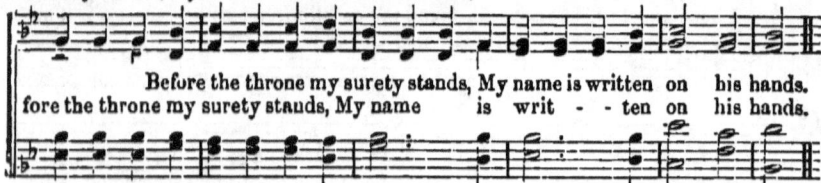

Before the throne my surety stands, My name is written on his hands.
fore the throne my surety stands, My name is writ - - ten on his hands.

name is written on his hands,

486.   *The Surety.*   (291)

2 The bleeding wounds he bears,
   Received on Calvary,
Now pour effectual prayers,
   And strongly speak for me;
" Forgive him, O, forgive," they cry,
" Nor let that ransomed sinner die."

3 The Father hears him pray,
   The dear Anointed One;—
He cannot turn away
   The pleading of his Son;
His Spirit answers to the blood,
And tells me I am born of God.

4 To God I'm reconciled;
   His pardoning voice I hear;
He owns me for his child;
   I can no longer fear:
With filial trust I now draw nigh,
And " Father, Abba Father," cry.
C. WESLEY.

487.   *My Father's House.*   (590)
      Tune LA MIRA, page 56.

1 THERE is a place of sacred rest,
   Far, far beyond the skies,
Where beauty smiles eternally,
   And pleasure never dies.

2 My Father's house, my heavenly home,
   Where " many mansions " stand,
Prepared, by hands divine, for all
   Who seek the better land.

3 In that pure home of tearless joy
   Earth's parted friends shall meet,
With smiles of love that never fade,
   And blessedness complete.

4 There, there adieus are sounds unknown
   Death frowns not on that scene,
But life, and glorious beauty, shine
   Untroubled and serene.
R. TURNBULL.

488. *The Jubilee Proclaimed.* (66)

1 Blow ye the trumpet, blow,
   The gladly-solemn sound;
 Let all the nations know,
   To earth's remotest bound,
 The year of jubilee is come;
 Return, ye ransomed sinners, home.

2 Exalt the Lamb of God,
   The sin-atoning Lamb;
 Redemption by his blood,
   Through all the lands proclaim
 The year of jubilee is come;
 Return, ye ransomed sinners, home.

3 Ye slaves of sin and hell,
   Your liberty receive,
 And safe in Jesus dwell,
   And blest in Jesus live:
 The year of jubilee is come;
 Return, ye ransomed sinners, home.

4 The gospel trumpet hear,
   The news of pardoning grace:
 Ye happy souls, draw near;
   Behold your Saviour's face:
 The year of jubilee is come;
 Return, ye ransomed sinners, home.

5 Jesus, our great High Priest,
   Has full atonement made;
 Ye weary spirits, rest;
   Ye mourning souls, be glad:
 The year of jubilee is come;
 Return, ye ransomed sinners, home.
                              C. Wesley.

489. *Christ a Prophet, Priest, and King.* (259)

1 Join all the glorious names
   Of wisdom, love, and power,
 That ever mortals knew,
   Or angels ever bore:
 All are too mean to speak his worth,
 Too mean to set the Saviour forth.

2 Great prophet of our God,
   Our tongues shall bless thy name;
 By thee the joyful news
   Of our salvation came,—
 The joyful news of sins forgiven,
 Of hell subdued, and peace with heav'n.

3 Jesus, our great High Priest,
   Has shed his blood and died;
 Our guilty conscience needs
   No sacrifice beside:
 His precious blood did once atone,
 And now it pleads before the throne.

4 O, thou almighty Lord,
   Our Conqueror and our King,
 Thy sceptre and thy sword,
   Thy reigning grace, we sing.
 Thine is the power; O, make us sit
 In willing bonds beneath thy feet.
                              Watts.

490. *Government of God.* (178)

1 The Lord Jehovah reigns;
   His throne is built on high;
 The garments he assumes
   Are light and majesty;
 His glories shine with beams so bright,
 No mortal eye can bear the sight.

2 The thunders of his hand
   Keep all the world in awe;
 His wrath and justice stand
   To guard his holy law;
 And where his love resolves to bless,
 His truth confirms and seals the grace.

3 Through all his ancient works
   Surprising wisdom shines,
 Confounds the powers of hell,
   And breaks their fell designs:
 Strong is his arm, and shall fulfill
 His great decrees, his sovereign will.

4 And can this mighty King
   Of glory condescend?
 And will he write his name
   My father and my friend?
 I love his name; I love his word:
 Join, all my powers, and praise the Lord.
                              Watts.

DOXOLOGY.

 To God the Father's throne
   Your highest honors raise;
 Glory to God the Son;
   To God the Spirit, praise;
 With all our powers, Eternal King,
 Thy name we sing, while faith adores

OLIVET. 6s & 4s.

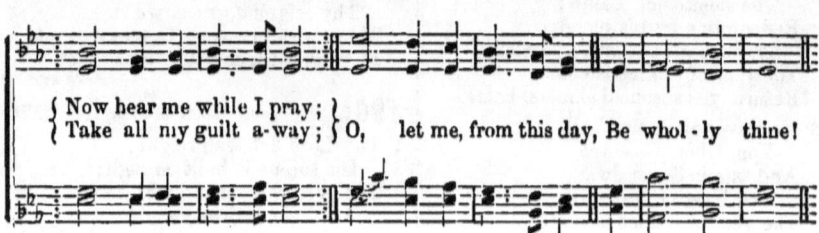

491. *Christ our Confidence.* (295)

2 May thy rich grace impart
  Strength to my fainting heart;
    My zeal inspire;
  As thou hast died for me,
  O, may my love to thee
  Pure, warm, and changeless be,
    A living fire!

3 While life's dark maze I tread
  And griefs around me spread,
    Be thou my Guide;
  Bid darkness turn to day,
  Wipe sorrow's tears away,
  Nor let me ever stray
    From thee aside.

4 When ends life's transient dream,
  When death's cold, sullen stream
    Shall o'er me roll,
  Blest Saviour, then, in love,
  Fear and distress remove
  O, bear me safe above,
    A ransomed soul.

RAY PALMER.

492. *Hymn for the National Anniversary.* (558)

1 AUSPICIOUS morning, hail!
  Voices from hill and vale
    Thy welcome sing;
  Joy on thy dawning breaks;
  Each heart that joy partakes,
  While cheerful music wakes,
    Its praise to bring.

2 When on the tyrant's rod
  Our patriot fathers trod,
    And dared be free,
  'Twas not in burning zeal,
  Firm nerves, and hearts of steel,
  Our country's joy to seal,
    But, Lord, in thee.

3 Thou, as a shield of power,
  In battle's awful hour,
    Didst round us stand;
  Our hopes were in thy throne,
  Strong in thy might alone,
  By thee our banners shone,
    God of our land.

S. F. SMITH.

NATIONAL HYMN.

1 My country, 'tis of thee, Sweet land of liberty, Of thee I sing: Land where my

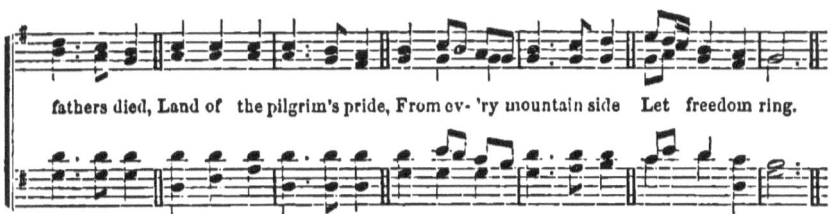

fathers died, Land of the pilgrim's pride, From ev-'ry mountain side Let freedom ring.

493. *National Hymn.* (556)

2 My native country, thee—
Land of the noble, free—
　Thy name I love;
I love thy rocks and rills,
Thy woods and templed hills;
My hearts with rapture thrills
　Like that above.

3 Let music swell the breeze,
And ring from all the trees
　Sweet freedom's song;
Let mortal tongues awake;
Let all that breathe partake;
Let rocks their silence break—
　The sound prolong.

4 Our fathers' God, to thee,
Author of liberty,
　To thee we sing:
Long may our land be bright
With freedom's holy light;
Protect us by thy might,
　Great God, our King.
　　　　　　　S. F. SMITH.

494. "God Save the State." (548)

1 GOD bless our native land!
Firm may she ever stand,
　Through storm and night;
When the wild tempests rave,
Ruler of winds and wave,
Do thou our country save
　By thy great might.

2 For her our prayer shall rise
To God, above the skies;
　On him we wait:
Thou who art ever nigh,
Guarding with watchful eye,
To thee aloud we cry,
　God save the State!

DOXOLOGY.

We praise, we worship thee,
Blessed and holy Three,
　Wisdom, Love, Might!
Boundless as ocean's tide,
Rolling in fullest pride,
O'er the world far and wide,
　"Let there be light!"

FOSTER. 8s. Single.

Wm. B. Bradbury.

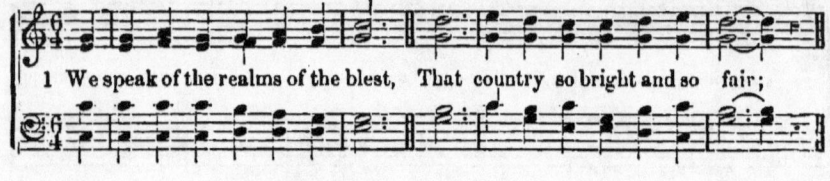

1 We speak of the realms of the blest, That country so bright and so fair;

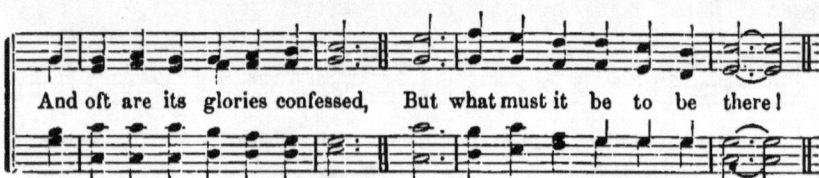

And oft are its glories confessed, But what must it be to be there!

495.   *Happiness of Heaven.*   (469)

2 We speak of its freedom from sin,
　From sorrow, temptation, and care,
　From trials without and within—
　But what must it be to be there!

3 We speak of its service of love,
　The robes which the glorified wear,
　The church of the first-born above—
　But what must it be to be there!

4 O, Lord, in this valley of wo,
　Our spirits for heaven prepare,
　And shortly we also shall know
　And feel what it is to be there!

496.   *The Believer Safe.*   (299)

1 A DEBTOR to mercy alone,
　Of covenant mercy I sing;
　Nor fear, with thy righteousness on,
　My person and off'ring to bring:

2 The terrors of law, and of God,
　With me can have nothing to do;
　My Saviour's obedience and blood
　Hide all my transgressions from view.

3 The work which his goodness began
　The arm of his strength will complete;
　His promise is yea, and amen,
　And never was forfeited yet;

4 My name from the palms of his hands
　Eternity will not erase;
　Impressed on his heart it remains,
　In marks of indelible grace.

5 Yes, I to the end shall endure,
　As sure as the earnest is given;
　More happy, but not more secure,
　The glorified spirit in heaven.
　　　　　　　　　　Toplady.

497.   *Our God Forever.*   (212)

1 This God is the God we adore,
　Our faithful, unchangeable Friend,
　Whose love is as large as his power,
　And neither knows measure nor end.

2 'Tis Jesus, the first and the last,
　Whose Spirit shall guide us safe home;
　We'll praise him for all that is past,
　And trust him for all that's to come.
　　　　　　　　　　Hart.

498.   *The Compassion of Christ.*   (153)
　　　Tune Avon, page 164.

1 How condescending and how kind
　Was God's eternal Son!
　Our misery reached his heavenly mind,
　And pity brought him down.

2 He sunk beneath our heavy woes,
　To raise us to his throne;
　There's ne'er a gift his hand bestows
　But cost his heart a groan.

3 This was compassion like a God—
   That when the Saviour knew
   The price of pardon was his blood,
   His pity ne'er withdrew.
4 Now, though he reigns exalted high,
   His love is still as great;

Well he remembers Calvary,
   Nor lets his saints forget.
5 Here let our hearts begin to melt,
   While we his death record;
   And with our joy for pardoned guilt,
   Mourn that we pierced the Lord.
                              WATTS.

MERCY'S FREE.

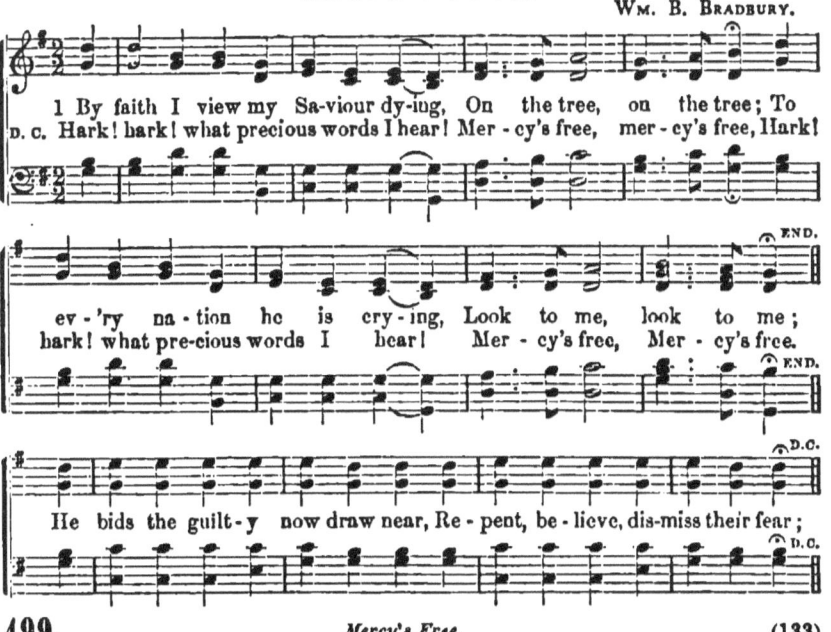

1 By faith I view my Saviour dying, On the tree, on the tree; To
D. C. Hark! hark! what precious words I hear! Mer-cy's free, mer-cy's free, Hark!

ev-'ry na-tion he is cry-ing, Look to me, look to me;
hark! what pre-cious words I hear! Mer-cy's free, Mer-cy's free.

He bids the guilt-y now draw near, Re-pent, be-lieve, dis-miss their fear;

499.   *Mercy's Free.*   (133)

2 Did Christ, when I was sin pursuing,
   Pity me, pity me?
   And did he snatch my soul from ruin?
   Can it be, can it be?
   Oh, yes! he did salvation bring,
   He is my Prophet, Priest, and King,
   And now my happy soul can sing,
   Mercy's free, mercy's free.
3 Jesus, the mighty God hath spoken
   Peace to me, peace to me;
   Now all my chains of sin are broken,
   I am free, I am free:

Soon as I in his name believed,
   The Holy Spirit I received,
   And Christ from death my soul retrieved;
   Mercy's free, mercy's free.
4 Jesus my weary soul refreshes:
   Mercy's free, mercy's free;
   And every moment Christ is precious
   Unto me, unto me:
   None can describe the bliss I prove,
   While through this wilderness I rove:
   All may enjoy the Saviour's love;
   Mercy's free, mercy's free.

WELLS. L. M.

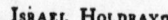

1 Show pi-ty, Lord; O Lord, forgive; Let a re-pent-ing reb-el live; Are not thy mer-cies large and free? May not a sin-ner trust in thee?

500. *Pardon Penitently Implored.* (83)

2 My crimes, though great, cannot surpass
  The power and glory of thy grace;
  Great God, thy nature hath no bound;
  So let thy pardoning love be found.

3 O, wash my soul from every sin,
  And make my guilty conscience clean;
  Here, on my heart, the burden lies,
  And past offences pain mine eyes.

4 My lips, with shame, my sins confess,
  Against thy law, against thy grace;
  Lord, should thy judgment grow severe,
  I am condemned, but thou art clear.

5 Should sudden vengeance seize my breath,
  I must pronounce thee just in death;
  And if my soul were sent to hell,
  Thy righteous law approves it well.

6 Yet save a trembling sinner, Lord!
  Whose hope, still hov'ring round thy word,
  Would light on some sweet promise there,
  Some sure support against despair.
  WATTS.

501. *The Spirit Entreated not to Depart.* (376)

1 STAY, thou insulted Spirit, stay,
  Though I have done thee such despite;
  Cast not a sinner quite away,
  Nor take thine everlasting flight.

2 Though I have most unfaithful been
  Of all who e'er thy grace received,—
  Ten thousand times thy goodness seen,
  Ten thousand times thy goodness grieved,

3 Yet, O, the chief of sinners spare,
  In honor of my great High Priest;
  Nor, in thy righteous anger, swear
  I shall not see thy people's rest.

4 My weary soul, O God release;
  Uphold me with thy gracious hand;
  O, guide me into perfect peace,
  And bring me to the promised land.
  C. WESLEY.

502. *Atoning Blood.* (80)

1 How shall the sons of men appear,
  Great God, before thine awful bar?
  How may the guilty hope to find
  Acceptance with th' Eternal Mind?

2 Not vows, nor groans, nor broken cries
  Not the most costly sacrifice,
  Not infant blood profusely spilt,
  Will expiate a sinner's guilt.

3 Thy blood, dear Jesus, thine alone,
  Hath sovereign virtue to atone:
  Here will we rest our only plea,
  When we approach, great God, to thee.
  JOSEPH STENNETT.

WINDHAM. L. M.

DANIEL READ.

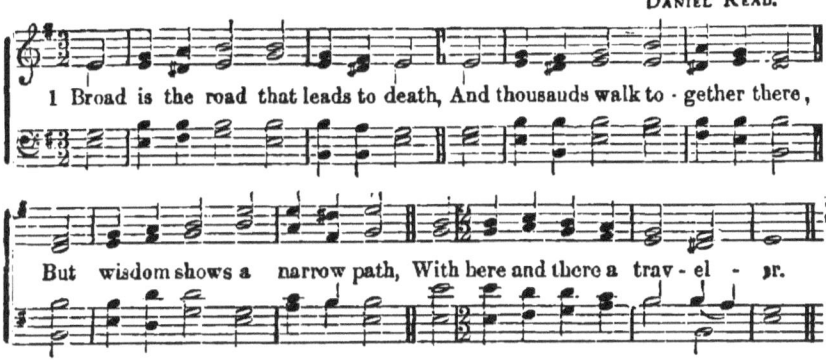

503. *The Broad Road.* (35)

1 Broad is the road that leads to death,
   And thousands walk together there;
   But wisdom shows a narrow path,
   With here and there a traveler.

2 "Deny thyself and take thy cross,"
   Is the Redeemer's great command:
   Nature must count her gold but dross,
   If she would gain this heavenly land.

3 The fearful soul that tires and faints,
   And walks the ways of God no more,
   Is but esteemed almost a saint,
   And makes his own destruction sure.

4 Lord, let not all my hopes be vain;
   Create my heart entirely new—
   Which hypocrites could ne'er attain,
   Which false apostates never knew.
   WATTS.

504. *The Spirit Striving.* (50)

1 O, sinner, hear the heavenly voice!
   O, hear the Spirit's gracious call!
   It bids thee make the better choice,
   And haste to seek in Christ thine all.

2 God's Spirit will not always strive
   With hardened, self-destroying man;
   Ye, who persist his love to grieve,
   May never hear his voice again.

3 Sinner, perhaps this very day
   Thy last accepted time may be;
   O, shouldst thou grieve him now away,
   Then hope may never beam on thee!

505. *Expostulation.* (24)

1 O, sinner, why so thoughtless grown!
   Why in such dreadful haste to die!—
   Daring to leap to worlds unknown!
   Heedless against thy God to fly!

2 Wilt thou despise eternal fate,
   Urged on by sin's delusive dreams!
   Madly attempt th' infernal gate,
   And force thy passage to the flames?

3 Stay, sinner, on the gospel plains,
   And hear the Lord of life unfold
   The glories of his dying pains—
   Forever telling, yet untold.
   WATTS.

506. *Prayer for Sincerity.* (400)
   Tune AVON, page 164.

1 Lord, when we bow before thy throne,
   And our confessions pour,
   O, may we feel the sins we own,
   And hate what we deplore!

2 Our contrite spirits, pitying, see;
   True penitence impart;
   And let a healing ray from thee
   Beam hope on every heart.

3 When we disclose our wants in prayer
   O, let our wills resign,
   And not a thought our bosoms share
   Which is not wholly thine.

4 Let faith each meek petition fill,
   And waft it to the skies,
   And teach our hearts 'tis goodness, still,
   That grants it or denies. CARLISLE.

WEBB. 7s & 6s.

G. J. Webb.

1 The morn-ing light is break-ing; The dark-ness dis-ap-pears;
The sons of earth are wak-ing To pen-i-ten-tial tears:
D. s. Of na-tions in com-mo-tion, Pre-pared for Zi-on's war.
Each breeze that sweeps the o-cean Brings ti-dings from a-far

507. *"The Morning Cometh."* (533)

2 Rich dews of grace come o'er us,
   In many a gentle shower,
And brighter scenes before us
   Are opening every hour:
Each cry, to heaven going,
   Abundant answers brings,
And heavenly gales are blowing,
   With peace upon their wings.

3 See heathen nations bending
   Before the God we love,
And thousand hearts ascending
   In gratitude above;
While sinners, now confessing,
   The gospel call obey,
And seek the Saviour's blessing,—
   A nation in a day.

4 Blest river of salvation,
   Pursue thy onward way;

Flow thou to every nation,
   Nor in thy richness stay:
Stay not till all the lowly
   Triumphant reach their home;
Stay not till all the holy
   Proclaim, "The Lord is come."
                  S. F. Smith.

508. *Guidance and Help Sought.*
   Tune OLIPHANT, page 14. (271)

1 Gently, Lord, O, gently lead us
   Through this lonely vale of tears!
And, O Lord, in mercy give us
   Thy rich grace in all our fears.
     O refresh us!
Traveling through this wilderness.

2 When temptation's darts assail us,
   When in devious paths we stray,
Let thy goodness never fail us,
   Lead us in thy perfect way.
     O refresh us!—
Traveling through this wilderness!

HYMNS. 195

3 In the hour of pain and anguish,
  In the hour when death draws near,
Suffer not our hearts to languish,
Suffer not our souls to fear.
  O refresh us!—
Traveling through this wilderness.

4 When this mortal life is ended,
  Bid us in thine arms to rest,
Till, by angel bands attended,
We awake among the blest.
  O refresh us!—
When we've passed the wilderness.

MISSIONARY HYMN. 7s & 6s.
Dr. Lowell Mason.

1 From Greenland's icy mountains, From India's coral strand, Where Afric's sunny foun-tains Roll down their golden sand: From many an an-cient riv-er, From many a palmy plain They call us to de-liv-er Their land from error's chain.

509.   *The Appeal.*   (537)

2 What though the spicy breezes
    Blow soft o'er Ceylon's isle,
  Though every prospect pleases,
    And only man is vile;
  In vain with lavish kindness
    The gifts of God are strown;
  The heathen, in his blindness,
    Bows down to wood and stone.

3 Can we whose souls are lighted
    By wisdom from on high,
  Can we to men benighted
    The lamp of life deny?

  Salvation, O salvation!
    The joyful sound proclaim,
  Till earth's remotest nation
    Has learned Messiah's name.

4 Waft, waft, ye winds, his story
    And you, ye waters, roll,
  Till, like a sea of glory,
    It spreads from pole to pole:
  Till o'er our ransomed nature,
    The Lamb for sinners slain,
  Redeemer, King, Creator,
    In bliss returns to reign.   Heber.

CROSS AND CROWN. C. M.

510. *The Cross and the Crown.* (336)

1 MUST Jesus bear the cross alone,
   And all the world go free?
  No: there's a cross for every one,
   And there's a cross for me.

2 How happy are the saints above
   Who once went sorrowing here;
  But now they taste unmingled love,
   And joy without a tear.

3 The consecrated cross I'll bear,
   Till death shall set me free,
  And then go home my crown to wear,—
   For there's a crown for me!
                                G. N. ALLEN.

511. *Choice of Deacons.* (161)

1 VOUCHSAFE, O Lord, thy presence now,
   Direct us in thy fear;
  Before thy throne we humbly bow,
   And offer fervent prayer.

2 Give us the men whom thou shalt choose,
   Thy house on earth to guide;
  Those who shall ne'er their power abuse,
   Or rule with haughty pride.

3 Inspired with wisdom from above,
   And with discretion blest;
  Displaying meekness, temperance, love,
   Of every grace possessed;

4 These are the men we seek of thee,
   O God of righteousness;
  Such may our deacons ever be,
   With such thy people bless.

512. *Redemption by Christ.* (251)

1 BEHOLD what pity touched the heart
   Of God's eternal Son;
  Descending from the heavenly court,
   He left his Father's throne.

2 His living power, and dying love,
   Redeemed unhappy men,
  And raised the ruins of our race
   To life and God again.

3 To thee, O Lord, our noblest powers
   We joyfully resign;
  Blest Jesus, take us for thine own,
   For we are doubly thine.   WATTS.

513. *Repentance in View of the Cross.* (91)

1 AND can mine eyes, without a tear,
   A weeping Saviour see?
  Shall I not weep his groans to hear,
   Who groaned and died for me?

3 Blest Jesus, let those tears of thine
   Subdue each stubborn foe;
  Come, fill my heart with love divine
   And bid my sorrows flow.

SUFFERING SAVIOUR. C. M. 197

1. A-las! and did my Saviour bleed? And did my Sovereign die?
Would he devote that sa-cred head For such a worm as I?

Chorus. Oh! the Lamb, the lov-ing Lamb, The Lamb on Cal-va-ry,
The Lamb was slain, but lives a-gain, To in-ter-cede for me.

514. *Godly Sorrow at the Cross.* (223)

2 Was it for crimes that I had done,
   He groaned upon the tree!
Amazing pity! grace unknown,
   And love beyond degree!

3 Well might the sun in darkness hide,
   And shut his glories in,
When Christ, the mighty Maker, died,
   For man the creature's sin.

4 Thus might I hide my blushing face
   While his dear cross appears,
Dissolve my heart in thankfulness,
   And melt mine eyes to tears.

5 But drops of grief can ne'er repay
   The debt of love I owe;
Here, Lord, I give myself away,
   'Tis all that I can do. WATTS.

515. *Humiliation of Christ.* (218)

1 AND did the holy and the just,
   The Sovereign of the skies,
Stoop down to wretchedness and dust,
   That guilty man might rise?

2 Yes, the Redeemer left his throne,
   His radiant throne on high,—
Surprising mercy! love unknown!
   To suffer, bleed, and die!

3 He took the dying traitor's place,
   And suffered in his stead;
For sinful man,—Oh, wondrous grace!
   For sinful man he bled!

4 O Lord, what heavenly wonders dwell
   In thine atoning blood!
By this are sinners saved from hell,
   And rebels brought to God! STEELE.

516. *Sweet Name of Jesus.* (265)

1 How sweet the name of Jesus sounds
   In a believer's ear!
It soothes his sorrows, heals his wounds,
   And drives away his fear.

2 It makes the wounded spirit whole,
   And calms the troubled breast;
'Tis manna to the hungry soul,
   And to the weary rest.

3 Weak is the effort of my heart,
   And cold my warmest thought;
But when I see thee as thou art,
   I'll praise thee as I ought.

4 Till then I would thy love proclaim
   With every fleeting breath;
And may the music of thy name
   Refresh my soul in death. NEWTON.

OH, HOW HAPPY ARE THEY.

1 Oh! how happy are they Who their Saviour obey, And have laid up their treasure above! Tongue can never express The sweet comfort and peace Of a soul in its earliest love.

517.   *Joy of a Convert.*   (112)

1 Oh! how happy are they
  Who their Saviour obey,
And have laid up their treasure above!
  Tongue can never express
  The sweet comfort and peace
Of a soul in its earliest love.

2 That sweet comfort was mine
  When the favor divine
I had found in the blood of the Lamb.
  When at first I believed,
  What true joy I received!
What a heaven in Jesus' sweet name!

3 'Twas a heaven below
  My Redeemer to know;
And the angels could do nothing more
  Than to fall at his feet,
  And the story repeat,
And the Lover of sinners adore.

4 Jesus, all the day long,
  Was my joy and my song:
O, that all his salvation might see!
  He hath loved me, I cried,
  He hath suffered and died
To redeem such a rebel as me!

5 Oh! the rapturous height
  Of that holy delight
Which I felt in the life-giving blood?
  Of my Saviour possessed,
  I was perfectly blest,
As if filled with the fullness of God.
C. Wesley.

518.   *Sinners Flocking to Jesus.*   (131)
    Tune Autumn, page 82.

1 See! the Scriptures are fulfilling—
    Sinners flocking to their home:
  Times the prophets were foretelling,
    Signs and wonders now are come.
  Gospel trumpets loud are sounding
    Here and there on every hand:
  God's own Spirit is descending,
    Christians joining heart and hand!

2 Thousands fall before Jehovah—
"Mercy, mercy," loud they cry!
Then with shouts of "Hallelujah,"
"Glory be to God on high!"
Many say, "'Tis all disorder,"
Disbelieve God's holy word;
Still these cry and shout the louder—
"Glory, glory to the Lord!"

3 "Come," is heard in each direction,
"Young and old, and rich and poor;"
These are "days of visitation;"
Gospel grace may soon be o'er,
Sinners, hear the invitation;
O, thou dead and dying one,
Fly to Jesus for salvation,
Ere he shut the judgment throne!

HERE IS NO REST.

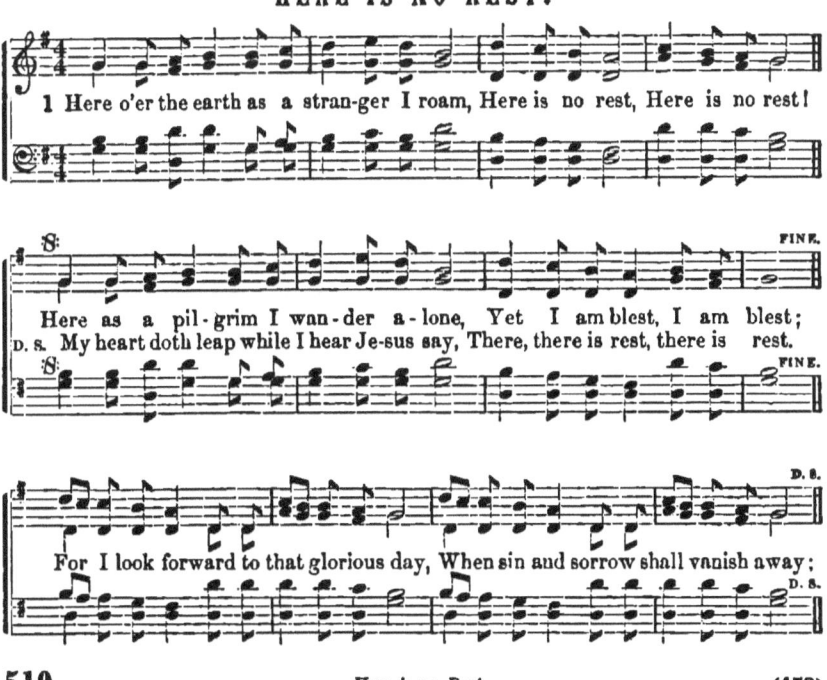

1 Here o'er the earth as a stran-ger I roam, Here is no rest, Here is no rest!
Here as a pil-grim I wan-der a-lone, Yet I am blest, I am blest;
D. S. My heart doth leap while I hear Je-sus say, There, there is rest, there is rest.
For I look forward to that glorious day, When sin and sorrow shall vanish away;

519. *Here is no Rest.* (479)

2 Here are afflictions and trials severe,
Here is no rest, here is no rest!
Here I must part with the friends I hold dear,
Yet I am blest, I am blest!
Sweet is the promise I read in his word:
Blessed are those who have died in the Lord:
They have been called to receive their reward,
There, there is rest; there is rest!

3 This world of care is a wilderness state,
Here is no rest, here is no rest!
Here must I bear from the world all its hate,
Yet I am blest, I am blest!
Soon shall I be from the wicked released,
Soon shall the weary forever be blest,
Soon shall I lean upon Jesus' own breast.
There, there is rest; there is rest!

NORTHFIELD. C. M.
J. INGALLS.

1 O, for a thousand tongues to sing
My dear Redeemer's praise,—
The glories of my God and King,
The triumphs of his grace.

520. *Praise to the Saviour.* (272)

2 My gracious Master and my God,
   Assist me to proclaim,
To spread through all the earth abroad,
   The honors of thy name.

3 Jesus! the name that calms our fears,
   That bids our sorrows cease;
'Tis music in the sinner's ears;
   'Tis life, and health, and peace.

4 He breaks the power of reigning sin;
   He sets the prisoner free;
His blood can make the foulest clean;
   His blood availed for me.
                    C. WESLEY.

521. *Delight in God's Word.* (184)

1 THOU art my portion, O, my God;
   Soon as I know thy way,
My heart makes haste t' obey thy word,
   And suffers no delay.

2 I choose the path of heavenly truth,
   And glory in my choice;
Not all the riches of the earth
   Could make me so rejoice.

3 Thy precepts and thy heavenly grace
   I set before my eyes;
Thence I derive my daily strength,
   And there my comfort lies.

4 If once I wander from thy path,
   I think upon my ways,
Then turn my feet to thy commands,
   And trust thy pardoning grace.

5 Now I am thine, forever thine,
   O, save thy servant, Lord;
Thou art my shield, my hiding-place,
   My hope is in thy word.   WATTS.

ST. MARTINS. C. M.
TANSUR.

1 O God, our help in ages past, Our hope for years to come, Our shelter from the stormy blast, And our eternal home.

522. *Support in God.* (190)

2 Beneath the shadow of thy throne
Thy saints have dwelt secure;
Sufficient is thine arm alone,
And our defense is sure.

3 Before the hills in order stood,
Or earth received her frame,
From everlasting thou art God,
To endless years the same.

4 Thy word commands our flesh to dust,—
"Return, ye sons of men;"
All nations rose from earth at first,
And turn to earth again.

5 O God, our help in ages past,
Our hope for years to come,
Be thou our guard while troubles last,
And our eternal home. WATTS.

523. *The Way, the Truth, and the Life.* (221)

1 Thou art the way; to thee alone
From sin and death we flee;
And he who would the Father seek,
Must seek him, Lord, through thee.

2 Thou art the truth; thy word alone
True wisdom can impart;
Thou, only, canst instruct the mind,
And purify the heart.

3 Thou art the life; the rending tomb
Proclaims thy conquering arm:
And those who put their trust in thee,
Nor death nor hell shall harm.

4 Thou art the way, the truth, the life;
Grant us to know that way,
That truth to keep, that life to win,
Which lead to endless day. DOANE.

524. *Prayer for Children's Conversion.* (418)

1 O LORD, behold us at thy feet,
A needy, sinful band;
As suppliants round thy mercy-seat,
We come at thy command.

2 'T is for our children we would plead,
The offspring thou hast given;
Where shall we go, in time of need,
But to the God of heaven?

3 We ask not for them wealth or fame
Amid the worldly strife;
But, in the all-prevailing Name,
We ask eternal life.

4 We crave the Spirit's quickening grace,
To make them pure in heart;
That they may stand before thy face,
And see thee as thou art.

202 THE PENITENT. WM. B. BRADBURY.

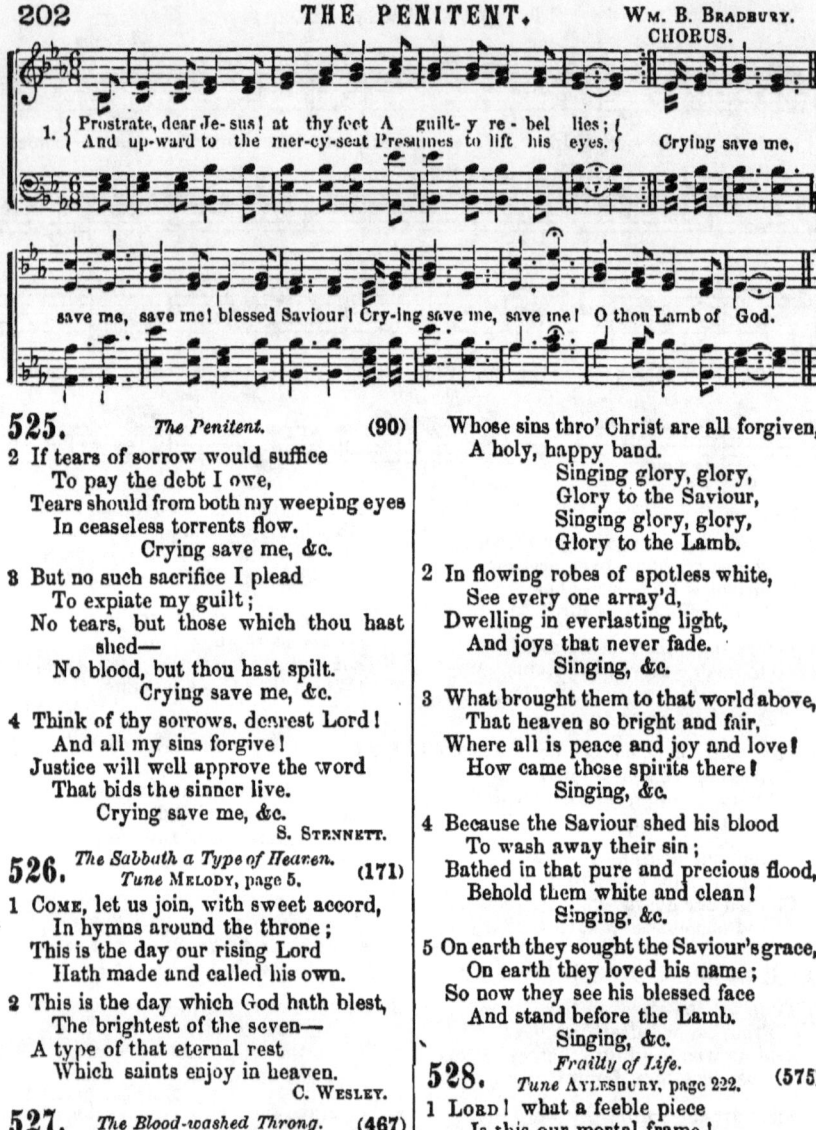

525. *The Penitent.* (90)
2 If tears of sorrow would suffice
    To pay the debt I owe,
Tears should from both my weeping eyes
    In ceaseless torrents flow.
        Crying save me, &c.

3 But no such sacrifice I plead
    To expiate my guilt;
No tears, but those which thou hast shed—
    No blood, but thou hast spilt.
        Crying save me, &c.

4 Think of thy sorrows, dearest Lord!
    And all my sins forgive!
Justice will well approve the word
    That bids the sinner live.
        Crying save me, &c.
                S. STENNETT.

526. *The Sabbath a Type of Heaven.*
    Tune MELODY, page 5. (171)
1 COME, let us join, with sweet accord,
    In hymns around the throne;
This is the day our rising Lord
    Hath made and called his own.

2 This is the day which God hath blest,
    The brightest of the seven—
A type of that eternal rest
    Which saints enjoy in heaven.
                C. WESLEY.

527. *The Blood-washed Throng.* (467)
1 AROUND the throne of God in heaven
    Thousands of saints now stand:

Whose sins thro' Christ are all forgiven,
    A holy, happy band.
        Singing glory, glory,
        Glory to the Saviour,
        Singing glory, glory,
        Glory to the Lamb.

2 In flowing robes of spotless white,
    See every one array'd,
Dwelling in everlasting light,
    And joys that never fade.
        Singing, &c.

3 What brought them to that world above,
    That heaven so bright and fair,
Where all is peace and joy and love!
    How came those spirits there?
        Singing, &c.

4 Because the Saviour shed his blood
    To wash away their sin;
Bathed in that pure and precious flood,
    Behold them white and clean!
        Singing, &c.

5 On earth they sought the Saviour's grace,
    On earth they loved his name;
So now they see his blessed face
    And stand before the Lamb.
        Singing, &c.

528. *Frailty of Life.*
    Tune AYLESBURY, page 222. (575)
1 LORD! what a feeble piece
    Is this our mortal frame!
Our life—how poor a trifle 'tis,
    That scarce deserves the name!

2 Alas! the brittle clay,
   That built our body first!
  And every month, and every day,
   'Tis moldering back to dust.

3 Our moments fly apace,
   Nor will our minutes stay;
  Just like a flood, our hasty days
   Are sweeping us away.

4 Well, if our days must fly,
   We'll keep their end in sight;
  We'll spend them all in wisdom's way,
   And let them speed their flight.

5 They'll waft us sooner o'er
   This life's tempestuous sea,
  Soon we shall reach the peaceful shore
   Of blest eternity.   WATTS.

HEAVEN IS MY HOME. Dr. L. MASON.

1 { I'm but a traveler here, Heav'n is my home;
    Earth is a desert drear, Heav'n is my home; } Danger and sorrow stand
  Round me on ev-'ry hand; Heav'n is my fatherland, Heav'n is my home.

529. *Heaven is my Home.* (461)

2 What tho' the tempest rage,
   Heav'n is my home;
  Short is my pilgrimage,
   Heav'n is my home;
  Time's cold and wintry blast,
  Soon will be over past,
  I shall reach home at last,
   Heav'n is my home.

3 There at my Saviour's side,
   Heav'n is my home,
  I shall be glorified,
   Heav'n is my home.
  There are the good and blest,
  Those I loved most and best,
  There, too, I soon shall rest,
   Heav'n is my home.

530. *Encouraging Prospects.* (534)
Tune ZION, page 130.

1 YES, we trust the day is breaking;
   Joyful times are near at hand;
  God, the mighty God, is speaking,
   By his word, in every land:
    When he chooses,
   Darkness flies at his command.

2 While the foe becomes more daring,
   While he enters like a flood,
  God, the Saviour, is preparing
   Means to spread his truth abroad:
    Every language
   Soon shall tell the love of God.

3 O, 'tis pleasant, 'tis reviving
   To our hearts, to hear, each day,
  Joyful news, from far arriving,
   How the gospel wins its way,
    Those enlightening
   Who in death and darkness lay.
            KELLY.

WEEP AND MOURN. C. M.

WM. B. BRADBURY.

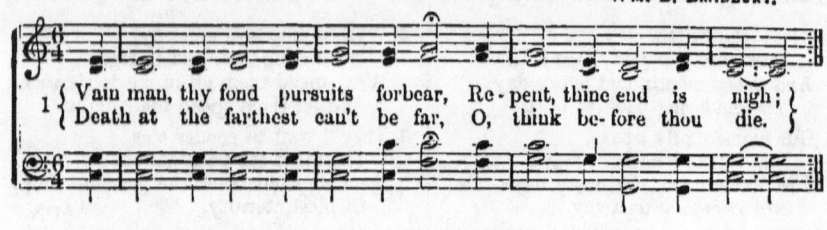

531. *The End Nigh.* (46)

2 Reflect, thou hast a soul to save;
  Thy sins, how high they mount!
 What are thy hopes beyond the grave?
  How stands that dark account?
    Weep, weep, mourn, mourn, &c.

3 Death enters, and there's no defense;
  His time there's none can tell:
 He'll in a moment call thee hence
  To heaven, or down to hell.
    Weep, weep, mourn, mourn, &c.

4 Thy flesh, perhaps thy greatest care,
  Shall unto dust consume:
 But, ah! destruction stops not there;
  Sin kills beyond the tomb.
    Weep, weep, mourn, mourn, &c.

532. *Remembering Christ.* (152)
  Tune HEBER, page 34.

1 IF human kindness meets return,
  And owns the grateful tie;
 If tender thoughts within us burn
  To feel a friend is nigh;—

2 O, shall not warmer accents tell
  The gratitude we owe
 To Him who died our fears to quell,
  And save from endless woe?

3 While yet his anguished soul surveyed
  Those pangs he would not flee,
 What love his latest words displayed!—
  "Meet, and remember me."

4 Remember thee! thy death, thy shame,
  The griefs which thou didst bear!
 O, memory, leave no other name
  But his recorded there. B. W. NOEL.

AVON. C. M.

205

Scottish.

1 How short and hast-y is our life! How vast our soul's af-fairs! Yet fool-ish mor-tals vain-ly strive To lav-ish out their years.

533. *Brevity and Frailty of Life.* (52)

2 Our days run thoughtlessly along,
 Without a moment's stay;
 Just like a story or a song,
 We pass our lives away.

3 God from on high invites us home;
 But we march heedless on,
 And, ever hastening to the tomb,
 Stoop downward as we run.

4 Draw us, O God, with sovereign grace,
 And lift our thoughts on high,
 That we may end this mortal race,
 And see salvation nigh.
         WATTS.

534. *The Vanity of Man.* (53)

1 TEACH me the measure of my days,
 Thou Maker of my frame;
 I would survey life's narrow space,
 And learn how frail I am.

2 A span is all that we can boast,
 An inch or two of time;
 Man is but vanity and dust,
 In all his flower and prime.

What should I wish, or wait for then,
 From creatures, earth and dust?
They make our expectations vain,
 And disappoint our trust.

4 Now I forbid my carnal hope,
 My fond desires recall;
 I give my mortal interest up,
 And make my God my all.
         WATTS.

535. *The Great High Priest.* (236)

1 Now let our cheerful eyes survey
 Our great High Priest above,
 And celebrate his constant care,
 And sympathetic love.

2 Though raised to a superior throne,
 Where angels bow around,
 And high o'er all the shining train,
 With matchless honors crowned;—

3 The names of all his saints he bears,
 Deep graven on his heart;
 Nor shall the meanest Christian say,
 That he hath lost his part.

4 Those characters shall fair abide,
 Our everlasting trust,
 When gems, and monuments, and crowns,
 Are mouldered down to dust.

5 So, gracious Saviour, on my breast,
 May thy dear name be worn,
 A sacred ornament and guard,
 To endless ages borne.
         DODDRIDGE.

OLMUTZ. S. M.

Arr., by Dr. L. Mason.

1 Ye servants of the Lord, Each in his office wait;

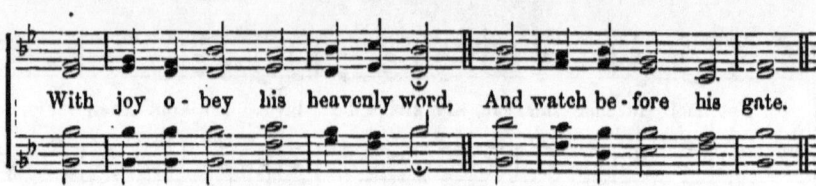

With joy obey his heavenly word, And watch before his gate.

536. *The Christian a Watcher.* (318)

2 Let all your lamps be bright,
 And trim the golden flame;
Gird up your loins, as in his sight,
 For awful is his name.

3 Watch!—'tis your Lord's command;
 And while we speak, he's near,
Mark every signal of his hand,
 And ready all appear.

4 Oh, happy servant, he,
 In such a posture found!
He shall his Lord with rapture see,
 And be with honor crowned.
  DODDRIDGE.

537. *Diffusion of the Gospel.* (523)

1 O Lord our God, arise,
 The cause of truth maintain,
And wide o'er all the peopled world,
 Extend her blessed reign.

2 Thou, Prince of life, arise;
 Nor let thy glory cease;
Far spread the conquests of thy grace,
 And bless the earth with peace.

3 Spirit of grace, arise,
 Extend thy healing wing,
And o'er a dark and ruined world,
 Let light and order spring.

4 Let all on earth arise,
 To God, the Saviour, sing;
From shore to shore, from earth to heaven,
 Let echoing anthems ring.

538. *Life and Death Eternal.* (49)

1 O, where shall rest be found—
 Rest for the weary soul!
'Twere vain the ocean's depths to sound,
 Or pierce to either pole.

2 The world can never give
 The bliss for which we sigh;
'Tis not the whole of life to live,
 Nor all of death to die.

3 Beyond this vale of tears
 There is a life above,
Unmeasured by the flight of years;
 And all that life is love.

4 There is a death whose pang
 Outlasts the fleeting breath;
O, what eternal horrors hang
 Around "the second death!"

5 Lord God of truth and grace,
 Teach us that death to shun,
Lest we be banished from thy face,
 And evermore undone.
  MONTGOMERY.

539. *Active Piety.* (317)

1 Laborers of Christ, arise,
 And gird you for the toil;
The dew of promise from the skies
 Already cheers the soil.

2 Go where the sick recline,
   Where mourning hearts deplore;
   And where the sons of sorrow pine,
   Dispense your hallowed lore.

3 Urge, with a tender zeal,
   The erring child along
   Where peaceful congregations kneel,
   And pious teachers throng.

4 Be faith, which looks above,
   With prayer, your constant guest,
   And wrap the Saviour's changeless love
   A mantle round your breast.

5 So shall you share the wealth
   That earth may ne'er despoil,
   And the blest gospel's saving health
   Repay your arduous toil.
                              L. H. SIGOURNEY.

540.   *Confession of Sin.*   (4)

1 ONCE more we meet to pray,
   Once more our guilt confess;
   Turn not, O Lord, thine ear away
   From creatures in distress.

2 Our sins to heaven ascend,
   And there for vengeance cry;
   O God, behold the sinner's Friend,
   Who intercedes on high.

3 Though we are vile indeed,
   And well deserve thy curse,
   The merits of thy Son we plead,
   Who lived and died for us.

4 Now let thy bosom yearn,
   As it hath done before;
   Return to us, O God, return,
   And ne'er forsake us more.

541.   *Reliance on God.*   (191)

1 MY God, permit my tongue
   This joy—to call thee mine;
   And let my early cries prevail
   To taste thy love divine.

2 For l'fe, without thy love,
   No r lish can afford;
   No joy can be compared with this,—
   To serve and please the Lord.

3 In wakeful hours of night,
   I call my God to mind;
   I think how wise thy counsels are,
   And all thy dealings kind.

4 Since thou hast been my help,
   To thee my spirit flies;
   And on thy watchful providence
   My cheerful hope relies.

5 The shadow of thy wings
   My soul in safety keeps;
   I follow where my Father leads,
   And he supports my steps.
                              WATTS.

542.   *God the Fount of all Good.*   (182)

1 GOD is the fountain whence
   Ten thousand blessings flow;
   To him my life, my health, and friends,
   And every good, I owe.

2 The comforts he affords
   Are neither few nor small;
   He is the source of fresh delights,
   My portion and my all.

3 He fills my heart with joy,
   My lips attunes for praise;
   And to his glory I'll devote
   The remnant of my days.
                              BEDDOME.

543.   *Office of Faith.*   (343)

1 FAITH is a precious grace,
   Where'er it is bestowed;
   It boasts a high, celestial birth,
   And is the gift of God.

2 Jesus it owns as King,
   And all-atoning Priest;
   It claims no merit of its own,
   But looks for all in Christ.

3 To him it leads the soul,
   When filled with deep distress,
   Flies to the fountain of his blood,
   And trusts his righteousness.

4 Since 'tis thy work alone,
   And that divinely free,
   Lord, send the Spirit of thy Son,
   To work this faith in me.
                              BEDDOME.

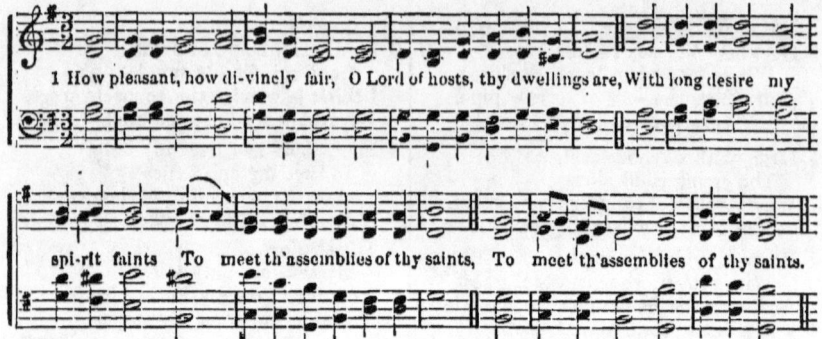

WM. B. BRADBURY.

1 How pleasant, how divinely fair, O Lord of hosts, thy dwellings are, With long desire my spirit faints To meet th' assemblies of thy saints, To meet th' assemblies of thy saints.

544. *Blessedness of Worshiping God in his Temple.* (173)

1 How pleasant, how divinely fair,
  O Lord of hosts, thy dwellings are!
  With long desire my spirit faints
  To meet th' assemblies of thy saints.

2 My flesh would rest in thine abode;
  My panting heart cries out for God;
  My God, my King, why should I be
  So far from all my joys and thee?

3 Blest are the saints, who dwell on high,
  Around thy throne, above the sky;
  Thy brightest glories shine above,
  And all their work is praise and love.

4 Blest are the souls who find a place
  Within the temple of thy grace;
  There they behold thy gentler rays,
  And seek thy face, and learn thy praise.

5 Blest are the men whose hearts are set
  To find the way to Zion's gate;
  God is their strength, and, through the road,
  They lean upon their helper, God.

6 Cheerful they walk, with growing strength,
  Till all shall meet in heaven at length;
  Till all before thy face appear,
  And join in nobler worship there.
  WATTS.

545. *The place where Jesus lay.* (143)

1 COME, happy souls, adore the Lamb,
  Who loved our race ere time began,
  Who vailed his Godhead in our clay,
  And in an humble manger lay.

2 To Jordan's stream the Spirit led,
  To mark the path his saints should tread;
  With joy they trace the sacred way,
  To see the place where Jesus lay.

3 Baptized by John in Jordan's wave,
  The Saviour left his watery grave;
  Heaven owned the deed, approved the way,
  And blessed the place where Jesus lay.

4 Come, all who love his precious name,
  Come, tread his steps, and learn of him;
  Happy beyond expression they
  Who find the place where Jesus lay.
  BALDWIN.

546. *Christ ever present in his Churches.* (414)

1 JESUS, where'er thy people meet,
  There they behold thy mercy-seat;
  Where'er they seek thee, thou art found,
  And every place is hallowed ground.

2 For thou, within no walls confined,
  Dost dwell within the humble mind;
  Such ever bring thee where they come
  And, going, take thee to their home.

3 Dear Shepherd of thy chosen few,
  Thy former mercies here renew;
  Here, to our waiting hearts proclaim
  The sweetness of thy saving name.
  COWPER.

547. *Prayer for General Peace.* (549)
1 THY footsteps, Lord, with joy we trace,
And mark the conquests of thy grace;
Complete the work thou hast begun,
And let thy will on earth be done.

2 O, show thyself the Prince of Peace;
Command the din of war to cease!
O, bid contending nations rest,
And let thy love rule every breast!

3 Then peace returns with balmy wing;
Glad plenty laughs, the valleys sing;
Reviving commerce lifts her head,
And want, and woe and hate have fled.

4 Thou good, and wise, and righteous Lord,
All move subservient to thy word;
O, soon let every nation prove
The perfect joy of Christian love!

548. *Praise for Divine Protection.* (208)
1 WITH all my powers of heart and tongue,
I'll praise my Maker in my song;
Angels shall hear the notes I raise,
Approve the song, and join the praise.

2 To God I cried when troubles rose;
He heard me, and subdued my foes;
He did my rising fears control,
And strength diffused through all my soul.

3 Amidst a thousand snares I stand,
Upheld and guarded by his hand;
His words my fainting soul revive,
And keep my dying faith alive.

4 Grace will complete what grace begins
To save from sorrows or from sins;
The work that wisdom undertakes,
Eternal mercy ne'er forsakes. WATTS.

549. *Christ's Invitation.* (58)
1 COME hither, all ye weary souls;
Ye heavy-laden sinners, come;
I'll give you rest from all your toils,
And raise you to my heavenly home.

2 They shall find rest that learn of me;
I'm of a meek and lowly mind;
But passion rages like the sea,
And pride is restless as the wind.

3 Blest is the man whose shoulders take
My yoke, and bear it with delight:
My yoke is easy to his neck,
My grace shall make the burden light.

4 Jesus, we come at thy command,
With faith, and hope, and cheerful zeal;
Resign our spirits to thy hand,
To mould and guide us at thy will.
WATTS.

550. *Prayer for more Laborers.* (497)
1 THROUGH many climes, o'er many lands,
How wide the growing harvest spreads!
But few the men, and weak the hands,
To reap where Heaven its bounty sheds.

2 O Thou, whose matchless love and power,
Thy sovereign counsels onward bear,
Raise up, in this important hour,
A sacred host, the work to share.

3 Call forth, from vale and mountain height,
The minds on which thy grace hath shone,
Richly imbue with holy light,
And consecrate them all thy own.

4 With knowledge fraught, and hallowed lore,
May they the cross of Christ proclaim;
From realm to realm, from shore to shore,
Till earth shall bless his saving name.
G. B. IDE.

551. *The Year Crowned with Goodness.* (552)
1 ETERNAL Source of every joy,
Thy praise may well our lips employ,
While in thy temple we appear,
Whose goodness crowns the circling year.

2 Wide as the wheels of nature roll,
Thy hand supports the steady pole;
The sun is taught by thee to rise,
And darkness when to vail the skies.

3 The flowery spring, at thy command,
Embalms the air and paints the land;
The summer rays with vigor shine,
To raise the corn and cheer the vine.

4 Thy hand in autumn richly pours
Through all our coasts abundant stores;
And winters, softened by thy care,
No more a dreary aspect wear.

5 Still be the cheerful homage paid
With morning light and evening shade;
Seasons, and months, and weeks, and days
Demand successive songs of praise.
DODDRIDGE.

GOD CALLING YET. L. M.

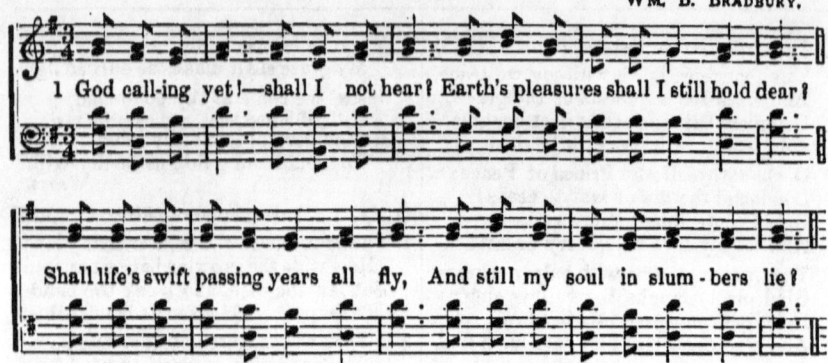

552. *"God Calling Yet."* (70)

1 God calling yet!—shall I not hear?
Earth's pleasures shall I still hold dear?
Shall life's swift passing years all fly,
And still my soul in slumbers lie?

2 God calling yet!—shall I not rise?
Can I his loving voice despise,
And basely his kind care repay?
He calls me still: can I delay?

3 God calling yet!—and shall I give
No heed, but still in bondage live?
I wait, but he does not forsake;
He calls me still!—my heart awake!

4 God calling yet!—I cannot stay;
My heart I yield without delay:
Vain world, farewell! from thee I part;
The voice of God hath reached my heart!

553. *Awake! Awake!* (55)

1 Awake, awake, each drowsy soul!
Awake, and view the setting sun!
See how the shades of death advance,
Ere half the task of life is done.

2 Soon will he close all drowsy eyes,
Nor shall we hear these warnings more;
Soon will the mighty Judge approach;
E'en now he stands before the door.

3 To-day, attend his gracious voice!
This is the summons which he sends—
"Awake! for on this passing hour
Thy long eternity depends."
HIGINBOTHAM.

554. *Invocation of the Spirit.* (310)

1 Come, sacred Spirit, from above,
And fill the coldest heart with love;
Soften to flesh the flinty stone,
And let thy Godlike power be known.

2 O, let a holy flock await
In crowds around thy temple gate;
Each pressing on, with zeal, to be
A living sacrifice to thee. DODDRIDGE.

555. *Light for the Heathen.* (517)

1 Though now the nations sit beneath
The darkness of o'erspreading death;
God will arise with light divine,
On Zion's holy towers to shine.

2 That light shall shine on distant lands,
And wandering tribes, in joyful bands,
Shall come, thy glory, Lord, to see,
And in thy courts to worship thee.

3 O light of Zion, now arise!
Let the glad morning bless our eyes!
Ye nations, catch the kindling ray,
And hail the splendors of the day.
L. BACON.

NEARER TO THEE.

R. LOWRY. *Harmonized for this work.*

1 Nearer, my God, to thee,—Nearer to thee! E'en though it be a cross That raiseth me; Still all my song shall be, Nearer, my God, to thee, Nearer, Nearer, Nearer to thee!

556. *Nearer to God.* (354)

1 NEARER, my God, to thee,—
Nearer to thee!
E'en though it be a cross
That raiseth me;
Still all my song shall be,
Nearer, my God, to thee,
Nearer to thee!

2 Though like a wanderer,
The sun gone down,
Darkness comes over me,
My rest a stone,
Yet in my dreams I'd be
Nearer, my God, to thee,
Nearer to thee!

3 There let my way appear
Steps unto heaven;
All that thou sendest me
In mercy given;
Angels to beckon me
Nearer, my God, to thee,
Nearer to thee!

4 Then with my waking thoughts
Bright with thy praise,
Out of my stony griefs
Bethel I'll raise;
So by my woes to be
Nearer, my God, to thee,
Nearer to thee!

5 And when on joyful wing
Cleaving the sky,
Sun, moon, and stars forgot,
Upward I fly;
Still all my song shall be,
Nearer, my God, to thee,
Nearer to thee!

SARAH F. ADAMS

212   CORINTH. C. M.
Dr. L. Mason.

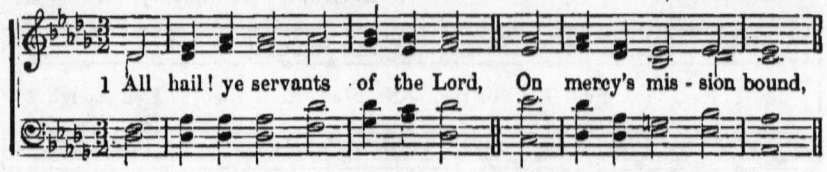
1 All hail! ye servants of the Lord, On mercy's mis-sion bound,

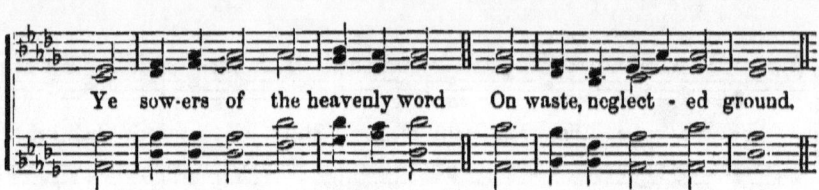
Ye sow-ers of the heavenly word On waste, neglect-ed ground.

557. *Home Missionaries Encouraged.* (502)
2 What though your seed 'mid thorns be sown
   Where tares and brambles thrive,
Still One is able, One alone,
   To save its germ alive.

3 Ye fear what falls on stony earth
   Will mock your prayerful toil,
But sometimes plants of holiest birth
   Bear fruit in sterile soil.

4 The seed that by the wayside fell
   Perchance you counted dead:
Yet souls that sing in heaven may tell,
   They on its sweetness fed.

5 And some a hundred fold shall bear
   Unto the harvest's Lord;
How blessed, then, will be your care;
   How glorious your reward!
                   L. H. Sigourney.

558. *Deploring Ingratitude.* (375)
1 With tears of anguish I lament,
   Here, at thy feet, my God,
My passion, pride, and discontent,
   And vile ingratitude.

2 Sure there was ne'er a heart so base,
   So false as mine has been;
So faithless to its promises,
   So prone to every sin!

3 My reason tells me thy commands
   Are holy, just, and true;
Tells me whate'er my God demands
   Is his most righteous due.

4 Reason I hear, her counsels weigh,
   And all her words approve;
But still I find it hard t' obey,
   And harder yet to love.

5 How long, dear Saviour, shall I feel
   These struggles in my breast!
When wilt thou bow my stubborn will,
   And give my conscience rest?
                   Stennett.

559. *The Spirit's Power.* (311)
1 Come, Holy Spirit, from above,
   With thy celestial fire;
Come, and with flames of zeal and love,
   Our hearts and tongues inspire.

2 The Spirit, by his heavenly breath,
   New life creates within;
He quickens sinners from the death
   Of trespasses and sin.

3 The things of Christ the Spirit takes
   And to our hearts reveals;
Our bodies he his temple makes,
   And our redemption seals.

560. *The Pledge of Fidelity.* (136)

1 YE men and angels, witness now,
   Before the Lord we speak;
   To him we make our solemn vow,
   A vow we dare not break,

2 That, long as life itself shall last,
   Ourselves to Christ we yield;
   Nor from his cause will we depart,
   Or ever quit the field.

3 We trust not in our native strength,
   But on his grace rely;
   May he, with our returning wants,
   All needful aid supply.

4 O, guide our doubtful feet aright,
   And keep us in thy ways;
   And, while we turn our vows to prayer,
   Turn thou our prayers to praise.
   BEDDOME.

561. *Hinder me Not.* (477)

1 IN all my Lord's appointed ways
   My journey I'll pursue;
   "Hinder me not," ye much-loved saints,
   For I must go with you.

2 Through floods and flames, if Jesus lead,
   I'll follow where he goes;
   "Hinder me not," shall be my cry,
   Though earth and hell oppose.

3 Through duties, and through trials too,
   I'll go at his command;
   "Hinder me not;" for I am bound
   To my Immanuel's land.

4 And, when my Saviour calls me home,
   Still this my cry shall be—
   "Hinder me not;" come, welcome death;
   I'll gladly go with thee.
   J. RYLAND.

562. *Gentleness to the Erring.* (504)

1 THINK gently of the erring one!
   O, let us not forget,
   However darkly stained by sin,
   He is our brother yet!

2 Heir of the same inheritance,
   Child of the self-same God,
   He hath but stumbled in the path
   We have in weakness trod.

3 Speak gently to the erring ones!
   We yet may lead them back,
   With holy words, and tones of love,
   From misery's thorny track.

4 Forget not, brother, thou hast sinned,
   And sinful yet may'st be;
   Deal gently with the erring heart,
   As God has dealt with thee.
   MISS FLETCHER.

563. *Christ's Condescending Regard to Little Children.* (415)

1 SEE Israel's gentle Shepherd stand,
   With all-engaging charms;
   Hark! how he calls the tender lambs,
   And folds them in his arms!

2 "Permit them to approach," he cries,
   "Nor scorn their humble name;
   For 'twas to bless such souls as these
   The Lord of angels came."

3 We bring them, Lord, by fervent prayer,
   And yield them up to thee;
   With humble trust that we are thine,
   Thine let our offspring be.

4 If orphans they are left behind,
   Thy guardian care we trust;
   That care shall heal our bleeding hearts,
   If weeping o'er their dust.
   DODDRIDGE.

564. *"Early will I Seek Thee."* (408)

1 EARLY, my God, without delay,
   I haste to seek thy face;
   My thirsty spirit faints away,
   Without thy cheering grace.

2 So pilgrims on the scorching sand,
   Beneath a burning sky,
   Long for a cooling stream at hand,
   And they must drink, or die.

3 I've seen thy glory and thy power
   Through all thy temple shine;
   My God, repeat that heavenly hour,
   That vision so divine!

4 Thus till my last expiring day,
   I'll bless my God and King;
   Thus will I lift my hands to pray,
   And tune my lips to sing.
   WATTS.

REST. L. M.

Wm. B. Bradbury.

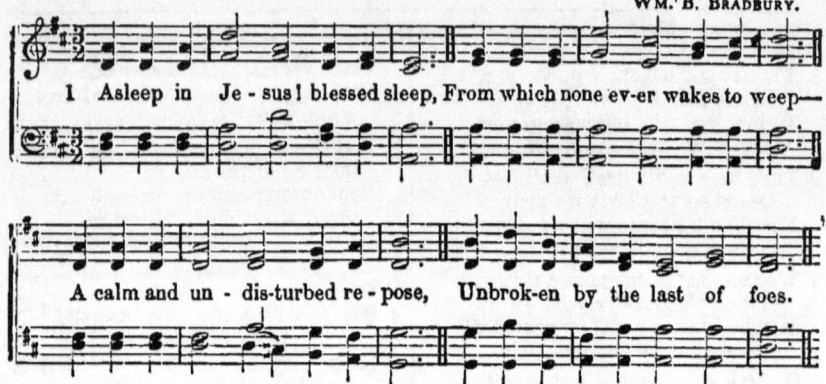

1 Asleep in Je-sus! blessed sleep, From which none ev-er wakes to weep— A calm and un-dis-turbed re-pose, Unbrok-en by the last of foes.

565. *Asleep in Jesus.* (581)

2 Asleep in Jesus! O, how sweet
To be for such a slumber meet!
With holy confidence to sing
That death has lost his venomed sting!

3 Asleep in Jesus! peaceful rest,
Whose waking is supremely blest;
No fear, no woe, shall dim that hour
That manifests the Saviour's power!

4 Asleep in Jesus! O, for me
May such a blissful refuge be:
Securely shall my ashes lie,
And wait the summons from on high.

5 Asleep in Jesus! time nor space
Affects this precious hiding-place:
On Indian plains or Lapland snows
Believers find the same repose.

6 Asleep in Jesus! far from thee
Thy kindred and their graves may be:
But thine is still a blessed sleep,
From which none ever wakes to weep.
Mrs. Mackay.

566. *The Example of Christ.* (219)

1 My dear Redeemer, and my Lord,
I read my duty in thy word;
But in thy life, the law appears
Drawn out in living characters.

2 Such was thy truth, and such thy zeal,
Such deference to thy Father's will,
Such love, and meekness so divine,
I would transcribe, and make them mine.

3 Cold mountains and the midnight air
Witnessed the fervor of thy prayer:
The desert thy temptations knew,
Thy conflict, and thy victory too.

4 Be thou my pattern; make me bear
More of thy gracious image here;
Then God, the Judge, shall own my name
Among the followers of the Lamb.
Watts.

567. *Deriving Strength from Christ.* (282)

1 Let me but hear my Saviour say,
"Strength shall be equal to thy day;"—
Then I rejoice in deep distress,
Upheld by all-sufficient grace.

2 I can do all things, or can bear
All suffering, if my Lord be there;
Sweet pleasures mingle with the pains,
While he my sinking head sustains.

3 I glory in infirmity,
That Christ's own power may rest on me;
When I am weak, then am I strong;
Grace is my shield, and Christ my song.
Watts.

568. *Choosing Christ's Service.* (254)

1 May I resolve, with all my heart,
With all my powers to serve the Lord;
Nor from his precepts e'er depart,
Whose service is a rich reward.

2 O, be his service all my joy!
Around let my example shine,
Till others love the blest employ,
And join in labors so divine.

3 Be this the purpose of my soul,
My solemn, my determined choice—
To yield to his supreme control,
And in his kind commands rejoice.

4 O, may I never faint nor tire,
Nor, wandering, leave his sacred ways;
Great God, accept my soul's desire,
And give me strength to live thy praise.
Steele.

569. *Living to Christ.* (256)

1 My gracious Lord, I own thy right
To every service I can pay,
And call it my supreme delight
To hear thy dictates and obey.

2 What is my being but for thee—
Its sure support, its noblest end?
'Tis my delight thy face to see,
And serve the cause of such a Friend.

3 'Tis to my Saviour I would live—
To him who for my ransom died;
Nor could all worldly honor give
Such bliss as crowns me at his side.

4 His work my hoary age shall bless,
When youthful vigor is no more,
And my last hour of life confess
His saving love, his glorious power.
Doddridge.

570. *Christian Stability.* (194)

1 O Lord, thy heavenly grace impart,
And fix my frail, inconstant heart;
Henceforth my chief desire shall be,
To dedicate myself to thee.

2 Whate'er pursuits my time employ,
One thought shall fill my soul with joy;
That silent, secret thought shall be,
That all my hopes are fixed on thee.

3 Thy glorious eye pervadeth space;
Thy presence, Lord, fills every place;
And, wheresoe'er my lot may be,
Still shall my spirit cleave to thee.

4 Renouncing every worldly thing,
And safe beneath thy spreading wing,
My sweetest thought henceforth shall be,
That all I want I find in thee.
J. F. Oberlin.

571. *The Better Land.* (589)

1 There is a land mine eye hath seen,
In visions of enraptured thought,
So bright that all which spreads between
Is with its radiant glory fraught;

2 A land upon whose blissful shore
There rests no shadow, falls no stain;
There those who meet shall part no more,
And those long parted meet again.

3 Its skies are not like earthly skies,
With varying hues of shade and light;
It hath no need of suns to rise,
To dissipate the gloom of night.

4 There sweeps no desolating wind
Across that calm, serene abode;
The wanderer there a home may find,
Within the Paradise of God.

572. *The Great Commission.* (158)

1 "Go, preach my gospel," saith the Lord,
"Bid the whole earth my grace receive,
He shall be saved that trusts my word,
And be condemned who'll not believe.

2 "I'll make your great commission known,
And ye shall prove my gospel true,
By all the works that I have done,
By all the wonders ye shall do.

3 "Teach all the nations my commands;
I'm with you till the world shall end;
All power is trusted in my hands;
I can destroy, and I defend."

4 He spake, and light shone round his head;
On a bright cloud to heaven he rode;
They to the farthest nations spread
The grace of their ascended God.
Watts.

NAOMI. C. M.
Dr. L. Mason. *By permission.*

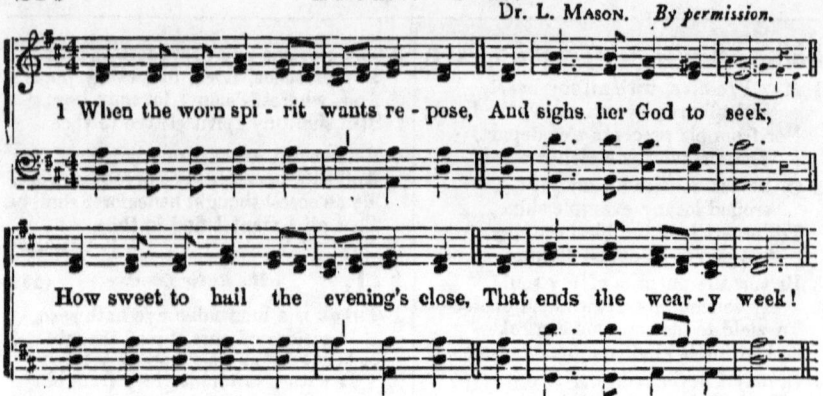

1 When the worn spi-rit wants re-pose, And sighs her God to seek, How sweet to hail the evening's close, That ends the wear-y week!

573. *Lord's Day Sweet to the Weary.* (166)

2 How sweet to hail the early dawn,
    That opens on the sight,
When first that soul-reviving morn
    Sheds forth new rays of light!

3 Sweet day, thine hours too soon will cease,
    Yet, while they gently roll,
Breathe, heavenly Spirit, source of peace,
    A Sabbath o'er my soul.

4 When will my pilgrimage be done,
    The world's long week be o'er,
That Sabbath dawn, which needs no sun,
    That day which fades no more?
                                    EDMESTON.

574. *Regeneration by the Spirit.* (89)

1 Nor all the outward forms on earth,
    Nor rites that God has given,
Nor will of man, nor blood, nor birth,
    Can raise a soul to heaven.

2 The sovereign will of God alone
    Creates us heirs of grace,
Born in the image of his Son,
    A new, peculiar race.

3 The Spirit, like some heavenly wind,
    Breathes on the sons of flesh,
Creates anew the carnal mind,
    And forms the man afresh.

4 Our quickened souls awake and rise
    From their long sleep of death;
On heavenly things we fix our eyes,
    And praise employs our breath.
                                    WATTS.

575. *Finding God in all Things.* (198)

1 While thee I seek, protecting Power!
    Be my vain wishes stilled;
And may this consecrated hour
    With better hopes be filled.

2 Thy love the power of thought bestow'd,
    To thee my thoughts would soar;
Thy mercy o'er my life has flowed,
    That mercy I adore.

3 In each event of life how clear
    Thy ruling hand I see!
Each blessing to my soul most dear,
    Because conferred by thee.

4 In every joy that crowns my days,
    In every pain I bear,
My heart shall find delight in praise,
    Or seek relief in prayer.

5 When gladness wings my favored hour,
    Thy love my thoughts shall fill;
Resigned, when storms of sorrow lower
    My soul shall meet thy will.
                                    WILLIAMS.

CROYDON. C. M.

From "The Jubilee."

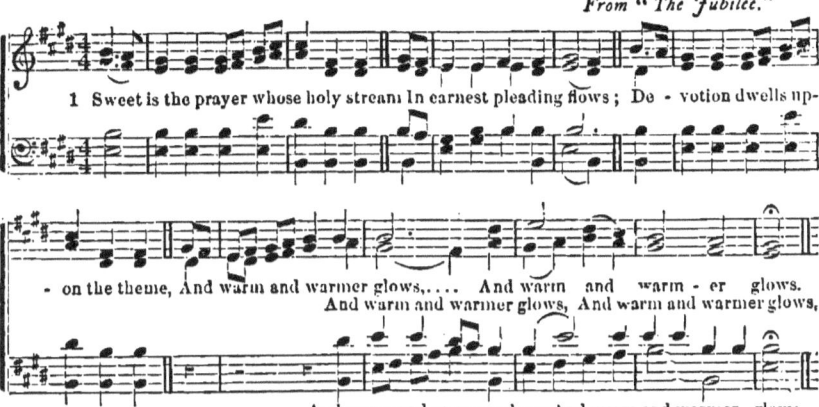

1 Sweet is the prayer whose holy stream In earnest pleading flows; Devotion dwells upon the theme, And warm and warmer glows,.... And warm and warmer glows.

576. *Secret Prayer.* (384)

2 Faith grasps the blessing she desires;
Hope points the upward gaze;
And Love, celestial Love, inspires
The eloquence of praise.

3 But sweeter far the still small voice
Unheard by human ear,
When God has made the heart rejoice,
And dried the bitter tear.

4 No accents flow, no words ascend;
All utterance faileth there;
But sainted spirits comprehend,
And God accepts the prayer!

577. *Heaven Happy.* (592)

1 There is a land of pure delight,
Where saints immortal reign;
Infinite day excludes the night,
And pleasures banish pain.

2 There everlasting spring abides,
And never-withering flowers;
Death, like a narrow sea, divides
This heavenly land from ours.

3 Sweet fields beyond the swelling flood,
Stand dressed in living green;
So to the Jews old Canaan stood,
While Jordan rolled between.

4 But tim'rous mortals start and shrink
To cross this narrow sea,
And linger, shivering on the brink,
And fear to launch away.

5 Oh! could we make our doubts remove,
Those gloomy doubts that rise,—
And see the Canaan that we love,
With unbeclouded eyes,—

6 Could we but climb where Moses stood,
And view the landscape o'er.—
Not Jordan's stream, nor death's cold flood,
Should fright us from the shore.
WATTS.

578. *Saints in the Hands of Christ.* (288.

1 Firm as the earth thy gospel stands,
My Lord, my hope, my trust:
If I am found in Jesus' hands,
My soul can ne'er be lost.

2 His honor is engaged to save
The meanest of his sheep;
All, whom his heavenly Father gave.
His hands securely keep.

3 Nor death, nor hell, shall e'er remove
His favorites from his breast;
Within the bosom of his love
They must for ever rest.
WATTS.

BROWN. C. M.

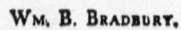

1 This is the day the Lord hath made, He calls the hours his own;
Let heaven rejoice, let earth be glad, And praise surround the throne;

579. *Lord's Day Morning.* (175)

1 This is the day the Lord hath made,
   He calls the hours his own;
Let heaven rejoice, let earth be glad,
   And praise surround the throne.

2 To-day he rose and left the dead,
   And Satan's empire fell;
To-day the saints his triumphs spread,
   And all his wonders tell.

3 Blest be the Lord, who comes to men
   With messages of grace;
Who comes in God, his Father's name,
   To save our sinful race.

4 Hosanna in the highest strains
   The church on earth can raise;
The highest heavens in which he reigns,
   Shall give him nobler praise.
                                   WATTS.

580. *Not Ashamed of Christ.* (330)

1 I'm not ashamed to own my Lord,
   Or to defend his cause;
Maintain the honor of his word,
   The glory of his cross.

2 Jesus, my God, I know his name—
   His name is all my trust;
Nor will he put my soul to shame,
   Nor let my hope be lost.

3 Firm as his throne his promise stands
   And he can well secure
What I've committed to his hands,
   Till the decisive hour.

4 Then will he own my worthless name
   Before his Father's face,
And in the new Jerusalem
   Appoint my soul a place.
                                   WATTS.

581. *Prayer for Special Favor.* (2)

1 Within thy house, O Lord, our God,
   In glory now appear;
Make this a place of thine abode,
   And shed thy blessings here.

2 When we thy mercy seat surround,
   Thy Spirit, Lord, impart;
And let thy gospel's joyful sound
   With power reach every heart.

3 Here let the blind their sight obtain;
   Here give the mourners rest;
Let Jesus here triumphant reign,
   Enthroned in every breast.

4 Here let the voice of sacred joy
   And humble prayer arise,
Till higher strains our tongues employ
   In realms beyond the skies.

582. *The Society of Heaven.* (424)

1 JERUSALEM, my happy home,
Name ever dear to me!
When shall my labors have an end,
In joy, and peace, and thee?

2 When shall these eyes thy heaven-built walls
And pearly gates behold?
Thy bulwarks with salvation strong,
And streets of shining gold?

3 O, when, thou city of my God,
Shall I thy courts ascend,
Where congregations ne'er break up,
And Sabbaths have no end?

There happier bowers than Eden's bloom,
Nor sin nor sorrow know:
Blest seats! through rude and stormy scenes
I onward press to you.

5 Why should I shrink at pain and woe,
Or feel at death dismay?
I've Canaan's goodly land in view,
And realms of endless day.

6 Apostles, martyrs, prophets, there,
Around my Saviour stand;
And soon my friends in Christ below
Will join the glorious band.

7 Jerusalem, my happy home!
My soul still pants for thee;
Then shall my labors have an end,
When I thy joys shall see.

583. *Pressing to the Goal.* (322)

1 AWAKE, my soul; stretch every nerve,
And press with vigor on;
A heavenly race demands thy zeal,
And an immortal crown.

2 A cloud of witnesses around,
Hold thee in full survey;
Forget the steps already trod,
And onward urge thy way.

3 'Tis God's all-animating voice
That calls thee from on high;
'Tis his own hand presents the prize,
To thine uplifted eye.

4 That prize, with peerless glories bright,
Which shall new lustre boast,
When victors' wreaths and monarch's gems
Shall blend in common dust.
DODDRIDGE.

584. *The Name of Jesus.* (289)

1 THERE is a name I love to hear:
I love to sing its worth;
It sounds like music in mine ear,
The sweetest name on earth.

2 It tells me of a Saviour's love,
Who died to set me free;
It tells me of his precious blood,
The sinner's perfect plea.

3 It tells of One whose loving heart
Can feel my smallest woe;
Who in each sorrow bears a part
That none can bear below.

4 Jesus! the name I love so well,
The name I love to hear!
No saint on earth its worth can tell,
No heart conceive how dear.

5 This name shall shed its fragrance still
Along this thorny road—
Shall sweetly smooth the rugged hill
That leads me up to God:

6 And there, with all the blood-bought throng,
From sin and sorrow free,
I'll sing the new eternal song
Of Jesus' love to me.

585. *The Joyful Sound.* (536)

1 LORD, send thy word and let it fly
The spacious earth around;
Till every soul beneath the sky
Shall hear the joyful sound.

2 From sea to sea, from shore to shore,
May Jesus be adored!
And earth, with all her millions, shout
Hosanna to the Lord!

DOXOLOGY.

To Father, Son, and Holy Ghost,
One God, whom we adore,
Be glory as it was, is now,
And shall be evermore.

NEARER MY HOME.

JOHN M. EVANS.

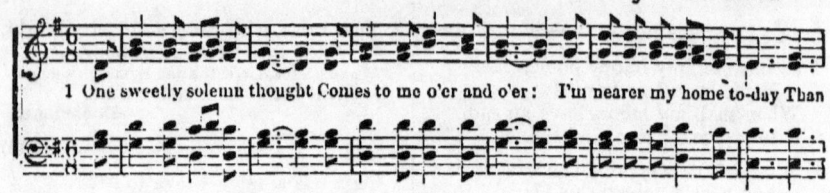

1 One sweetly solemn thought Comes to me o'er and o'er: I'm nearer my home to-day Than I've ev-er been be-fore.

CHORUS.

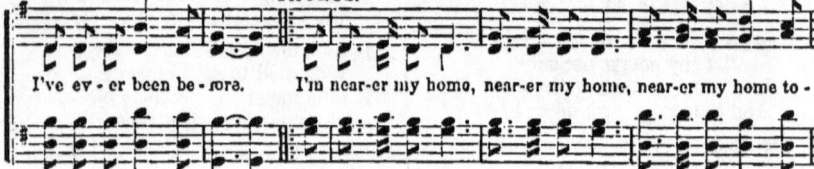

I'm near-er my home, near-er my home, near-er my home to-day; Yes! near-er my home in heav'n to-day, Than ev-er I've been be-fore.

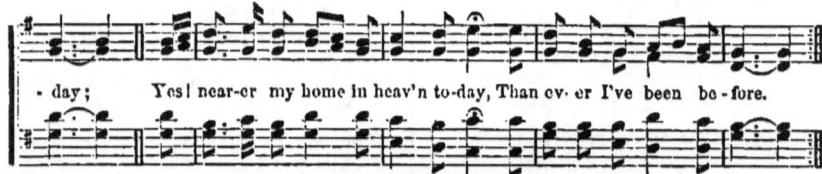

586.   *"Nearer my Home."*   (423)

2 Nearer my Father's house,
  Where the many mansions be;
Nearer the great white throne,
  Nearer the jasper sea.

3 Nearer the bound of life
  Where we lay our burdens down,
Nearer leaving my cross,
  Nearer wearing my crown.

4 But lying darkly between,
  Winding down through the night,
Is that dim and unknown stream
  Which leads at last to light.

For even now my feet
  May stand upon its brink;
I may be nearer my home,
  Nearer now, than I think.

587.   *The Dreadful End.*   (39)
    Tune WINDHAM, page 193.

1 LORD, what a thoughtless wretch was I
  To mourn, and murmur, and repine,
To see the wicked, placed on high,
  In pride and robes of honor shine!

2 But oh, their end, their dreadful end!
  Thy sanctuary taught me so:
On slippery rocks I see them stand,
  And fiery billows roll below.

3 Their fancied joys—how fast they flee;
  Just like a dream when man awakes!
Their songs of softest harmony
  Are but a prelude to their plagues.

4 Now I esteem their mirth and wine
  Too dear to purchase with my blood;
Lord, 'tis enough that thou art mine,
  My life, my portion, and my God!
                        WATTS.

THE CHRISTIAN HERO.

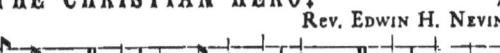

588. *The Christian Hero.* (338)

2 Watch on the field of battle!
    The foe is everywhere;
    His fiery darts fly thickly,
      Like lightning thro' the air,
        Watch! watch! watch! watch!
    On the field of battle!

3 Pray on the field of battle!
    God works with those who pray,
    His mighty arm can nerve us,
      And make us win the day.
        Pray! pray! pray! pray!
    On the field of battle.

4 Die on the field of battle!
    'Tis noble thus to die;
    God smiles on valiant soldiers.
      Their record is on high.
        Die! die! die! die!
    On the field of battle!   E. H. NEVIN.

589. *Death and Resurrection of Christ.*
    Tune ZEPHYR, page 46. (229)

1 He dies!—the friend of sinners dies!
    Lo! Salem's daughters weep around;
    A solemn darkness vails the skies;
    A sudden trembling shakes the ground.

2 Ye saints, approach!—the anguish view
    Of him who groans beneath your load;
    He gives his precious life for you;
    For you he sheds his precious blood.

3 Here's love and grief beyond degree;
    The Lord of glory dies for men;
    But, lo! what sudden joys we see!
    Jesus, the dead, revives again!

4 The rising God forsakes the tomb;
    Up to his Father's court he flies;
    Cherubic legions guard him home,
    And shout him welcome to the skies.

5 Break off your tears, ye saints, and tell
    How high our great deliverer reigns;
    Sing how he spoiled the hosts of hell,
    And led the tyrant death in chains.

6 Say, "Live for ever, glorious King,
    Born to redeem, and strong to save!"
    Then ask, "O, death, where is thy sting?
    And where thy victory, boasting grave?"
                        WATTS.

590. *Universal Praise to God.*
    Tune DUKE ST., page 78. (211)

1 From all that dwell below the skies
    Let the Creator's praise arise,
    Let the Redeemer's name be sung,
    Through every land, by every tongue.

2 Eternal are thy mercies, Lord,
    Eternal truth attends thy word;
    Thy praise shall sound from shore to shore,
    Till suns shall rise and set no more.
                        WATTS.

AYLESBURY. S. M.

1 Ah, how shall fallen man Be just before his God!
If he contend in righteousness, We fall beneath his rod.

591. *Man Condemned before God.* (79)

1 Ah, how shall fallen man
  Be just before his God!
If he contend in righteousness,
  We fall beneath his rod.

2 If he our ways should mark
    With strict, inquiring eyes,
  Could we for one of thousand faults
    A just excuse devise?

3 All-seeing, powerful God,
    Who can with thee contend?
  Or who that tries th' unequal strife
    Shall prosper in the end?

4 The mountains, in thy wrath,
    Their ancient seats forsake;
  The trembling earth deserts her place;
    Her rooted pillars shake.

5 Ah, how shall guilty man
    Contend with such a God?
  None, none can meet him, and escape
    But through the Saviour's blood.
                                  WATTS.

592. *Importance of To-day.* (27)

1 To-morrow, Lord, is thine,
    Lodged in thy sovereign hand;
  And if its sun arise and shine,
    It shines by thy command.

2 The present moment flies,
    And bears our life away;
  O, make thy servants truly wise,
    That they may live to-day.

3 Since on this fleeting hour
    Eternity is hung,
  Awake, by thy almighty power,
    The aged and the young.

4 One thing demands our care;
    O, be it still pursued,
  Lest, slighted once, the season fair
    Should never be renewed.

5 To Jesus may we fly,
    Swift as the morning light,
  Lest life's young, golden beams should die
    In sudden, endless night.
                                DODDRIDGE.

593. *At the Cross.* (471)

1 HERE will I ever lie,
    And tell thee all my care,
  And "Father! Abba, Father!" cry
    And pour a ceaseless prayer:

2 Till thou my sins subdue,
    Till thou my sins destroy,
  My spirit after God renew,
    And fill with peace and joy.
                              C. WESLEY.

LEBANON. S. M. 223
J. ZUNDEL.

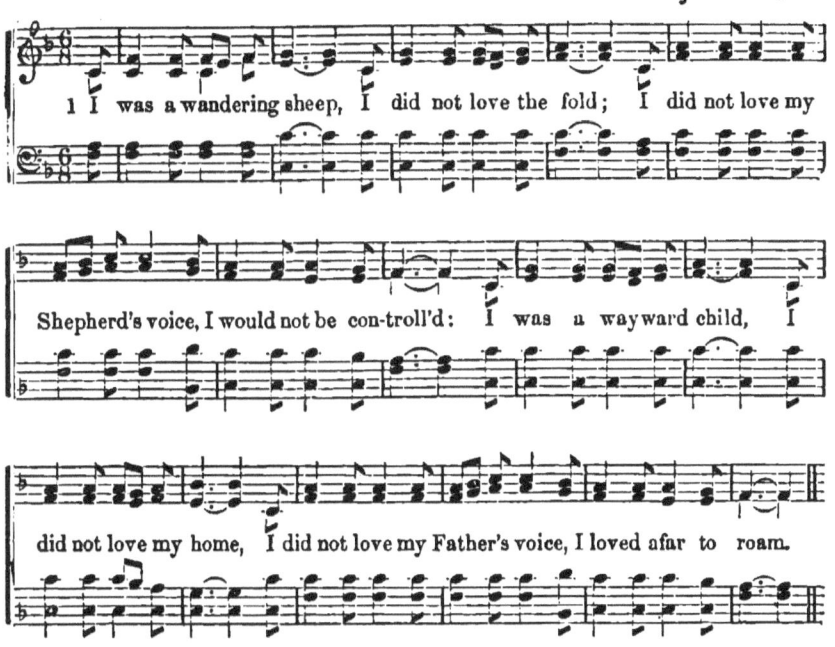

1 I was a wandering sheep, I did not love the fold; I did not love my Shepherd's voice, I would not be con-troll'd: I was a wayward child, I did not love my home, I did not love my Father's voice, I loved afar to roam.

594. *The Good Shepherd.* (127)

2 The Shepherd sought his sheep,
  The Father sought his child;
They followed me o'er vale and hill,
  O'er deserts waste and wild:
They found me nigh to death,
  Famish'd, and faint, and lone;
They bound me with the bands of love,
  They saved the wandering one.

3 Jesus my Shepherd is,
  'Twas he that loved my soul,
'Twas he that washed me in his blood,
  'Twas he that made me whole:
'Twas he that sought the lost,
  That found the wandering sheep,
'Twas he that brought me to the fold—
  'Tis he that still doth keep.
                              BONAR.

595. *Lord's Day Welcomed.* (167)
   Tune ST. THOMAS, page 85.

1 WELCOME, sweet day of rest,
  That saw the Lord arise:
Welcome to this reviving breast,
  And these rejoicing eyes!

2 The King himself comes near,
  And feasts his saints to-day;
Here we may sit, and see him here,
  And love, and praise, and pray.

3 One day amidst the place
  Where my dear Lord has been,
Is sweeter than ten thousand days
  Of pleasure and of sin.

4 My willing soul would stay
  In such a frame as this,
And sit and sing herself away
  To everlasting bliss.   WATTS.

WE'LL BE THERE.

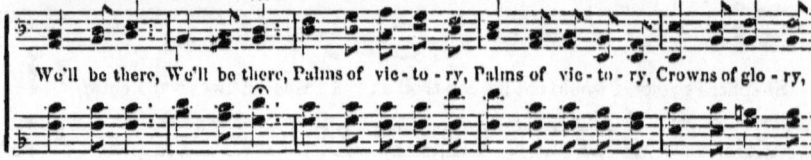

596. *"There is a Beautiful World."* (593)

2 There is a beautiful world,
   Where sorrow never comes;
A world where tears shall never fall,
   In sighing for our home.—*Refrain.*

3 There is a beautiful world,
   Unseen to mortal sight,
And darkness never enters there—
   That home is fair and bright.—*Refrain.*

4 There is a beautiful world,
   Of harmony and love;
O, may we safely enter there,
   And dwell with God above.—*Refrain.*

597. *Dismission.*
   Tune GREENVILLE, page 89. (600)

1 LORD, dismiss us with thy blessing,
   Fill our hearts with joy and peace;
Let us, each thy love possessing,
   Triumph in redeeming grace;
     O, refresh us,
   Traveling through this wilderness.

2 Thanks we give and adoration,
   For thy gospel's joyful sound;
May the fruits of thy salvation
   In our hearts and lives abound;
     May thy presence
   With us evermore be found.

3 So, whene'er the signal's given,
   Us from earth to call away,
Borne on angels' wings to heaven,
   Glad the summons to obey—
     May we, ready,
   Rise and reign in endless day.
                    BURDER.

598. *Christian Liberality.* (505)
   Tune OLD HUNDRED, page 6.

1 WHEN Jesus dwelt in mortal clay,
What were his works from day to day,
But miracles of power and grace,
That spread salvation through our race.

2 Teach us, O Lord, to keep in view
Thy pattern, and thy steps pursue;
Let alms bestowed, let kindness done,
Be witnessed by each rolling sun.

3 That man may last, but never lives,
Who much receives, but nothing gives;
Whom none can love, whom none can thank,
Creation's blot, creation's blank!

4 But he who marks, from day to day,
In generous acts his radiant way,
Treads the same path his Saviour trod,
The path to glory and to God.

HE LEADETH ME.

599. *He Leadeth Me.*

2 Sometimes 'mid scenes of deepest gloom,
Sometimes where Eden's bowers bloom,
By waters still, o'er troubled sea—
Still 'tis his hand that leadeth me!
He leadeth me, &c.

3 Lord, I would clasp thy hand in mine,
Nor ever murmur nor repine—
Content, whatever lot I see,
Since 'tis my God that leadeth me,
He leadeth me, &c.

4 And when my task on earth is done,
When, by thy grace, the victory's won,
E'en death's cold wave I will not flee,
Since God through Jordan leadeth me,
He leadeth me, &c.

600. *The Lord's Supper Instituted.*
   Tune WINDHAM, page 193.   (149)

1 'Twas on that dark, that doleful night,
When powers of earth and hell arose
Against the Son, of God's delight,
And friends betrayed him to his foes,—

2 Before the mournful scene began,
He took the bread, and blessed, and brake;
What love through all his actions ran!
What wondrous words of grace he spake!

3 "This is my body, broke for sin;
Receive and eat the living food;"
Then took the cup and blessed the wine;
"'Tis the new covenant in my blood.

4 "Do this," he cried, "till time shall end,
In memory of your dying Friend;
Meet at my table, and record
The love of your departed Lord."

5 Jesus, thy feast we celebrate;
We show thy death, we sing thy name,
Till thou return, and we shall eat
The marriage supper of the Lamb.

WATTS.

226 SHALL WE KNOW EACH OTHER THERE?

R. Lowry.

1. When we hear the music ringing Through the bright celestial dome,
When the angel voices ringing Gladly bid us welcome home
To the land of ancient story, Where the spirit knows no care;
In that land of light and glory, Shall we know each other there?

Shall we know each other? Shall we know each other?
Shall we know each other? Shall we know each other there?
We shall know each other, We shall know each other
We shall know each other, We shall know each other there.

601. *Recognition in Heaven.* (406)

1 When we hear the music ringing
 Through the bright celestial dome,
When the angel voices ringing
 Gladly bid us welcome home
To the land of ancient story,
 Where the spirit knows no care;
In that land of light and glory,
 Shall we know each other there?
  Shall we know, &c.

HYMNS.

2 Yes, my earth-worn soul rejoices,
　　And my weary heart grows light,
　For the thrilling angel-voices,
　　And the angel-faces bright,
　That shall welcome us in heaven,
　　Are the loved of long ago,
　And to them 'tis kindly given
　　Thus their mortal friends to know.
　　　We shall know, &c.

3 O! ye weary, heavy laden,
　　Droop not, faint not by the way;
　Ye shall join the loved departed
　　In the land of perfect day.
　Harp-strings touched by angel fingers,
　　Murmur in my raptured ear;
　Evermore their sweet tone lingers,
　　We shall know each other there.
　　　We shall know, &c.

SHALL WE SING IN HEAVEN?

Wm. B. Bradbury.

602. *Shall We Sing in Heaven.* (463)

2 Shall we sing with holy angels
　　In that land?
　Shall we sing with holy angels
　　In that happy land?
　Yes! oh, yes! in that land, that happy land,
　Saints and angels sing for ever
　Far beyond the rolling river,
　Meet to sing, and love for ever
　　In that happy land.

3 Shall we rest from care and sorrow,
　　In that land?
　Shall we rest from care and sorrow
　　In that happy land?
　Yes! oh, yes! in that land, that happy land,
　They that meet shall rest for ever
　Far beyond the rolling river,
　Meet to sing, and love for ever,
　　In that happy land!

INDEX OF FIRST LINES.

	HYMN.
A BEAUTIFUL land by faith I see	340
A broken heart, my God, my King	291
A charge to keep I have	64
A debtor to mercy alone	496
A Friend there is, your voices join	175
Ah! how shall fallen man	591
Ah! this heart is void and chill	91
Alas! and did my Saviour bleed	514
Alas! what hourly dangers rise	192
All hail! the power of Jesus' name	343
All hail! ye servants of the Lord	557
All yesterday is gone	287
Almighty Lord, before thy throne	323
Always with us, always with us	213
Amazing grace, how sweet the sound	485
Amazing sight! the Saviour stands	275
Am I a soldier of the cross	270
Amid the joyous scenes of earth	303
And are we wretches yet alive	422
And can I yet delay	477
And can mine eyes without a tear	513
And can my heart aspire so high	61
And canst thou, sinner, slight	65
And did the holy and the just	515
And have I, Christ, no love for thee	83
And must I be to judgment brought	278
And must I part with all I have	88
And must this body die	81
And now, my soul, another year	84
And will the Judge descend	481
And will the Lord thus condescend	146
Approach, my soul, the mercy seat	54
Arise, arise; with joy survey	45
Arise, my soul, arise	486
Arm of the Lord, awake, awake	75
Around the throne of God in heaven	527
Ask, and ye shall receive	474
Asleep in Jesus! blessed sleep	565
Assembled at thy great command	268
A throne of grace! then let us go	450
Auspicious morning, hail	492
Awake, and sing the song	820
Awake, awake each drowsy soul	553
Awaked by Sinai's awful sound	53
Awake, my drowsy soul, awake	326
Awake, my soul, in joyful lays	152
Awake, my soul; stretch every nerve	583
Awake, our souls; away our fears	76
BEFORE Jehovah's awful throne	3
Begone, unbelief, my Saviour is near	353
Behold! a stranger's at the door	481
Behold the Lamb of God who bore	322
Behold the sin atoning Lamb	265
Behold the throne of grace	370
Behold what pity touched the heart	512
Behold what wondrous grace	14
Believing souls, of Christ beloved	7

	HYMN.
Beneath our feet, and o'er our head	426
Beset with snares on every hand	373
Bestow, O Lord, upon our youth	196
Be thou, O God, exalted high	4
Blessed Bible! how I love it	223
Bless, O my soul, the living God	40
Blest be the everlasting God	33
Blest be the tie that binds	363
Blest hour, when earthly cares resign	141
Blest hour, when mortal man retires	407
Blow ye the trumpet, blow	488
Brethren, while we sojourn here	249
Brightest and best of the sons of the morning	418
Broad is the road that leads to death	503
Buried beneath the yielding wave	34
By faith I view my Saviour dying	499
CHILDREN of the Heavenly King	174
Christ and his cross are all our theme	144
Christ, of all my hopes the ground	380
Come, brethren, don't grow weary	177
Come, friends, and let our hearts awake	443
Come, gracious Lord, descend and dwell	5
Come, gracious Spirit, heavenly Dove	241
Come, happy souls, adore the Lamb	545
Come hither, all ye weary souls	549
Come, Holy Spirit, come	16
Come, Holy Spirit, Dove divine	433
Come, Holy Spirit, from above	529
Come, Holy Spirit, heavenly Dove	1
Come in, thou blessed of the Lord	197
Come, let us join our cheerful songs	450
Come, let us join our friends above	433
Come, let us join with sweet accord	526
Come, let us lift our joyful eyes	179
Come, Lord, in mercy come again	24
Come, my soul, thy suit prepare	382
Come, sacred Spirit, from above	554
Come, sinner, to the gospel feast	151
Come, sound his praise abroad	318
Come, thou Fount of every blessing	214
Come, thou soul-transforming Spirit	29
Come to Calvary's holy mountain	456
Come, trembling sinner, in whose breast	25
Come, weary souls, with sin distressed	162
Come, we that love the Lord	167
Come, ye disconsolate, where'er ye languish	206
Come, ye sinners, poor and wretched	46
Come, ye that know and fear the Lord	92
Come, ye that love the Saviour's name	393
DAUGHTER of Zion, awake from thy sadness	410
Dear as thou wast, and justly dear	453
Dearest of all the names above	22
Dear Father, to thy mercy seat	36
Dear refuge of my weary soul	369
Dear Saviour, we rejoice to hear	199
Dear Shepherd of thy people, here	100

228

INDEX OF FIRST LINES.

HYMN.
Deep are the wounds which sin has made... 243
Deep in our hearts, let us record............ 125
Delay not, delay not; O sinner draw near... 446
Depth of mercy! can there be............... 356
Did Christ o'er sinners weep................ 77
Did Jesus weep for me...................... 395
Dismiss us with thy blessing, Lord.......... 357
Do not I love thee, O my Lord.............. 176
Down to the sacred wave.................... 284
Dread Jehovah! God of nations............. 249
EARLY, my God, without delay............. 564
Eternal source of every joy.................. 551
Eternal Spirit, we confess................... 122
Eternity is just at hand..................... 376
FAITH is a precious grace................... 543
Far from mortal cares retreating............ 228
Far from my thoughts, vain world, begone.. 71
Father, I stretch my hands to thee.......... 271
Father of glory, to thy name................ 452
Father of mercies, in thy word.............. 460
Father, whate'er of earthly bliss............. 27
Firm as the earth thy gospel stands......... 578
For a season called to part.................. 333
Forever with the Lord...................... 159
From all that dwell below the skies......... 590
From every stormy wind that blows......... 6
From Greenland's icy mountains............ 509
From whence doth this union arise.......... 132
GENTLY, Lord, O gently lead us............ 508
Give me the wings of faith to rise........... 434
Glorious things of thee are spoken.......... 212
Glory to thee, my God, this night.......... 239
God bless our native land................... 494
God calling yet! shall I not hear............ 552
God, in the gospel of his Son................ 266
God is love; his mercy brightens............ 226
God is the fountain whence.................. 542
God is the refuge of his saints............... 161
God moves in a mysterious way............. 251
God of mercy, God of grace................. 388
God of my life; through all my days........ 202
God's holy law transgressed................ 78
Go forth, on wings of faith and prayer...... 177
Go, labor on; your hands are weak......... 409
Go, preach my gospel, saith the Lord....... 572
Grace! 'tis a charming sound................ 319
Grant the abundance of the sea............. 153
Great God, attend while Zion sings......... 42
Great God, is not thy promise pledged....... 403
Great God, now condescend................ 17
Great God, we sing that mighty hand....... 200
Great Shepherd of thine Israel.............. 345
Guide me, O thou great Jehovah............ 31
HAD I the tongues of Greeks and Jews..... 73
Hail, sovereign love, that first began........ 165
Happy the heart where graces reign......... 324
Hark! from the tombs a doleful sound...... 279
Hark! my soul, it is the Lord............... 389
Hark! the glad sound! the Saviour comes.. 451
Hark! the voice of love and mercy.......... 339
Hark! what mean these lamentations....... 211

HYMN.
Hasten, Lord, the glorious time............. 168
Haste, O sinner: now be wise............... 381
Hastening on to death's dark river.......... 801
Hear, O sinner! Mercy hails you........... 139
Heart of stone, relent, relent................ 411
Hear us, O Lord, in time of need............ 264
He dies! the friend of sinners dies........... 589
He leadeth me! Oh! blessed thought!...... 599
He lives! the great Redeemer lives......... 472
Here at thy table, Lord, we meet........... 58
Here at thy cross, incarnate God............ 288
Here, o'er the earth as a stranger I roam.... 519
Here will I ever lie......................... 593
He that goeth forth with weeping........... 191
Holy Ghost, with light divine............... 336
Holy source of consolation.................. 216
How beauteous are their feet................ 131
How blest the righteous when he dies....... 121
How blest the sacred tie that binds.......... 372
How can I sink with such a prop............ 236
How can we see the children, Lord.......... 23
How charming is the place.................. 316
How condescending and how kind.......... 493
How firm a foundation, ye saints of the Lord 352
How happy every child of grace............. 105
How happy is the Christian's state.......... 253
How helpless guilty nature lies.............. 310
How lost was my condition.................. 185
How loving is Jesus, who came from the sky 351
How oft, alas! this wretched heart.......... 87
How oft have sin and Satan strove.......... 432
How pleasant, how divinely fair............. 544
How pleasant thus to dwell below........... 342
How precious is the book divine............. 57
How sad our state by nature is.............. 421
How shall the sons of men appear........... 502
How shall the young secure their hearts.... 427
How short and hasty is our life.............. 533
How sweet and awful is the place........... 424
How sweet, how heavenly is the sight....... 145
How sweetly flowed the gospel sound....... 408
How sweet the name of Jesus sounds....... 516
How sweet, upon this sacred day........... 464
How tedious and tasteless the hours........ 134
I ASKED the Lord, that I might grow....... 405
I cannot call affliction sweet................ 85
If human kindness meets return............. 532
If I must die, O, let me die.................. 86
I have a Father in the promised land........ 455
I lay my sins on Jesus....................... 184
I love thy kingdom, Lord.................... 219
I love to steal awhile away.................. 353
I love to think of heaven.................... 394
I love to think of the heavenly land......... 10
I'm a pilgrim, and I'm a stranger........... 11
I'm but a traveler here..................... 529
I'm not ashamed to own my Lord........... 580
In all my Lord's appointed ways............. 561
In all my vast concerns with thee............ 143
In duties and in sufferings too............... 233
In evil long I took delight................... 425
Inquiring souls, who long to find............ 240
Inscribed upon the cross we see............. 406
In the Christian's home in glory............. 444

INDEX OF FIRST LINES.

HYMN		HYMN	
In the cross of Christ I glory	245	MAJESTIC sweetness sits enthroned	111
In thy name, O Lord, assembling	28	Mary to the Saviour's tomb	205
In vain I trace creation o'er	808	May I resolve with all my heart	568
In vain we seek for peace with God	195	Meekly in Jordan's holy stream	439
I send the joys of earth away	127	Mercy, O thou son of David	246
Is this the kind return	19	Mourn for the thousands slain	475
It is not death to die	129	Must Jesus bear the cross alone	510
I was a wandering sheep	594	My country, 'tis of thee	493
I would not live alway; I ask not to stay	445	My days are gliding swiftly by	50
		My dear Redeemer, and my Lord	506
JERUSALEM! my happy home	582	My drowsy powers, why sleep ye so	193
Jesus, and shall it ever be	242	My faith looks up to thee	491
Jesus! delightful charming name	327	My former hopes are fled	66
Jesus demands this heart of mine	126	My God, how endless is thy love	70
Jesus, I love thy charming name	2	My God, permit me not to be	292
Jesus, I my cross have taken	225	My God, permit my tongue	541
Jesus, in thy transporting name	402	My God, the spring of all my joys	463
Jesus, let thy pitying eye	415	My gracious Lord, I own thy right	569
Jesus! lover of my soul	207	My heavenly home is bright and fair	164
Jesus, my all, to heaven is gone	203	My hope is built on nothing less	135
Jesus shall reign where'er the sun	201	My opening eyes with rapture see	108
Jesus, thou art the sinner's friend	321	My rest is in heaven, my rest is not here	877
Jesus, thou joy of loving hearts	293	My son, know thou the Lord	62
Jesus, thy boundless love to me	375	My soul, be on thy guard	815
Jesus, where'er thy people meet	546	My soul, repeat his praise	222
Jesus, who knows full well	13		
Join all the glorious names	489	NEARER, my God, to thee	556
Joyfully, joyfully onward I move	258	No more, my God, I boast no more	871
Joy to the world! the Lord is come	449	Nor eye has seen, nor ear has heard	56
Just as I am, without one plea	43	Not all the blood of beasts	864
Just as thou art, without one trace	44	Not all the outward forms on earth	574
		Nothing but leaves! the Spirit grieves	189
KINDRED in Christ for his dear sake	262	Nothing, either great or small	829
Know, my soul, thy full salvation	215	Not to condemn the sons of men	151
		Not what I feel or do	866
LABORERS of Christ, arise	539	Now for a tune of lofty praise	204
Let every mortal ear attend	397	Now, gracious Lord, thine arm reveal	85
Let me but hear my Saviour say	567	Now is the accepted time	288
Let sinners take their course	18	Now let our cheerful eyes survey	535
Let Zion's watchmen all awake	399	Now mercy's light-winged page	82
Life's journey we have started	224	Now the Saviour standeth pleading	247
Live on the field of battle	588		
Look, ye saints, the sight is glorious	49	O, BLESS the Lord, my soul	368
Lo! on a narrow neck of land	98	O, cease my wandering soul	67
Lord, dismiss us with thy blessing, Fill	597	O could I find from day to day	114
" " " " Bid	158	O could I speak the matchless worth	97
Lord, I hear of showers of blessing	188	O'er the gloomy hills of darkness	329
Lord, in the morning thou shalt hear	453	O'er the realms of Pagan darkness	841
Lord, lead the way the Saviour went	103	O for a closer walk with God	482
Lord, look on all assembled here	440	O for a faith that will not shrink	483
Lord, may our sympathizing breasts	26	O for a heart to praise my God	178
Lord, may thy goodness cause our land	150	O for a thousand tongues to sing	520
Lord of my life, O may thy praise	147	O for that tenderness of heart	193
Lord, send thy servants forth	217	O for the death of those	470
Lord, send thy word and let it fly	583	O God of sovereign grace	367
Lord, 'tis sweet to mingle where	884	O God, our help in ages past	522
Lord, we come before thee now	879	O happy day that fixed my choice	8.3
Lord! what a feeble piece	528	O how happy are they	517
Lord, what a thoughtless wretch was I	587	Oh how divine, how sweet the joy	182
Lord, when we bow before thy throne	500	Oh, how the hearts of those revive	359
Lord, while for all mankind we pray	254	O Lord, behold us at thy feet	524
Love is the fountain whence	213	O Lord, our God, arise	527

INDEX OF FIRST LINES.

	HYMN.
O Lord, thy heavenly grace impart	570
O Lord, thy work revive	63
Once I thought my mountain strong	412
Once more, my soul, the rising day	82
Once more we meet to pray	540
O ce, O Lord, thy garden flourished	230
C e th e is above all others	243
One sweetly solemn thought	586
On Jordan's stormy banks I stand	361
On the mountain's top appearing	887
Onward, herald of the Gospel	393
O righteous God, thou Judge supreme	244
O sing to me of heaven	396
O, sinner, hear the heavenly voice	504
O, sinner, why so thoughtless grown	505
O speed thee, Christian, on thy way	454
O that I could repent	282
Oh, that I knew the secret place	441
O that my load of sin were gone	290
O thou, my soul, forget no more	346
O thou, that hear'st when sinners cry	473
O thou, that hear'st the prayer of faith	96
O thou, who in Jordan did'st bow thy meek head	350
O turn ye, O turn ye, for why will ye die	354
Our country's voice is pleading	186
Our helper, God, we bless thy name	470
Out on an ocean all boundless we ride	873
Oh, what amazing words of grace	59
O, when shall I see Jesus	183
O, where is now that glowing love	120
O, where shall rest be found	538
Oh, who can part our ransomed souls	102
People of the living God	173
Pilgrims we are, to Canaan bound	330
Pity the nations, O our God	401
Planted in Christ, the living vine	90
Plunged in a gulf of dark despair	325
Prayer is appointed to convey	408
Prayer is the breath of God in man	256
Prayer is the contrite sinner's voice	180
Prayer is the soul's sincere desire	117
Precious Bible! what a treasure	457
Prostrate, dear Jesus, at thy feet	525
Religion is the chief concern	232
Remark, my soul, the narrow bound	306
Remember thy Creator now	142
Repent; the voice celestial cries	234
Return, O wanderer, now return	471
Rise, my soul, and stretch thy wings	420
Rock of ages, cleft for me	413
Safely through another week	335
Salvation! oh the joyful sound	485
Saved by grace, I live to tell	208
Saved ourselves by Jesus' blood	414
Saviour, breathe an evening blessing	229
Saviour, like a shepherd lead us	30
Saviour, visit thy plantation	110
Say, brothers, will you meet us	813
Say, sinner, hath a voice within	124
Say, why should friendship grieve for those	263
See the ransomed millions stand	210

	HYMN.
See! another year is gone	172
See how the fruitless fig-tree stands	238
See Israel's gentle Shepherd stand	563
See! the Scriptures are fulfilling	518
Shall we meet beyond the river	392
Shall we sing in heaven for ever	602
Show pity, Lord; O Lord, forgive	500
Since all the varying scenes of time	436
Sinner, art thou still secure	890
Sinner, rouse thee from thy sleep	391
Sinners, turn; why will ye die	206
Sinners, will you scorn the message	47
Sinner, the voice of God regard	484
Sinner, what has earth to show	887
Soldiers of Christ, arise	221
So let our lips and lives express	267
Sons we are through God's election	157
Soon as I heard my Father say	255
Soon shall the trump of God	220
Sow in the morn thy seed	80
Spirit divine, attend our prayer	89
Stand up, my soul, shake off thy fears	74
Stay, thou insulted Spirit, stay	501
Stop, poor sinner, stop and think	416
Strait is the way, the door is strait	423
Strange and mysterious is my life	136
Sweet hour of prayer, sweet hour of prayer	304
Sweet is the prayer whose holy stream	576
Sweet is the work, my God, my King	41
Sweet land of rest! for thee I sigh	160
Sweet the moments, rich in blessing	227
Sweet was the time when first I felt	448
Swell the anthem, raise the song	169
Teach me the measure of my days	534
That awful day will surely come	311
That warning voice, O sinner, hear	94
That was a time of wondrous love	467
The billows swell; the winds are high	874
The blessed Spirit, like the wind	437
The day approaches, O my soul	89
The day is past and gone	281
Thee we adore, eternal name	280
The heathen perish, day by day	429
The Lord can clear the darkest skies	101
The Lord into his garden comes	52
The Lord is risen indeed	817
The Lord Jehovah reigns	490
The morning light is breaking	507
The people are gathering from near and from	68
The pity of the Lord	479
There is a beautiful world	596
There is a fountain filled with blood	272
There is a land mine eye hath seen	571
There is a land of pure delight	577
There is a name I love to hear	584
There is an hour of peaceful rest	299
There is a place of sacred rest	487
There is a realm where Jesus reigns	294
There is a time we know not when	245
There is no name so sweet on earth	190
There's a friend above all others	93
There's a light in the window for thee, brother	312

INDEX OF FIRST LINES.

HYMN.		HYMN.	
The Saviour bids us watch and pray	39	We're traveling home to heaven above	69
The Saviour calls; let every ear	104	We sing the Saviour's love	285
The Saviour! Oh, what endless charms	99	We speak of the realms of the blest	493
The Spirit in our hearts	286	What courteous stranger at the door	800
The swift declining day	129	Whatever cross the world may bring	19
The time is short! sinners, beware	277	What glory gilds the sacred page	116
The voice of free grace cries, escape to the mountain	155	What is the thing of greatest price	20
Think gently of the erring one	562	What shall I render to my God	465
This God is the God we adore	497	What shall the dying sinner do	289
This is the day the Lord hath made	579	What sinners value I resign	349
This rite our blest Redeemer gave	51	What various hindrances we meet	466
Tho' the days are dark with trouble	417	When across the ocean wide	166
Thou art my portion, O my God	521	When all thy mercies, O my God	807
Thou art the way; to thee alone	523	When any turn from Zion's way	257
Though now the nations sit beneath	555	When driven by oppression's rod	805
Thou hast said, exalted Jesus	48	When God revealed his gracious name	106
Thou Lord of all the worlds on high	55	When I can read my title clear	344
Thou lovely source of true delight	115	When I survey the wondrous cross	149
Thou only sovereign of my heart	347	When Jesus dwelt in mortal clay	598
Through the love of God our Saviour	274	When marshaled on the nightly plain	843
Through all the changing scenes of life	462	When shall the voice of singing	187
Through many climes, o'er many lands	550	When shall we meet again	297
Thus far the Lord hath led me on	260	When sins and fears prevailing rise	404
Thy bounties, gracious Lord	865	When the worn spirit wants repose	573
Thy footsteps, Lord, with joy we trace	547	When thou, my righteous Judge, shalt come	96
'Tis a point I long to know	332	When thy mortal life is fled	298
'Tis faith that lays the sinner low	21	When torn is the bosom by sorrow or care	447
'Tis God the Spirit leads	130	When we hear the music ringing	601
'Tis religion that can give	395	Where is my God? does he retire	469
'Tis sweet in the trials of conflict and sin	831	Where two or three with sweet accord	79
To-day if you will hear his voice	423	While life prolongs its precious light	123
To-day the Saviour calls	189	While o'er the deep thy servants sail	2
Together let us sweetly live	442	While thee I seek, protecting Power	575
To God, the only wise	869	While, with ceaseless course, the sun	134
To Him who loved the souls of men	461	Who are these in bright array	295
To-morrow, Lord, is thine	592	Who can describe the joys that rise	148
To our Redeemer's glorious name	250	Who can forbear to sing	15
To thee this temple we devote	112	Why do we mourn departing friends	309
'Twas on that dark, that doleful night	600	Why should the children of a King	113
		Why should we start, and fear to die	110
		Why sleep we, my brethren! come let us arise	855
Vain are the hopes, the sons of men	276	Why will ye waste on trifling cares	430
Vain man, thy fond pursuits forbear	531	With all my powers of heart and tongue	543
Vouchsafe, O Lord, thy presence now	511	Within thy house, O Lord, our God	581
		With joy we meditate the grace	400
Wait, my soul, upon the Lord	388	With tears of anguish I lament	558
Wait, O my soul, thy Maker's will	261		
Waked by the trumpet's sound	79	Ye angels, who stand round the throne	183
Wake the song of jubilee	334	Ye dying sons of men	154
Watchman! tell us of the night	170	Ye glittering toys of earth, adieu	118
We are coming, blessed Saviour	356	Ye hearts, with youthful vigor warm	252
We are going, we are going	140	Ye humble souls, approach your God	87
We are joyously voyaging over the main	273	Ye men and angels, witness now	560
We are living, we are dwelling	137	Ye servants of the Lord	536
We are out on the ocean, sailing	259	Ye sinners, fear the Lord	478
We bless thy name, Almighty God	163	Yes, my native land, I love thee	12
We come, O Lord, before thy throne	194	Yes, we trust the day is breaking	580
We come to his courts, where so often we prove	314	Ye valiant soldiers of the cross	269
Weep for the lost! thy Saviour wept	237	Ye wretched, hungry, starving poor	60
Weeping soul, no longer mourn	410	Your harps, ye trembling saints	480
Welcome, delightful morn	156		
Welcome, O Saviour, to my heart	862	Zion, awake; thy strength renew	4
Welcome, sweet day of rest	595	Zion's King shall reign victorious	521
		Zion stands with hills surrounded	522

CLASSIFICATION OF HYMNS.

The Figures indicate the Hymns.

INTRODUCTORY, 5, 28, 29, 71, 379, 540, 581.

REVIVALS.
- I. REVIVAL SOUGHT, 24, 52, 63, 77, 101, 110, 230, 237, 414.
- II. SINNERS WARNED, 20, 47, 65, 94, 98, 123, 124, 128, 206, 232, 234, 235, 238, 247, 277, 283, 287, 298, 376, 381, 387, 390, 391, 416, 430, 446, 478, 481, 484, 503–505, 531, 533, 534, 538, 553, 587, 592.
- III. SINNERS INVITED, 46, 59, 60, 104, 139, 154, 162, 181, 189, 246, 275, 286, 354, 397, 428, 431, 456, 471, 488, 548, 552.
- IV. INQUIRERS, 22, 25, 43, 44, 66, 78, 96, 151, 188, 195, 198, 243, 265, 271, 272, 276, 282, 289, 290, 321, 366, 386, 388, 410, 411, 421, 422, 477, 500, 502, 513, 525, 574, 591.
- V. CONVERTS, 15, 53, 106, 148, 157, 165, 182, 185, 203, 208, 246, 302, 351, 359, 364, 371, 425, 435, 467, 485, 499, 517, 518, 594.
- VI. HEARING CANDIDATES, 173, 199, 560.
- VII. CONVERTS BAPTIZED, 34, 48, 51, 284, 350, 433, 439, 545.
- VIII. CONVERTS WELCOMED, 7, 197, 262.
- IX. CONVERTS AT THE LORD'S TABLE, 58, 424, 461, 498, 532, 600.

THE CHURCH.
- I. ORGANIZATION, 90, 219, 338.
- II. OFFICERS, 131, 399, 511, 572.
- III. PLACES OF WORSHIP, 39, 100, 112.

THE LORD'S DAY, 41, 42, 108, 141, 156, 316, 335, 464, 526, 544, 573, 579, 595.

CLASSIFICATION OF HYMNS.

PRAISE TO GOD, 3, 4, 14, 37, 40, 55, 92, 143, 161, 202, 222, 226, 251, 255, 261, 307, 308, 318, 360, 368, 369, 436, 462, 463, 465, 479, 490. 497, 521, 522, 541, 542, 548, 570, 575, 590.

PRAISE TO CHRIST.
   I. ADVENT OF CHRIST, 204, 418, 449, 451.
   II. LIFE OF CHRIST, 408, 515, 523, 566.
   III. SUFFERINGS AND DEATH OF CHRIST, 99, 125, 227, 245, 288, 406, 514.
   IV. RESURRECTION OF CHRIST, 317, 589.
   V. INTERCESSION OF CHRIST, 49, 179, 400, 469, 472, 535.
   VI. THE LOVE OF CHRIST, 83, 93, 102, 176, 325, 343, 389, 395.
   VII. INDEBTEDNESS TO CHRIST, 88, 111, 113, 152, 215, 233, 242, 258, 320, 322, 346, 362, 375, 489, 512, 568, 569.
   VIII. PRECIOUSNESS OF CHRIST, 2, 97, 134, 144, 155, 175, 190, 225, 250, 293, 327, 339, 398, 402, 450, 508, 516, 520.
   IX. LOOKING TO CHRIST, 107, 109, 126, 135, 149, 184, 207, 213, 214, 285, 347, 383, 404, 413, 432, 486, 491, 496, 567, 578, 584.

PRAISE TO THE HOLY SPIRIT, 1, 16, 118, 122, 130, 216, 241, 310, 336, 437, 452, 554, 559.

CHRISTIAN LIFE.
   I. CHRISTIAN ACTIVITY, 18, 64, 68, 74, 76, 80, 127, 137, 138, 191–193, 209, 221, 267, 269, 270, 315, 326, 355, 380, 434, 454, 510, 536, 539, 580, 583, 588.
   II. CHRISTIAN GRACES, 21, 27, 56, 61, 73, 85, 114, 178, 218, 324, 353, 423, 482, 483, 543, 556.
   III. CHRISTIAN FELLOWSHIP, 132, 145, 342, 363, 372.
   IV. DECLENSION, 19, 87, 95, 120, 136, 146, 257, 291, 332, 412, 415, 448, 473, 501, 558.
   V. PRAYER, 6, 13, 17, 23, 32, 36, 38, 54, 62, 70, 72, 117, 142, 147, 180, 196, 229, 239, 256, 260, 281, 292, 296, 304, 358, 370, 382, 384, 405, 407, 441, 447, 453, 459, 466, 468, 474, 506, 524, 546, 563, 564, 576.

CHRISTIAN LIFE—CONTINUED.

VI. CHRISTIAN REJOICING, 10, 11, 30, 31, 50, 69, 91, 105, 115, 133, 140, 159, 160, 164, 167, 174, 183, 205, 224, 228, 236, 253, 258, 259, 273, 274, 301, 303, 312–314, 319, 328, 330, 331, 344, 348, 349, 352, 356, 361, 377, 378, 385, 392, 394, 417, 420, 438, 442–444, 455, 480, 495, 519, 527, 529, 561, 582, 586, 593, 601, 602.

SPREAD OF THE GOSPEL.

I. COLPORTAGE, 82, 177, 300.

II. BIBLE DISTRIBUTION, 57, 223, 266, 427, 457, 460.

III. MINISTERIAL EDUCATION, 252, 305, 550.

IV. HOME MISSIONS, 26, 103, 186, 210, 334, 345, 393, 409, 475, 557, 562, 598.

V. SEAMEN, 9, 67, 153, 194, 373, 374.

VI. FOREIGN MISSIONS, 8, 12, 45, 78, 168, 170, 187, 201, 211, 212, 217, 231, 268, 329, 337, 341, 367, 401, 403, 419, 429, 507, 509, 530, 537, 555, 585.

SPECIAL OCCASIONS.

I. FASTS, 244, 249, 254, 264, 323, 440, 494, 547.

II. THANKSGIVINGS, 150, 163, 166, 169, 365, 492, 493, 551.

III. CLOSING OF THE YEAR, 84, 200, 280, 306, 470.

IV. NEW YEAR, 35, 171, 172.

THE FUTURE STATE.

I. DEATH, 86, 119, 121, 129, 263, 279, 309, 396, 426, 445, 458, 476, 528, 565.

II. THE RESURRECTION, 33, 79, 81, 220.

III. THE JUDGMENT, 89, 278, 311.

IV. HEAVEN, 294, 295, 297, 299, 340, 487, 571, 577, 596.

PARTING HYMNS, 158, 333, 357, 597.

INDEX OF SUBJECTS.

The Figures indicate the Numbers of the Hymns.

ABSENCE, from Christ deprecated, 134.
   from God forever intolerable, 311.
Accepted time, 123, 235, 283.
Access to God, 179.
Adoption, 14, 55, 486.
Advent of Christ, 449, 451.
   second, 267, 443.
Advocate, Christ an, 46, 175, 321, 469, 472.
Affliction, benefit of, 85.
   encouragement in, 417.
   patience in, 202, 233, 243.
   rejoicing in, 567.
   submission in, 27, 61.
   support in, 109, 183, 213, 327.
All will be well, 274.
Amazing grace, 185, 485.
Armor of Christian, 188, 315, 448, 454.
Atonement, finished, 339.
   relying on, 22, 43, 96, 135, 184, 195, 208, 265, 272, 283, 289, 364, 366, 371, 404, 413, 421, 472, 477, 491, 496, 502, 525.
   sufficiency of, 22, 44, 195, 265, 502.

BACKSLIDING confessed, 19, 87, 120, 146, 291, 412, 415, 448, 473, 501, 553.
   return from, 87, 120, 291, 473.
Baptism, a burial with Christ, 34, 48, 433.
   emblem of Christ's death, 48, 51.
   following Christ in, 284, 350.
   joy in, 34, 43, 302, 350, 545.
   Spirit invoked in, 433, 439.
   symbol of regeneration, 350.
Barren fig-tree, 238.
Believer, security of, 135, 157, 233, 352, 353, 369, 389, 404, 432, 485, 496 580, 584.
Bethlehem, star of, 343.
Blood of Christ, cleanses from sin, 43, 155, 184, 272, 330, 364, 413, 421, 443.
   peace with God by, 227, 486.
   relying on, 43, 135, 195, 227, 272, 283, 364, 366, 421, 486, 489, 502.
   salvation only by, 195, 240, 322, 364, 366, 489, 502, 515, 591.
Blood shed for sin, 411, 425.
Bound for land of Canaan, 442.
Broad and narrow way, 508.
Broken heart, 19, 291, 411, 415.
Brotherly love, 132, 145, 342, 363, 372.
Brothers, will you meet us, 313.

CARE of God for his saints, 255, 436, 462.
Casting care on the Lord, 188, 184, 358.
Charity, for the erring and the poor, 539.
Chastisement, use of, 258.
Child, come home, 209.
Children, Christ blessing, 563.
   prayer for our, 17, 21, 196, 524 563.
   solicitude for, 23.
Christ, advent of, 418, 449, 451.
   advent, second, 267.
   our advocate, 46, 179, 321, 469, 472.
   atonement of, 98, 515.
   all-sufficiency of, 184, 321, 349, 477, 502.
   ascension of, 204, 572.
   birth of, 418.
   blood of. See BLOOD.
   compassion of, 46, 111, 325, 431, 498, 499.
   condescension of, 99, 111, 498, 515.
   coronation of, 49.
   crucified, 78, 499.
   death of, 125, 514, 515.
   death and resurrection, 317, 589.
   enthroned and worshiped, 321.
   exaltation of, 204.
   our example, 233, 566.
   fountain of life, 59, 397.
   friend, 93, 104, 175, 248, 346, 417, 431, 472, 589.
   all fullness in, 184.
   God incarnate, 22, 46, 99, 204, 288, 589.
   guide, 467, 508.
   hiding place, 54, 95, 165.
   high-priest, 46, 400, 472, 488, 489, 535.

Christ, hosanna to, 289, 451, 579.
   humiliation of, 515.
   humiliation and triumph of, 204.
   intercession of, 46, 256, 472, 488.
   inviting sinners, 44, 104, 154, 162, 189, 275, 354, 391, 431, 499, 549.
   King of saints, 155, 190, 398, 489, 499.
   knocking at the door, 275, 431.
   Lamb of God, 43, 184, 265, 322, 364, 488.
   life by his death, 195.
   life eternal in, 157.
   love of, 43, 46, 58, 59, 60, 83, 98, 102, 154, 162, 250, 275, 325, 351, 364, 366, 386, 477, 498, 549, 584.
   love to, 2, 83, 68, 97, 102, 109, 111, 113, 114, 126, 134, 149, 175, 176, 184, 190, 207, 225, 250, 285, 299, 327, 346, 347, 362, 366, 389, 398, 402, 450, 477, 491, 516, 520, 567, 584.
   loving kindness of, 568.
   matchless worth of, 97.
   mediation of, 179.
   name of, sweet, 2, 134, 190, 327, 402, 516, 520.
   new song to, 320.
   pardon in, 99, 498.
   peace by faith in, 22, 195, 243, 265.
   physician, 184, 243.
   praise to, 22, 152, 461.
   precious, 2, 351, 499, 516.
   prince, 190.
   prophet, priest, and king, 489, 499.
   ransom, 488.
   refuge, 207, 347.
   resurrection of, 204, 205.
   resurrection and ascension of, 210, 276.
   our righteousness, 96, 135, 371, 421, 496.
   rock of ages, 383, 413.
   rock, the solid, 185.
   sacrifice. 99, 151, 195, 285, 364, 411.
   Saviour, 151, 190, 289, 321, 362, 366.

INDEX OF SUBJECTS. 237

ist, Shepherd, 333, 594.
sin bearer, 184, 411, 425.
sinner's friend, 109.
submission to, 411, 477.
sufferings of, 125, 411, 514, 515.
teachings of, 408.
trust in. See DEPENDENCE.
union to, 90, 102, 302.
victory and exaltation of, 49.
way, truth, and life. 523.
weeping over sinners, 77, 237. 395.
welcomed as a Saviour, 243, 362, 411
with us ever, 213.
worthy of praise, 49, 175, 285, 343. 398. 450, 489, 520.
istian, active, 193, 599.
not ashamed of Christ, 242, 317.
backsliding and returning, 136, 448.
bearing the cross, 225, 269, 510.
bearing shame for Christ, 225.
blessedness of. 105, 106, 208, 253, 467, 485, 499, 517.
breathing after God, 469.
casting care on the Lord, 183. 184, 358.
Christ his strength, 76, 383, 467, 560. 567.
Christ, all in all to. 99, 207.
clinging to the cross, 413.
coldness lamented, 87, 120, 126, 448.
delighting in Christ, 2, 97, 111, 113, 1 4. 207. 29 1, 327, 346, 375. 398, 516, 584.
delighting in God, 308, 463, 541, 542.
delighting in worship, 28, 41, 42, 71, 141, 316, 464, 544. 595.
desiring to be like Christ, 184, 566.
desiring to be with Christ, 133, 184, 361, 463.
diligence. 64, 193, 326, 539.
dying, 119, 121, 129, 396.
encouraged, 14, 161, 251, 261. 369. 436, 462. 575.
enjoying love of Christ, 375.
enjoying presence of Christ, 2, 71.
exemplifying the gospel, 267.
filial trust of. 61.
following Christ, 203, 561.
following example of saints, 434.

Christian forgiven, 40, 208, 222, 368, 467.
frames not trusted, 135.
glorying in infirmity, 567.
godly sorrow of. 19, 87, 95, 120, 146, 257, 291, 411, 412, 415, 425, 448, 473, 501, 513, 514, 558.
gratitude of, 88, 111, 149, 202, 208, 307, 368, 532, 549.
hoping in God, 255, 349, 522, 541.
imitating Christ, 233, 566.
lamenting indwelling sin, 126. 473, 540.
lamenting inconstancy, 19, 120, 214, 448.
living to Christ, 568, 569.
looking towards home, 91, 164, 207.
looking to Jesus, 491, 593.
loving the children of God, 132, 145, 342, 363, 372.
obeying Christ, 561.
parting with all for Christ, 88, 118, 225, 269, 371, 477.
patient in suffering, 202, 358, 417, 548.
profited by affliction. 85.
rejoicing in Christ, 71, 115, 185, 208, 302, 517.
rejoicing in revival, 15, 52, 182, 359.
resignation of, 27.
resorting to God in trouble, 522, 548.
safety of, in Christ, 195, 157, 288, 369, 389, 404, 432, 485, 496, 578.
safety of, in God alone, 37, 143, 161, 255, 360, 462, 522, 541, 570.
salvation of. secure. See SAFETY of, in CHRIST.
self-denial, 88, 423, 503.
a sol'dier. 183, 270.
steadfastness of. 570.
supported by hope, 236.
sustained by grace 130.
thoughts of, in affliction, 27, 61, 85.
trusting in Christ. See DEPENDENCE.
trusting in God. 143, 236, 239, 253, 300, 479, 522, 541.
united to Christ. 64, 326, 536.
warfare, 68, 74, 209, 221, 269. 270, 315, 454.
washed in blood of Christ, 272, 461.
welcoming Christ, 477.
Church, admission sought, 173.
beauty of. 8, 212.
below and above, 488.

Church, love to, 219.
new members welcomed, 7, 197, 262.
unity of, 90.
victorious, 419.
Colportage, 82, 177, 300.
Commission. the great, 572.
Confession of sin, 78, 386, 388, 421, 422, 500, 525, 540.
Contrite heart. 354.
prayer for. 198, 282, 415.
Conversion of sinners, desired, 16, 130, 270.
of sinners, rejoicing over, 15, 182, 359, 518.
of the world, 9.
Conviction of sin, 78, 151, 276, 411, 425.
Coronation of Christ, 343.
Country, fathers of our, 166, 492.
God its defense, 166.
love of, 254, 493.
prayer for, 249, 254, 494.
Cross of Christ, 406.
glorying in, 149, 245.
joy at, 227.
repentance at, 153, 364, 411, 425. 513, 514.
safety in, 228.
subdued by, 208, 411, 425, 513.

DANGER of delay, 65, 123, 235, 287, 298, 381, 390, 446, 592.
Day of judgment, 79, 89, 278, 306, 311, 481.
strength equal to, 352, 383, 567.
Deacons, choice of, 511.
Death, believers triumph in, 119
of Christian friends, 263, 3 9.
hastening on, 171, 280, 306, 426, 528.
and judgment. 79, 89.
prayer for support in, 86, 279.
preparation for. 86, 89, 280.
presence of Christ makes easy. 119.
of righteous blessed. 86, 476.
saints happy in, 119, 121.
sleep in Jesus, 565.
welcome. 374.
Debt paid, 208, 328.
Dependence on Christ, 22, 25, 43, 44, 54, 78, 96, 135, 151, 195, 240, 243, 265, 274, 289, 321, 347, 366, 411, 421, 477, 491.
on mercy of God, 162, 271, 388, 500.
Dismission, 158, 383.

EARTHLY joys powerless, 347.
Election of grace, 157, 208.

INDEX OF SUBJECTS.

Encouragement to believers, 14, 161, 251, 261, 369, 486, 462, 575.
to Zion, 8, 45, 212, 219, 231, 337, 338.
Eternity, 98, 280, 376.
Example of Christ, 233, 566.
Expostulation with sinners, 47, 65, 247, 298, 376, 387, 390, 430, 484, 504, 505, 531, 553.
Evangelization of our country, 186.

FAITH, call to exercise, 25, 46, 104, 151, 154, 410.
excellence of, 543.
exercise of, 364, 499.
gift of God, 271, 543.
looking to Jesus, 491.
power of, 21.
prayer for, 198, 271, 410, 483, 543.
precious grace, 543.
Faithfulness of God, 456.
Favor of God, the chief good, 18, 308.
Feelings not trusted, 135.
Fellowship, Christian, 90, 132, 145, 342, 363, 372.
church, welcome to, 7, 197, 262.
Fig tree, barren, 238.
Filial confidence, 14, 255, 436, 499.
love, 55.
submission, 61, 215.
Finished work of Christ, 46, 328, 339.
Firm foundation, 352.
Following Christ in ordinances, 34, 48, 51, 284, 350, 545.
Forsaking all for Christ, 88, 113, 225, 371, 477.
Fount of blessing, 214.
Frailty of man, 528, 534.
Friend above all others, 93, 175, 248, 346, 417.

GETHSEMANE, 46.
Glorying in the cross, 149, 245.
God, all things found in, 542, 575.
author of salvation, 37, 40.
character seen in gospel, 266.
confidence in, 37, 40, 161, 202, 222, 226, 236, 251, 255, 261, 353, 369, 436, 462, 463, 479, 521, 541, 542, 548, 570, 575.
delight in, 308, 463, 541, 542.
eternal, 522.

God, faithfulness of, 432.
goodness of, acknowledged, 37, 40, 163, 200, 226, 261, 365, 436, 542.
goodness of, universal, 37, 551.
government of, 490.
greatness of, 490, 551.
guardian, 37, 200, 239, 470.
guide, 31, 470.
helper, 271, 470.
kindness of, 92, 307, 368, 465, 479.
love of, 92, 226, 369, 462, 470.
love as seen in Christ, 37, 92, 151, 406.
majesty of, 3.
mercy of, 4, 40, 169, 172, 222, 307, 363, 465.
omnipotent, 143, 551.
providence of, 307, 542, 548, 551.
refuge and portion, 161, 254, 360, 528, 542.
safety in, 37, 143, 462, 522, 541, 548.
sovereignty of, 3, 490.
unchangeable, 432.
wisdom of, 226, 261, 369, 436, 490.
Good old way, 240.
Gospel, diffusion of, 367, 537.
excellence of, 116, 266.
exemplified in life, 267.
glad tidings of, 47, 457.
glory of, 116, 266.
prayer for spread of, 75, 168, 187, 329, 341, 367, 401, 403, 429, 585.
savor of life or death, 144.
success of, 9, 170, 261, 329, 507, 530.
a support, 432.
Grace, constraining, 319, 485.
salvation by, 44, 46, 60, 195, 236, 289, 354, 366.
sovereign, 165, 208, 366, 421, 565.
Gratitude, national, 150, 169, 365, 551.
for spiritual good, 40, 208, 222, 368, 532.
for temporal good, 202, 307, 465, 548.
Guilt, confessed, 78, 290, 386, 422, 500, 525.
confessed, national, 244, 249, 323, 440.

HAPPINESS in God only, 308.
Harvest home, 80.
spiritual, expected 101.
Heart of stone, 282, 411.
Heathen, calling, 211.

Heathen, perishing, 429.
prayer for, 75, 403, 587.
Heaven, desiring, 91, 105, 133, 152, 184.
enjoyments of, 602.
glory of, 116, 361, 434, 582.
happiness of, 495, 577, 596.
hope of, 183, 301, 344, 408.
meeting in, 297, 313, 85, 342, 363, 487, 544, 571.
no parting there, 140, 487, 571.
prospect of, 10, 74, 159, 320, 340, 358, 389, 480, 586.
recognition in, 487, 601.
rest in, 225, 299, 340, 544, 377, 444, 519.
society of, 56, 295, 582.
songs of, 132, 155.
no sorrow there, 394, 396.
welcome home to, 294.
Heavenly joy on earth, 105, 167.
Help of God, 271.
Hinder me not, 561.
Holy aspirations, 157.
Holy Spirit, breathing after, 16, 29.
calling, 44, 286, 354, 504.
comforter, 55, 241.
earnest of heaven, 118.
grieved, 473, 482, 501.
guide, 130, 241.
illuminating, 16, 122, 241.
indwelling, 16, 118, 215, 216, 336, 473.
invoked, 1, 16, 29, 216, 241, 336, 554, 559.
invoked at baptism, 433, 439.
power of, needed, 144, 188, 310.
prayer for, 29.
quickening by, 1, 559, 574.
regeneration by, 437, 574.
sanctifier, 16, 336.
sovereignty of, 251.
teachings of, 122.
Homeward bound, 228, 259, 378
Hope, the believer's, 185.
rejoicing in, 517.
Humility, 21, 178, 405.
Hypocrisy, 56.

IMITATION of Christ, 233, 566.
Indwelling of Spirit. See Holy Spirit.
sin lamented, 126, 473, 540
Ingratitude deprecated, 83.
lamented, 19, 87, 386, 42. 500, 558.
Intemperance, evils of, 475.
Intercession of Christ, 46, 256, 472, 488.
Internal conflicts, 136, 832.

INDEX OF SUBJECTS. 239

Invitations to sinners, 46, 59, 60, 94, 104, 139, 154, 162. 181, 189, 240, 275, 286, 354, 891, 397, 428, 431, 456, 471, 488, 549, 552

JERUSALEM, Christ wept over, 77.
Jews, prayer for, 75, 217.
Jubilee, proclaimed, 489.
song of, 834.
Judgment, day of, 79, 89, 278, 306, 311, 431.
sinner at the, 284, 298, 416, 481.
Just as I am, 43, 203.
you are, 44, 46, 154, 354.
Justification by faith, 21.

LABORERS, more, prayed for, 550.
Lamb of God, 43, 184, 265, 322, 364, 488.
Latter day, glory of, 45, 201.
living in, 137.
Law, conviction by, 53, 66, 78, 195, 276.
and gospel, 53, 276.
threatenings of, 66, 195.
Liberality, Christian, 598.
Light in window, 312.
Looking home, 163.
Looking to Jesus, saint, 491, 593.
to Jesus, sinner, 22, 185, 265, 272, 276, 321, 411, 502, 513, 525.
Lord's Day, delight in, 41, 464, 573.
morning, 108, 156, 579.
in the sanctuary, 385.
welcomed, 141, 156 526, 595.
worship on the, 42, 385, 544.
Lord's Supper instituted, 600.
compassion of Christ in, 498.
gratitude for a place at, 424.
love of Christ in, 58, 498.
memorial of Christ's death, 600.
presence of Christ at, 424.
Love, importance of, 73, 218, 324.

MANSIONS of glory, bound for, 331.
Marching along, 68.
Mary at the Saviour's tomb, 205.
Meditation, evening, 260, 281.
Mercy acknowledged, 271, 386, 422, 499, 513.
calling, 104, 139, 446.
free, 499.
sought, 25, 188, 386, 500, 525.
trusted in, 162, 271, 388, 500.

Mercy seat, 6, 36, 54, 316, 466, 525, 546.
Ministers, 181, 399.
Missionaries, 572.
farewell of, 12.
Missions, foreign, 8, 12, 45, 75, 168, 170, 187, 201 211, 212, 217, 231, 268, 329, 337, 341, 367, 401, 403, 419, 429, 507, 509, 530, 587, 585.
home, 26, 103, 186, 210, 334, 345, 393, 409, 475, 557, 562, 598.

NATIONAL anniversary, 498.
blessings invoked, 254, 494.
deliverance sought, 264.
gratitude. 150, 169, 365, 551.
humiliation, 440.
judgments deprecated, 244, 823.
praise, 163.
sins, pardon asked, 249.
thanksgiving, 169, 551.
Narrow way, 483.
Nearer my home, 62, 480.
Nearness to God, 114, 349, 482, 556.
New birth, 58, 574.
Newness of life, 433.
New Year, 171, 172, 200, 306.
No cross no crown, 443.
Not lost but gone before, 263.
Nothing but leaves, 139.

PARDON through blood of Christ, 46, 240, 265, 272, 456, 502, 591.
implored, 87, 96, 388, 500, 525.
Parental prayer, 17, 23, 196, 524, 563.
Passing away, 428.
Patience in trial, 27, 61, 85.
Peace, universal, 547.
Perseverance, 128, 174, 228, 236, 319, 352, 496.
Pilgrim songs, 11, 81, 50, 69, 91, 160, 174, 258, 380, 392, 488, 442, 443, 455, 529.
Poor, kindness to, 103.
Praise to Christ, 22, 152, 461.
Christ the King, 489.
Christ the Lamb, 450.
Christ the Redeemer, 152, 250, 461, 520.
continual, 261.
the Creator, 3.
exhortation to, 318.
to God, 4, 37, 490.
for revival, 199.
for salvation, 15, 157, 208, 435, 485.
universal, 590.

Prayer for acceptance, 95.
answered by crosses, 405.
at beginning of worship, 28, 29. 385.
evening, 70, 229, 239, 858.
morning, 32, 70, 147, 458.
secret, 292, 441, 576.
for conversion of sinners, 156, 250, 385, 554. 581.
efficacious, 54, 468.
encouragement to, 72, 382, 474.
for faith, 55, 198, 271, 410, 488, 506, 543.
for growth in grace, 143, 188, 405.
for guardian care, 30, 200, 239, 241, 281, 522, 541.
for guidance, 122, 501, 503, 560.
for heathen. See GOSPEL, spread of.
for help in temptation, 308, 374, 412.
for holy affections, 198, 491, 513, 559.
hour of, 141, 304, 407.
for humility 178.
importunity in, 453.
invitation to, 296, 466.
for the Jews, 348, 582.
for the nation, 244, 249, 254, 264, 323, 440, 494, 547.
nature of, 117, 180, 256.
for pardon, 87, 96, 388, 500, 525.
for perseverance, 87, 572.
for presence of Christ, 71, 126, 207, 298.
for presence of God, 5, 27, 531.
for repentance, 198, 290, 386, 411, 506
for resignation, 27.
for restoring grace, 87, 415, 473.
for revival, 24, 52, 63, 110, 230, 414.
for sanctification, 114, 157, 178, 336, 473, 566.
for seamen, 153, 555.
for sincerity, 506.
for steadfastness, 362, 563, 570.
for submission, 27, 178.
for support in death, 27, 491, 508.
sweet, 447.
Presence of Christ desired, 24 71, 110, 115, 207, 213, 230, 293
Procrastination, 65, 128, 234, 235, 277, 287, 298, 390, 446, 592.
Promised land, 455, 485.

INDEX OF SUBJECTS.

Promises, trusting, 432, 496, 580.
Providences, 251, 261, 369.
Purity of heart, 178.

QUICKENING grace sought, 198, 290.

RACE, the Christian, 76, 583.
Reconciliation to God, 248, 486, 515.
Regeneration, 53, 574.
Reign of Christ, 168, 201.
Religion, importance of. 232, 385.
Repentance, 77, 234, 235, 500, 525.
  at the cross, 364, 411, 425, 498, 513, 514.
  from goodness of God, 422.
  prayer for, 198, 290, 386, 411, 506.
Repenting sinner, joy over, 148, 182.
Rest in heaven. See HEAVEN.
  for the weary, 138, 162, 444, 538, 549.
Resurrection of believer, 309, 349.
  of Christ. 205, 309, 515.
  of dead, 220.
  hope of, 33, 105, 349.
  and judgment, 79.
Revival, prayer for, 24, 52, 63, 110, 230, 414.
  rejoicing in, 15, 52, 182, 359, 518.
Righteousness, Christ our, 96, 135, 240, 276, 371, 421, 496.
  no trust in our, 135, 276, 502, 591.
Rock of ages, 383, 413.
  the solid, 135.
Room for all, 60, 181.

SACRIFICE of Christ. See CHRIST.
Safety of believers. See BELIEVER.
Salvation through Christ, 43, 44, 78, 96, 195, 240, 265, 278, 296, 421, 502, 591.
  complete in Christ, 102, 111, 215, 322.
  through faith, 21, 272, 276, 502.
  by grace. See GRACE.
Sanctification, 14.
  needed, 56.
Sanctuary, delight in, 41, 314, 316, 544.
  God present in, 42, 141, 316.
  prayer for blessings in, 100, 112.
Scriptures, delight in, 57, 110, 223, 457, 460, 521.

Scriptures, love of. 223.
  precious, 57, 161, 457.
  sufficiency of. 457.
Seamen, prayer for, 153, 555.
  prayer of, 373.
Security in God, 37, 143, 464, 522, 541.
Self-confidence, false, 412.
Self-denial, 88, 423, 503.
Shore, evergreen, 273.
  golden, 259.
  happy. 342.
  shining, 50.
Sin, caused death of Christ, 411, 425.
  confession of, 78, 386, 388, 421, 422, 500, 525, 540.
  conviction of, 78, 151, 276, 411, 425.
  indwelling lamented, 126, 473, 545.
  grieves the Holy Spirit, 473, 482, 501.
Sinners admonished, 20, 47, 65, 123, 128, 234, 238, 247, 283, 287, 376, 381, 390, 391, 416, 430, 456, 481, 484, 504, 505, 531, 583, 534, 538, 553.
  awakened, 66.
  entreated, 124, 206, 234, 387.
  going to Jesus, 25, 43, 421.
  helpless, 53, 96, 185, 191, 243, 366, 421.
  invited to Christ, 44, 46, 59, 60, 104, 139, 151, 154, 162, 181, 189, 240, 243, 247, 265, 275, 286, 354, 397, 428, 431, 456, 471, 488, 504, 549, 552.
  invitations to. 94, 391.
  at judgment, 234, 298, 416, 481.
  looking to Jesus. See LOOKING.
  saved by grace, 208, 276, 328, 485.
Sinner trusting in Christ, 43, 96, 195, 421.
Slumberers admonished, 198, 326, 355.
Sons of God, 14, 55, 157.
Soul, worth of, 20.
Sovereign grace, 208, 366, 421.
Sowing and reaping, 80, 191.
Spiritual blindness, 246.
Strength in Christ, 76, 388, 467, 500, 507.

TEMPTATION, 331, 374.
  prayer for help in, 374, 412, 503.
Throne of grace, 370, 459.
Time, the accepted, 123, 275, 283.
  and eternity, 93, 171, 280, 306.

Time, flight of, 123, 128, 171, 306, 533.
  importance of present, 123, 128, 235, 280, 381, 478, 504, 531, 553, 592.
  of love, 467.
  shortness of, 277, 533, 534, 553.
Trinity, praise to, 452.
  rejoicing over conversion of sinners, 148.
Trouble, God a help in, 161, 522.

UNBELIEF, banished, 358.
  mistakes God, 251.
Uncertainty of life, 35, 171, 172, 280.
Union with Christ, 90, 102, 302.
  among Christians, 90, 132, 145, 342, 363, 372.
Universal Hallelujah, 187.

VINE, the living, 90.
Voice of free grace, 155.

WANDERER from God, 408, 471, 594.
Warfare, Christian, 68, 74, 209, 221, 269, 270, 315, 454.
Warning to sinners, 65, 123, 234, 247, 287, 390, 391, 430, 505.
Watch and pray, 88.
We are coming, 356
Weary, rest for, 162, 408, 444, 538, 549.
Weeping over sinners, 77, 237.
What of the night, 170, 329, 507, 530.
Will ye also go away, 257, 347.
Worship, Christ present in, 156, 316, 595.
  commencement of, 5, 28, 29, 71, 379, 540, 581.
  delight in, 41, 42, 71, 141, 316, 464, 544, 595.
Wrath of God intolerable, 390, 416, 481.

YEAR, close of, 84.
  crowned with mercy, 470.
  new, 171, 172, 200, 806.
Young, exhorted, 62, 142, 252.
  importance of Bible to, 427.
  pilgrims, 224.
  prayer for, 17, 23, 196, 524, 563.
  prayer of, 142.

ZEAL, prayer for, 491.
Zion encouraged, 8, 45, 212, 281, 337, 388, 572.
  loved of God, 388, 491, 572.
  promises to, 212.
  prospects of, 219.
  safety of, 161, 242, 383.

SUPPLEMENT:

CONSISTING OF

OLD AND FAMILIAR TUNES AND CHORUSES.

INSERTED BY REQUEST.

INVITATION. C. M.

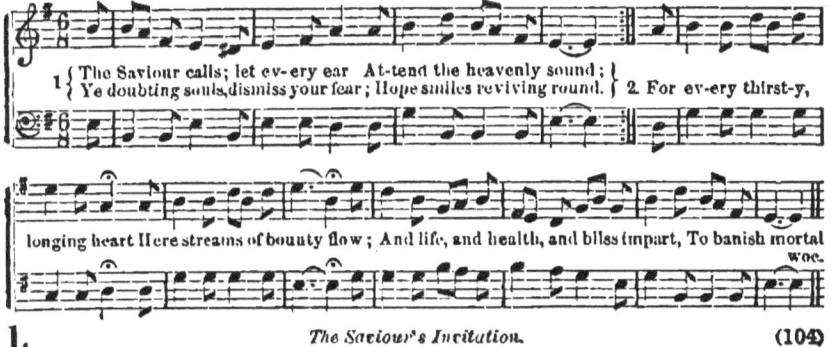

1 { The Saviour calls; let ev-ery ear At-tend the heavenly sound; }
  { Ye doubting souls, dismiss your fear; Hope smiles reviving round. } 2. For ev-ery thirst-y, longing heart Here streams of bounty flow; And life, and health, and bliss impart, To banish mortal woe.

1. *The Saviour's Invitation.* (104)

3 Ye sinners, come; 'tis mercy's voice;
  That gracious voice obey;
  'Tis Jesus calls to heavenly joys
  And can you yet delay?

4 Dear Saviour, draw reluctant hearts;
  To thee let sinners fly,
  And take the bliss thy love imparts,
  And drink, and never die.

SOVEREIGN GRACE. 7s.

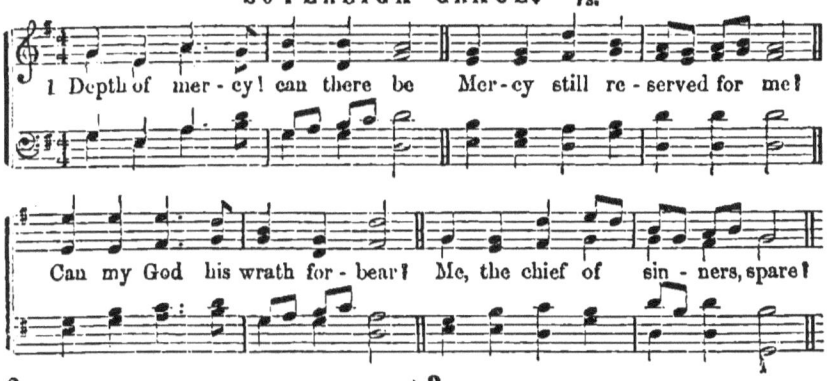

1 Depth of mer-cy! can there be Mer-cy still re-served for me? Can my God his wrath for-bear? Me, the chief of sin-ners, spare?

2. *The Penitent Inquirer.* (386) | **3.** *Prayer for the Spirit.* (336)

2 I have long withstood his grace;
  Long provoked him to his face;
  Would not hear his gracious calls;
  Grieved him by a thousand falls.

1 Holy Ghost! with light divine,
  Shine upon this heart of mine;
  Chase the shades of night away,
  Turn my darkness into day.

RESOLVE. C. M. Double.

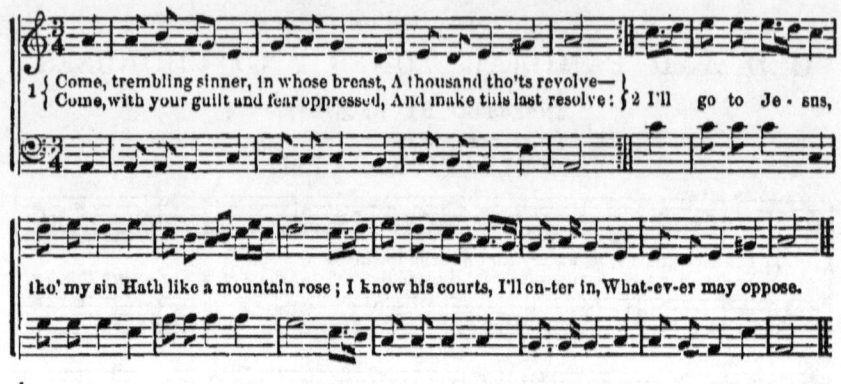

1 Come, trembling sinner, in whose breast, A thousand tho'ts revolve—
  Come, with your guilt and fear oppressed, And make this last resolve: 2 I'll go to Jesus, tho' my sin Hath like a mountain rose; I know his courts, I'll enter in, What-ev-er may oppose.

4. *Resolving to go to Jesus.* (25)

3 Prostrate I'll lie before his throne,
  And there my guilt confess;
  I'll tell him I'm a wretch undone,
  Without his sovereign grace.

4 I'll to the gracious King approach,
  Whose sceptre pardon gives;
  Perhaps he will command my touch—
  And then the suppliant lives.

SUPPLICATION. L. M. *Arranged.*

1 Show pi-ty, Lord; O Lord, forgive; Let a re-pent-ing reb-el live; Are not thy mer-cies large and free May not a sin-ner trust in thee?

5. *Pardon Penitently Implored.* (500)

2 My crimes, though great, cannot surpass
  The power and glory of thy grace;
  Great God, thy nature hath no bound;
  So let thy pardoning love be found.

3 O, wash my soul from every sin,
  And make my guilty conscience clean;

Here, on my heart, the burden lies,
  And past offences pain mine eyes.

4 My lips, with shame, my sins confess,
  Against thy law, against thy grace;
  Lord, should thy judgment grow severe,
  I am condemned, but thou art clear.

REPENTANCE. C. M.

1 A-las! and did my Sav-iour bleed? And did my Sovereign die?
Would he de-vote that sa-cred head For such a worm as I?

Chorus. Oh! the Lamb, the lov-ing Lamb, The Lamb on Cal-va-ry,
The Lamb was slain, but lives a-gain, To in-ter-cede for me.

6. *Godly Sorrow at the Cross.* (514)

2 Was it for crimes that I had done,
He groaned upon the tree!
Amazing pity! grace unknown,
And love beyond degree!

3 Well might the sun in darkness hide,
And shut his glories in,
When Christ, the mighty Maker, died,
For man the creature's sin.

ENCOURAGEMENT. 7s.

Arranged and harmonized by W. B. B.

1 Weeping soul, no longer mourn, Jesus all thy griefs hath borne; View him bleeding on the tree,
Pouring out his life for thee; There thy ev-ery sin he bore, Weeping soul, lament no more.

7. *"He hath Borne our Griefs."* (410)

2 All thy crimes on him were laid;
See upon his blameless head
Wrath its utmost vengeance pours,
Due to my offense and yours;
Weary sinner, keep thine eyes
On the atoning sacrifice.

3 Cast thy guilty soul on him,
Find him mighty to redeem;
At his feet thy burden lay,
Look thy doubts and fears away;
Now by faith the Son embrace,
Plead his promise, trust his grace.

ATONEMENT. C. M.

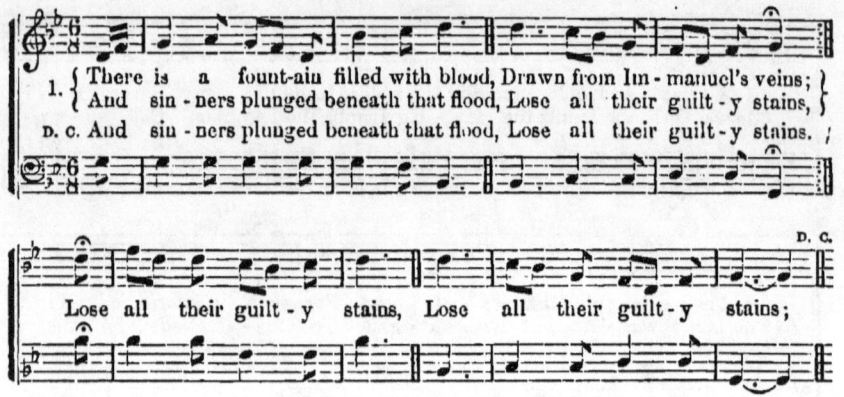

1. There is a fount-ain filled with blood, Drawn from Im-manuel's veins;
And sin-ners plunged beneath that flood, Lose all their guilt-y stains.
D. C. And sin-ners plunged beneath that flood, Lose all their guilt-y stains.
Lose all their guilt-y stains, Lose all their guilt-y stains;

8. *"There is a Fountain filled with Blood."* (272)

2 The dying thief rejoiced to see
That fountain in his day;
And there have I, as vile as he,
Washed all my sins away.

3 Dear, dying Lamb! Thy precious blood
Shall never lose its power,
Till all the ransomed church of God
Be saved to sin no more.

DISCIPLE. 8s & 7s. Mozart.

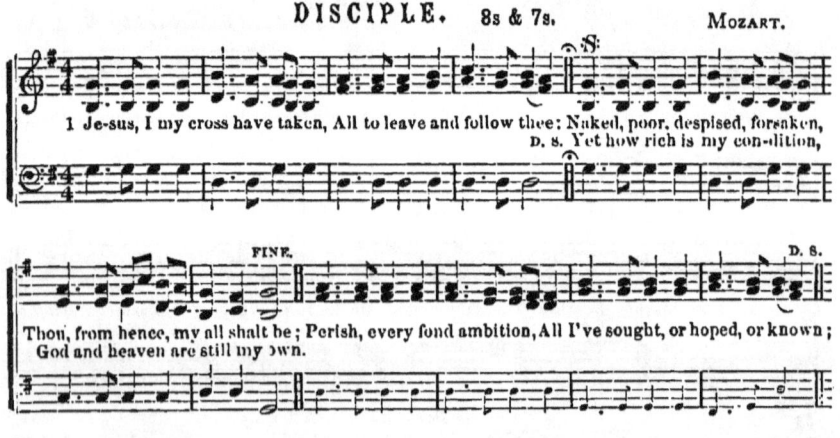

1 Je-sus, I my cross have taken, All to leave and follow thee: Naked, poor, despised, forsaken,
D. S. Yet how rich is my con-dition,
Thou, from hence, my all shalt be; Perish, every fond ambition, All I've sought, or hoped, or known;
God and heaven are still my own.

9. *"Jesus, I my Cross have taken."* (225)

2 Let the world despise and leave me,
They have left my Saviour, too;
Human hearts and looks deceive me
Thou art not, like them, untrue:

And while thou shalt smile upon me,
God of wisdom, love, and might,
Foes may hate, and friends may scorn me;
Show thy face, and all is bright.

AMAZING GRACE. C. M. 5

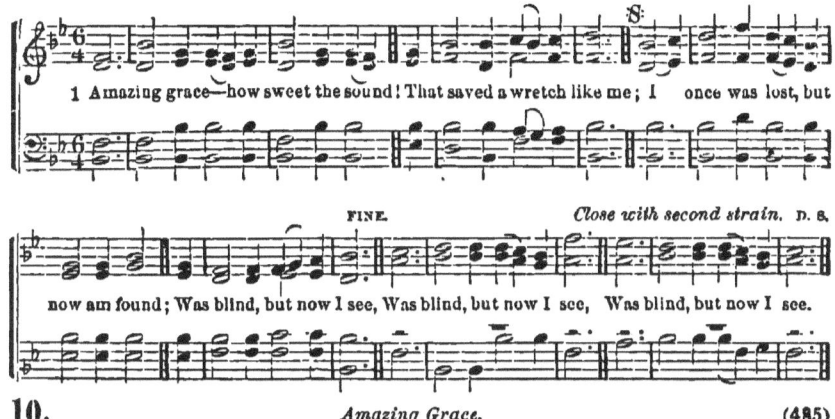

10. *Amazing Grace.* (485)

2 'Twas grace that taught my heart to fear,
 And grace my fears relieved:
 How precious did that grace appear,
 The hour I first believed!

3 Through many dangers, toils, and snares,
 I have already come;
 'Tis grace has brought me safe thus far,
 And grace will lead me home.

SALVATION FREE. S. M.

REV. E. W. DUNBAR.

11. *Heavenly Joy on Earth.* (167)

2 The sorrows of the mind
 Be banished from the place;
 Religion never was designed
 To make our pleasures less.

3 Let those refuse to sing,
 That never knew our God;
 But favorites of the heavenly King
 May speak their joys abroad.

I LOVE JESUS. 8s & 7s.

Arranged by Wm. B. Bradbury.

{ Come, thou Fount of every blessing, Tune our hearts to grateful lays:
Streams of mercy, never ceasing, Call for songs of loudest praise. } I love Jesus, Halle-lu-jah,

I love Je-sus, yes, I do, I do love Je-sus, he's my Saviour, Jesus smiles and loves me too.

12. *The Fount of Blessing.* (214)

2 Teach me some melodious sonnet,
  Sung by flaming tongues above:
  Praise the mount—O, fix me on it,
  Mount of God's unchanging love.

3 Here I raise my Ebenezer;
  Hither, by thy help I'm come;
  And I hope, by thy good pleasure,
  Safely to arrive at home.

MOUNT PISGAH. C. M.

1 Am I a sol-dier of the cross, A follower of the Lamb;.... And shall I fear to

CHORUS.

own his cause, Or blush to speak his name? Or blush to speak his name? Or blush to speak his name?

13. *Christian Soldier.* (270)

2 Must I be carried to the skies,
  On flowery beds of ease,
  While others fought to win the prize,
  And sailed through bloody seas?

3 Are there no foes for me to face?
  Must I not stem the flood?
  Is this vile world a friend to grace,
  To help me on to God?

REMEMBER ME. C. M.

1 Je-sus, thou art the sinner's friend, As such I look to thee;
Cho. Re-mem-ber me, re-mem-ber me, Dear Lord! re-mem-ber me.
Now, in the full-ness of thy love, O Lord, re-mem-ber me.

14. "*Lord, Remember Me.*" (321)

2 Remember thy pure word of grace,
Remember Calvary;
Remember all thy dying groans,
And then remember me.

3 Thou wondrous advocate with God,
I yield myself to thee,
While thou art sitting on thy throne,
Dear Lord, remember me.

MERCY-SEAT. L. M. Double.

1 From ev-ery stormy wind that blows, From every swelling tide of woes,
There is a calm, a sure re-treat; 'Tis found be-fore the mer-cy-seat.
D. C. A place of all on earth most sweet; It is the blood-bought mer-cy-seat.

2 There is a place where Je-sus sheds The oil of glad-ness on our heads—

15. *The Mercy-Seat.* (6)

3 There is a scene where spirits blend,
Where friend holds fellowship with friend;
Though sundered far, by faith they meet
Around one common mercy-seat.

4 There, there, on eagle wings we soar,
And sin and sense molest no more;
And heaven comes down, our souls to greet,
And glory crowns the mercy-seat.

16. *The Firm Foundation.* (352)

2 In every condition—in sickness, in health,
In poverty's vale, or abounding in wealth,
At home and abroad, on the land, on the sea,—
As thy day may demand, shall thy strength ever be.

BETHANY. 6s & 4s.

By permission, Dr. L. Mason.

17. *Nearer to God.* (556.

2 Though, like a wanderer,
   The sun gone down,
Darkness comes over me,
   My rest a stone;
Yet in my dreams I'd be
Nearer, my God, to thee,
   Nearer to thee!

3 There let my way appear
   Steps unto heaven;
All that thou sendest me
   In mercy given;
Angels to beckon me
Nearer, my God, to thee,
   Nearer to thee!

BLEST MORN. 11s & 10s.

1. Hail! thou blest morn, when the Great Media-tor, Down from the re-gions of glory descends;
Shepherds, go worship the Babe in the Man-ger, Lo! for his guard the bright angels attend.
D.C. Star in the East, the ho-ri-zon a-dorn-ing, Guide where our in-fant Re-deemer is laid.

Brightest and best of the sons of the morning, Dawn on our darkness, and lend us thine aid;

18.   *The Infant Saviour.*   (418)

2 Cold, on his cradle, the dew-drops are shining;
Low lies his bed with the beasts of the stall;
Angels adore him in slumbers reclining,
Maker, and Monarch, and Saviour of all.

EVENING. S. M.

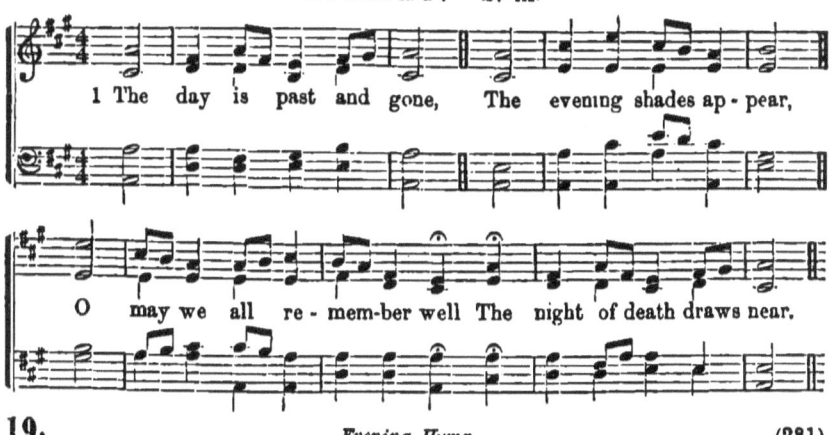

1 The day is past and gone, The evening shades ap-pear,
O may we all re-mem-ber well The night of death draws near.

19.   *Evening Hymn.*   (281)

2 We lay our garments by,
  Upon our beds to rest;
So death will soon disrobe us all
  Of what we here possess.

3 Lord, keep us safe this night,
  Secure from all our fears;
May angels guard us while we sleep,
  Till morning light appears.

HYACINTH. 7s.

1 Hark, my soul, it is the Lord; 'Tis thy Saviour, hear his word; Jesus speaks, and speaks to thee: "Say, poor sinner, lov'st thou me?

20. *Lovest thou Me?* (389)

2 "I delivered thee when bound,
And when wounded, healed thy wound;
Sought thee wandering, set thee right,
Turned thy darkness into light."

6 Lord, it is my chief complaint,
That my love is weak and faint;
Yet I love thee and adore,
O, for grace to love thee more!

NEWTON.

ADVENT. C. P. M.

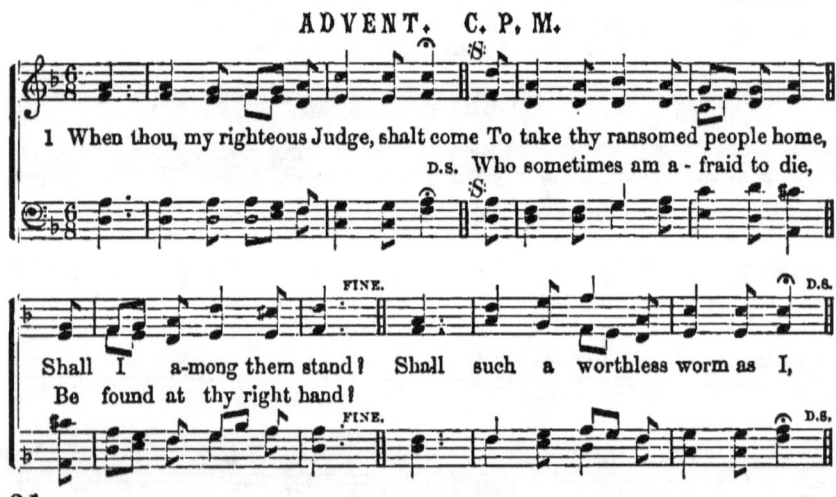

1 When thou, my righteous Judge, shalt come To take thy ransomed people home,
D.S. Who sometimes am afraid to die,
Shall I among them stand? Shall such a worthless worm as I,
Be found at thy right hand?

21. *Pleading for Acceptance.* (95)

2 I love to meet among them now,
Before thy gracious feet to bow,
Though vilest of them all;
But—can I bear the piercing thought?—
What if my name should be left out,
When thou for them shalt call!

3 Prevent, prevent it by thy grace;
Be thou, dear Lord, my hiding-place,
In this, th' accepted day;
Thy pardoning voice, O, let me hear,
To still my unbelieving fear,
Nor let me fall, I pray.

MERDIN. 7s.

L. MASON. *By permission.*

1 { Brethren, while we sojourn here, Fight we must, but should not fear; / Foes we have, but we've a Friend, One that loves us to the end. } Forward, then, with courage [go,
Long we shall not dwell below; Soon the joyful news will come, "Child, your Father calls, come home."

22. *We shall soon be at Home.* (209)

2 In our way, a thousand snares
Lie to take us unawares;
Satan, with malicious art,
Watches each unguarded heart;

But from Satan's malice free,
Saints shall soon in glory be;
Soon the joyful news will come,
"Child, your Father calls, come home."

MEAR. C. M.

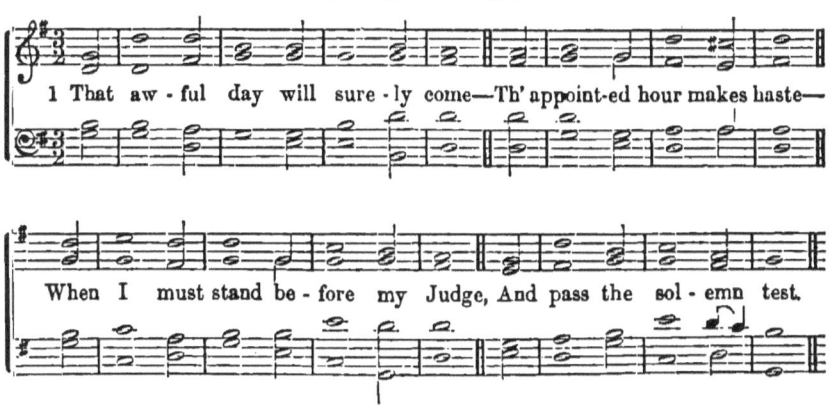

1 That awful day will surely come—Th' appointed hour makes haste—
When I must stand before my Judge, And pass the solemn test.

23. *Everlasting Absence of God Intolerable.* (311)

2 Thou lovely Chief of all my joys,
Thou Sovereign of my heart,
How could I bear to hear thy voice
Pronounce the sound, "Depart!"

24. *I must go to the Judgment.* (278)

1 And must I be to judgment brought,
And answer, in that day,
For every vain and idle thought,
And every word I say?

STEM THE STORM. C. M.

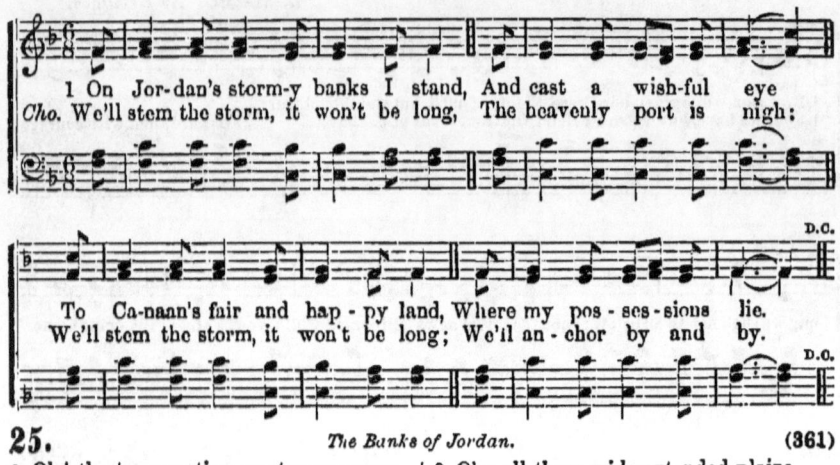

1 On Jor-dan's storm-y banks I stand, And cast a wish-ful eye
To Ca-naan's fair and hap-py land, Where my pos-ses-sions lie.
Cho. We'll stem the storm, it won't be long, The heavenly port is nigh;
We'll stem the storm, it won't be long; We'll an-chor by and by.

25. *The Banks of Jordan.* (361)

2 Oh! the transporting, rapturous scene,
That rises to my sight!
Sweet fields, arrayed in living green,
And rivers of delight.

3 O'er all those wide-extended plains
Shines one eternal day;
There God the Son forever reigns,
And scatters night away.

WE'LL WAIT. L. M.

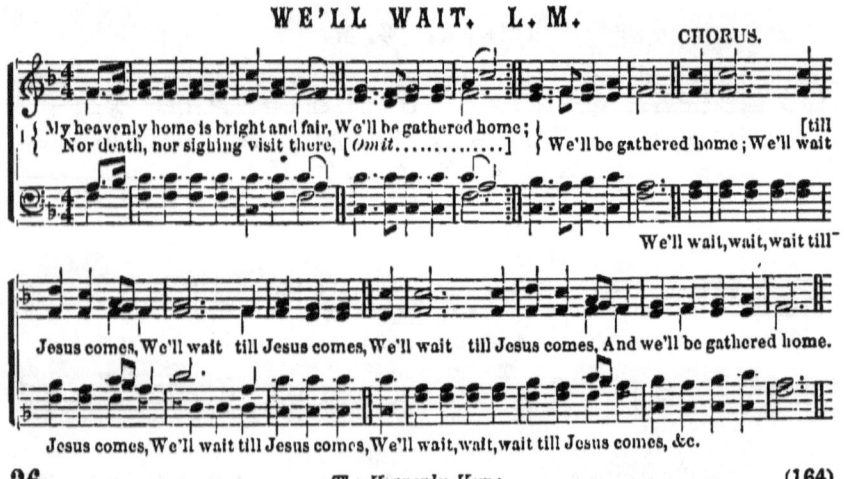

CHORUS.

{ My heavenly home is bright and fair, We'll be gathered home; }
{ Nor death, nor sighing visit there, [Omit............] } We'll be gathered home; We'll wait [till

We'll wait, wait, wait till Jesus comes, We'll wait till Jesus comes, We'll wait till Jesus comes, And we'll be gathered home.
Jesus comes, We'll wait till Jesus comes, We'll wait, wait, wait till Jesus comes, &c.

26. *The Heavenly Home.* (164)

1 My heavenly home is bright and fair;
Nor pain, nor death can enter there;
Its glitt'ring towers the sun outshine;
That heav'nly mansion shall be mine.

2 My Father's house is built on high,
Far, far above the starry sky;
When from this early prison free,
That heavenly mansion mine shall be.

HAPPY HOME. C. M. D. 13

1 Je-ru-sa-lem, my hap-py home, Name ever dear to me! When shall my labors have an end, In joy, and peace, and thee. 2 When shall these eyes thy heav'n-built walls, And streets of shining gold? And pearly gates behold?

D.S. Thy bulwarks with salvation strong,

27. *The Society of Heaven.* (582)

3 O, when, thou city of my God,
   Shall I thy courts ascend,
Where congregations ne'er break up,
   And Sabbaths have no end?

4 There happier bowers than Eden's bloom,
   Nor sin nor sorrow know:
Blest seats! through rude and stormy scenes
   I onward press to you.

LAND OF REST. C. M. D.

1 { Sweet land of rest! for thee I sigh: When will the mo-ment come,
   And dwell with Christ at home,...... And dwell with Christ at home.
When I shall lay my ar-mor by, And dwell with Christ at home, }
When I shall lay my ar-mor by, And dwell with Christ at home.

28. *Sweet Land of Rest.* (160)

2 No tranquil joys on earth I know,
   No peaceful sheltering home;
This world's a wilderness of woe,
   This world is not my home.

3 To Jesus Christ I sought for rest,
   He bade me cease to roam,
But fly for succor to his breast,
   And he'd conduct me home.

EXHORTATION. 5s, 6s, & 11s.

1 Come, let us a-new Our journey pursue, Roll round with the year, And never stand still till the Mas-ter ap-pear: His a-dor-a-ble will Let us glad-ly ful-fill, And our talents improve, By the patience of hope, and the la-bor of love, By the patience of hope, and the la-bor of love.

29. *Exhortation to Faithfulness.*

2 Our life is a dream;
Our time, as a stream,
Glides swiftly away,
And the fugitive moment refuses to stay;
The arrow is flown;
The moment is gone;
The millennial year
Rushes on to our view, and eternity's near.

3 O that each, in the day
Of his coming, may say,
"I have fought my way through;
I have finished the work thou didst give me to do;"
O that each from his Lord
May receive the glad word,
"Well and faithfully done;
Enter into thy joy, and sit down on thy throne."

SOLDIERS OF THE CROSS.

1 Ye soldiers of the cross, rise and put your armor on; March to the cit-y of the New Je-ru-sa-lem; Je-sus gives the or-der, and leads his people on Till vic-to-ry is won.

CHORUS.

Glo-ry, glory, hal-le-lu-jah! Glo-ry, glory, hal-le-lu-jah! Glo-ry, glo-ry, hal-le-lu-jah! We are marching on.

30.   *The Summons to the Conflict.*

2 The watchmen they are crying, attend the trumpet's sound;
Take the gospel banner, and the powers of hell surround;
Hearts and arms make ready, the battle is at hand;
Go forth at Christ's command.—*Ch.*

3 Lay hold upon the Saviour by faith's victorious shield,
March on in order till you win the glorious field;
Faint not by the way till you've gained that peaceful shore,
Where war shall be no more.—*Cho.*

4 Ne'er think the victory won, nor lay your armor down;
March on in duty, till you gain the starry crown;
When the war is o'er, and the battle you have won,
Jesus will say, "Well done."—*Cho.*

SUPPLEMENT.

INDEX OF TUNES.

		PAGE			PAGE
Advent,	C. P. M.	10	Land of Rest,	C. M.	13
Amazing Grace,	C. M.	5	Mear,	C. M.	11
Atonement,	C. M.	4	Mercy-Seat	L. M.	7
Bethany	6s & 4s.	8	Merdin	7s.	11
Blest Morn,	11s & 10s.	9	Mount Pisgah,	C. M.	6
Confidence,	11s.	8	Remember Me,	C. M.	7
Disciple,	8s & 7s.	4	Repentance,	C. M.	3
Encouragement,	7s.	3	Resolve,	C. M.	2
Evening,	S. M.	9	Salvation's Free,	S. M.	5
Exhortation,	5s, 6s, & 11s.	14	Soldiers of the Cross,		15
Happy Home,	C. M.	13	Sovereign Grace,	7s.	1
Hyacinth,	7s.	10	Stem the Storm,	C. M.	12
I love Jesus,	8s & 7s.	6	Supplication,	L. M.	2
Invitation,	C. M.	1	We'll Wait,	L. M.	12

INDEX OF FIRST LINES.

	NO.		NO
Alas! and did my Saviour bleed,	6	Jerusalem, my happy home,	27
Amazing grace! how sweet the sound!	10	Jesus, I my cross have taken,	9
Am I a soldier of the cross?	13	Jesus, thou art the sinner's Friend,	14
And must I be to judgment brought,	24	My heavenly home is bright and fair,	26
Brethren, while we sojourn here,	22	Nearer, my God, to thee,	17
Come, let us anew,	29	On Jordan's stormy banks I stand,	25
Come, thou Fount of every blessing,	12	Show pity, Lord, O Lord, forgive,	5
Come, trembling sinner, in whose breast,	4	Sweet land of rest, for thee I sigh,	28
Come, we that love the Lord,	11	That awful day will surely come,	23
Depth of mercy! can there be,	2	The day is past and gone,	19
From every stormy wind that blows,	15	There is a fountain filled with blood,	8
Hail! thou blest morn, when the great	18	The Saviour calls, let every ear,	1
Hark, my soul! it is the Lord,	20	Weeping soul, no longer mourn,	7
Holy Ghost, with light divine,	3	When thou, my righteous Judge, shalt come.	21
How firm a foundation, ye saints of the Lord,	16	Ye soldiers of the Cross,	30

NOTICE.

☞ The numbers in parenthesis at the right hand, under the tunes, indicate the number of the hymns *complete* in the body of the Devotional Hymn and Tune Book.

www.ingramcontent.com/pod-product-compliance
Lightning Source LLC
Chambersburg PA
CBHW021358230426
43666CB00006B/568